MEAN DEVIATION

MEAN DEVIATION

FOUR DECADES OF PROGRESSIVE HEAVY METAL

JEFF WAGNER

Bazillion Points

Mean Deviation: Four Decades of Progressive Heavy Metal
Copyright © 2010 Jeff Wagner
All rights reserved.

http://www.mean-deviation.com

Cover artwork and interior illustrations by Michel "Away" Langevin
Photographs as credited
Book design by Bazillion Points
Supervised by Ian Christe
Edited by Polly Watson

First published in the United States in 2010 by

BAZILLION POINTS BOOKS
61 Greenpoint Ave. #504
Brooklyn, NY 11222
USA

www.bazillionpoints.com

ISBN 978-0-9796163-3-4

Printed in China

"Without deviation from the norm, progress is not possible."

—Frank Zappa

CONTENTS

FOREWORD

W AY BACK IN THE CULTURAL DESERT OF THE EARLY 1980s, I was barely into my teens when I fell in love with music. More specifically, I fell in love with two kinds of music: heavy metal and progressive rock. Laying ears on the former was easy, since the New Wave of British Heavy Metal was in full flow, but the latter was almost impossible to hear. Progressive music was banished, only heard by pillaging your best friend's big brother's record collection, or exploring secondhand record stores and taking a chance on anything with an interesting cover and/or long songs—preferably divided into movements.

At that time there wasn't much fusion between the worlds of metal and progressive music, aside from the occasional extended metal epic on an Iron Maiden or Diamond Head album. This new wave of heavy metal was largely centered on a back-to-basics approach, combining recycled Led Zeppelin or Judas Priest riffs with a barroom punk rock aesthetic. Ultimately, the "anyone can play guitar" philosophy didn't really appeal to me, so while my love of progressive music stayed with me, my interest in the apparently unambitious metal genre faded to nothing. A new album by Saxon just didn't have the same appeal once I discovered Frank Zappa and King Crimson. Yes, I became a music snob!

Fast forward to 2000, and I had been making music professionally myself for ten years, with a number of projects in various different musical styles. One of these bands was Porcupine Tree, which was very much in the tradition of the progressive bands I'd grown up listening to. Over the course of several albums, Porcupine Tree had touched on a lot of musical styles—but not metal. Metal remained something I thought I'd left behind in my teens.

When meeting music journalists, we would often discuss what I saw as the poor state of contemporary progressive music, wondering where all the really ambitious musicians had gone. Maybe those kinds of people were just more inclined to be filmmakers or writers nowadays. One day, one of these journalists handed me an Opeth CD called *Still Life*, saying: "You should listen to this; these guys are big fans of yours."

When I played the CD at a sound check a couple days later, what I heard forced me to completely revise my assumptions about both metal and progressive music. This wasn't the barroom heavy metal I remembered from my youth, and neither was it like the nostalgic Genesis clones I'd become accustomed to hearing passed off as "progressive" rock. Opeth's music was inventive, brutal, rhythmically complex, conceptual, technically astonishing, beautiful, textured, powerful, and, above all, ambitious. I was blown away.

I sent an e-mail to Opeth's main man, Mikael Åkerfeldt, complimenting him on *Still Life*, and received an invitation by return. Within a few more weeks I was in the studio working with the band on their groundbreaking *Blackwater Park* album. What made the music so special to me was that while it drew heavily from the great progressive era of the '70s, it was made by musicians who had grown up listening to death metal. Mikael was as influenced by the nihilistic folk of '70s band Comus as he was by black metallers Bathory, as in love with the sonic experiments of Scott Walker as he was with the bludgeoning riffing of Black Sabbath.

My discovery of Opeth was just the start of a trail that led to my discovery of many fantastic bands fusing heavy music with a totally progressive outlook. Soon I discovered the music of another Swedish band, Meshuggah, whose polyrhythmic complexities were not simply about showing off, but were fundamental to their brutal power. This band, perhaps more than any other, began to influence my own music. And it went on. In a very short time, I found a whole network of bands creating new forms of ambitious, album-oriented music with metal at its core. This combination of brutality and sophistication seemed to make perfect sense to me.

In Jeff Wagner's *Mean Deviation*, we now have a definitive book on the relationship between metal and progressive music, and the myriad variation of styles that it has given rise to. "Progressive metal" is now well established as a style and an approach, so much so that it has become a recognized genre in itself. In some ways this is unfortunate. When a blueprint for a style of music becomes established, what follows tends to include a lot of imitation—but to copy Mastodon, Tool, or Dream Theater is, of course, to miss the point of "progressive" music. The truly innovative bands simply play the music that comes naturally to them, by listening eclectically and seeing nothing strange in combining their influences. In doing so—whether by accident or design—they create new musical hybrids, which for me (along with an allegiance to the idea of the album as a musical journey) is one of the basic tenets of any music that can call itself progressive. In the meantime, metal continues to mutate and evolve, sometimes in the most unexpected ways, demonstrating that it is far from spent and is, in fact, the most flexible of musical forms.

It's some kind of strange, brutal beauty.

—Steven Wilson, London, 2010

PROLOGUE: CRIMES AGAINST GOOD TASTE?

A MASS OF BRUTE FORCE RIDING ON WHIRLWINDS. A sound from deep down in the churning guts of its creator, aiming at the listener/victim in the same region and parts below. Kicks you in the nuts and sweeps you off your feet. Mean. Ugly. Raw. Primal. Inhuman and otherworldly. This is the killing art of heavy metal.

So what happens when heavy metal, now entering its fifth decade of existence, grows up, leaves home, and progresses? What does it sound like when sex and violence are forgotten in favor of sax and violins? Or when time signatures mutate into quirky mathematical headaches, song lengths peak out at fifty-five minutes, and Pink Floyd informs a metal band's sound more than Black Sabbath? What happens when the barbarian impulse is sublimated—when the lowly beast is pulled from its cave, lured by a vast array of state-of-the-art tools and unlimited access to technology? Is "progressive" metal still even metal?

Quite possibly, progressive heavy metal should have never happened. Maybe it's an anomaly, an oxymoronic freak of evolution—or perhaps the mutation was inevitable. Many other music genres branched from their source at some point—witness avant-garde jazz and avant-garde classical music. Prog rock, one of the earliest perturbations of the rock-and-roll form, is an infamous manipulation of rock basics. Even decidedly anti-progressive outcast genres such as punk and hardcore claim their own progressive outgrowths. Why not heavy metal?

Heavy metal *is* a legitimate art form, after all. Outsiders took a while to admit as much, but metal has proven its resilience and viability and has earned its place in modern culture. In the 1980s, music critics too good for the likes of Judas Priest and Metallica dismissed the genre, misunderstanding it entirely, even as metal bands packed stadiums and racked up sales in the tens of millions. Inspired youngsters around the world blasted out their takes on the genre, and the form morphed and mutated into a zillion different subgenres, splicing some rather interesting, experimental outgrowths onto the tangled family tree.

Since the very beginning, the 1970s, early (or proto-metal) bands Black Sabbath and Rush emerged from primordial thuds to create remarkable and elaborate pieces of nascent progressive metal. That's just what happens with art. The creators eke out crude blueprints then improve upon them—they discover, experiment, and grow. They deviate.

Growing up an enthusiastic, some would say obsessed, fan of metal music— *hi, Mom!*—I picked up very early on bands that offered a deeper, more involved take on heavy metal. In the 1980s, I was attracted to Iron Maiden, Queensrÿche, and Fates Warning—bands that brought what I loved about 1970s bands such as Rush into heavier, darker realms. With *Seventh Son of a Seventh Son*, *Rage for Order*, and *Awaken the Guardian*, respectively, those new bands pushed metal into illuminating, fascinating realms; they were, in essence, progressive.

Bands whose growth is marked by constant change always intrigue me. I make impossible demands on my favorite ones. I want to have no idea where they will go next. I want surprises, challenges, new things to grapple with each time around. Fans like me were the nerdy train spotters who canvassed every page of *Metal Forces* magazine in the 1980s, seeking out the new and unusual, eagerly awaiting records by oddities such as Mekong Delta, Disharmonic Orchestra, and Psychotic Waltz.

I have also followed more straightforward bands. Once stricken with the metal disease, there's no shaking it. Sometimes you need immersion in the purest, most primitive metal available—and a blast of Bolt Thrower or Motörhead does the trick. Yet over time I found myself anticipating their new albums less and less. I knew what was coming before I even got the record out of the sleeve. It got to the point where I would rather pay for a failure—Celtic Frost's *Cold Lake* or Crimson Glory's *Strange and*

Beautiful—than a carbon copy of an album I already owned. If not a step forward, at least those stumbles were a step *somewhere*.

Voivod's *Angel Rat* was very much a step into *somewhere else*, especially considering where that band had started. The worth of the album is still hotly debated, nearly two decades after its late 1991 release. To some, *Angel Rat* was the ultimate in heavy metal treason. To others, its completely unexpected left turn made Voivod the ultimate avatars of musical bravery, in metal or any other genre.

I brought *Angel Rat* home from the record store with insanely high expectations. I'd followed Voivod since their 1984 debut, *War and Pain*, and the quantum leaps they made with each successive album were unparalleled by any other metal band. By the early 1990s, their clattering, primordial nuclear thrash had mutated into cold, cybernetic constructs. Voivod melted bizarre X-flat and Z-sharp chords onto total screwball time signatures. I found it incredibly impressive that the same four Canadian youngsters who had churned out the barbaric "Condemned to the Gallows" and "Nuclear War" produced obtuse sci-fi epics such as "Missing Sequences" and "Into My Hypercube" just a few short years later.

Talk about high expectations: The dawn of the 1990s found Voivod on major label MCA and touring successfully with Soundgarden and Faith No More, with Rush producer Terry Brown brought in to produce their sixth album. The band's clout had never been stronger. So when the laser made its first run through *Angel Rat* that memorable morning—I was the first person in Iowa City's BJ Records that day—I was taken completely by surprise. *Angel Rat* was not the Voivod I once knew. The songs were shorter, more accessible, more...rock. Psychedelia still lurked in the margins, but I wasn't prepared for this sharp change of direction.

In that era before the Internet could spoil the fun of a blind purchase, most of us rarely heard any of an album before actually buying it. Through tape trading, I sometimes unearthed rehearsal recordings for as-yet-unreleased Voivod albums, but that wasn't the case with *Angel Rat*. After finally hearing it, I was confused but enthralled. I listened to it again immediately after the first spin. I couldn't get enough. The CD had depth and subtlety unlike anything I'd heard. Still weirder than most other bands, songs such as "The Prow" and "Golem" also had a catchy, unusually human element running through them. I probably listened to *Angel Rat* two or three times a day for the first few weeks, getting familiar with its unique character and unexpected accessibility.

My roommate Tom was also a Voivod fan, and he hated *Angel Rat*. His bedroom was below mine. When I woke him to the sounds of this foreign, unknown album on the morning of its release, he later told me he thought I was playing "the new Ozzy or something." He was disappointed with the album's lack of sci-fi themes and Voivodian terminology. "Best Regards" and "None of the Above" bummed him out by addressing the real world instead of Voivod's fictional universe. I think he wanted this follow-up to *Nothingface* to sound pretty much like *Nothingface*. So did my other friends and acquaintances among Voivod's Iowa City fan base. Almost everyone thought *Angel Rat* was a sell-out. To them, Voivod were pandering to the mainstream, swimming with the musical tide they previously swam against.

I didn't hear the album like that, and I debated with my friends for months. Their disappointment seemed hypocritical. How could they expect stasis from a band like Voivod, who they loved because the *only* sure artistic move they ever made was forward? How could they ask Voivod to remain the same—or to go backwards? Talk about selling out—isn't willful artistic inertia the ultimate surrender?

Angel Rat seemed to me the very essence of progressive music. To others, it was the antithesis. So it is in the world of heavy metal, where dependability, consistency, and loyalty to fan expectations remain core values. Voivod never apologized for what was basically a commercial failure, even though *Angel Rat* knocked them off a career pedestal to which they never again ascended.

Progressive metal hardly revolves solely around Voivod and *Angel Rat*, but the curveball the band threw with this album does represent, to me, the principles—or anti-principles—at the very heart of progressive metal. Playing progressive metal means never looking back. It means taking precarious, dangerous steps in the unending search for new avenues of metallic expression—commercial, critical, and fan acceptance be damned. Young death metal bands can totally emulate their death metal heroes and still be 100 percent death metal. That's obvious. But can a young metal band emulate a legendary progressive metal band and still be considered truly progressive? That's a stickier, more difficult issue.

Then there's progressive rock. Back in the late '80s, I devoured any magazine article I could find about Voivod, Fates Warning, Iron Maiden, and my other metal favorites, and I noticed the recurring mentions by all of them of several '70s bands that inspired their playing and writing. The old band names were then completely unknown to me, but naturally I wanted to dig in and find out more. King Crimson, Van der Graaf Generator, Camel, Nektar, and Eloy were my first discoveries. At first their world seemed wholly different from metal, offering completely new terrain to explore. Yet prog rock paralleled the evolutionary arc and long-form escapist listening experience I valued so much in great metal bands. Eventually I started to see parallels between prog rock and my own taste in metal. With time, I noticed more metal bands looking back not only to metal's founding fathers for inspiration, but to bands such as Pink Floyd and Genesis. And with further delving, I learned those bands were about much more than radio hits such as "Money" and "Invisible Touch."

The links connecting prog rock and metal appeared more frequently as I made my personal musical discoveries. And over time, a torrent of hybridization occurred. After the pioneering prog rock and heavy metal of the '70s, and the growth of a more progressive metal strain in the '80s, the metal genre expanded its boundaries phenomenally. Metal is no longer exclusively about brute force and pure primal power. At its gut level, metal is still metal. Beyond that, anything goes.

Mean Deviation highlights many impossibly scattered bands and movements that widened the scope of the heavy metal genre. For lack of a better term, much of the music covered here will be referred to as "progressive metal," a term that means different things to different people. To some, it starts with Dream Theater and ends with an interminable stream of bands that sound like Dream Theater. By my interpretation, progressive metal is a catch-all term that allows for consideration of cosmic post–black metal band In the Woods, avant-garde metal surrealists Thought Industry, and those obscure purveyors of corrupted Swedish death metal, Carbonized—along with more obvious entries such as Fates Warning, Opeth, and, of course, Dream Theater.

To me, the bands with the most interesting stories were the ones that began humbly, playing crude, simple forms of metal, and later expanded way beyond that.

On the other hand, many modern progressive or technical metal bands begin life already sounding as mature as their final albums will years down the road, as if the early research-and-development phase of many other prog bands was skipped over entirely. There is no growing up in public for many newer bands, no important mistakes being made, no happy accidents stumbled upon. These kinds of bands are playing safe "progressive" music. Even if they offer worthwhile listening, there's not enough forward evolution to warrant closer inspection here.

Some legitimately progressive modern bands lack the coverage in this book that they admittedly deserve, but after careful consideration I decided that Mastodon, Hammers of Misfortune, Nachtmystium, and Between the Buried and Me—to cite just a few examples—are still too much in flux to properly place in the historical timeline. They are, in fact, bands whose histories are still very much in the making.

While writing this book, I realized that various strains of progressive metal I initially hoped to cover must wait for a future book written by someone else. The story of progressive metal takes a different arc for each individual fan, and *Mean Deviation* is just one man's view of progressive metal—part history, part personal comment. Fact and opinion will intersect and sometimes clash, but be assured that an Orwellian redrafting of history is not my aim.

Two criteria decided the bands spotlighted here. First—do they sound like no other metal band? They must be unique. I don't accept, for example, "like Queensrÿche only faster" as a qualifier. Second, refer to the Frank Zappa quote that opens this book, and also consult the dictionary definition of "progress" or "progressive." Does a band deviate from the norm? Does the artist approach metal using an innovative, ingenious, and/or novel angle of attack? Like Voivod with *Angel Rat*, does the band compel, confound, and/or piss people off with their unorthodox creative pursuits?

The biggest challenge in writing this book was not whom to spotlight, but whom to leave out. Many wonderful, valued, execrable friends made my job even harder, dropping in with suggestions or flat-out orders for their own pet prog metal band: "Don't forget Heads or Tales." "You have to get Albino Slug in there." "What about End Amen?" "You're giving Slauter Xstroyes a page, right?" "Last Crack!" This was not budgeted as a thousand-page A-to-Z prog metal encyclopedia. In that case, not even a dreadful band like Metrical Charms would be left behind.

In his careful dissection of the initial English progressive rock wave, *The Music's All That Matters*, Paul Stump writes: "Progressive [rock]'s chief crimes against good taste, its excess and bombast, are wildly magnified in heavy metal." What of *progressive* metal then? There doesn't seem to be much bad taste, excess, or bombast in a band like Pain of Salvation, yet they are decidedly progressive, and metal enough to earn the title.

Prog metal is a vast field, and its most interesting bands are the hardest to define. Even a metal newbie can identify NWOBHM or Swedish death metal from one or two opening riffs. Defining what prog metal is, or isn't, is more problematic. Prog metal benefits from *not* being easily placed into a specific sound or geographic category. It's an approach but not a methodology. It isn't a movement of consciously unified bands with any kind of official mission statement. Progressive metal doesn't necessarily define itself by long songs, high-pitched vocals, keyboards, a zillion different parts, and odd time signatures. These are sometimes its main features, but they can also be entirely absent. It doesn't necessarily require technical musicianship— it's more about big ideas and grand ambition. Breaking away from the norm doesn't necessarily require mind-boggling polyrhythms or arpeggio sweeps in 12/8 time. But those are cool too.

One thing prog metal certainly is, is metal. Hard and bold and brash, but refined, adulterated, and mutated; it is heavy metal taken somewhere illuminating and sometimes bizarre.

Ultimately, if progressive metal *is* a load of bombast, and if the exaggeration and excess of metal reveal themselves too loudly, so what? Is there no value in that? Since when did any form of rock and roll play it safe? Bring on the bombast, I say.

Audacity...excess...overindulgence? Yeah, bring it on.

PART I:
Atmospheric Disturbance

1. INVENTION / REINVENTION

October 29, 1969, Goddard College, Plainfield, Vermont: "King Crimson's first U.S. gig, to an audience with a high proportion tripping and expecting a happy soul band. We began with '21st Century Schizoid Man.' The audience never recovered from the first shock, their condition being delicate anyway. I had the impression of the crowd being squashed."
—Robert Fripp, King Crimson

ANY SURVEY OF HOW HEAVY METAL FANS ARE FIRST DRAWN to progressive rock will likely reveal King Crimson as the gateway. Crimson's abrasive and unpredictable character appeals to metal fans. Even into the 2000s, their twelfth album, *The ConstruKction of Light*, summoned moments of utterly demonic instrumental shred that were amply sinister to lay most hotshot metal guitarists flat on their backs.

The discography of King Crimson defines the very essence of any progressive music—rock, metal, or otherwise. "The fundamental aim of Crimson is to organize anarchy," says Fripp, "to utilize the latent power of chaos, and to allow the varying influences to interact and find their own equilibrium. The music therefore naturally evolves rather than develops along predetermined lines."

King Crimson's 1969 debut, *In the Court of the Crimson King*, is an indelibly iconic progressive rock album. Red with fright, the face screaming out from the cover painting appears haunted by paranoia and trapped in isolation. The effect is eerie and uneasy—rather like the sound of the music. Opening track "21st Century Schizoid Man" reveals a hybrid of rock, jazz, blues, and classical music. Fluid guitar lines weave through hyper-jazz rhythms, while a blaring sax and muffled voice pile on

At paranoia's poison door: Barry Godber's anguished cover painting for King Crimson's *In the Court of the Crimson King*, 1969

the dread. Finally, at the seven-minute mark, the song crashes with the sound of twisted steel—an ugly heap of noise made of earthier stuff: wood and string. First came the Beatles' "Helter Skelter," then the primal thud of Led Zeppelin, and then this band vowing rape and ruin upon the conventions of contemporary rock and roll.

Born as Giles, Giles and Fripp, the trio added sax/flute player Ian McDonald and bassist/vocalist Greg Lake to become King Crimson. While early Crimson could sound as infernal as its name, the fire was balanced by delicacy and tempered by discipline. In a single show the band would build a bridge between the bouncing beatnik/hippie jazz of "Drop In" and the dramatic, apocalyptic pounding of "Mars"—a selection taken from Gustav Holst's *The Planets*—all of it revealing the far-reaching ambitions of the iconoclastic young Englishmen.

Heads swam and ears rang during Crimson's devastating late-'60s club appearances. One popular Newcastle nightclub, Change Is, featured a rotating weekly theme; one week brought "Love," with another came "Fun." King Crimson performed its inaugural shows at Change Is in late February 1969, during a week whose theme was "Horror." Had heavy metal been already born and named, King Crimson would have fit right in. At least, Robert Fripp thought so.

"'21st Century Schizoid Man,' for me, was intelligent heavy metal," he says. "It was very hard to play. It was so hard to play and it was so terrifying." But heavy metal—equally as misunderstood and maligned as progressive rock—was not even yet a mark on history's pages.

King Crimson's debut is considered one of the first true progressive rock albums, but the radicalization of rock had been brewing for the second half of the 1960s. Some San Francisco weirdos named the Mothers of Invention blindsided the listening public with *Freak Out!* in 1966. The brainchild of Frank Zappa, the album

Serious psychedelia: A young Pink Floyd visits the BBC in 1967
(*Chris Walter*)

taunted mainstream pop music and defied good taste at every opportunity. *Freak Out!*
took ridiculousness seriously, perverting common perceptions of popular music with
over-the-top weirdness and a huge sardonic grin. There no clear precedent for such
poignant and witty rock, but the inspirations listed in the liner notes told the tale:
Maurice Ravel, Buddy Guy, Dalí, Lenny Bruce, Ravi Shankar, Brian Epstein, James
Joyce, Wolfman Jack, Bob Dylan, Joan Baez, Don Van Vliet (aka Captain Beefheart),
Phil Spector, Charlie Mingus, Igor Stravinsky, Karlheinz Stockhausen, John Wayne,
Bram Stoker—and scores more. *Freak Out!* was excessive. The second-ever studio
double album, after Bob Dylan's *Blonde on Blonde*, *Freak Out!* presaged the elaborate
extended-length opuses to come by Pink Floyd, Led Zeppelin, Genesis, and Yes.

During the following year, 1967, Pink Floyd released *The Piper at the Gates of
Dawn* and the Beatles brought *Sgt. Pepper's Lonely Hearts Club Band*. Previously, long-
players had merely been vehicles for singles. The journey of a deep, thirty-five-minute
album experience remained unexplored territory. Starting in the late 1960s, progressive bands changed all that. Following Frank Zappa, Pink Floyd, and the Beatles, others such as the Who, the Pretty Things, Procol Harum, and the Moody Blues pushed
the pop album format to its breaking point. *Sgt. Pepper's* and Procol Harum's *Shine on
Brightly* felt more like slowly unfolding films than mere pop albums.

In 1968, Deep Purple released its groundbreaking classical album, *Deep Purple & the Royal Philharmonic Orchestra*. Soon after, Led Zeppelin fused aspects of folk, reggae, and jazz to their esoteric hard rock core. And as Jethro Tull's bluesy roots quickly grew into a dynamic heavy prog sound, by the early '70s parts of their albums, even whole songs, sounded indistinguishable from early heavy metal. Ironically, Tull's parody of the prog rock concept album, 1972's *Thick as a Brick*, is now considered a seminal work of the initial prog rock wave.

A mass of bands soon experimented much further with rock. Upstarts Genesis, Yes, Gentle Giant, and Van der Graaf Generator emboldened the long-haired intelligentsia and formed a new foundation. As players evolved rapidly through creative periods, there was a sense of restlessness at the wheel. Discovery became the only rule during this careening, mad race of ambition and anti-commercial risk taking.

The infusion of folk, psychedelic, electronic, classical, and jazz elements into standard rock music created the miasmic melting pot eventually known as "prog." But according to Gentle Giant's Derek Shulman, they didn't know what "prog" was: "We started in 1970," he says, "and toward the end of the ten years we were together there became a name for it: 'progressive.' When we started it was just: 'Let's make some good music.'"

While the first Yes and Genesis albums were not as ornate as their more notorious later efforts, King Crimson's debut scaled the heights of hybridization and instrumental prowess. Just as mature at the earliest stage was supergroup Emerson, Lake and Palmer, which released its self-titled album in 1970. The trio—Keith Emerson, Greg Lake, and Carl Palmer—had respectively fled the Nice, King Crimson, and Atomic Rooster. A phenomenon—and big business—in the new decade, their albums were diversely arranged marriages of all the most bombastic elements of classical and rock music. ELP's early live shows were cacophonous. Onstage, Emerson and his Hammond organ convulsed in a ritual of mock fucking, climaxing with the keyboardist stabbing groups of keys with a knife, creating a dissonant drone over which he madly improvised. According to legend, that very knife was given to Emerson by none other than Lemmy Kilmister—former roadie for the Nice, later the bad-boy bassist of Hawkwind, and today revered in metal circles as the leader of Motörhead.

ELP's raucousness was initially only slightly tempered by Emerson's classical training. By the late '70s, ELP's raw material was spit-shined by maturity. Their peers in King Crimson rose quickly to legendary status; but even if Crimson also played large venues and sold a ridiculous amount of albums, Fripp's crew seemed more like the biggest cult band in the world than a huge commercial conglomerate like ELP.

After the big names established their enormous global audiences, doors opened for like-minded acts, and the branches of the prog tree became numerous. Fusion and prog met in the middle as Brand X and Colosseum II exploded onto the scene. Another pioneering English band, Queen, gave rise to "art rock"; that term took its share of beatings, but the music was indeed smart, thoughtful, and conceptual. Art rock bands Be-Bop Deluxe, 10cc, and Crack the Sky snipped the fat from prog excess while maintaining a sense of hybridization and exploration. Art rock consciously and deliberately sublimated rock's base elements. Its slick, smart, meticulous approach appealed to some prog fans but avoided the demanding, sometimes bloated journeys into fantasia taken by the big prog bands. Art rock was song-oriented yet avoided the disposability of the pop formula by virtue of quirk and intelligence.

Throughout the majority of the 1970s, prog rock was defined by adventure. Bands usually remained quite distinct, alike only in their will to move forward. Leaders Yes and Genesis maxed their prog muscle with massive concept double albums *Tales from Topographic Oceans* and *The Lamb Lies Down on Broadway*, respectively. These works demanded total attention from listeners, testing casual fans with uncompromising and intense flights of fancy.

The classical influence on many of the U.K.'s pioneering acts was a mere starting point. Caravan played a quirky, whimsical jazz/rock hybrid that came to be known as "Canterbury," named after the area in England where they and similar others originated; the Netherlands' Supersister took that sound a step further, coming off like an eccentric/experimental, Zappa-esque Canterbury offshoot. Meanwhile, Gryphon and Comus spearheaded folk-influenced prog sounds. Magma's Christian Vander took influence from John Coltrane and such twentieth-century composers as Igor Stravinsky and Béla Bartók, constructed his own language (Kobaïan), and banged out oppressive, epic, peerless orchestral rock.

But the heavily populated prog movements in Italy, Germany, Scandinavia, and the U.S. deserve special attention. With their country's rich heritage of opera and classical music, young Italian fans easily grasped the grandiosity of English bands Genesis and Van der Graaf Generator. Soon, homegrown units including Banco del Mutuo Soccorso, Le Orme, Premiata Forneria Marconi (aka P.F.M.), and loads of others emerged to great acclaim, within and outside of Italy.

Germany was just as prolific. Krautrock—so named by the English press, who saw the country's output as an organized, intentional movement—wasn't so much a particular sound as a geographical blitz of creativity. The country birthed a huge variety of bands. Some played experimental/improvisational music (Can, Faust, Guru Guru); many were outgrowths of the earlier psych movement (Os Mundi, Embryo, Amon Düül II); some pioneered electronic/synth-pop music (Tangerine Dream, Kraftwerk); and others were inspired by classic English prog bands (Eloy, Novalis, Triumvirat). Nektar were unique among all of the German bands, comprised exclusively of Englishmen living in Germany. Also dubbed "Kosmische Musik," or "Cosmic Musick," by Tangerine Dream's Edgar Froese, "Krautrock" was the term that stuck—even if it was vaguely offensive to some people. This prolific national scene also spawned Hannover's Scorpions, who eventually transformed into an arena rock sensation.

From English-style prog to improv/experimental music to early electronic and synth-pop, Krautrock bands as different as Eloy, Kraftwerk, and Amon Düül II made a significant mark on the '70s. Simultaneously, dark wizards such as England's Henry Cow and Belgium's Univers Zero created grave, forbidding music, using expanded lineups, varied instrumentation, and even sheet music scores. They also tightened prog's association with jazz and classical by drawing lineage to musique concrete and to such groundbreaking twentieth-century composers as Karlheinz Stockhausen.

Sweden, Norway, and Denmark were productive on an underground level, with bands varying significantly in style, ranging from jazz-rock/fusion to folk/prog to space-rock to quirky, angular weirdness. Finland offered its own mutations on the prog rock sound—as did Japan and Argentina.

In the U.S., Yezda Urfa, Babylon, and Cathedral never climbed out of the underground, but Virginia's eclectic Happy the Man ended up on Arista Records, while

Indiana's Ethos—modeled after the big English bands—landed on the giant Capitol label. The biggest success story in U.S. prog rock was undoubtedly Kansas—like their heroes in King Crimson, they were one of the first bands to weld metallic elements to a sturdy prog framework.

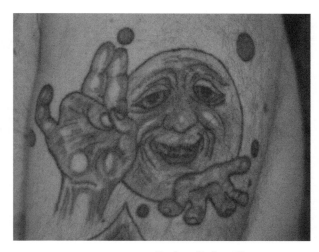

Enslaved's Ivar Bjørnson wears the mark of the Crimson King (*Tonje Elisabeth Peersen*)

Written by guitarist Kerry Livgren, the first Kansas songs were an amalgam of Crimson, Frank Zappa, Van der Graaf Generator, and Soft Machine. Early tracks "Nactolos 21" and "Totus Nemesis" were monolithic and intimidating. Revamping their lineup, Kansas signed to CBS imprint Kirshner (founded by mogul Don Kirshner) and released a few directionless albums spanning barroom boogie, hard rock, and English-influenced prog. The band was clearly best when heavy tendencies collided with more epic ambitions. "Incomudro—Hymn to the Atman" and "Journey from Mariabronn" easily eclipse such basic, boogie-driven tunes as "Bringing It Back" and "It Takes a Woman's Love (to Make a Man)."

One of the earliest and clearest mergers of prog rock and heavy metal appeared on Kansas's 1975 album *Masque*. "Icarus (Borne on Wings of Steel)"—soaring and sublime, but also gutsy and sharp—pointed the way to the sturdier, more focused following two albums, *Leftoverture* and *Point of Know Return*. Once Kansas found its comfort zone, hordes of people rallied around them—the singles "Carry On Wayward Son" and "Dust in the Wind" sold more than a million copies each, and placed their respective albums high on the charts. As the English greats had proven previously, intelligent and challenging rock music could sell large without selling out.

Whether or not the pioneers of progressive rock's first wave would approve, their work birthed and nurtured many in the weird, wild world of heavy metal. For example, Mikael Åkerfeldt of Opeth passionately praises the influence of Andy Latimer and Camel on his playing and compositional approach. Christofer Johnsson, leader of modern-day opera metal pioneers Therion, sees a clear lineage leading back to the innovators of prog. "There are loads of '70s progressive rock influences in Therion," he says. "A lot of the things we do are practically the same as the '70s, just a bit more dressed up in a modern sound. Many of our own songs could have been played in the '70s. Like 'Lemuria,' which even has a Mellotron and those '70s sounds. If that song would have been recorded in the '70s, it would have been completely normal."

As unlikely as it might have seemed then, the prog/metal crossover was bound to happen. The Beatles' experimental period led twenty-five years later to the avant-garde psychedelic death metal of Sweden's Pan-Thy-Monium—even if the path is roundabout. The link between Kansas and Jethro Tull and modern progressive metal legends Dream Theater and Fates Warning is more obvious.

Robert Fripp of King Crimson hardly denied his band's similarity to metal—he even encouraged it. On the departure of Crimson violinist David Cross in 1974, Fripp declared, "The violin is not an instrument of heavy metal."

Then Crimson recorded *Red*, featuring their heaviest, most complex and frightening music but retaining their more refined, textured characteristics. "I think 'Red' was a beautiful piece of heavy metal—in 5/8 time," says Fripp. "I hadn't heard heavy metal in 5 before, but for me that was it."

2. ALL MOVING PARTS

"Black Sabbath was extraordinary, because it had roots in progressive rock and blues and jazz. Some of that early Sabbath work is extraordinary to listen to because it has all those elements, but it's wrapped up in this new sound, this new way to write music." —Rob Halford, Judas Priest

LONG THE BLACK SHEEP OF THE GREATER ROCK SCENE, prog rock and metal have been inextricably linked since their beginnings. Both endured critical dismissal; neither were taken seriously, and tastemakers had little use for either. The two styles were bound to intersect, clash, and conspire.

Throughout the 1970s, progressive rock and early heavy metal moved in tandem, spinning on axes of wildness, escapism, and anti-commercial methods. They shared many similarities, and much of metal's family tree even stems from progressive rock. Black Sabbath guitarist Tony Iommi was a member of Jethro Tull for a few fleeting seconds in late 1968 but returned to his mates in Earth, who rechristened the band Black Sabbath in 1969.

Good old heavy metal in the 1970s was ugly, beastly stuff that couldn't get respect and wasn't looking for any—just a misunderstood mass of unkempt hair and ridiculous volume. Many bands of the era made great art and a good living sticking to the reliable adage, "If it ain't broke, don't fix it." Amidst the storm and bluster, others morphed the form into a zillion different shapes; the result of bravery, talent, vision, restlessness, perhaps even boredom. Even during its earliest years, metal proved to be a surprisingly viable and malleable form of music, paralleling the birth and subsequent growth of jazz in the early twentieth century.

The exact point where heavy metal became distinct from rock and roll is debatable, but Black Sabbath's early 1970 debut, *Black Sabbath*, is the generally accepted starting point. The seminal album's rape and plunder of blues rock, reshaped and made into something uglier, found deeper gravity via mournful singing and a sinister rhythmic pulse. As soon as the band arrived on the scene, they obliterated notions of rock and roll as mere entertainment. Their throbbing downer sound was frightening to outsiders but much-needed therapy for the members of the band and their young listeners. *Black Sabbath* faced personal and global problems head-on—this was not another artist spoon-feeding the public easily digestible ear candy. Their music still provided escape, which all good rock and roll should do, but was altogether more jarring and sobering than what had come before.

Black Sabbath quickly gained notoriety for its uncompromising heavy brand of rock. Successive albums *Paranoid* (1970), *Master of Reality* (1971), and *Vol. 4* (1972) painted bleak pictures of the world—the band's reaction to life on this planet. The albums also wrote the first and most important chapters in the history of doom metal. Then in 1973 a curiously different Black Sabbath emerged. After just five years of existence, the band largely credited with inventing metal took its primordial thud into prog territory. Having done everything they could with the basic formula, they had clearly decided it was time to move on.

Black Sabbath's first four albums were total musical thunder, without the nuance and subtlety of Led Zeppelin and Deep Purple. Even decades after the genre's genesis, many modern bands still plod along a Neanderthal line. But as soon as Sabbath and other early metal bands had the resources to spend entire years in the studio, toying with melodramatic sensitivity and grandiose sonic imagery, the genre proved uncommonly pliable.

For their fifth album, Black Sabbath remained sequestered in the studio many months, obsessing over the tiniest details and widening each song's sonic range. The result, *Sabbath Bloody Sabbath*, is one of the earliest proofs of metal's remarkable potential.

Sabbath Bloody Sabbath marked the first time Black Sabbath produced one of its own albums. This new freedom showed throughout its eight songs. Drugs also played their role. They had been part of Sabbath's inner workings since the beginning, and were no doubt a catalyst in the band's move toward broader sonic territory.

Going through changes: Black Sabbath in 1973
(*Chris Walter*)

Alcohol, pot, and cocaine were particular favorites, and while one could argue they may have actually stunted the band's progression, Sabbath's creative growth spurt in the mid-'70s seems to state otherwise. The liner notes in *Vol. 4* give a not very veiled thanks to one of their favorite substances: "We wish to thank the great COKE-cola company of Los Angeles."

Arguably the first progressive metal album, *Sabbath Bloody Sabbath* was full of sublime atmosphere and exotic texture. The band successfully pulled its leaden iconoclasm into more cerebral realms. Recorded only a single year after the largely sluggish, muddy *Vol. 4*, the record surprised fans. "I was already listening to Black Sabbath, and I bought *Sabbath Bloody Sabbath* when it came out," says future Dream Theater manager and Inside Out label boss Jim Pitulski. "It took awhile to get into, because it was different than what I had come to expect. I could tell the band was trying to go someplace else, and I wasn't sure I approved. I was just a kid, and I wanted to hear what I had become comfortable with. That's the nature of progressive music—to surprise people and keep them on their toes, and carry the fans along with it."

Where *Vol. 4*'s "Wheels of Confusion," *Paranoid*'s "Planet Caravan," and other forays prepared the way for a wiser, more thoughtful Sabbath, no one could have predicted a song like the elaborate "Spiral Architect." Closing *Sabbath Bloody Sabbath*, it paints an airy, dreamlike picture with lyrics that are appropriately abstract and surreal. A string section, mysteriously credited to the "Phantom Fiddlers," enhances its ethereal texture. The extra instrumentation throughout the song and the rest of the album—most of it played by the members themselves—expands on the traditional setup: steel guitar, piano, harpsichord, synthesizer, Mellotron, organ, timpani, flute, and bagpipes.

BLACK SABBATH

TECHNICAL ECSTASY

Far from tolling bells and hands of doom:
Sabbath's Hipgnosis-designed *Technical Ecstasy*, 1976

Bassist Geezer Butler is even inexplicably credited on "Spiral Architect" with "nose," perhaps part of what Tony Iommi called "the Rhythm Box." "It had all these little things in it, like maracas and triangles and stuff," says Iommi. "We tried all kinds of stuff. *Sabbath Bloody Sabbath* was the album where we started going for more, trying to keep things from sounding the same as what had come before."

Enhancing the members' own adventures outside the basic guitar/bass/drums lineup, in came legendary keyboardist Rick Wakeman, known from prog folkies Strawbs, quintessential prog gods Yes, and his ambitious solo output. His piano and synthesizer sounds on psych-blues number "Sabbra Cadabra" are magical. Surprisingly, Wakeman wasn't employed on the synth-drenched "Who Are You." The normally microphone-bound Ozzy Osbourne is credited with synthesizer, as is bassist Butler. "Fluff" gives further depth to the album with its serene, almost aloof tone. The song—four minutes of tranquility that out-mellowed the previous album's "Changes"—features Iommi on acoustic and steel guitar, piano and harpsichord, with Butler handling bass.

Sabbath Bloody Sabbath was a rare departure that struck a chord with the record-buying public, coinciding with the most experimental phase rock music had yet been through. The album went gold instantly and continues to be one of the best-selling albums in the Sabbath catalog. The usually metal-phobic *Rolling Stone* even gave the record an excellent review, with Gordon Fletcher calling it "an extraordinarily gripping affair."

The commercial success of *Sabbath Bloody Sabbath* encouraged this brighter, braver Black Sabbath. The band spent even more time recording their next album, 1975's *Sabotage*. Their experimental mode was at its height, and *Sabotage* took nearly eighteen months to make. According to Iommi, "In those days you couldn't borrow samples or have that many effects, so you had to make your own by more organic means. And that took a lot longer. Especially when [drummer] Bill [Ward] would start farting about, making some sort of weird rig to lower anvils into water and recording the sound of that. We tried all these different ideas, physically challenging stuff. Those were the things that took time. Today you press a button and it just comes out."

Sabotage is the creative apex of the original Black Sabbath's eight-album run. It has all the charm and experimentation of its predecessor, but expands and broadens everything. Produced with remarkable depth once again by the band (with Mike Butcher coproducing this time), Sabbath's trademark bludgeon is treated with rounded warmth, while the adventurous tangents are more thoroughly explored than before. The band had become studio wizards, and the songwriting was more heavily layered, as demonstrated on epics "Megalomania" and "The Writ."

Bloodthirsty metal opens *Sabotage* in the form of "Hole in the Sky" and "Symptom of the Universe." But if the Santana-like final moments of "Symptom of the Universe" didn't scare away fans wanting the old Sabbath back, maybe the *Fantasia*-meets-Third-Reich drone of "Supertzar" did. And then there was the completely odd "Am I Going Insane (Radio)." Synth-driven, with irrepressible bouncing bass, its bizarre beauty was based on a paranoid pop refrain, hummable yet full of unease. The album's most ambitious compositions, "Megalomania" and "The Writ," set a benchmark for bending metal into strange new shapes.

The time spent fussing around in the studio paid off. *Sabbath Bloody Sabbath* and *Sabotage* continue to attract young fans venturing beyond the band's first four records. Geezer Butler remains proud of Sabbath's most adventurous period. "A lot of bands could record two or three albums in the time it used to take us to do a couple songs," he says. "But you can still listen to those songs and hear them a different way every time."

Although the question of who first applied the term "heavy metal" to music has been much debated, Sandy Pearlman may deserve the credit. First a writer for underground '70s rock rag *Crawdaddy!* and later the Svengali/mentor/conceptualist for Blue Öyster Cult, Pearlman often used the term to describe the nascent heavy music of the time: Black Sabbath, Deep Purple, Led Zeppelin, and more obscure acts such as Bang, Captain Beyond, Budgie, and Sir Lord Baltimore. These bands came from the darkness and sent the raw energy of distorted guitars to their limits. And when the term "heavy metal" came to widespread use later in the decade, Scorpions and especially Judas Priest solidified its essence through ever more ballsy, explosive sounds.

Hailing from Long Island, Blue Öyster Cult enjoyed enormous popularity while holding fast to a unique and not necessarily commercial vision. They found success on the level of Black Sabbath in 1976, with the complex and compelling "(Don't Fear) the Reaper"—still a staple of classic rock radio. B.Ö.C. explored esoteric concepts and arcane practices, mixing alchemy, modern science, and philosophy within an eclectic brew of hard rock, art rock, heavy metal, and prog. Columbia Records attempted to brand them "the American Black Sabbath," touting their self-titled 1972 debut album as "a panorama of violence and suffering." But B.Ö.C. was never quite so harrowing. Their methods were more subtle, and their sound less blunt. As drummer and cofounder Albert Bouchard recalls, they couldn't do straight Sabbath: "'Cities on Flame with Rock and Roll' was our attempt at imitating Black Sabbath," he says. "We stole the first part from Black Sabbath's 'The Wizard' and the second part from King Crimson's '21st Century Schizoid Man.'"

Most of B.Ö.C.'s output is not that derivative. Whatever tracks such as "Wings Wetted Down" and "Flaming Telepaths" are; whatever *Tyranny & Mutation*, *Secret Treaties*, and *Cultosaurus Erectus* convey in all their subtext; the Blue Öyster Cult discography runs thick with sublimity and allure. The band certainly aided in the merger of progressive rock and heavy metal.

A black and white Rainbow, 1978
(*Chris Walter*)

In the early 1970s, future Black Sabbath vocalist Ronnie James Dio was play-ing in the Electric Elves, who morphed over several years into The Elves and, finally, just plain Elf. In 1974 Deep Purple bassist Roger Glover recruited Dio to sing on Glover's ambitious solo album, *The Butterfly Ball and the Grasshopper's Feast*. Between this album and Elf's stints as live opener for Deep Purple, guitarist Ritchie Blackmore became enamored of Dio's vocal capabilities. Blackmore left Deep Purple in 1975 and replaced his old mates with nearly the entire Elf lineup, calling the new group Rain-bow. Rainbow made three albums with Dio between 1975 and 1978, chasing a sound somewhere between the smart hard rock of Blackmore's previous band, keyboard-dominant English prog, and the finessed early metal of Rush and Black Sabbath.

Rainbow was a key influence on Opeth's Mikael Åkerfeldt. He names them a much greater inspiration than the more popular Rush. "I respect Rush as progressive innovators," says Åkerfeldt. "I always liked the instrumental bits but was turned off by the vocals. For me, Rainbow was much more important. They were progressive, even though they didn't have many time changes or odd beats, but they had an epic feel to their sound."

Two Rainbow songs in particular stand as prog metal cornerstones. "Stargaz-er," from 1976's *Rising*, is less a song and more a journey. Majestic and dreamlike, its atmosphere has rarely been duplicated. The song probably trumped anything else the band ever did, but the mystical "Gates of Babylon" from 1978's *Long Live Rock 'n' Roll* is nearly its equal. Dio left in 1979 to join up with the fractured, Ozzy-less Black Sabbath, and recorded two unbendable works of metal greatness with them, *Heaven and Hell* and *Mob Rules*. But Sabbath would never again exercise the unfettered creative freedom of their mid- to late -'70s period, and Rainbow would move onto decidedly more radio-friendly pastures in the '80s.

Like the earliest progressive rock bands, in the 1970s the earliest metal bands didn't even have a name for the new musical strain they were pioneering. Heavy metal back then was just a newer, heavier form of hard rock that came naturally to its practitioners. Equipment was more versatile, amps were able to handle louder volumes, the world was becoming scarier, and people's ears were more attuned to bizarre, disturbing music. It was only sometime around 1977 or 1978 that the term "heavy metal" was regularly applied to music on a global scale.

The first band that defined metal as a unique branch of the rock-and-roll tree and a significant leap beyond hard rock was Judas Priest. Hailing from Birmingham, England, the birthplace of Black Sabbath, Judas Priest's early material provided inspiration for future progressive metal bands Voivod and Fates Warning, among many other more traditional metal acts. The band's best-known albums are streamlined hell-bent-for-leather killers, but their earliest recordings showed a grandiose streak that remains one of the most compelling "what if"s in progressive music history.

Rocka Rolla debuted in 1974, inspired by fellow Birmingham peers Black Sabbath while taking a page from the Wishbone Ash school of twin guitar harmony. Judas Priest were one of the first bands to utilize two lead guitarists for trade-off and tandem soloing, as opposed to the more common single-guitar approach of bands such as Deep Purple and Black Sabbath or the rhythm/lead teams of Scorpions and Kiss.

Rocka Rolla sounds quaint compared to Judas Priest's later, more popular work. The band sounds unaware of its destiny and unencumbered by expectation. After sludgy openers "One for the Road" and "Rocka Rolla," the band is warmed up and ready to offer more radical ideas. The four-part "Winter/Deep Freeze/Winter Retreat/ Cheater" offers hazy psychedelic doom, harrowing Hendrix-like guitar torture, sullen melancholy, and barroom blues metal, respectively. The second half's "Run of the

Mill" and "Dying to Meet You" are broad in scope and arrangement; brooding, epic, and majestic compositions that, in hindsight, seem ahead of their time. Vocalist Rob Halford's wailing in the final moments of both "Never Satisfied" and "Run of the Mill" is not obviously rooted in rock at all, coming more from an operatic influence and certainly of an even higher pitch than fellow screamers Ian Gillan and Robert Plant.

Rocka Rolla is to Judas Priest's discography what *Fly by Night* and *Caress of Steel* are to Rush's, and can be considered a companion to those efforts. But Priest clearly had a heavier touch, with mournful, dark atmospheres deeply permeating the drama. The band's theatrical side would be fully explored on its next studio visit.

Priest's *Sad Wings of Destiny* (1976) arrived just as Black Sabbath's musical wanderlust was fading. The time was right for a revival or reinstatement of what Sabbath had started and what Rush and Rainbow were carrying into the future. Bright, punchy, and propulsive, *Sad Wings* contrasted with *Rocka Rolla*'s foggy downbeat plod. Amidst the searing vocals of Halford and distinctive twin guitar trade-offs of Glenn Tipton and K.K. Downing, shades of Queen-level pomp could be heard. The operatic range Halford exhibited on the first album was made crystalline on "Dreamer Deceiver," an autumnal ballad that expanded the epic melancholy of the debut, and "Epitaph," which veered into a precarious Beatles-meets-Broadway mode that Priest would never again revisit. Elsewhere, the band shot forth sparks of state-of-the-art metalwork with the slashing "Ripper"; medieval metal blueprints "Tyrant" and "Genocide"; and epic opener "Victim of Changes," which shaped expanded song structure, performance finesse, and heightened aggression into a career cornerstone. Halford and Downing still name "Victim of Changes" as the ultimate Priest composition.

Subsequent albums saw less ambitious writing from Judas Priest, although *Sin After Sin* and *Stained Class* hold their share of early progressive metal moments. Beginning with 1978's *Hell Bent for Leather*, the band streamlined and found its legendary signature sound. The songwriting was no less excellent, the playing no less impressive, but their commitment to bravery and exploration began to fall off considerably. (The 2008 double album *Nostradamus* arguably resurrects Priest's penchant for prog, although it will likely never be considered their *Tales from Topographic Oceans*.)

The 1970s gave birth to heavy metal, and the new form's restless spirit didn't take long to liberate itself from the shackles of three-chord thud. The most ambitious material by metal's pioneers may not be considered experimental or avant-garde in light of what came later, but their push at the edges of the sonic spectrum showed that the genre, even at that early stage, was not just a raw, thrilling experience, but a malleable form of music with limitless possibility.

O o O o

If Judas Priest's *Rocka Rolla* seems quaint compared to more popular later albums, Scorpions' 1972 debut sounds positively alien. *Lonesome Crow* is clearly a product of Germany's fertile psych scene: loose, bluesy, brimming with hippie spirit. It sounds more like German brethren Hairy Chapter or Jane than the arena balladeers Scorpions became in the 1980s. Thus the disgust of '80s teenagers who picked up *Lonesome Crow* after being turned on to slicker, more polished Scorpions albums *Blackout* or *Love at First Sting*.

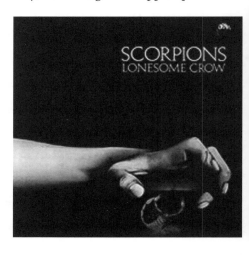

Lonesome Crow was largely inspired by Jimi Hendrix and Cream. Clearly the work of a band still searching for its identity, the album is probably most noteworthy as the launching pad for guitar legend Michael Schenker. Seventeen years old at the time of recording, Schenker was lured away by England's UFO shortly after the album's release,

Scorpions' proggy debut, *Lonesome Crow*, 1972

leaving Scorpions in the hands of vocalist Klaus Meine and Michael's brother Rudolf.

Originally released on seminal Krautrock label Brain Records, *Lonesome Crow* was a product of its time and place. Scorpions did not embrace the eclectic direction of fellow Brain artists such as Grobschnitt or Novalis, leaving the label after *Lonesome Crow* for major RCA and recording two early progressive metal cornerstones, *Fly to the Rainbow* (1974) and *In Trance* (1975). With Hendrix devotee Uli Jon Roth replacing Michael Schenker on guitar, songs such as the spectral "Fly to the Rainbow," the contemplative "Life's Like a River," and the psychedelic doom monster "Evening Wind" showed that, even at this early stage, metal could inhabit both the primal and sublime.

The Roth-penned "Drifting Sun" exhibits an ahead-of-its-time heaviness and nods to the band's '60s roots—presaging another seminal Roth composition, 1978's classic "Sails of Charon." These and more direct songs "Speedy's Coming" and "Robot Man" laid the blueprint for students such as Queensrÿche and Fates Warning. With celestial lead guitar melodies, Meine's expressiveness, thick background harmony vocals, and an uninhibited approach to composition, early Scorpions stands alongside Rush, Black Sabbath, Rainbow, and Judas Priest as an important building block of prog metal's basic foundation.

Unfortunately, internal struggles and external pressures made the final two Black Sabbath albums of the 1970s uneven and, in spots, downright awful. But Sabbath still thrust laudably into new areas, despite the turmoil. *Technical Ecstasy* contorted in two very different directions. Some songs ("Back Street Kids," "Rock and Roll Doctor") found the band reverting to their blues roots, minus the depressive, gloomy atmosphere. Others, such as the emotive, multifaceted "Gypsy" and the cosmically funky "All Moving Parts (Stand Still)" showed a band still exploring. Sabbath's gloomy center hadn't completely disappeared—it had just changed shape. Both "You Won't Change Me" and "She's Gone" are neurotic/narcotic updates of their early downer vibe. "It's Alright," a ballad sung by drummer Bill Ward, was the odd song out this time, a mix of Elton John and the Beatles that was hardly even recognizable as Black Sabbath.

Technical Ecstasy's recording sounded more basic and impromptu than the previous production pieces, although plenty of nuances still separated this Black Sabbath from their early bare-bones aesthetic. The album cover itself is unusual, a cartoon/art deco depiction of two robots passing each other on an escalator. Designed by Storm Thorgerson's company Hipgnosis—a hot commodity in prog circles at the time—the image looked more like an Alan Parsons Project cover. This was clearly not your older brother's Black Sabbath.

Sabbath lurched into 1978 with *Never Say Die*, the final album recorded with their original lineup. While its diversity is beyond anything they'd previously attempted, the album is as unbalanced as it is eclectic. Driving upbeat rock ("Never Say Die," "Over to You"), beer-hall chant-along ("A Hard Road"), piano-laden jazz-rock ("Air Dance"), surly blue-collar swagger ("Swinging the Chain"), an instrumental full of blaring brass ("Breakout"), and one song of typical Sabbath heaviness ("Shock Wave")—this is *Never Say Die* in all its scattered glory. The band pulled itself in too many directions for one album, yet two songs have aged particularly well. "Johnny Blade" and "Junior's Eyes" are vivid lyrical plays with plenty of musical substance, and the album's bright recording highlights their detail and texture. The songs come back-to-back after the boisterous opening title track—an early climax on this fascinating, uneven album. *Never Say Die* is a mishmash, but an admirable step forward for a band that refused to let their music atrophy owing to repetition.

Black Sabbath was definitely the first heavy metal band—were they also metal's first progressive band? *Sabbath Bloody Sabbath* predates Rush's *Fly by Night* by two years. The band that defined the simplistic appeal of heavy metal—music based on pure blunt force—broke their own mold in a quest for the unknowns that lay around the next corner. Whoever was first, or the biggest inspiration to metal's future progressives, at their genre-blurring best, Black Sabbath deserve to have their name uttered along with that of King Crimson—and the soon-to-arrive Rush—when laying down the bedrock of big ideas to come.

3. BY-TOR AT THE GATES OF DELIRIUM

"The question that we tend to ask most often is 'What if?' I think if you had to simplify our motivation or simplify a moving force in our music, that would probably suffice."—Neil Peart, Rush

As early metal and prog bands in Europe and America were busy defining their nascent genres—occasionally dabbling in one another's methods—a trio of Canadians sat on the edge of that stream, watching and listening, waiting for their turn and practicing like hell. Their name was Rush, and they would most successfully hybridize prog rock and heavy metal.

From 1968 to 1973, a young Rush worked the clubs, tracing the blueprints of heroes such as Cream, the Who, Blue Cheer, and Led Zeppelin. After years of paying dues and discovering their own songwriting talents, the band released their self-titled debut album in 1974. Neither Sabbath nor Crimson had anything to worry about. *Rush* was a workmanlike display of the band's influences, and while it was tight, capable, even enjoyable, it was hardly the stuff of legend. No review of the album failed to note similarities to Led Zeppelin: heavy blues riffing, thunderous rhythmic bludgeon, and the wailing of vocalist/bassist Geddy Lee. Rush could hardly make much impact, considering the real deal was still very much alive and kicking. And despite some of the ethereal touches within "Before and After," *Rush* offered no obvious clue of what was to come.

Immediately after the album's release, drummer John Rutsey bowed out due to health concerns and his dislike of touring. His departure was the best thing that ever happened to the band, forcing founding Rush members Lee and guitarist Alex

Lifeson to audition drummers so they could tour in support of their debut. On the second day, good fortune brought them Neil Peart. Not only did Peart have a meticulous, detailed approach to his playing that Rutsey lacked, but his love of literature and generally intellectual disposition set Rush on a high-minded course. His presence brought cranial substance to the songwriting and sensitivity to their instrumental chemistry. Fortunately, Lee and Lifeson's interests had been moving along a similar line—together the revamped trio pushed the band's primordial poundings several evolutionary steps ahead.

With a new lineup in place and some roadwork behind the band, second album *Fly by Night* clearly defined Rush's developing sound as something they could call their own. Only traces of the first album's approach remained. The songs that pointed the way forward shined brightest and have been remembered the longest. Leadoff song "Anthem" shoved Peart's propulsive drum work to the foreground. The riffs were more involved, the melodies more intricate, the singing more insistent. Peart immediately assumed the bulk of lyric duties. At the time, the drummer was heavily into the writings of author Ayn Rand. Based on the Rand book of the same name, "Anthem" became Rush's mission statement, conveying a quest for integrity and individuality in a world that rewarded the meek and mediocre.

As they expanded their own playing and writing, the three members of Rush remained engaged fans of other artists. They remained aware of changing musical tides through every step of their career, and so their ever-evolving sound stayed modern and relevant. In the mid-'70s, the trio was swept up in the English progressive rock wave. Under the influence of Yes, Genesis, Van der Graaf Generator, Gentle Giant, and ELP, Rush fused the thunderous heaviness of their early work with the musical complexity of the prog elite.

"They were progressive in every sense of the word," says Geddy Lee, "and we were influenced by that kind of playing and structure. We started admiring bands like Cream and the Who, and when the progressive movement came along, we were so impressed with the musicality and complexity. We became complexity freaks. So we wanted to write things that were heavy but complex."

Early 1975's *Fly by Night* heralded Rush's style of epic song craft that served them well into the early '80s. "By-Tor and the Snow Dog," at eight minutes and forty seconds, might have been conservative compared to later twenty-minute works, but its aims were clear. The song's vivid storytelling was weighty and multifaceted without feeling overwrought. Its midsection musical battle between By-Tor (stabbing, steely guitar) and the Snow Dog (flanged, effects-laden bass growling) was the most memorable moment—even if it wasn't exactly original. Just a year earlier, Yes's *Relayer* album opened with the twenty-two-minute workout "The Gates of Delirium," which exhibited something very similar to "By-Tor" in its clashing, clanging midsection duel. It was obvious where Rush got the idea. Still wearing their influences on the outside, Rush upped the ante and merged the complexity of their prog teachers with their own innate heaviness. "By-Tor and the Snow Dog" was the first tangible result, a crucial early intersection between progressive rock and heavy metal.

With literary/fantasy themes, nimble yet attacking drum work, fat guitar tones, melodic sensitivity, and otherworldly banshee vocals welded to their overall bludgeoning approach, Rush was, probably unwittingly, crafting a new kind of musical expression. This was progressive metal in its infancy, played by musicians eager to prove their worth, pushing forward with each album in an effort to better themselves and expand their scope. Together with producer Terry Brown, they attained high standards of sonic excellence with each new endeavor, balancing power and grace with increasingly state-of-the-art productions.

The prog metal blueprint laid down on "Anthem" and "By-Tor..." was built onto and expanded further in the coming years. Late 1975 brought *Caress of Steel*, which opened with "Bastille Day," a burning early metal classic somewhere between murky hard rock and the kind of neoclassical glory later dubbed "power metal." *Caress of Steel*—bearing blooper artwork of muddy gold instead of the intended steely silver—introduced two long-form works in "The Necromancer" and "The Fountain of Lamneth." They showed the band moving in a heady direction that made the *Rush* debut seem not two years but two decades distant.

Rush's darkest song yet, the impressive twelve-minute-plus "The Necromancer" deftly demonstrated their seamless merging of metal and prog, a mash-up of Black Sabbath and Genesis. A direct line to Rush-inspired bands of the future can be heard in the heavy, spacious early metal workout introduced after the song's four-minute mark. Indeed, the Canadian teenagers who would later form Voivod were lis-

Rush's iconic "Starman," first seen on *2112*. "In Rush's lyrics, there are good forces–creativity and free expression–and bad things contrary to that," says artist Hugh Syme. "The man is the hero of that story. The pureness of his person and creativity without the trappings of elements like clothing is classic. The red star is the evil red star of the Federation, one of Neil Peart's symbols"

tening. "The first progressive band that I heard was Rush," states Voivod drummer Michel "Away" Langevin, "and that's really where I noticed you could be very intricate yet still heavy."

Paul Masvidal of progressive metal band Cynic also considers Rush a game-changer. "They married really interesting musical ideas with three completely separate musicians and created this mishmash that became the Rush sound," he says. "They changed a whole generation in terms of musicians, and shaped a style and influenced so many acts. It's just phenomenal what Rush has done."

Sadly, *Caress of Steel* remains the most overlooked of Rush's classic '70s-era albums. The band's label, Mercury Records, got cold feet after relatively disappointing sales, and told Rush in so many words that their epic direction wasn't appreciated. The idea of a hit single was discussed by the label and band management—curious, considering Rush had been given total creative control in their contract. In this era, major labels were actually willing to encourage a band's wildest, most extravagant musical whims. But slowing momentum—poor record sales, dropping concert attendance, media disinterest—found Rush dubbing the *Caress of Steel* tour the "Down the Tubes" tour. They seemed to be sliding quickly downhill toward obscurity.

"There was a lot of pressure from the record company and management to go back to our roots, make another *Rush* album," Alex Lifeson recalls. "And we basically said, 'You know what? That's not what we're about. If that's what everybody wants, then that's what they're not going to get. If we go down, then we're going to go down in flames.'"

Inspired again by the writings and objectivist philosophy of Ayn Rand, Rush's fourth album, *2112*, featured the side-long title opus. A well-written, fully realized epic, "2112" flowed easily, and its concept was not hard to digest, despite its extended length. The song showed the young band gaining maturity well beyond their years. "2112" is segmented into seven distinct chapters; yet for all its complexity, it captures the listener's interest, from the first waves of cosmic synth to the cacophonous conclusion more than twenty minutes later. Neil Peart called it "the first real blend of our diverse and schizophrenic influences."

Opening their make-or-break album with such a demanding composition was beyond risky. The very idea drew the consternation of their record label and management, who preferred they take an easier road. It was Rush against the world, and Peart remembers their mind-set: "It was uncertain whether we would fight or fall, but finally we got mad. We came back with a vengeance. We were talking about freedom from tyranny in '2112,' and we *meant* it."

The other half of *2112* could have paled next to the title track, but Rush's fountain of creativity was overflowing. Thundering ganja ode "A Passage to Bangkok" incorporated Eastern melodies, the mellow "The Twilight Zone" was veiled in melancholic mystery, and the wailing of "Something for Nothing" took the approach of their debut and injected it with the metal disease. Another production better than its predecessor, another album better than the one before it, *2112* was a perfect cap to the band's first era. The album might have been the exact opposite of what their record company was asking for, but it sold a hundred thousand copies in its first week of release in March 1976. The record company finally agreed with something their fans had known all along: This odd new band was onto something.

Jim Pitulski points to *2112* as a pivotal moment. "Rush's first three albums were really good. They did some stuff with odd time signatures and sci-fi lyrics, and the song structures were kind of complex, but *2112* was the one. The concept, the instrumentation, production—it was sort of like a movie on vinyl. It was very theatrical. I just climbed into that record and let it transport me."

Underscoring their four-album progression, Rush immortalized the *2112* tour with the live album *All the World's a Stage*. They then began another four-album campaign that culminated in the most advanced compositions of their career.

The next step for Rush was 1977's *A Farewell to Kings*. The album revealed an even tighter, wiser band. *Farewell*'s regal atmosphere was adorned with plenty of sonic pomp, as if recorded in a pastoral residential studio in the gorgeous Welsh countryside. (It actually was.) "Cygnus X-1" and "Xanadu" were highlights. The latter is a grand recalling of Samuel Taylor Coleridge's *Kubla Khan* poem, musically more ornate than previous epics, and "Cygnus X-1"details a harrowing cosmic drama. With sensitive drum work, monstrous bass lines, robotic riffing, and strange dissonant chords, "Cygnus X-1" might just be the ultimate prog metal epic. The middle of the album contained the short yet sublime "Closer to the Heart," which was Rush's first Top 40 hit. Bringing philosophy and sublimity to FM radio's baser instincts, the song still features highly on classic rock radio today. *A Farewell to Kings* showcases the band's wide appeal better than any other Rush album, and proved their unique ability to write complex works of art for the egghead rocker while maintaining mainstream appeal.

Hemispheres in 1978 introduced the final side-long epic of Rush's career. "Cygnus X-1 Book II: Hemispheres" came with six additional subtitles and a wandering, mazelike arrangement. Despite wonderful moments, the convoluted and overly wordy track didn't live up to previous long-form pieces, its sublime musical moments buried under a torrent of text. The song was no doubt as cerebral as early metal got.

Though the reference to the first "Cygnus X-1" provided conceptual continuity, the album's other three songs propelled Rush higher and farther. Clocking in at a concise 4:46, "The Trees," with its lyrical scope and dramatic arrangement, could have justifiably been another twenty-minute monster—but the band resisted. Despite the elongated epic on side one, Rush was getting better at communicating a lot of information in less time, an ideal they would move swiftly toward on successive albums.

Still, much of *Hemispheres* finds Rush at its most meticulous—as on the nine-and-a-half-minute "La Villa Strangiato." "We wanted to put together a very complex song that had a lot of different time changes and had a lot of really radical changes in mood and rhythm," says Neil Peart. "We spent more time recording 'La Villa Strangiato' than the entire *Fly by Night* album."

As adept as Rush had become as players, it's remarkable that they resisted writing an entirely instrumental piece until "La Villa Strangiato." Comprising twelve distinct movements, each flowing easily into the next, the track is a fantastic example of wordless musical storytelling, with the band's collaborative chemistry at its peak.

Hemispheres represents Rush at its most ambitious. "Certainly the music was over-decorated and so were the lyrics," Peart said sixteen years later. "And the lyrics were often dealing with very abstract themes—but where do you start? As a lyricist, I started with abstract themes. And I was young, too, enamored of fantasy and science fiction and all this stuff that maybe I don't have use for any longer, but I did then, so it was perfectly

Alex Lifeson and Geddy Lee of Rush, 1977: Four hands, six necks, and thirty-four strings (*Frank White*)

sincere. Also, a lot of the grand allegories that I used at the time were about exploring—'Hemispheres' was a grand allegory of reason and emotion, and in Nietzsche-esque terms of Apollo and Dionysus. So yeah, I was very cerebral and very remote from life, but it is still about life, and it's a theme that I've been able to personalize over the years and refine. What's the possible excuse? We were doing what we wanted to do the way we wanted to do it, and the critics be damned."

By 1980, Rush was making slow steps toward a more concise methodology. *Permanent Waves* would do for Rush what "Closer to the Heart" did three years earlier: put them on the radio and into the ears of the mainstream. Both "The Spirit of Radio" and "Freewill" brought the band household-name status, if they hadn't already achieved it. *Permanent Waves* contains six tracks, but maybe more correctly it consists of three pairs: Two smart radio-friendly songs, two subdued balladic numbers, and two ambitious epics. Of the epics, "Jacob's Ladder" is dense and tense, a slowly unfold-ing, darkly atmospheric drama; the tech-y "Natural Science" shifts through a number of cosmic panoramas—a more personal, urgent distillation of the profound concepts Peart explored with "Hemispheres." Performances by all three members, notably on "Natural Science," are at an all-time high, and the musical chemistry seems to have become intuitive. Terry Brown's production is detailed and sumptuous.

Each element of the Rush machine—writing, performance, production—climaxed with *Moving Pictures* in 1981, the capper to the second distinctive Rush era.

Rush's *Hemispheres*, 1978, art by Hugh Syme

Not only is *Moving Pictures* their most com-mercially successful album, but it remains an artistic watershed. Six of seven songs show the trio moving toward the compact songwriting that became their modus operandi ("The Cam-era Eye" was the only elongated piece, at ex-actly eleven minutes). Yet there was still plenty of complexity tucked within the clever writing, magnificent playing, and warm, textured pro-duction.

Moving Pictures is as enjoyable for the recording as it is for the songs themselves. Ter-ry Brown, engineer Paul Northfield, and the band achieved a remarkably round, rich atmosphere with the band's eighth album, which pulled the darkness of "Witch Hunt" into contrast against brighter tracks such as "Limelight." From the esoteric lyrics of "Tom Sawyer" (a more unlikely hit single is hard to find) and musician's favorite "YYZ" to the cinematic elegance of "Red Barchetta" and menacing cautionary tale "Witch Hunt," *Moving Pictures* is Rush's absolute peak. The curious "Vital Signs" closed the album, foreshadowing the band's future direction with synthetic drums, jumpy reggae rhythms, and slick new-wave sheen. Focused, en-ergetic, and compositionally airtight, *Moving Pictures* is at once the apex and the end of the most important and influential string of albums in progressive metal's early era.

Rush didn't bother trying to top *Moving Pictures*. Rarely stagnant, they moved quickly toward new ideas and different sounds, embracing the technology of the '80s and writing with a deliberate concision. Their next several albums were full of cold digital synths, electronic drums and impossibly crisp productions. The heavy guitar sound of the band's early days mutated into subtle background texture; Lee's growling bass mellowed and even got funky; multipart twenty-minute epics were banished forever to the past.

Along with their openness to cutting-edge technology, Rush continually absorbed contemporary influences. Their affinity for '70s prog rock waned as younger bands of the '80s such as the Police, the Fixx, and Ultravox grabbed their attention. Rush continued to move directly forward in the middle of changing musical climates. They remained as individualistic as ever, but never were caught out of time—Rush never became a relic.

By 1982's *Signals*, Rush's songs had become remarkably compact. A few months before the album's release, Neil Peart told Rush biographer Bill Banasiewicz: "Although we have always been interested in a more stylistic approach to music, in terms of putting more into a song than it really needs, we've found ourselves changing. We've started streamlining. Our songwriting now comes from a stronger rhythmic point of view. We find a pulse that feels really good and build our changes around it, whereas in the past we tended to do the reverse. We would find a melodic passage that we liked and go nuts on it rhythmically, and put so many time changes and meter changes in it that it became like an octopus." Peart cited Peter Gabriel and Talking Heads, who were, in his words, "going after fresh rhythmic approaches. They're stripping the music down and getting rid of unnecessary decoration."

As *Signals* and 1984's *Grace Under Pressure* introduced a sleeker Rush, some fans and critics dismissed the band as has-beens or a second-rate Police. Perpetually on Rush's case, *Rolling Stone* magazine was probably quite happy to print critic J.D. Considine's blasting of *Signals* in 1982: "*Signals* is chockablock with state-of-the-studio gadgetry...none of these electronic add-ons enhances the group's music. If anything, Rush emerges from this jungle of wires and gizmos sounding duller than ever."

Throughout much of the '80s, Alex Lifeson's guitar was relegated to the background by banks of cold digital synths. Peart's Simmons SDSV electronic drum module was pushed forward in the mix of 1986's *Power Windows*, which sounded contemporary then, but now dates the album considerably. By 1988's *Hold Your Fire*,

Rush was firmly set in their reversed polarity, and they remained in that realm, to some degree or another, for more than two decades. They can still play rings around kids young enough to be their grandchildren—they're just long past the point of needing to prove it.

Rush's later material might not be as obviously ambitious on the surface, but there are subtleties in the songs that remain challenging for the seasoned musicians. "'Animate' is just as hard to play as 'Tom Sawyer,' which is more of an overtly complex drum part," Peart explains. "Over the years I've spent more time on details and ironing out things, so it's a deceptive simplicity. You want to take the extremely difficult and make it look easy."

Rush was often considered pretentious and self-indulgent—even humorless—by a media often vicious to cerebral rock music. The band absolutely did take its music seriously, yet built into it a release valve that critics were apparently blind to—the band members could, and often did, laugh at themselves. Sometimes they did so flagrantly. "La Villa Strangiato," the insanely ambitious 1978 composition, was subtitled "An Exercise in Self-Indulgence." A later instrumental had fun with its title—1991's "Where's My Thing?" was subtitled "Part IV, 'Gangster of Boats' Trilogy." Various texts in the liner notes of many Rush albums exhibit a similarly knowing grin; they seem to use humor as levity against the seriousness on the surface. That lightheartedness rarely revealed itself in the actual music, but in interviews, tour programs, and even some band photos, it was clear that Rush were much less uptight than their critics.

Rush often demonstrates its playfulness onstage. Even performing to enormous crowds, they seem more carefree than during their early days. Lee and Lifeson goof with each other and dance stupid dances while big screens blast silly short films in time with "By-Tor and the Snow Dog." Comedian Jerry Stiller even introduced the band from the big screen on their thirtieth-anniversary tour. And what could be more ridiculous than throwing Rush T-shirts into the crowd, fresh and hot from an arsenal of onstage clothes dryers (a novelty introduced in the early 2000s to take the place of bass cabinets after Geddy Lee switched to digital signal processing in concert).

Progressive music, in whatever form, has long taken a beating for being "self-indulgent" and "pretentious." Critics call for the willful restraint of the musician, as if invention, ingenuity, skill, and even excess have no place in art. Yet the evolution of modern music could never have made significant forward progress if artists had stuck to tradition rather than indulging in the "self." The act of learning an instrument and nurturing unique talent is inherently self-indulgent. Without self-indulgence, pioneers such as the Beatles, King Crimson, and Rush would never have pushed into undiscovered musical areas. And without them, the many metal bands that aspire to virtuosity and grand imagination might never have evolved from their primal core.

Opeth's Mikael Åkerfeldt is proud to be called pretentious. "It's a positive word," he says. "If it's a personality thing, if someone called me pretentious, I would take it as an insult, but for music, something you create, it's good. We as a band have been called that a million times. It shows you're ambitious. That you care."

Kevin Hufnagel—guitarist in hard-to-categorize instrumental band Dysrhythmia, and a Rush fan—agrees with Åkerfeldt. "When I read criticisms like that, it comes across as a lazy cop-out," he says. "Like they wrote it off without having given the music a serious listen, or thought about what the artist is trying to express. Music should be an outlet for escape, and if that's the way you escape, then more power to you."

Critics and fans of progressive music alike can probably agree that no band, not even Rush, can continue on the path of complication and intellectualization forever. At some point exhaustion sets in. The need to flaunt talent fades, and the music eventually becomes more visceral, more direct. But cycles continue to churn, as younger bands in the '80s, inspired by Rush's elaborate epics, took up the mantle of grandiosity that the Canadian trio left behind.

In a way, Rush's widespread and ongoing popularity is perplexing. Although Lee, Lifeson, and Peart are clearly excellent musicians, great writers, and still creative well into their fifties, their early period is full of such inaccessible elements as arrangements made only for long attention spans, instrumental complexity, and high-pitched vocal warbling that turned off as many as it turned on. Yet Rush has been rewarded for stubborn individuality in a musical world that more often rewards conformity.

Their legacy is that of a band who persevered and never compromised. Once inspired by the English prog rock movement, they provided a bright flame that guided early hard rock and heavy metal out of their primordial cave and into the blinding daylight of total creative abandon.

4. OPEN MIND FOR A DIFFERENT VIEW

"I listen to what's out there, but I wouldn't think of going out and getting a Bon Jovi or Mötley Crüe album and putting it on my turntable. That stuff doesn't excite me. If I'm gonna spend time listening to music, it's gonna be something very wild like Paganini, a classical violinist from the eighteenth century. That kind of stuff gets your head spinning and your blood boiling faster than any metal I could listen to." —Dave Mustaine, Megadeth

ROCK AND ROLL WAS AN AMERICAN INVENTION born in the 1950s from the intersection of black rhythm-and-blues artists and white crooners. Figures such as Bill Haley, Buddy Holly, Chuck Berry, and Elvis Presley defined the new genre. However, most major rock movements since have emerged from the U.K. The British Invasion began with Liverpool's Beatles, who reinvented pop iconography and paved the way for the Rolling Stones and the Who. Midlands bands Deep Purple and Led Zeppelin added weight to rock's propulsive undertow, and prog rock emerged with Pink Floyd, Procol Harum, and the Moody Blues. Black Sabbath birthed the heavy metal beast in Birmingham, with fellow Brummies Judas Priest following in their wake. Then came the fashionable London punk explosion of Sex Pistols and the Clash. Later, significant movements and bands, from Britpop to Radiohead and Coldplay, reinvented rock and pop formulas and found massive acclaim.

In 1979, an especially vehement musical movement appeared in the U.K. First referred to in print as the "New Wave of British Heavy Metal"—or NWOBHM— by *Sounds* editor Geoff Barton, this incredibly prolific era was the explosive output of kids raised on Black Sabbath, UFO, and Judas Priest. Though punks and metalheads were socially warring factions, new British metal bands took the speed and intensity inherent in punk and built something tighter. Melding tough-as-nails riffing, raw velocity, and short, catchy songs, these young metal bands offered hundreds of indie-label or even self-released singles and albums. Speed metal was born here, thanks to the off-the-rails energy of prototypes such as Jaguar, Savage, and Raven, following a trail freshly blazed by elder statesmen Motörhead.

Of the two biggest bands that rose from the NWOBHM, Def Leppard shot quickly to pop superstardom, while Iron Maiden merged the grand imagination of a band like Rush with a merciless intensity that left all others in the dust. Steve Harris formed the first version of Iron Maiden at the tail end of 1975, inspired by English bands of various stripes. For years, Iron Maiden weathered the storms of punk and then new wave. They constantly changed lineups, persevering against anti-metal prejudice until they became one of the biggest success stories of the genre.

While the punks attempted to extinguish "dinosaur rock," Harris reveled in its excesses, even ratcheting up the bar a few notches. The energy of punk and local London heroes Motörhead was fundamental to the early Iron Maiden sound, but so were Uriah Heep, Wishbone Ash, UFO, and Jethro Tull.

Equally influential were prog albums Harris grew up with, such as Genesis's *Foxtrot* and *Nursery Cryme*, and Nektar's *A Tab in the Ocean* and *Recycled*. "Stuff like Genesis's 'The Musical Box' still gives me goose bumps," says Harris. "It just completely changed my life. I thought it was fucking amazing, and I immediately wanted to have a go at trying to play this stuff myself."

When Yes and Genesis tunes proved too difficult a start for the young bassist, Harris practiced to Deep Purple and Free records instead. Yet the directness of early metal and the escapist elements of classic prog eventually coalesced in his songwriting. Fusing fantasy, horror, and sci-fi themes with multitiered arrangements and the blunt savagery of metal, Iron Maiden led the way for progressive metal in the '80s.

Maiden's enormous global success was founded on a broad appeal. Their intensity pulled in demanding headbangers, while epic storytelling and songwriting lured older prog rockers looking for a meatier version of their vanished '70s heroes. Yet the group remained approachable as people, just five regular blokes. Iron Maiden let the music, lyrics, and wild album covers stamp the band's identity.

Lyrics have never been heavy metal's primary selling point. The rush of musical power and scream-therapy catharsis are key elements of many a metal band's sound, while lyrics often get smeared and blurred by over-the-top vocal delivery. Already by the early 1980s, trashy sex-and-party lyrics were an overused

Of prog mind and metal heart: Iron Maiden's Steve Harris (*Michael J. Mulley*)

metal cliché. Yet even in their earliest days, Iron Maiden presented a total package: All that storm and stress came complete with well-researched, thought-provoking subject matter. Their 1980 debut offered "Strange World," which seemed straight from an old-school fantasy novel—an exotic realm where girls drink "plasma wine" and no one ever grows old. Battalions of teenagers undoubtedly picked up books by Edgar Allan Poe and Frank Herbert after listening to "Murders in the Rue Morgue" and "To Tame a Land," Maiden songs inspired by those authors. Likewise, high school libraries in 1984 certainly saw a rise in interest in Samuel Taylor Coleridge's *Lyrical Ballads* collection after Maiden crafted a thirteen-minute song around Coleridge's epic poem "The Rime of the Ancient Mariner."

Iron Maiden brought a smarter approach to metal—they were the great paradigm-shifters that Rush had been for hard rock, and that Metallica would later become. Harris's horde moved relentlessly forward with each album, in the spirit of the bassist's prog rock favorites, searching and stretching further and further, until peaking on 1988's *Seventh Son of a Seventh Son*.

Throughout the seven albums of Iron Maiden's first and most important phase, their songs were based on a variety of interesting and unusual subjects: Alexander the Great, *The Phantom of the Opera*, ancient Egypt, the Bible (particularly the book of Revelations), the abstract British TV show *The Prisoner*, and even "The Loneliness of the Long Distance Runner," an obscure short story by British author Alan Sillitoe. Attending carefully to deeply flowing musical and lyrical narratives, Harris and the band's other prominent songwriters, vocalist Bruce Dickinson and guitarist Adrian Smith, avoided cartoonishness despite their youthful enthusiasm.

Iron Maiden's *Seventh Son of a Seventh Son*, 1988

Just as zealous when it came to touring, by the end of the globe-trotting 1984–'85 campaign for *Powerslave*, the members of Iron Maiden were exhausted. After recovering from the grueling 193-date blur, Dickinson approached the drawing board with grand ideas. "If I had my way, the sixth album would have sounded very different," he says. "I felt we had to come up with our *Physical Graffiti*. We had to get it onto another level, or we'd stagnate and just drift away. I thought the time was right for us to do something audacious, something vast and daring."

Dickinson—a great admirer of Van der Graaf Generator and their front man, Peter Hammill—might have expected he would have an easy time convincing fellow prog fan Harris of his ideas. But it wasn't to be. Harris and the rest of the band swiftly rejected Bruce's acoustic-based songs. "He came in with a few which didn't really suit," remembers Harris. "It wasn't because it was acoustic, or even that it was very different sort of stuff. We didn't think it was good enough, really."

Somewhat crestfallen, Dickinson still sounds disappointed: "We just made another Iron Maiden album."

But the resulting *Somewhere in Time* wasn't exactly the same old Maiden. Guitar synths were introduced, shocking many fans. Back on 1983's *Piece of Mind*, Maiden had flaunted metal purity with the credo: "No synthesizers or ulterior motives." On *Somewhere in Time*, however, they embraced modern technology, resulting in a more subdued sound. The guitars were cosmic and distant, while Martin Birch's production lent a curiously soft texture. It was a mature, adult Iron Maiden. At a time when bands such as Slayer and Kreator were pushing metal to new limits of intensity, Maiden didn't bother to compete—they even went the other way.

Though he had no writing credits on *Somewhere in Time*, Dickinson continued pushing for a radical change in sound. The reinvention he hoped for never entirely came, but 1988's *Seventh Son of a Seventh Son* made a step toward something new and different. Now largely recognized as the band's creative peak, *Seventh Son* was closer to Dickinson's vision for the previous album. This time, Harris approached Dickinson about making a full-blown conceptual work. Although the final outcome wasn't as grand as the vocalist had envisioned—he fought for a double album—the reinvigorated songwriting chemistry yielded impressive results. *Seventh Son* instantly became a fan favorite, and the album performed well on commercial and critical levels. Martin Birch's production gave the album an appropriately fantastical aura, while some of the songs found the band stretching to the furthest. Acoustic guitars entered the picture, the songwriting was more collaborative than before, and the scope of songs such as "Moonchild," "Infinite Dreams," and the ten-minute title track saw Maiden claiming a new high point.

Seventh Son of a Seventh Son could have been a spectacular flop. Despite its compromised nature, it reached further than *Somewhere in Time* in terms of melody, elaboration, technology, and conceptual complexity. Its success proved that Iron Maiden's audience was ready to explore uncharted waters with them. Tellingly, *Seventh Son*'s follow-up, the much simpler *No Prayer for the Dying*, is looked upon as a lesser album than the ones before it. Perhaps Maiden thought fans were ready for a rawer, more stripped-down album, but reaction to *No Prayer* indicated otherwise.

What if Iron Maiden, as Bruce Dickinson proposed, would have stretched out over a prog-inspired extended-length high-concept album? The world will never know, but the bands that came in their wake and under their influence, such as Fates Warning and Dream Theater, presented their own answers to that question.

Eastward from England across the North Sea, Denmark's underground metal movement was also roaring loudly by 1983. Spandex-and-leather metal bands such as Witch Cross, Evil, and Maltese Falcon were active in the territory, and the country later became a progressive metal hotbed thanks to the likes of Royal Hunt, Wuthering Heights, and Beyond Twilight. But Denmark's most important metal export to this day remains the influential and rather bizarre Mercyful Fate.

Mercyful Fate's '80s-era material pushed the limits of the metal form. Their eccentric frontman, King Diamond, portrayed multiple characters and covered a variety of vocal registers, the most remarkable being a piercing, eerie falsetto. Born Kim Petersen, King Diamond's image was derived from theatrical rock gods Arthur Brown and Alice Cooper. A thoughtful, well-spoken individual offstage, Petersen developed the King Diamond alter ego around his love of horror fiction and his alignment with Anton LaVey's philosophical brand of Satanism. Ghastly facial paint and a microphone mounted on an inverted crucifix fashioned from human femur and tibia bones provided a strong visual identity for the band's music—which was exceptional even without the theatrical trappings.

Bizarre Mercyful Fate ringmaster King Diamond (*Mike Coles*)

Mercyful Fate's eleven-minute "Satan's Fall," from 1983's *Melissa*, took cues from '70s prog for both its scope and its numerous time changes. Often toying with harmonic dissonance and unusual time signatures, the band, with its dark occult tone, was miles away from such reckless satanic peers as Venom. The guitar work of Hank Shermann and Michael Denner proved a fortunate pairing; their complementary styles, imaginative playing, and melodic sensibility elevated the band's musicality to sublime levels. Anyone willing to look past Mercyful Fate's controversial imagery and lyrics found metal of a remarkably sophisticated nature.

Mercyful Fate's legend continued long after their 1985 breakup. Members of Metallica, Megadeth, Watchtower, and Dream Theater have eagerly noted the Danish band's impact. "One of the big influences for us that often gets overlooked, and a band that should be considered one of the progressive metal pioneers, is Mercyful Fate," says Fates Warning guitarist Jim Matheos. "We all thought the music was incredible. They were doing new and interesting things way before us."

As work began in 1985 on a third Mercyful Fate album, Diamond's songwriting partner Hank Shermann started bringing pop songs to the table. Disagreements over the band's direction soon led to Mercyful Fate's fall. Diamond took guitarist Denner and bassist Timi Hansen and forged ahead with a new band bearing his stage name. With two talented new members completing the quintet, the King Diamond material jumped several technical leaps ahead of Mercyful Fate, peaking on late-'80s albums *Them* and *Conspiracy*. Despite a revolving door of musicians and some less-than-legendary later albums, King Diamond remained prolific and kept the performance caliber high. In particular, his guitarist and writing partner, Andy LaRocque, remained a constant throughout the band's two-decade run.

Mike Portnoy of Dream Theater also cites the Danes as an early influence. "They were progressive, absolutely," he says. "In the mid-'80s, when I was looking for bands that were heavy and progressive, those Mercyful Fate and King Diamond albums were huge influences for me. At the same time that I was discovering Fates Warning and Watchtower, I was also loving King Diamond's *Abigail* and *Them*."

Inspired by both the bigger and lesser-known names of the NWOBHM, early-'80s American metal bands soon followed the operating model of recording demos, releasing seven-inch records, and signing deals with the new independent labels sprouting up everywhere. Most of these were straightforward denim-and-leather-clad keepers of the flame. A few, such as San Francisco's Anvil Chorus, moved from the basics to a more challenging hybrid of prog rock and the increasingly intense new metal. Taking inspiration from the NWOBHM and fusing it with influence from such then-contemporary prog rock bands as U.K., Saga, and FM, songs such as "Blue Flames," "European," and "Tales" offered a kind of metal that would have received more praise a decade later, after the success of Long Island band Dream Theater opened the floodgates for this approach. Anvil Chorus were way ahead of the curve, playing truly progressive metal when Queensrÿche and Fates Warning were still getting the Iron Maiden and Judas Priest influences out of their systems.

In 2009, Anvil Chorus finally released their debut album, *The Killing Sun*—fresh recordings of songs from their early- to mid-'80s demos. The band's failure to gain any sort of record deal in their initial phase stunted their growth and limited their impact. However, others from the healthy California underground soon had their chance to push metal's boundaries farther. Like Iron Maiden before them, Metallica and Megadeth elevated the ambition level and performance standards of their genre. Arising from a shared Los Angeles family tree, both bands became prime movers and standard-bearers in the nascent thrash metal underground.

Metallica's early story is legendary and well documented: Formed in Los Angeles in 1981, and relocating to San Francisco by early 1983, Metallica was made up of young kids full of enthusiasm and inspiration, pioneers of a new metal sound, who, against all odds, became one of the biggest bands in rock history. Between the youthful energy of 1983 speed metal classic *Kill 'Em All* and 1991's multiplatinum monument *Metallica* (aka "the Black Album"), Metallica recorded three albums that cannot be ignored in any discussion of metal's cutting edge.

Spanning 1984 through 1988, *Ride the Lightning, Master of Puppets*, and *...And Justice for All* melded intensity with intelligence. Many other thrash bands took their work seriously, but Metallica projected a confidence and depth that others lacked. The band fused the rawness of their punk and Motörhead inspirations with the ambitious songwriting prowess of NWOBHM heroes Diamond Head. And then they pushed it further. Metallica dealt in detailed and propulsive rhythms, but there was a unique underlying melodic sensibility. Early Metallica was foreboding and epic, like Wagnerian opera, but its ferocity went far beyond classical compositions. In fact, Metallica were one of the very first metal bands to be compared to classical music, due to the suitelike movements of their most complex arrangements; the bombastic melodic sense; the multitude of time changes and mood swings; and the sweeping grandiosity. They also bypassed genre clichés with socially relevant and introverted/introspective lyrics—underscored by the taut, abrasive riffing of James Hetfield and, for too short a time, the groundbreaking bass work of Cliff Burton.

Cliff Burton's sensitive yet bestial approach to the bass was unusual. While Iron Maiden's Steve Harris led his band with his bass, Burton went a few steps further. A knowledge of classical music informed Burton's writing and playing on epic Metallica instrumentals "The Call of Ktulu," "Orion," and "To Live Is to Die." With his unorthodox approach, his love for bands as varied as Misfits, Rush, and Lynyrd Skynyrd, and his one-of-a-kind personality, Burton left an invaluable imprint on Metallica's sound.

Drummer Lars Ulrich remembers Burton's songwriting impact. "Cliff was responsible for a lot of the things that happened between *Kill 'Em All* and *Ride the Lightning*," he says. "He exposed me and James to a whole new musical horizon of harmonies and melodies, and obviously that's something that greatly influenced our songwriting abilities. He was a great part of the way Metallica has turned out, even after he is no longer with us."

Metallica pushed at the boundaries; they proved massively influential inside and outside the world of metal. They became ambassadors of the genre, turning many non-metal listeners onto the genre's possibilities, and they forced other thrash bands to tighten their approaches and get serious—to evolve or rot in stagnation. Burton's tragic death in September 1986 was a huge personal blow to the band members, and a musical loss all around—prompting much speculation about what directions he could have had in store for Metallica.

At the peak of their artistic output in the 1980s, Metallica was a refreshingly smart metal band. And they were totally progressive. Once they perfected thrash metal, they left it behind and moved on to explore other areas. Thanks in large part to Metallica, skeptics had to finally accept metal as a legitimate and lasting art form. When *Metal Forces* writer Dave Constable reviewed *Master of Puppets* upon its release in 1986, he claimed that Metallica had become as essential as Led Zeppelin, Deep Purple, and Iron Maiden. What might have seemed like hyperbole then has certainly been borne out by time.

Too good to last: Megadeth's formidable early lineup in December 1986
L-R: Dave Mustaine, Chris Poland, Dave Ellefson, Gar Samuelson
(*Chris Walter*)

Like many bands, Metallica experienced early growing pains, moving through several lineups before finding the perfect chemistry. One discarded member was guitarist Dave Mustaine. Bitter after being unexpectedly dismissed from Metallica shortly before they began recording their first album, Mustaine vowed revenge, and his weapon of reprisal was Megadeth. Their mission: To play faster, tighter, heavier, and better than Metallica—and anyone else. To that end, Mustaine selected the unlikely pair of guitarist Chris Poland and drummer Gar Samuelson, already lock-tight from playing in jazz fusion bands together. Completed by bassist Dave Ellefson, Megadeth released two albums with this lineup, setting a new standard for thrash metal.

Killing Is My Business...and Business Is Good (1985) and *Peace Sells...but Who's Buying?* (1986) exhibited unusual rhythmic ideas and unorthodox guitar riffs. While the rhythm section careened like a runaway train, the riffs sounded like records being spun backwards on a turntable. Whether or not Megadeth bested Metallica is debatable, but the dual lead guitars of Mustaine and Poland certainly outclassed Metallica. With Mustaine providing dexterity at hellish speeds and Poland plucking bizarre notes from the ether, Megadeth's approach was compelling and groundbreaking. But plagued by drug addiction and personality clashes, the original lineup was doomed.

Poland and Samuelson exited, setting off a series of lineup changes. Throughout, the two Daves maintained high performance and songwriting standards that peaked with 1990's *Rust in Peace*. Introducing new members Marty Friedman and Nick Menza, *Rust in Peace* was a flurry of precision and fluidity, making good on Megadeth's claim to being "the world's state-of-the-art speed metal band."

The original Megadeth cast-offs moved into projects that further displayed their enormous talents. Poland disappeared for a few years but then returned in 1990 with the instrumental solo album *Return to Metalopolis*, and he revisited the instrumental format ten years later with *Chasing the Sun*. Meanwhile, he spent the first half of the 1990s working in Damn the Machine, a band he formed with drumming brother Mark Poland. Damn the Machine's only album, 1993's self-titled debut, featured politically charged lyrics and slick, textured metal that was in some ways ahead of its time. Smart, melodic, and mature, and bearing artwork by longtime Rush artist Hugh Syme, *Damn the Machine* failed to gain much attention beyond cult level. A European tour with Dream Theater and an American jaunt with Voivod helped increase the band's visibility, but Damn the Machine folded too early—they were entirely defunct by 1995.

Later, in Ohm, Poland found the kind of acclaim he hadn't received since leaving Megadeth. Ohm's albums were well received by jazz, metal, and prog fans alike. Derived from jazz fusion greats such as Return to Forever, Brand X, and Mahavishnu Orchestra, Ohm brought Poland full circle, back to the music he played before he and Samuelson joined Mustaine's hellish crew.

The late Gar Samuelson was less prolific after Megadeth. He resurfaced in the mid-'90s with Fatal Opera, whose left-field thrash was featured on two full-length albums. By the end of the decade, they had already faded into obscurity. Fatal Opera called themselves "fusion metal," a combination of thrash, traditional metal, and hard rock, spiced up with pop, jazz, and alternative elements—the outcome not nearly as confusing as it sounds.

While no Megadeth album pushed metal as far forward as Metallica's best work, a million tasteful details in the songs put Mustaine and company miles ahead of most. Amidst the thrashing clatter are found a variety of odd, complicated riffs and arrangements. The tense din of "Black Friday" has Mustaine and Poland entangled in dense guitars and trance-inducing jazz-from-hell pacing. The song's intro, "Good Mourning," offers epic theatricality on par with Metallica's album-opening movements. Tech metal fans disagree whether the puzzling syncopation of "Loved to Deth" is sloppy or plain genius. "Set the World Afire" and "Holy Wars...The Punishment Due" are crafted of seriously crazy riff mazes. Nowhere is there a more inspiring display of rhythmic dexterity and blazing twin guitar duels than the final minutes of "Hangar 18." Examples of Megadeth's metallic perplexity are nearly countless.

Though Dave Mustaine's riffing style is largely derived from Mercyful Fate and Diamond Head, his ideas about songwriting depth go a little further back. "Led Zeppelin's *Presence*," he says. "I must have listened to that record a hundred times and heard something different every time. It's like if you listen to a Rush record, you hear all this stuff, but then the next time you hear something different. And a lot of that kind of thinking came from me listening to Pink Floyd so much. It's tucked away in there. It's ear candy."

The exploratory steps of Black Sabbath, Rainbow, Judas Priest, and Scorpions—and the all-out prog/metal hybridization of Rush—were already in heavy metal's past. The groundwork was in place, allowing for the complete adulteration of metal's basic formulas. While Iron Maiden, Mercyful Fate, Metallica, and Megadeth may not be the first bands summoned by the term "progressive metal," they delivered smarter, more sophisticated metal to the masses throughout the 1980s. These bands pushed metal onto awesome plateaus with albums that shattered the stiff stereotypes associated with the genre. The path was paved for radical reinvention—and other bands soon appeared that made metal revolution their sole mission.

PART II:
The Science of the Day

5. PASSING THE THRESHOLD

"I saw Queensrÿche and Fates Warning play together in 1986. I was drawn to Queensrÿche because they combined the metal of Judas Priest with the theatrics of Pink Floyd. And the way Fates Warning was doing an Iron-Maiden-meets-Rush—these were all favorites of mine at the time, and those bands had an immediate impact on me." —Mike Portnoy, Dream Theater

ACCESSIBLE DIGITAL TECHNOLOGY, THE POPULARITY OF PUNK AND NEW WAVE, and musical complexity fatigue brought prog rock gods such as Genesis and Yes to simpler, brighter sounds at the dawn of the 1980s. Critics like to claim that punk killed prog in the late 1970s, always failing to mention that Genesis's *Abacab* and Yes's *90125* were among the biggest commercial successes of the early '80s. Those albums cultivated entirely new fan bases, many of whose members didn't know or care about weird recordings of the distant past such as *The Lamb Lies Down on Broadway* or *Tales from Topographic Oceans*. Lots of prog bands from the golden '70s era either simplified in the '80s or disbanded. Time marched relentlessly forward, and many elder prog rock statesmen went from being treated like royalty to being dismissed as dinosaurs.

The '80s were intolerant of '70s prog values—so most of the revered English prog bands traded excess and ambition for pop sensibility and dinner-jacket smooth. As the mantra seemed to be "move with the times or die," the dependably iconoclastic King Crimson moved with the times while remaining on the cutting edge. Leader Robert Fripp linked back up with drummer Bill Bruford and introduced new members Adrian Belew and Tony Levin. The result was 1981's *Discipline*, which found the renewed Crimson adopting a sound that drew comparisons to Talking Heads, mostly due to Belew's vocal similarity to David Byrne. The music was as clean as it was complex, balancing song craft and modern polish with top-notch musicianship and fresh technical approaches. The brain-numbing rhythmic complications of "Indiscipline" and the eccentric "Elephant Talk" remain highlights of the vast Crimson catalog, songs very much aligned with their basic ethos—yet neither song ever could have been born in the '70s.

Meanwhile, that pimply teenage beast heavy metal landed in the '80s with a multitiered agenda. Staking its claim as a legitimate art form, crude as it was, metal expanded upon its myriad possibilities, thanks to leaders such as Metallica and Megadeth. And some metal practitioners injected the spirit of the most grandiose prog rock of the '70s.

Nothing could stop metal's spread in the early 1980s. For many early metal loyalists, punk rock was already old hat, new wave was impossibly lame, and the old hard rock bands had lost their edge. A new legion of bands, fans, fanzines, and independent record labels dotted the landscape, energized by the founding fathers and the more contemporary NWOBHM. Popularity and participation were at a peak. In the U.S., each state seemed to boast its own answer to Judas Priest. Clad in leather, spandex, bullet belts, and animal pelts, hellions such as Wild Dogs from Oregon, Armored Saint from California, Jag Panzer from Colorado, Znowhite from Illinois, and Manowar from New York helped lead the charge. Alongside these purists, metal swiftly branched off into a variety of subgenres, from the sleazy glam of the Hollywood scene to the thrash metal that erupted via Metallica, Exodus, and Slayer on the Pacific Coast and Anthrax and Overkill on the Atlantic. Wherever the metal lust demanded, record stores were importing albums from far-flung places such as Sweden and Japan. This metal machine was everywhere, fueled by youthful adrenaline and a desire for something newer, heavier, and more radical than plain old radio rock.

From this frenetic miasma emerged Washington State's Queensrÿche and Connecticut's Fates Warning, two bands that came to define progressive metal. The youths who formed these bands learned their craft through Black Sabbath, Rush, Scorpions, and Iron Maiden. Both recorded their first albums by 1984. Both claimed influence from prog rock and other non-metal sources, but above all, early prog metal pioneers such as Rush and Iron Maiden dominated each band's sound. With Queensrÿche and Fates Warning, the torch was about to be passed, as they soon developed more ambitious and original forms of forward-thinking metal.

Queensrÿche transcended the metal genre altogether in later years, but their early sound is pure heavy metal—and overwhelmingly influenced by Iron Maiden and Judas Priest, at that. From the arrival of their four-song self-titled EP in 1983, Queensrÿche—the umlauts merely cosmetic—proved they had learned the right lessons and how to apply them. Vocalist Geoff Tate out-wailed Maiden's "air raid siren" Bruce Dickinson, while guitarists Chris DeGarmo and Michael Wilton built their teamwork along the Priest and Maiden models.

Queensrÿche's rise to infamy was one of the quickest in metal history. The four shadowy and theatrical songs of *Queensrÿche* were initially a demo tape hinting at grand designs. When the underground started buzzing, the band launched their own label, 206 Records, and pressed the eighteen-minute demo onto vinyl—which was subsequently picked up by big boys EMI. Despite the members' young age, the band's music was already mature in terms of precision and detail.

That Orwellian year of 1984 brought Queensrÿche's debut full-length. The young band had evolved significantly. Taking large leaps with each new phase was a modus operandi they embraced even in their earliest incarnation. Produced by James Guthrie—best known for coproducing Pink Floyd's *The Wall*—*The Warning* expanded on the medieval vibe of the EP, yet the songwriting felt elevated, scaling back on the velocity and raw energy of earlier material. The guitars of *The Warning* had a silky texture, more regal than raucous. Geoff Tate's vocal control and melodramatic range of expression were undeniable, compounded by the thickly layered and richly over-dubbed production. Iron Maiden's Bruce Dickinson and Judas Priest's Rob Halford had made high-register singing into a metal art form—now Tate brought it to a theatrical new level. Formal training with Maestro David Kyle in Tate's early days had sharpened his talent. His mother had also sung professionally, and his cousin sang in the Cincinnati Opera. Bombastic vocal prowess seemed to be in the man's blood.

The Warning was slick, the subject matter devoid of cliché, the performances and writing obsessively exacting. The album's ambitious songwriting was raised to a sublime level by Guthrie's ornate production work, creating a rounded, warm sound atypical for metal. "Roads to Madness" was ten minutes of gargantuan melodrama, putting Tate's lamenting, tragic wails to great use. The forward-thinking band leapt over the trapdoors of dungeon-metal stereotypes, most remarkably in the sci-fi quirk of "NM 156," a tale of paranoid future shock that employed sonic effects largely alien to the genre at the time. Queensrÿche seemed to be consciously mining the more intellectual faction of the metal audience, and soon their meticulous ways paid off.

In a career where perpetual forward motion was key, Queensrÿche made its longest leap ahead in late 1986 with *Rage for Order.* The album was an obvious departure, and even the band's new image was weird and different. The back cover displayed the five members in a kind of Japanese visual *kei* mode, dressed in elaborate robes and coats. Their hairstyles and makeup morphed the previously masculine members into effeminate-looking divas—more Duran Duran than Iron Maiden.

Their look wasn't the only thing that underwent a face-lift. Bringing in producer Neil Kernon, who had worked previously with Kansas, Brand X, and Hall & Oates, the band was clearly going for something outside the heavy metal norm. *Rage for Order* is a masterpiece of production, slick without feeling antiseptic, clean with no lack of vitality. The futuristic digital sheen and variety of studio tricks further suggested the band wasn't remotely interested in adhering to metal's then-rigid guidelines. Anything that made the album a more complete experience, they attempted. Instead of letting tradition dictate their course, they drafted new blueprints.

Even decades after its release, the cold synth effects, lush beds of keyboards, cinematic shadings, and various other subtleties of *Rage for Order* give it a unique atmosphere for a metal album. The song titles alone are unusual: "Neue Regel," "Screaming in Digital," and "Chemical Youth (We Are Rebellion)." The album blurred the lines between naked human emotion and cold mechanical futurism, while Tate's mournful, melancholy timbre draped a gothic veil over tracks such as "I Dream in Infrared" and "London."

The dramatic stalker song "Gonna Get Close to You," originally by Canadian pop/new wave artist Lisa Dalbello, was a brave and curious inclusion. The song matched the album's somber and paranoid mood, and avoided sounding like a tossed-off novelty. The daring band selected "Gonna Get Close to You" as the one and only music video from the album, and received generous play on MTV throughout 1987—putting *Rage for Order* in the hands and ears of a demographic who may not have noticed otherwise. Although not a huge hit at the time, *Rage for Order* gathered remarkable respect as the years passed. Its finely detailed approach and futuristic at-

New sound, new look: Queensryche's 1986 game-changer, *Rage for Order*

titude beat the rest of the pack in 1986; the album rightfully remains a milestone of progressive metal.

Rage for Order's follow-up, *Operation: Mindcrime*, considerably expanded the band's popularity, but its May 3, 1988, arrival was only greeted enthusiastically by the previously converted—at first. *Mindcrime* sits at the peak of Queensrÿche's most progressive period. In producer Peter Collins, Queensrÿche's clarity and cleanliness met its perfect match. Collins had been responsible for the slick, almost antiseptic sheen of Rush's *Power Windows* and *Hold Your Fire*, and his methods worked equally well for *Operation: Mindcrime*. The album was based on an ambitious narrative story line that was thankfully easy to follow and clearly communicated. While many concept albums are mired in messy, clichéd, or overcomplicated storytelling, this story of prostitute-turned-nun Mary, junkie Nikki, and the manipulative Dr. X flowed persuasively from beginning to end. The music had room to breathe, never entirely harnessed in service to the voluminous lyrics.

The more challenging elements of *Operation: Mindcrime* exist mostly in the margins, properly digested only with focused listening. The whole piece was ambitious, even for this band, but whittled down to bare components the songs were the most streamlined Queensrÿche to date. Only the eleven-minute "Suite Sister Mary" explores expanded structuring instead of traditional songwriting patterns. Songs such as "I Don't Believe in Love" and "Eyes of a Stranger" hinted at a more mainstream rock approach—something the band fully embraced on their next album.

Prime 'Rÿche: Geoff Tate and Chris DeGarmo
(*Frank White*)

Ten full songs formed the foundation of *Operation: Mindcrime*, filled out with five dialogue and sound effect interludes, some veering into experimental terrain. "Electric Requiem" is not exactly Stockhausen, but it did show the band liberally coloring outside the lines. All the extra conceptual themes, sound effects, and segues created an album-length journey, much better absorbed in its entirety than in pieces. The story line, its airtight presentation, the lifelike scenery, and the vivid characterization all screamed for expansion into multimedia. Nine of the album's fifteen tracks spawned music videos—collectively released as *Video: Mindcrime* in 1989—but the band waited several years before performing the entire album live.

Queensrÿche were still basically a cult band when *Operation: Mindcrime* was released in mid-1988. They continued paying their dues as an opening act while seeking a larger audience. Opening for Metallica on their North American "Damaged Justice" tour was not a bad gig, and it was partly responsible for starting the groundswell of interest in the album. Finally, well into 1989, *Operation: Mindcrime* took a firm hold with the masses. Just as the band were ready to come off the road to write their next album, MTV began airing the "Eyes of a Stranger" video. Sales of the album shot through the roof. *Operation: Mindcrime* went gold a year after its release and garnered platinum status in 1991 as its legend continued to grow.

Despite the quality of much of their other work, *Operation: Mindcrime* still eclipses all of Queensrÿche's other recordings. The album's plot is open to a broader interpretation that touches on political conspiracy, religious hypocrisy, terrorism, and a belief that nothing in life is black-and-white. The story grapples with the evil in good, the good in evil, and the messy gray area in between. *Operation: Mindcrime*'s exploration of universal themes caught the interest of Tony Award–nominated actor/singer Adam Pascal (*Rent*) two decades after its release, and in 2009 Pascal announced that, with the blessing of the band, *Operation: Mindcrime* would be developed as a Broadway-style musical production, opening the band's music to an entirely new audience.

The temptation to record a sequel to *Operation: Mindcrime* followed Queensrÿche around for years. In 2006, they finally gave in. *Operation: Mindcrime II* was only a shadow of the first installment, though it became their best-received album in years. Too much time had passed, along with a string of albums that were not exactly hailed as great works. *Operation: Mindcrime II* proved yet again that sequels to enormously successful movies, books or albums usually lack the grand inspiration that gave rise to the originals.

In retrospect, though the band's origins never vanished, *Operation: Mindcrime* proved to be the final full-on metal Queensrÿche album. Their desire to branch off from the genre strongly reared its head on 1990's *Empire*, and eventually the departure became complete. "We're always trying to experiment," Geoff Tate confirmed in 1988. "We get bored always doing the same things. We solve this by trying to be different, doing things differently. Sometimes it works, sometimes it doesn't, but that's how you learn. A great example is AC/DC—they put out a similar album each year. That's sort of nice, but with us, people never really know what we're gonna do next. It's that surprise element. We've been exploring this ever since the EP."

Queensrÿche's stretch into more commercial waters on *Empire* paid off handsomely. The spacious and orchestral hit song "Silent Lucidity"—very Pink Floyd–like with its affected English accent and soaring, David Gilmour–esque guitar solo—exposed the band to a whole new audience oblivious to their early medieval metal. Slick, radio-ready songs such as "Another Rainy Night (Without You)" and uncomplicated rockers such as "Jet City Woman" furthered their mainstream appeal. Not much of *Empire* resembled its heady predecessor. While still clearly the work of a cerebral outfit, *Empire* was remarkably accessible. Much as Metallica did on their eponymous turning-point album, Queensrÿche reached a wider audience with *Empire* by honing their sound toward mainstream accessibility, maintaining their meticulousness but clipping off the overt complexities of past work.

Multiplatinum sales of *Empire* finally endowed Queensrÿche with ample resources to take *Operation: Mindcrime* on the road. Lasting eighteen months and spanning three continents, the "Building Empires" tour balanced songs from *Empire* with a couple of obligatory older gems, while the entire *Operation: Mindcrime* album formed its centerpiece. With video backdrops and a full headlining slot, *Operation: Mindcrime* finally got its due. The album has since become hallowed in the band's discography, often named alongside other legendary concept albums such as the Who's *Tommy* and Pink Floyd's *The Wall*.

Massive success in the early '90s bought resting time for Queensrÿche's exhausted members, and a long break after the *Empire* campaign brought a more introspective band back to the drawing board. Recorded slowly between mid-1992 and mid-1994, *Promised Land* fell short of the commercial heights of its predecessor but still sold more than a million copies. Artistically, it can only be seen as a success. *Promised Land* is a relatively subdued album, devoid of the roar from Queensrÿche's old metal days, more introspective than the let's-solve-the-world's-problems vibe of *Empire*, and still as cerebral and fine-tuned as ever. Brooding atmosphere, reflective lyrics, and looser performances indicated that Seattle's whiz kids were letting go of their youth and their metal past.

Promised Land capped the band's first evolutionary arc and set the wheels in motion for the next. After this, Queensrÿche stripped down considerably and wrote music with a lighter, looser modern rock attitude. They had done much to widen the parameters of metal, but for their part, they were done with all that.

"We're much more mature and have explored a lot of musical areas," Geoff Tate said later. "It's been an interesting journey being part of this band and this musical growth, this musical change. We started from the metal scene, being influenced by that, and over time we took our influences and shaped them into our own significant style that is very recognizable. We're interested in breaking new ground. If we leave some people behind, so be it. Our life work has not been to appease people. We write music for our own reasons for our own selves—we don't write it for anybody else."

Dogged by comparisons to Queensrÿche for much of the '80s, Connecticut's Fates Warning remains legendary in progressive metal. Many judged Fates Warning inferior to 'Rÿche in nearly all aspects—*except* music. Major-label contract, radio airplay, stadium tours, huge profile—Queensrÿche always had more of those things. But musically, Fates Warning's accomplishments could fill a book. Since forming in 1982, the band have generated catalog sales totaling well over a million albums—all with long-running independent label Metal Blade. And guitarist Jim Matheos alone has overseen every second of their long and interesting journey.

Like many of their early-'80s contemporaries, Fates Warning intently studied the work of masters such as Iron Maiden, Judas Priest, and Scorpions. Yet instead of covering the most popular songs in early rehearsals, Fates showed an affinity for these bands' more esoteric material: not "Run to the Hills," but "Strange World"; not "Breaking the Law," but "Beyond the Realms of Death"; not "Rock You Like a Hurricane," but "Pictured Life." Their standards were high and they learned their lessons well. Soon Fates Warning were writing originals that stood strong against those of their heroes.

Led by Matheos and lyricist/vocalist John Arch, early Fates Warning was obviously derivative of its teachers. Their first album, 1984's *Night on Bröcken*, was a promising start with some glaring flaws. The band's gifts barely broke aboveground. Despite some gems—the title track, "The Calling," and especially "Damnation"—*Night on Bröcken* was crippled by weak recording and tacky cover art. The record was actually released with two different covers, both horrendous. A later reissue brought a third and much better cover image, a simple photograph of the moon.

The band's leap from *Night on Bröcken* to 1985's *The Spectre Within* was extraordinary, markedly improved in all departments. Fates Warning's perennial war with stagnation had begun. *Spectre's* lead track, "Traveler in Time," seemed to contain more parts and tempo changes than the entire first side of their debut. Raw energy was still inherent, but the guitars were rounded, with a thicker bottom end, and the production brought out the band's doom-laden essence. Somberness cloaked the song's ornate arrangement, and Arch added gravity with expressive, mournful wailing. "Traveler in Time" found the band attempting to cram tons of musical information into a small space, which they had not really done on the debut. They sounded like Iron Maiden blasted through a cosmic kaleidoscope and infused with the spirit of Rush. And this was only the first song on the album, already hoisting the bar.

The following two songs backpedaled a bit toward the first album, but afterward Fates Warning never again looked back. "Pirates of the Underground" was a riff-crammed commentary on the band's musical neighborhood. Lyrically, it was heavy with symbolism and double entendre, soon to be Arch trademarks. With this song the vocalist began playing with alliteration, a tradition upheld by the band on several subsequent albums.

The three songs of *The Spectre Within*'s latter half define the band's ambitious early period. First among them is "The Apparition," a tale of life from birth to death. For all its potential triteness, Arch's poetic prose rose above clichéd pitfalls. Carried by stirring riffing and soaring guitar melodies, the song is haunting and emotionally effective. "Kyrie Eleison" begins with the low drone of chanting monks, building to frantic momentum that conveys doom and sadness despite its fast pace. Closer "Epitaph" took metal into new realms of drama and despair over an exotic and ornate twelve minutes.

The Spectre Within set Fates Warning apart from just about everyone else in the metal underground, although parallels could be drawn to Danish band Mercyful Fate, an early influence on Matheos. *Spectre* was darker and more complex than even Iron Maiden or Queensrÿche, and it handled its fantasy imagery intelligently, passing over the clichéd traps of wizards, dragons, and ham-fisted, second-rate riffs.

Once *Awaken the Guardian* was released in 1986, *The Spectre Within* seemed like a mere warm-up. New whiz kid guitarist Frank Aresti, a continually underrated player, reinvigorated the core of Matheos, Arch, and rhythm section Steve Zimmerman (drums) and Joe DiBiase (bass). The band was now well equipped to attain greatness. The atmosphere of *Awaken the Guardian* was thick, full of strange rhythmic shifts and unorthodox riff patterns, asking listeners to process an almost oppressive amount of information in forty-eight minutes. It was a sublime step forward, equally modern and medieval—at once advanced and ancient.

Throughout *Awaken the Guardian*, arrangements are woven of complex patterns using impossibly dense riffs. Though the music was busy, Arch's vocal patterns were absolutely frantic. Using his voice artistically, he often painted pictures with phonetic "aaahhs" and contorted words into strange pronunciations—never stumbling as he crammed piles of lyrics into each stanza. The album's flow is remarkable considering its high detail and complexity.

Crafting a classic: John Arch recording Fates Warning's *Awaken the Guardian*, Preferred Sound Studios, 1986 (*Jim Matheos*)

Awaken's complicated nature is balanced with gentler, more linear moments. "Guardian" is as emotionally connective as the previous album's "The Apparition," though much more serene, with beautiful detailing by Arch. Only the sole Aresti composition, "Giant's Lore (Heart of Winter)," relaxes the frequent tempo changes. Before 1986, no band had transcended the heavy metal norm with the level of sensitivity and complexity inherent in *Awaken the Guardian*.

Fans were shocked by the dismissal of John Arch in 1987. After the vocalist put such a strong stamp on the band's identity, his firing was a risky decision. Arch was as shocked as the fans. "I'm gonna be truthful and candid—that night I downed close to half a liter of vodka. I was so out of it. I was in the shower and couldn't feel myself and it was a pretty bad experience."

Judging Fates Warning's 1980s material with Arch, Jim Matheos is characteristically critical: "I've always thought it was like looking at an old photo album. You look at yourself and say, 'Man, what a dork! What was I thinking?' On the other hand, I appreciate that people like it, because I listen to my favorite bands' old stuff, like the stuff Rush did in the '70s, and think, 'Wow, that's amazing.' I'm sure they're the same way; they listen to it and find all the things that are wrong with it. With the exception of a few spots here and there, I kind of cringe and don't want to listen to it."

Despite discomfort between the two parties, the departure never led to outright acrimony. Arch made a guest appearance onstage with the band several years later to sing "Guardian," and relations between the vocalist and Matheos have been friendly and, for a brief time, creatively productive. More than twenty years later, Fates

WHAT IF?

Comic book publisher Marvel Comics began a series in 1977 titled *What If?* Each issue explored an alternate reality, something that could have transpired in the Marvel Universe but ultimately failed to materialize. Issues such as "What If Spider-Man Had Joined the Fantastic Four?" and "What If Captain America Became President?" appealed to the hard-core Marvel geek.

There are many What If? scenarios in the Metal Universe worth pondering: What If Slayer's Kerry King Had Stayed in Megadeth? What If Paul Di'Anno Had Never Left Iron Maiden? What If Black Sabbath Had Never Discovered Drugs? One of the most intriguing: What If Ron Jarzombek Had Joined Fates Warning? (Get your geek helmet on, people, we're going in...)

In 1986, Fates Warning began the search for a guitarist to replace original member Victor Arduini. While Demonax guitarist Frank Aresti eventually got the job and entered the studio with the band to record a little album called *Awaken the Guardian*, a young six-string slinger in Texas named Ron Jarzombek was close to getting the gig instead.

S.A. Slayer had just broken up, and Ron, their guitarist, was back to messing around on his Tascam four-track machine. Approached by Fates Warning for an audition but lacking the funds to fly to Connecticut, Jarzombek sent the band a demo of a song he wrote, an attempt to prove he could write material in the Fates vein. Featuring his older brother Bobby on drums, Ron presented the five-minute track "Fishies on Leashes" (obviously meant as a working title only, and perhaps an answer to Accept's 1985 song "Dogs on Leads"?). The song is the greatest Fates Warning track that never was—lots of tempo shifts, doom-laden twin guitar harmonies, with an air of dark, fantasy-esque drama. But it wasn't to be, and Jarzombek soon found his calling by joining Texas legends Watchtower, and later birthing the Spastic Ink and Blotted Science projects.

Had Ron joined Fates Warning in 1986, it's likely he would have exited by 1991 anyway, when the band's *Parallels* album shifted toward more accessible, less technical territory—the same reason Ron gave up on Watchtower during the band's original sessions for the legendarily delayed *Mathematics* album.

Warning's Arch era maintains a loyal cult following. "It made some kind of difference," says Arch. "The whole point behind this is to spur people's imagination and to make contact with people, and hope that they got something out of it. I'm amazed that a lot of people are still into it."

True to form, Fates Warning marched ahead, assuring fans that Arch's replacement would be worthy. They plucked new vocalist Ray Alder from Texas metal band Syrus and recorded album number four. *No Exit* (1988) reached new musical and commercial highs for Fates, introducing the band to a whole new audience thanks to MTV *Headbangers Ball*'s occasional airings of the "Silent Cries" video. John Arch had not been the most accessible vocalist, and *Awaken the Guardian* was far from an easy listen. *No Exit* was an easier pill to swallow. While still 100 percent Fates Warning, this new version of the band sounded less arcane. Alder had fantastic power and control, and probably a wider range than Arch. His voice was perfect for the band's new, modernized approach.

Jim Matheos of Fates Warning pulling double duty, July 1988
(*Frank White*)

With a title inspired by the Jean-Paul Sartre play of the same name (Matheos's reading material at the time including thinkers such as Sartre and Arthur Rimbaud), *No Exit* found a sturdier, tougher Fates Warning distancing itself from more delicate, fantasy-laden elements. But they didn't quell their ambitious side—the twenty-two-minute "The Ivory Gate of Dreams" swallowed up *No Exit*'s entire second half. Nodding in the direction of Rush's epic songs of the 1970s, "The Ivory Gate of Dreams" challenged other progressive metal bands to write equally listenable, comprehensible extended-length tracks.

"The Ivory Gate of Dreams" left an indelible imprint on future progressive metal musicians, among them guitarist Jasun Tipton, who formed Zero Hour with his twin brother, Troy, in the early 1990s. "My brother and I really enjoyed *No Exit*," he says. "The first time one of our friends played us 'The Ivory Gate of Dreams,' we looked at each other and knew we had to make a run to the record store. We took a bus and bought the goods. It ruled!"

Again expanding and exploring, Fates Warning brought in Warlord drummer Mark Zonder for the follow-up to *No Exit*. There was no comparison between the newcomer and original pounder Steve Zimmerman. Zimmerman was capable, but Zonder was mind-blowing. He was very familiar with Fates Warning, having already worked in the studio with producer Bill Metoyer during the recording of *The Spectre Within* and *Awaken the Guardian*, even tuning Zimmerman's drums. But Zonder was not a fan of *No Exit*'s more aggressive songs, such as "Anarchy Divine" and "Shades of Heavenly Death." In fact, he hesitated when Matheos approached him to join.

"If you listen to *No Exit*," Zonder says, "there's some serious thrashing going on. I'm not comfortable playing in bands that I don't like. I gotta be into it. I can't just join a band to join a band. But Jim told me they wanted to get rid of Steve to go in a different direction. They knew he couldn't do it. But it takes all types. The drummers that have made the most money and played with the biggest bands in the world are not what you consider awesome drummers, like Peter Criss and Ringo Starr—they're not Vinnie Colaiuta and Steve Gadd, you know? So it's not that Steve's bad or that I'm good. For where Fates Warning went, I think a change was important."

Zonder's inspirations varied from soul/funk/R&B such as Tower of Power, to U.S. prog rockers Kansas, to the ubiquitous Rush. "I'd come home from high school and listen to Rush's *All the World's a Stage*—'Bastille Day,' 'In the Mood,' 'Anthem.' And *Grace Under Pressure* is one of my favorite albums ever," he says. "Actually, there hasn't been a disappointing Rush record for me."

The drummer's biggest influence, however, was not Neil Peart, but Aynsley Dunbar, particularly from the first three Journey albums. "That stuff was progressive, in my mind. 'Of a Lifetime,' from the first Journey record, all that drumming in that song, I used to come home from school and just rip it off. That's where I learned the whole hi-hat thing, where I learned those syncopated, linear kinds of things."

Zonder's approach had a tremendous effect on Fates Warning's music, and 1989's *Perfect Symmetry* marked a big change. The sleek cover art by Hugh Syme, who had worked with Rush since 1975, signaled that the band had turned a corner. With a new, streamlined logo replacing the bulky old one, the album did not look very metal. Goodbye old-school logo and fantasy art—hello polyrhythms and string quartets.

Perfect Symmetry's production was technical and clinical, a cold cradle for sour laments such as "Chasing Time" and the piercing "The Arena." The metal that coursed through Fates Warning's veins became finer and more detailed as the band balanced tunefulness with their most complex rhythmic work yet. The uniformity of the recording lent the album a monochromatic rainy-day atmosphere that matched the gray tones of the artwork—but a few songs escape into a more colorful world. For example, complicated rhythmic stutters and unpredictable timing introduced the Zonder-era sound on opener "Part of the Machine." "Through Different Eyes" was the band's catchiest, most radio-ready song yet. A string quartet led the band through the mostly instrumental "At Fates' Hands," revealing the prog rock influence of Rush and Kansas. King Crimson's edgy rhythms are also echoed in the instrumental torrent of the main section.

With *Perfect Symmetry*, Jim Matheos initiated a recurring lyrical theme: the trials of aging, feeling worn, and—as the song says—having "Nothing Left to Say." A line from the album's final track epitomizes Matheos's views on the passage of time: "And behind the disguise of a man with a cause / There's a child screaming / With nothing left to say." This was bitter-cold reality from a band that had sat in turreted towers of fantasy several years earlier.

With Arch long gone, bandleader Matheos took on the task of writing lyrics. "I'm not one to write fiction songs," he says. "I have to write about the things I think about. If you're playing long songs in minor keys, it doesn't really make sense to distill them with joyful lyrics. When I'm feeling happy or enjoying myself, it's not the time where I want to run to the studio and express myself. I want to enjoy the moment. But when you're depressed or contemplative, that's the time you want to express those thoughts."

Into the 1990s, Fates Warning streamlined further. Sixth album *Parallels* saw Rush producer Terry Brown at the helm, and Hugh Syme again creating cover art. The band now clearly saw a model in Rush. They pursued ever more direct, accessible lines, as their Canadian heroes had done in the '80s. Working with Brown—long considered the fourth member of Rush—was a career high-light for Fates Warning. "I love that guy," says Matheos. "He's great, and nowadays I consider him a friend. Those Rush albums were such a huge influence on me. Rush is probably one of my top three influences. And with Terry Brown, we really worked well together. It was very comfortable, and he's always got great ideas."

Parallels (1991) took the first step down a path that Fates Warning still walks today. While "Life in Still Water" and the tremendous "The Eleventh Hour" recalled the complexity of the previous album, the other six songs were remarkably slick, leaning toward pop on "We Only Say Goodbye" and "Eye to Eye."

This trend continued with 1994's *Inside Out*, where the complex "Monument" was surrounded by melodic, catchy fare such as "Down to the Wire" and "Shelter Me." True to the band's nature, much of the music was sedate, even gloomy, but in a modern-sounding, commercial context, akin to Queensrÿche's *Promised Land*. One of the album's standout songs, "Face the Fear," remained sharp and bright, with tasty melodic nuances and Zonder's tricky rhythms working stealthily beneath simple surface material.

Despite a dedicated following, loads of critical accolades, and seven excellent albums, mainstream success continued to elude Fates Warning. At this point, the band lineup—the most stable formation in the group's history—fragmented. Key members Joe DiBiase and Frank Aresti left after *Inside Out*'s release.

Fates Warning has continued to shift its lineup, even hiring temporary touring members such as guitarist Bernie Versailles—of speed metal merchants Agent Steel and modern proggers Redemption—and keyboardist/guitarist Shaun Michaud of new-school prog metal act Event. After the mostly straightforward approach of *Inside Out*, many thought the band's experimental days were behind them, but Fates Warning rebounded in 1997 with *A Pleasant Shade of Gray*. The album exploited the rainy-day melancholy that permeated their earlier work, again aided by producer Terry Brown. The album-length song was split into twelve movements, a demanding fifty-four-minute listen. *APSOG*—as the band's fans have since dubbed it—has proven to be one of the most lauded albums in the band's catalog. Even Zonder is unequivocal in his estimation of the album: "I think *A Pleasant Shade of Gray* is the best thing Fates Warning has ever done. Period. End of conversation."

Fates Warning's ace card, Frank Aresti, September 2009
(*Christina Ricciardi*)

Despite their split in 1987, Jim Matheos and former vocalist John Arch worked together again. The twenty-eight-minute 2003 solo release *A Twist of Fate* marked Arch's first trip to the recording studio in more than fifteen years. The two lengthy songs that comprise *A Twist of Fate* healed the wound of Arch's too-early dismissal from Fates Warning. It was easy to forget it was 2003, too tempting to imagine that this was what the fourth Arch-era Fates Warning album might have sounded like.

Matheos remains proud of *A Twist of Fate*. "I'd love to sit down with John Arch for six months and write a full-length record," he says. But even if some fans thought it filled the gap between *Awaken the Guardian* and *No Exit*, Matheos disagrees. "Remember, there are twenty years and a lot of life experiences between *Awaken the Guardian* and *A Twist of Fate*. Whatever 'FW4' with John Arch would have sounded like, it would have been nothing like *A Twist of Fate*."

Fates Warning and Queensrÿche moved in parallel to a variety of peers in the 1980s, sharing similar styles and in some cases influencing other bands directly. In the Pacific Northwest, Seattle's Heir Apparent drew plenty of comparisons to their royal brethren Queensrÿche. The band's 1986 debut, *Graceful Inheritance*, showcased a band already reaching for the sublime. There was some ingenuity on display, and the

Crimson Glory makes the cover of *Kerrang!*, 1989

album's atmosphere of epic majesty is still treasured by fans of the sound and era. Three years later Heir Apparent's second and final album, *One Small Voice*, revealed a slicker recording and a busier songwriting approach. Despite the maturity and memorability of originals "The Fifth Season" and "Cacophony of Anger," their decision to cover Simon & Garfunkel's "The Sound of Silence" eclipsed the rest of the songs in reviews and college radio airplay. Heir Apparent deserves credit for beating fellow Seattleites Nevermore to the cover by more than a decade.

In the Southeast, Florida's Crimson Glory modeled its 1986 self-titled debut after the usual Iron Maiden/Judas Priest influences, adding a slickness reminiscent of Queensrÿche. The first Crimson Glory album offered tight songwriting, tighter playing, and the piercing high-range style of vocalist Midnight, born John Patrick McDonald. The band's image was strange, and harkened to Genesis's theatrical stagecraft—each member wore a silver mask, hiding his face under cold, rigid steel.

Though the masks garnered attention, their music spoke for itself. When Crimson Glory's second album, *Transcendence*, arrived in 1988, the press almost forgot about the silver faces. The collection of ten songs was roundly praised by critics and fans and remains a hallowed prog metal cornerstone. *Transcendence* brought a Led Zeppelin aspect to "In Dark Places," "Painted Skies," and the mystical title track. Eastern melodies abound, and Midnight's Robert Plant–isms are undeniable. The band's steely melodies and stellar musicianship mesh with '70s influences and more mature, sublime songwriting. The album thrust the cold futurism of Queensrÿche's *Rage for Order* into a less claustrophobic and more ethereal place. From the time of its release, *Transcendence* had "classic" written all over it.

The follow-up, 1991's *Strange and Beautiful*, introduced an altered Crimson Glory lineup and a sound that brought together a simulacrum of Led Zeppelin, a more exotic Mötley Crüe, and the emerging alternative rock/metal scene. The trademark masks had also disappeared. The album flopped spectacularly. Vocalist Midnight left to pursue a solo career, while a new lineup offered poorly received 1999 comeback album, *Astronomica*. Afteward, the band, in various guises, continually threatened to return and pursue the legacy of their first two albums, to no avail. The death of Midnight in July 2009—due to total kidney and liver failure—insured that the original band would never regain its former glory.

Another Florida band, Savatage, has maintained a longer career than Crimson Glory, surviving substance abuse, shifting lineups, and outright tragedy. After beginning life as Avatar in 1979, the band changed its name and morphed from studs-and-leather metal to pioneering theatrical metal. With early recordings *Sirens* and *The Dungeons are Calling*, Savatage dished meat and muscle for young metallions across the planet, while hinting at grander ambitions. On 1987's *Hall of the Mountain King*, the band followed guitarist Criss Oliva through a spirited interpretation of Norwegian composer Edvard Grieg's "In the Hall of the Mountain King."

With *Gutter Ballet* in 1989, the band progressed further. Inspired by vocalist/keyboardist/main songwriter Jon Oliva's impressions of a Toronto performance of the musical *The Phantom of the Opera*, Savatage's music became more theatrical. Producer and de facto band member Paul O'Neill, who had toured as a guitarist with musicals *Hair* and *Jesus Christ Superstar*, encouraged Savatage toward the dramatic flourishes heard on "When the Crowds are Gone" and "Gutter Ballet."

O'Neill helped propel Savatage into grandiose realms. Following his days in musical theater, the New York City native worked for rock management giant Leber-Krebs Inc. As a successful concert promoter in Japan, he worked with Madonna and Sting. His overall business acumen was sharp, but his first loves were writing and performing, and Savatage was his chance to reenergize those creative impulses. O'Neill signed on as producer of *Hall of the Mountain King*. Two years later, he boasted as many songwriting credits on *Gutter Ballet* as Jon and Criss Oliva.

O'Neill considered the Oliva siblings incredibly talented, but thought they needed direction. He squeezed every ounce of vision from Criss and Jon while tapping into his own innate ability. "For some bands," O'Neill says, "all you can do is pound some nails and put a couple boards together, and that's fine—do it to the best of your ability. But these guys could build the Taj Mahal and create beautiful epic structures. While a lot of people were straining, they did it effortlessly. To me, Jon and Criss were on Michelangelo's artistic level."

By the album *Streets: A Rock Opera* in 1991, Savatage had practically become an off-Broadway metal band. Their grandiosity was met either with heaps of acclaim or complete derision, but the Oliva brothers and O'Neill had created a new niche for Savatage: Their curious mixture of traditional metal, bombast, Broadway, and balladry satisfied an audience that no one even knew existed up to that point.

Curiously, at this juncture Jon Oliva stepped aside to act as a behind-the-scenes consulting member, assuming a father-figure role similar to O'Neill's. Oliva's exit was controversial. He announced he would concentrate fully on his other band, Doctor Butcher, and on grand designs for a musical called *Romanov* —but after a well-publicized trip to rehab in 1988, some journalists and fans assumed his struggle with drug and alcohol addiction had threatened not only the quality of his voice but his ability to weather road life.

Fans were baffled when virtual unknown Zachary Stevens became the new Savatage vocalist. An obvious and unavoidable reinvention, 1993's *Edge of Thorns* was less ornamented than *Streets*, but continued on the same slick, melody-driven path.

Edge of Thorns was received surprisingly well, but everything was sidetracked after October 17, 1993, when Criss Oliva was killed by a drunk driver. Brother Jon admitted that the band might as well have died with Criss, but he continued to direct the group, along with O'Neill, in an effort to keep his brother's vision alive. Savatage's lineup shifted constantly, accommodating, among others, Jon, who wandered through different roles as needed.

Despite inconsistencies, the band released a clutch of albums that drew continued acclaim for dramatic and melodic heavy metal, the most revered being 1995's *Dead Winter Dead*. After 2001's *Poets and Madmen*, the band went on indefinite hiatus. But Savatage had made its mark—the band that started out with skull-cracking songs "The Whip" and "By the Grace of the Witch" ended up as a major influence on many bands populating the high-minded progressive metal movement of the 1990s.

Jon Oliva's *Romanov* never saw the light of day, but after 1996 he found enormous respect and success outside the metal world with Trans-Siberian Orchestra, which he founded with Paul O'Neill and several other longtime Savatage members. T-SO is essentially a metallic version of Germany's prog-turned-Christmas-music-sensation Mannheim Steamroller. The multi-member outfit has reaped huge sales and performed in front of more people than Savatage ever dreamed of. Their symphonic approach to traditional Christmas music, played mostly by seasoned metal musicians, has been wildly successful since its formation, reaching platinum sales with almost every release.

6. KILLED BY TECH

"'Tech metal' was a term we coined on our flyers without feeling like it was going to be some kind of genre. But we had to call it something. We knew it was different and we didn't want people to think that they were just coming to see a rock-and-roll band. So we were 'The Harvesters of Technical Thrash Metal: Watchtower!'" —Jason McMaster, Watchtower

AN INTERESTING VARIETY OF BANDS took melodic progressive metal to some wild places in the mid-'80s. As metal surged, the genre fragmented further into deeper subgenres. The outgrowths of Rush, Iron Maiden, and Metallica's influence on young musicians took myriad forms. Some newcomers went for the gut in a more traditional fashion. Others, such as Queensrÿche and Fates Warning, evolved rapidly, pulling a few influences from outside the metal genre. In 1986, both released finely crafted albums that would set new metal standards. *Rage for Order* by Queensrÿche and *Awaken the Guardian* by Fates Warning were both tagged "thinking man's metal" by a global media struggling to find new names for the genre's rapid expansion.

"Thinking man's metal" meant "progressive metal"—and was sometimes lamentably tagged "techno metal." "Thinking man's metal" didn't really stick, which is probably good, as there is something alienating and elitist about the term. "Techno metal" worked well enough until "industrial metal" came along in the early '90s, introducing into the genre the synthetic and repetitive machine sounds of industrial or techno music, something despised by many of the "thinking" men (and women) in the progressive metal audience. The shortened "tech metal" term eventually fell into common use; in the mid-'80s an entire subset of bands blasted off into the unknown

"Complex abstract techno-thrash";
an early Watchtower flyer

with complex metal sounds that made good on the "tech metal" tag. The craziest of them made even the most difficult Fates Warning material sound rudimentary.

Influenced by metal's most ambitious pioneers, and various jazz and prog rock artists, bands such as San Diego's Psychotic Waltz, Austin, Texas's caustic Watchtower, and their German doppelgängers, Sieges Even, emerged and took the genre into yet more technically demanding areas. Watchtower, particularly, touched off a movement and sound that focused obsessively on technicality, and their influence spread across the globe and across subgenres like wildfire. Indeed, metal's avant-garde was taking off, in a variety of different directions, on a global scale.

Tech metal is hectic and otherworldly, inhuman in atmosphere, and mercilessly demanding of the human channels through which it is delivered. Its rhythmic axis reveals influences that are sometimes seemingly at odds with metal—such as jazz fusion, classical and world music—along with the manic, precise thrust of metal's most hyperactive elements. Tech metal uses disorienting time signatures, 5/8ths and 51/32nds flying everywhere, with an occasional bone thrown to convention by an attacking 4/4. Transitions between individual parts are rapid and unpredictable. Vocals are impressive only because they exist at all—so much musical information is involved that squeezing vocals into the fray seems impossible. Some singers succeeded where other hapless ones failed. The atmosphere of tech metal is unerringly one of tension and paranoia. To listen to bands of this genre is to embark on a cliffhanging musical adventure that feels precarious but is carefully managed by ridiculously astute musicians. Everything is anal-retentively arranged and in place—there is no room for drifting improvisation.

As raw and scrappy as it was, "Meltdown," by the obscure Watchtower, marked the birth of tech metal. The song and band stealthily debuted on the 1983 album *Cottage Cheese from the Lips of Death: A Texas Hardcore Compilation*. Released on the tiny Ward-9 label, the fringe punk collection was an odd place to introduce Watchtower. Even for a band without a niche, "Meltdown" stuck out like a sore thumb—frantic early speed metal hell buried as the last of fourteen songs by the likes of D.R.I. and Butthole Surfers. Jason McMaster's vocals bore uncanny similarity to those of Raven's John Gallagher, and the crazed speed of

Demonstrations in chaos: Watchtower's *Meltdown* tape, 1984

the song was equally in line with those NWOBHM loonies. Bassist Doug Keyser and drummer Rick Colaluca played on the brink of disaster, threatening to collapse with each tempo change if not for their tremendous dexterity and chemistry. Guitarist Billy White rounded out the quartet, he alone still seemed rooted solely in metal.

Two years later, in 1985, Watchtower officially debuted with *Energetic Disassembly*, an eight-song album released on its own Zombo Records label. The title is a perfect distillation of the music's atomic weirdness, and an important descriptive cornerstone of metal's most confounding subgenre. While a few fanzine editors and tape traders were already avid followers of the band's 1984 *Meltdown* demo, most metal fans had trouble finding the album. Watchtower quickly became an entity most had heard of but never actually heard. Of course, the unintentional obscurity worked wonders for their cult status. Those metal fiends lucky enough to hear *Energetic Disassembly* had their ringing ears greeted by the bizarre, uneasy sounds of technical metal in its infancy.

Energetic Disassembly was an acquired taste, with a buzzing guitar sound buried under an avalanche of difficult, slippery rhythms and wailing fits of vocal hysteria. Watchtower's energy level could only have been maintained by teenagers, and only prodigies could have boasted their skill level. White and McMaster were deeper into the metal of the day than Watchtower's rhythm section—particularly bands like Metallica and Mercyful Fate, who, as McMaster says, "used ten riffs in a seven-minute song, and all these different movements."

McMaster endearingly calls Keyser and Colaluca "nerds in extreme metal." "They didn't really fit into the category of 'metalhead,'" he says. "They're very book-smart. Sure, they had Iron Maiden and Judas Priest albums, and maybe early Queensrÿche, but [they] never really got past that. They also had U.K. albums, and every Rush album. They even had Oingo Boingo and Frank Zappa in their collections, and this was in high school. They were in this weird metal band, but they were into all this other stuff." And so, the Watchtower sound was born.

Years before Dream Theater would be called a mixture of Rush and Metallica by their record label, *Energetic Disassembly* deserved the comparison. Even Dream Theater drummer Mike Portnoy concurs. "I saw Lars Ulrich wearing a Watchtower shirt in *Kerrang!* magazine," he says. "I was like, 'Who the hell are those guys?' Somehow I discovered their first album and got in touch with Jason McMaster. I was completely blown away by the musicianship. They sounded like Rush on steroids. I had never heard any bands playing like that at that time. It was just taking the musicianship to a whole other level."

Appropriately, the first song on *Energetic Disassembly* was "Violent Change." Its wiry jazzlike bass was reaffirmed in the Geddy Lee–like bass bounce of third song, "Tyrants in Distress." Drummer Colaluca threw ridiculously busy fills through the din, while pushing a solid, metronome-like beat. With only one guitar and no studio overdubbing, even during solo parts, the ensemble generated an atmosphere not unlike that of a berserk '70s fusion band. Plenty of mad metal was on display, of course. McMaster's singing stuck to a range that alternated between high and higher. His John Gallagher–meets–Geddy Lee screech added an extra layer of nervous energy to an already jumpy musical trio.

Billy White's angular and unorthodox guitar playing fueled Watchtower's odd machine. His metal fuzz was appropriately distorted, while the roughshod recording lent his guitar a ghastly hollow tone that telegraphed edgy caffeinated paranoia. His solos hinted at jazz legends like Allan Holdsworth, as well as rock heroes Eddie Van Halen and Rush's Alex Lifeson. *Energetic Disassembly* is a perplexing listen, with more *what the...?* moments blazing by than any earthbound listener would care to count.

Although *Energetic Disassembly* was his only full-length appearance with Watchtower, Billy White remains legendary in prog metal circles—particularly in Texas, where eyewitnesses to his prowess remain. "All the guitar players in town were followers of Billy White," recalls McMaster. "To this day he has so much respect, even though he's not a rock guitar player anymore—he plays flamenco guitar and is into all types of music. People still talk about Billy White as the creator of the prog metal riff: super-über-angular crazy fucked-up all-over-the-place metal riffs. He taught guitar to a lot of people around here who still play in bands and still play metal. He really made an impact."

Watchtower's artwork and lyrical imagery didn't bow to conservative metal norms. The cover art of their debut was simple but unorthodox for the genre: three triangular shapes bearing arcane symbols, like a rough sketch for a Rush cover. Although titles such as "Argonne Forest" and "Cimmerian Shadows" could have been stolen from Michael Moorcock novels, other subject matter addressed heady social and political topics. As with Metallica and other emerging thrashers, Watchtower's lyrics took on real-world ugliness, addressing the environment ("Violent Change"), nuclear technology ("Meltdown," "Energetic Disassembly"), human rights ("Asylum"), and political corruption ("Social Fears"). Along with Metallica, Iron Maiden, Queensrÿche, and Fates Warning, Watchtower widened the scope of metal by expanding its lyrical range and avoiding stereotypes such as skulls, swords, and scantily clad babes. A new intelligentsia was bubbling to life in the metal universe.

After *Energetic Disassembly,* Watchtower went through violent changes. Billy White shocked the band by resigning. "He decided he needed to play other styles of music," says McMaster. "We were thinking, 'How can we replace Billy White?' This guy spearheaded a whole movement, he and his guitar in his bedroom."

Fortune smiled on Watchtower, however, as they drafted another gifted guitarist from their neighborhood to fill White's big shoes. "In my mind the only replacement was Ron Jarzombek," says McMaster.

Ron Jarzombek had been seeking a new gig after the dissolution of San Antonio band Slayer (renamed S.A. Slayer after the L.A. thrashers surpassed them in popularity). S.A. Slayer sounded similar to early Watchtower, with obvious influence from Mercyful Fate, though lacking the Martian rhythm section of the former and the songwriting excellence of the latter. Their lone album with Jarzombek, recorded in 1984, bore the clichéd title *Go for the Throat*. Their material was frantic and unfocused, and front man Steve Cooper's vocals were total nails-on-chalkboard. In the end, S.A. Slayer's major contribution to metal was as a finishing school, as its members graduated into a variety of more successful acts: Juggernaut, featuring Jarzombek's equally talented older brother Bobby on drums; New York City legends Riot; Arizona thrashers Sacred Reich; and California aggro-mongers Machine Head.

While playing in S.A. Slayer, Ron Jarzombek witnessed Watchtower in its first incarnation. "Seeing the original lineup with Billy White on guitar was something," he says. "They floored me and inspired me. There wasn't another band doing what they were doing in '84 and '85, combining what was then the most extreme form of metal with a very progressive approach. Watchtower definitely deserve to be called early pioneers of technical metal or jazz metal or techno thrash or whatever labels people have come up with over the years to describe the band."

Jarzombek's unorthodox approach sounded bizarre to an unreal degree: The guitarist utilized unusual time signatures, unprecedented fluidity, and tonal scales he seemed to have invented himself.

On S.A. Slayer's *Go for the Throat,* the first indication of his mad genius appeared with "TLO 22," a short, multitracked guitar workout showcasing one very weird style. After Eddie Van Halen's "Eruption" in 1978, every bad-boy metal guitarist had to lay his own claim to six-string wizardry, and Jarzombek's effort was a thing of rare originality. Under a bed of whammy-bar dive-bombs, Jarzombek impressed not with an array of effects pedals and recording trickery, but with searing runs that crept up and down the fretboard in a fifty-seven-second series of strange melodic choices.

Jarzombek was perfect for Watchtower. His influences included Rush's Alex Lifeson, Steve Vai, Judas Priest's Glenn Tipton, and Scorpions alumni Michael Schenker and Uli Jon Roth. Even Frank Zappa left an impression. "I've seen lots of Zappa transcriptions," says the guitarist, "and his timing subdivisions really impacted my playing and writing."

After adding Jarzombek, Watchtower recorded the *Instruments of Random Murder* demo in 1987. Hugely inspired by Metallica's *Master of Puppets*, the guitar-

Screaming in 11/8: Jason McMaster of Watchtower (*Gerrie Lemmens*)

ist dug in and immediately began writing material. Watchtower's admiration of Rush also persisted. The Canadians had used Morse code to develop their classic 1981 instrumental "YYZ," and that technique left an indelible imprint on Jarzombek.

"We worked a lot with numbers and patterns," he says, "which came from Rush's 'YYZ.' That opened up a whole series of doors for us, and is something I use heavily with my writing today. I was just getting into listening to Bugs Bunny cartoons and film scores by Richard Band, and then Danny Elfman, Jerry Goldsmith, and Elliot Goldenthal." Building on the band's stated prog rock and fusion influences such as Yes, U.K., and Mahavishnu Orchestra, this lineup of Watchtower soon jumped leaps and bounds ahead of the first incarnation.

The broadened musical scope and completely left-field nature of the *Instruments of Random Murder* demo expanded the band's range considerably, but internal upheavals continued to alter Watchtower's treacherous course. With help from the constantly networking front man McMaster, bassist Doug Keyser auditioned for Metallica in the wake of Cliff Burton's untimely death. Unsurprisingly, he was one of the final contenders, though the golden ticket went to Jason Newsted of Arizona thrash band Flotsam and Jetsam.

Though dedicated to Watchtower, Jason McMaster also kept his options open, auditioning for California thrash bands Mordred and Bloodlust. Closer to home, McMaster was invited to join Pantera when the Abbott brothers Dimebag Darrell and Vinnie Paul sought a replacement for original vocalist Terrence Lee. McMaster declined, but soon departed his beloved Watchtower for party rockers Dangerous Toys. The band's ballsy good-time blues rock was a cross between Guns N' Roses and AC/DC—worlds away from Watchtower.

The decision to leave Watchtower was tough for McMaster, after six years of dedication, but, like the restless Billy White, he had to move on. "I like that primal state of rock," he says. "That's where it all comes from. So to actually go back and play something that rocks, and has groove and boogie, was interesting to me. It pissed off a lot of Watchtower fans."

With this new pursuit, McMaster fulfilled a dream. His new band landed a deal with Columbia Records, a major achievement for any band. Dangerous Toys had several videos played on MTV—"Scared" appeared on nostalgic VH1 shows years later—and toured relentlessly. The band enhanced its image with sneering evil clown mascot Bill Z. Bub, their own version of more popular figures such as Iron Maiden's Eddie and Megadeth's Vic Rattlehead. In the end, Dangerous Toys afforded McMaster opportunities that Watchtower, in all their crazy inaccessibility, never could have.

After leaving, McMaster recruited Mike Soliz from Texas power thrash act Militia to take over his vacant spot. "I felt like family," says McMaster. "I wanted them to succeed, so I actually helped them find a replacement for me." Soliz only stayed long enough to appear on the 1989 Noise Records compilation *Doomsday News 2* on the track "Dangerous Toy," obviously a reference to McMaster's new career choice.

Watchtower finally settled down with New Jersey boy Alan Tecchio—another singer recommended by McMaster. Alan had proven his versatility, strength, and melodic sensibility with adventurous power metal act Hades. The three Watchtower instrumentalists had already written the lion's share of second album *Control and Resistance*. Tecchio arrived at the last minute to record in Germany—home of their new label, Noise Records—and another chapter in progressive metal history began.

During Watchtower's down time between lineup shifts, various other bands appeared with similar inspirations. One of them, Germany's Sieges Even, recorded two demo tapes in 1986 and 1987 that their guitarist, Markus Steffen, describes as "heavily influenced by U.S. metal in the vein of Megadeth, Hades, Metal Church, and Tension, NWOBHM stuff like Iron Maiden, and traditional stuff like Judas Priest." By 1988 and the *Repression and Resistance* demo, the band was engulfed in technicality.

German label Steamhammer signed Sieges Even, and later in 1988 their first album, *Life Cycle*, appeared. Sporting two instrumentals among its eight tracks, *Life Cycle* featured the same instrumentation as Watchtower's debut, but with the addition of acoustic guitar and electronic percussion. *Life Cycle* clearly benefited from a punchier, fuller sound, as well as guitar overdubbing for a thickness that Watchtower's debut lacked. The band's rhythm section mirrored the Watchtower team--sharp attack and incredible finesse--with brothers Oliver and Alex Holzwarth having the advantage of musical intuition by blood relation. Sieges Even's wealth of talent and ambition asserted itself throughout the album's exhausting forty-three minutes, notably on the lengthy twelve-minute "Straggler from Atlantis."

Sieges Even's *Life Cycle*, 1988

The album artwork revealed Sieges Even's high-minded agenda, depicting a brain and heart linked to an electronic circuit board. Song titles such as "The Roads of Iliad," "David," and "Straggler from Atlantis" were far from cliché, and the members didn't look very metal. The inside cover featured a quote from German poet/playwright Bertolt Brecht. Cerebral stuff it was, though not without its problems. Vocalist Franz Herde's nasal yelp wandered in and mostly out of key, and he lacked the control of respected prog metal vocalists such as Ray Alder and Geoff Tate. Musically, flow and memorability were eclipsed by complication. Regardless, the talent on display was inarguably impressive.

Watchtower's *Control and Resistance* album of 1989 shared uncanny similarities with Sieges Even's debut. Rick Colaluca used electronic drums as early as Watchtower's debut—one of the first metal drummers to do so--and they were more prominent on *Control and Resistance*. Sieges drummer Alex Holzwarth used them liberally throughout *Life Cycle*. The title *Control and Resistance* was suspiciously close to Sieges Even's "Repression and Resistance." Watchtower's album even featured a song called "Life Cycles," almost exactly Sieges Even's album title. One wonders if the Germans, so obviously influenced by Watchtower, had in turn influenced the Texans. "None of us in Watchtower were remotely fans of Sieges Even," claims guitarist Ron Jarzombek, "so the chance of any of us ripping them off was zero. We had never heard of them until people started telling us we had been ripped off. Doug Keyser came up with the title 'Life Cycles' and he didn't even listen to any metal bands. Same thing with 'Repression and Resistance' versus *Control and Resistance*. We had done lots of interviews in 1988 and our new song titles were mentioned a lot. I guess that's how Sieges Even got their titles."

Markus Steffen denies this. "We liked Watchtower, no doubt about it. But what people claimed—including the guys in Watchtower—as far as stealing song titles and riffs, that overshot the mark by far. One reason for the similarities is we were based on similar influences, like Rush and Allan Holdsworth. And we had the same attitude—that was a time in our career when we wanted to write the most complicated music in the world, and this was something Watchtower were also trying to achieve."

Rush certainly played a huge part in Sieges Even's music. "Rush always stood for individuality," Steffen says. "No other band sounds like Rush, no other guitar player like Alex Lifeson. This is what makes them so inspiring. I've followed them throughout all their stages and I can't say which album I like best. I really dig *Hold Your Fire*—the songwriting is outstanding—and I even like their later output, especially *Vapor Trails*."

Sieges Even eventually abandoned their mind-boggling complexity, which ended accusations that they were ripping off Watchtower. However, their second album, 1990's *Steps*, was hardly easier on the ears than the debut. *Metal Forces* reviewer Rob Clymo said the album "lacks cohesiveness and has the awful tendency of becoming incredibly tedious. Worse than that, it hasn't got any real songs on it either... Sieges Even have committed the ultimate in commercial suicide."

Steps opened with the ludicrously titled twenty-five-minute "Tangerine Windows of Solace," illustrating the band's attitude, according to Steffen: "being radical and non-conformist to what people and even our record company expected from us."

Though the music was more refined, built less with aggression and more with elaborate textures, the writing itself was probably more complex. Elements of jazz and prime-era Rush were threaded into the compositions. The music felt less panicky, calling for a more sensitive vocal approach, but vocalist Franz Herde couldn't deliver. His misplaced yowling marred the instrumentalists' efforts and spelled his end. While Sieges Even was recording their next album, *A Sense of Change*, it became clear that something softer was needed, and Herde was summarily dismissed.

A Sense of Change introduced the smooth soulfulness of new vocalist Jogi Kaiser. Though the band still explored, they left their utterly technical material in the past. "That album is where we found our own style," says Steffen, "the contrast between heavy and soft parts; clean guitars, distorted guitars; more structured songs. When we continued with *The Art of Navigating by the Stars* more than ten years after *A Sense of Change*, we simply continued with the concept that we started on that album."

For ten years between those two albums, Sieges Even was in flux. Steffen left the band after *A Sense of Change*, and more new blood meant yet another new direction. "I think it would have been better if the Holzwarth brothers had continued under a different name," Steffen says. *Sophisticated* in 1995 and *Uneven* in 1997 were products of that tumultuous era. Though mostly ignored at the time, both albums received a second look with reissues in 2008.

After *Uneven*, Sieges Even went on hiatus for nearly eight years, until 2005. During this time, the band members sought new avenues of expression. The Holzwarth brothers became touring members of power metal band Blind Guardian in the 2000s, and Alex found steady work drumming with Italian symphonic metal sensations Rhapsody. Meanwhile, original guitarist Steffen busied himself writing chamber music and publishing a book on classical guitar.

The brothers eventually reunited with Steffen, forming Looking Glass Self in 1999. Fronted by vocalist Andre Matos of Brazilian progressive/power metal band Angra, Looking Glass Self replaced the metal influence of Sieges Even with an abundance of acoustic new age fluff. After one demo, the band parted ways with Matos, picked up vocalist Arno Menses, and mutated into the slightly sturdier Val'Paraiso.

Eventually, Val'Paraiso material felt enough like Sieges Even that the band switched back to their most familiar moniker. Under that banner they recorded two studio albums and one live album before yet again breaking up in the autumn of 2008. The live album, *Playgrounds*, closed the book on Sieges Even for good, drawing from their final two albums and also reaching back to *A Sense of Change*. *Playgrounds* even incorporated various Rush passages within "These Empty Places," acknowledging one of the band's biggest influences. After the split, Steffen and Menses forged ahead in a similar vein with new band Subsignal, while the Holzwarth brothers settled back into their careers as in-demand session players.

The alpha year of tech metal, 1985, found San Diego band Aslan taking their first steps. As Watchtower released their debut and Sieges Even formed, Aslan's three-song, sixteen-minute demo hit the underground. The tape bore similarities to the demo by pre–Dream Theater band Majesty, standing with one foot in Iron Maiden and early Queensrÿche, the other planted in the more complex arrangements favored by Fates Warning and classic Rush. All five members of Aslan—Buddy Lackey, Dan Rock, Brian McAlpin, Ward Evans, and Norm Leggio—continued into the band's next incarnation as Psychotic Waltz. Under that name, the band released a second demo in 1988, exposing tighter arrangements and increasing complexity. While Aslan's medieval, mystical edge remained, they were breaking through to something greater that would propel them on a wild four-album ride, defying cliché at every turn.

The year 1990 finally brought the debut album *A Social Grace*, released on tiny European label Rising Sun. Complex and busy with a psychedelic edge, the spiraling, hypnotic lines of guitarists Rock and McAlpin and the charismatic vocals of Buddy Lackey formed the core of the band's sound. Lackey occasionally busted out a flute, drawing inevitable comparisons to Jethro Tull's Ian Anderson. Typically, any rock band with a flute would draw comparison to Anderson and Tull, but Lackey welcomed the references, heard on *A Social Grace* in "I Remember" and in later Psychotic Waltz song "My Grave." Lackey clearly modeled his singing and flute playing on Anderson, who he has humbly called "my teacher"—itself a reference to Tull's 1970 song "The Teacher."

Psychotic Waltz's magnum opus, *Into the Everflow*, arrived in 1992. Produced by Ralph Hubert of German neoclassical tech thrashers Mekong Delta, the album saw the band's songwriting achieve a tighter focus, while maintaining the epic feel of the debut. Orchestral and haunting, the swirling guitars of Rock and McAlpin were now central to the band's compelling sound. The songs themselves were not boggling minds with the same crazy complexity as the debut—but their many individual parts combined into a larger whole worked marvelously.

As *Into the Everflow* expanded on the promise of *A Social Grace*, the band's following grew, especially in Europe. "I had pen pals all over Europe," remembers drummer Norm Leggio. "I ended up selling two thousand Psychotic Waltz demos out

Rare Psychotic Waltz 7-inch, circa 1990

of my bedroom, but we were so ahead of the curve that U.S. labels didn't know how to market us. So we concentrated on Europe. Another thing that helped was living in Germany for two months while recording *Into the Everflow*. Fans would see us taking the train to the studio or hanging out in pubs during our downtime, and we toured a lot for *Everflow*. We kind of became a local band over there."

Into the Everflow's psychedelic atmosphere and imagery set them apart from the colder approaches of Watchtower and Sieges Even, bands they otherwise had plenty in common with; deliberate references to the Doors, the Beatles, the Jimi Hendrix Experience, Jethro Tull, and Jane's Addiction in "Butterfly" made their inspirations clear. Yet Psychotic Waltz's dark, complex metal was still spinning on an axis of jarring tempo changes amid a myriad of songwriting curveballs. Fans—most of them concentrated in countries like Germany, the Netherlands, and Belgium—loved them; labels didn't know what to do with them; and their status as a hotly tipped cult band became their destiny.

The band's bad-luck streak didn't help matters. Before the release of *Into the Everflow*, and after an appearance at the Netherlands' Dynamo festival in 1991—where they shared the stage with Obituary, Morbid Angel, Primus, Metal Church, and Armored Saint—guitarist Dan Rock fell from a bridge while rappelling. The near-fatal accident left him unable to play for eight months. His guitar partner, McAlpin, had been wheelchair-bound since the age of sixteen, from injuries sustained in a car accident. As if the band wasn't cursed enough with bad record deals and physical derailments, the final straw came in the late '90s, when an actress filed a lawsuit against the band, claiming she was blinded by lights used during the filming of their "Faded" video. The litigation exhausted the band's financial resources. Faced with a fragmenting lineup whose musical interests were moving along different lines, Psychotic Waltz broke up 1998. Tensions during the recording process of their final two and much more streamlined albums, *Mosquito* (1994) and *Bleeding* (1996), and Lackey's desire to go solo—and, as Leggio puts it, "be the next Peter Gabriel"—indicated that the dam would eventually break.

Somewhere in a spiral tower:
Psychotic Waltz in the early '90s
(*Kevin Badami*)

Short careers and small discographies became the norm in tech metal, as evidenced by Watchtower's snail's-pace output and the brief time Sieges Even and Psychotic Waltz spent obsessing over musical technicality. Many later tech metal bands— like Cynic, Atheist, and Obliveon— repeated the pattern. Each recorded one or two albums of extremely technical material, then changed course by either simplifying or totally dissolving.

Hunter Ginn—drummer for modern tech metal band Canvas Solaris—understands the rapid burnout rate. "A band that feels they need to keep playing tech metal is going to get sick of playing the same thing over and over," he says. "Those guys are bursting with ideas, and they probably want to do something else. And the maintenance of that kind of facility is just exhausting. To keep playing at that kind of level and to keep writing music of that complexity, it just burns certain bands out. I think some people thrive on it and some people just get tired of it."

Lack of solid record company support for Psychotic Waltz led to poor distribution of their music, relegating them to eternal cult status. Each of their four albums was at some point released by the band itself, due to inexplicable lack of interest from labels. Help arrived years later from Metal Blade Records, who secured the rights to all four albums and released them in double packages, curiously pairing the first and third CDs in one set, the second and fourth in another. Posthumous vindication remains small consolation, since so few cared when the band disbanded.

Over four albums, Psychotic Waltz made compelling music where a listener could always find something new. Their overall vibe was unusual for a metal band, mingling messages of spirituality, enlightenment via marijuana, peace, human rights, and even a dash of humor. And their songwriting and playing were beyond reproach. Even among progressive metal bands, Psychotic Waltz stood apart—their blessing and their curse.

Despite all the talent in the band, post–Psychotic Waltz projects Teabag and Darkstar garnered curiously little attention. Psychotic Waltz/Deathrow collaboration End Amen also got the cold shoulder in 1992, brushed under the rug of obscurity. Only vocalist Buddy Lackey carried on with a remarkable degree of success, beginning with his eclectic 1993 solo album *The Strange Mind of Buddy Lackey*, produced by old friend Ralph Hubert, who had also overseen the recording of *Into the Everflow*.

In the late '90s, Lackey resurfaced in Austria, having changed his name to Devon Graves and formed a new band. Deadsoul Tribe carried on where *Bleeding* left off, even if the singer found the *Mosquito/Bleeding* era one of tension (mostly between him and producer Scott Burns). Deadsoul Tribe has received continual support from the Inside Out label and has gone further in many ways than Psychotic Waltz. Graves seems content to measure out musical progress in smaller increments than he did with the "thinking man's metal" of his previous band. "I'm not what you would call a 'progressive' player," he says. "Technique is a minor component in what I do. I deal in emotions."

The "thinking man's metal" tag was also thrown during the 1980s at short-lived upstate New York band Toxik. Their 1988 debut album, *World Circus*, brought other labels, like "tech speed," but at that point speed eclipsed the tech part of the equation. "Heart Attack," in particular, was a blazing fast song that bridged manic velocity with the prodigious guitar work of bandleader Josh Christian. The vocals of

Mike Sanders were high, screeching, and wailing, setting him apart from the many atonal growlers in the speed/thrash field.

Though Toxik sat on the more complex side of the thrash tracks, their debut did not put them in Watchtower's league. A vocalist change and 1989's *Think This* album put Toxik permanently in the halls of prog metal greats. With a more distinctive voice and a wider range, singer Charles Sabin wasn't the only thing that had improved on the second album. The music left speed metal behind in favor of ultra-powerful traditional metal, notable for myriad tempo changes, greater melodic depth, and Christian's superb playing.

"*Think This* is more accessible," says Toxik bassist Brian Bonini. "The combination of heavy, fast, and intricate just didn't mix. You can be more intricate when things are a little less heavy and a little slowed down. You can be more involved." A legion of highly technical speed/thrash bands would later prove Bonini wrong, but such was Toxik's path. As was common for so many tech metal bands, they fizzled early and never capitalized on their potential.

Watchtower gave birth to tech metal in 1985 with its debut, but the band's second album, *Control and Resistance*, came out four years later, when technicality in metal was increasingly common. Fates Warning's most technical album, *Perfect Symmetry*, was released in 1989. Dream Theater kicked off their wildly productive career that year. Sieges Even was well under way. Psychotic Waltz was gearing up for its first album. Even bands in the extreme thrash/death metal underground were evolving toward more complicated music by 1989. Just looking at the cover of *Metal Forces* from November 1989, it was clear that something big and strange was brewing. Amidst the usual magazine fare of the era—Bullet Boys and Faith No More—the cover promised articles on a pack of underdogs, including Watchtower, Toxik, Fates Warning, Voivod, and Atheist. Prog metal's time was at hand.

Though unlikely for a band so challenging, for a short time Watchtower were darlings of the metal media. *Control and Resistance* was insanely hyped, garnering effusive reviews in the European press, while smaller stateside fanzines recognized the album's importance. Some reviewers were dumbfounded. Likening the band to "Rush, thrash, and Herbie Hancock in the middle of an Exodus medley," Wayne Wayne of Minneapolis zine *Sheet Metal* confessed that *Control and Resistance* was "brilliant, completely fucking amazing, and I never want to hear it again." *Metal Forces'* Mike Exley cut to the chase: "Watchtower could be the next Rush."

Watchtower's high visibility was aided by their worldwide deal with Noise Records, who had already boosted careers for forward-thinkers like Voivod, Coroner, and Celtic Frost. In fact, Celtic Frost leader Thomas G. Fischer had first brought Watchtower to the attention of Noise back in 1986. The label obviously had the proper resources to push this extraordinary band through the right channels.

The press photos sent to the media upon the release of *Control and Resistance* showed a Watchtower that had discarded the leather-and-bullet-belt image of the first album for dress shirts, *Miami Vice* jackets, and hair spray. But the eight songs on *Control and Resistance* were far less conservative than the photos and even more confounding than the band's debut. Four insane musicians ripped apart the metal rulebook and replaced it with a blueprint few would be able to replicate. The album gave off a futuristic, antiseptic atmosphere, thrusting metal into entirely new realms. It was like Fates Warning playing songs by legendary fusion band Return to Forever at two hundred beats per minute. Alan Tecchio's vocals strained to keep up with the ridiculous rhythmic complexities. He mustered viable, memorable melodies in "Life Cycles" and "Mayday in Kiev" but got lost in the miasma of notes and rhythms elsewhere. Everything pivoted on the axis of the rhythm section, with Doug Keyser's punchy, clean-channel bass locking in with Rick Colaluca's intensely busy drumming. Their love of jazz players shone brightly, with the entire middle section of "Dangerous Toy" leaving all metal behind for a foray into pure fusion.

Credited only with "hands & feet," Colaluca was now using a variety of electronic drums in his arsenal. The artificial, plastic sounds coming from his new setup date the album to the late 1980s, though his unorthodox choice set the band apart from the metal hordes. Not being more than part-time metal fans at that point, Watchtower's all-important rhythm section didn't care much about obeying metal laws—which is why Ron Jarzombek locked into the scheme so well. Anything the formidable Keyser/Colaluca rhythm section threw at him, Jarzombek threw back with a

Raging tech: Watchtower live in 1990. Left to right: Ron Jarzombek, Alan Tecchio, Doug Keyser
(*Tanya*)

counterpointing yet complementary guitar part—decidedly metal, but nutty enough to hang with whatever they tossed his way. Credited with "electric, acoustic & backwards guitars," Jarzombek built himself a cult following with his one and only album with Watchtower, a following nearly as large as that of the band itself.

Sadly, Watchtower never capitalized on the hype. After touring America and playing some dates in Europe with Swiss tech thrashers Coroner, Tecchio left to rejoin old Hades bandmate Dan Lorenzo in Non-Fiction. Watchtower searched far and wide for a replacement. Ex–Fates Warning vocalist John Arch was offered the job but turned it down due to family commitments, a steady job, and his aversion to road life.

Scott Jeffreys of North Carolina technical doom band Confessor worked on several new songs with the band, including "Coming Home" and "Nightfall." The material was remarkably straightforward, built with a minimum of parts and tempo changes. Despite this obvious streamlining, the songs were clearly being played by musicians possessing extraordinary chops. Unfortunately, that lineup only existed virtually, with the audition tape being sent from Texas to North Carolina for vocal overdubbing, and then back to Texas.

The Watchtower machine soon came to a halt. Jarzombek began experiencing difficulties with his left hand due to overuse. "During the recording and touring

PROG ON A POGO STICK

WHO SAYS PROG BANDS HAVE NO SENSE OF HUMOR? This transcript, littered with in-jokes, comes from a Watchtower gig intro tape, circa 1990. Mission statement or meaningless mirth? The answer lies somewhere between mysticism and physics.

FEMALE VOICE:

The essence of belief lies somewhere between mysticism and physics.

PITCH-SHIFTED, DOUBLE-TRACKED MALE VOICE:

The essence of belief lies somewhere between mysticism and physics.
When in doubt, one can usually count on realistic answers from the keeper of the LongBurger. Though if one searches for such answers late at night, he is sure to find that the keeper has closed shop.

FEMALE VOICE:

Another path towards pure understanding is to hop repeatedly.

PITCH-SHIFTED, DOUBLE-TRACKED MALE VOICE:

Another path towards pure understanding is to hop repeatedly.
The effect is exaggerated if done on a pogo stick.

FEMALE VOICE:

On a pogo stick?

PITCH-SHIFTED, DOUBLE-TRACKED MALE VOICE:

The effect is exaggerated if done on a pogo stick.
Fact: Ron is Mr. Penis and not Taxi.
Fact: Rick is Satan Claus and BumperBoy.
Fact: Alan powders regularly and waits in the car.

FEMALE VOICE:

He waits in *my* car.

PITCH-SHIFTED, DOUBLE-TRACKED MALE VOICE:

Fact: Doug is Doogie Howser, R.G., in combat sneakers.
Together, they strive to destroy heavy metal as we know it: Watchtower.

of *Control and Resistance* I was having problems with my left hand's third and pinky fingers," he says, "and I didn't get the problem corrected until three years later. I think the fire died during that time. Even when I was having surgeries, I was trying to write and play at rehearsals with a splint on my hand, and it was pointless. During this time there was also a shift in the band's musical direction, something I didn't care for in the least. Everything got so watered down. I was finding that all of the cooler and more difficult things I was writing weren't fitting in with this new Watchtower."

Watchtower's Jarzombek and Keyser in 2004 at Headway Festival, The Netherlands (*Gerrie Lemmens*)

Ron Jarzombek soon formed Spastic Ink with his drumming brother, Bobby. Meanwhile, the Watchtower rhythm section worked in the spectacularly named funk/hip hop/rock band Retarted Elf. Complete with a brass section, Retarted Elf sporadically enchanted local Austin clubgoers but remained lost in a haze of obscurity outside their immediate environs.

Even as Watchtower drifted, a number of other metal musicians on the extreme end of the spectrum sang their praises and wore their T-shirts—always a high compliment. Florida hellions such as Death and Atheist exalted the Texans. Hot death metal producer Scott Burns announced he would jump at any opportunity to produce a third album by Watchtower. Unfortunately, that third album never materialized.

Not until 1999 did Watchtower reappear, when a fortunate blip in the band's continuum led to a series of reunion performances. The original *Instruments of Random Murder* demo lineup—the founding vocalist and rhythm section, plus Jarzombek—reworked Accept's "Run if You Can" on a tribute album to the German heavy metal gods. Their version was remarkably tame, and an unlikely catalyst for a reunion. Yet word spread about this casual regrouping, and offers to play European summer festivals rolled in. After a few warm-up shows in their home state—which were attended by longtime fan Chuck Schuldiner of Death, who traveled from Florida just to see them—Watchtower came back together for 2000's Bang Your Head festival in Germany. They also played a few well-received performances in Texas as guests of Dream Theater—handpicked by drummer and longtime fan Mike Portnoy. After the gigs with Dream Theater, recording of the long-awaited third Watchtower album seemed imminent.

More than a decade later, fans were still waiting. Virtually the *Chinese Democracy* of tech metal, *Mathematics* has gone through multiple fits and starts over a span of years. Although work on the band's third album started during the early '90s, when Jarzombek was experiencing medical woes, the 2000 reunion shows provided a renewed impetus. Starting with the "Coming Home" and "Nightfall" audition tracks and other post–*Control and Resistance* sketches, work on the long-promised album

Onetime doppelgängers meet: Watchtower and Sieges Even headline the Headway, 2004

began, progressed slowly, stalled—and then died. Jarzombek wasn't fond of the material in the first place. "Some lame songs were cut," he says. "I was trying to find some musical direction for the band but never did. Those sessions eventually stopped."

In 2004, Europe called again. The band was invited to the two-day Headway Festival in the Netherlands. Watchtower headlined one evening while onetime rivals Sieges Even headlined the other. After that excursion, according to Jarzombek, came "more writing sessions, more lame songs, and we finished writing the material for *Mathematics*. But things fizzled out again and the recordings never made much progress. I don't want the *Mathematics* material to ever see the light of day. If it gets reworked again, possibly, but we've done that twice and I'm done trying to revive the whole thing."

Jason McMaster agrees with Jarzombek on the doomed *Mathematics*. "I don't want to put the legacy we have in danger," he says. "If it's not going to be top-notch material, would our fans still want it? It was written so long ago now that Doug and Rick aren't even connected to the material. They're not in that place anymore. I don't know if they can write that kind of crazy, fucked-up heavy metal."

McMaster developed a stock response for the wearying "When is *Mathematics* coming out?" question. "I tell people, 'Buy Spastic Ink's *Ink Compatible*.' It's got Doug on a song or two, it's got me on five songs, it's got Bobby Jarzombek all over it. It's going to appease people more than *Mathematics* probably would."

But in 2008, the reappearance of one of Watchtower's acolytes set the wheels of *Mathematics* spinning again. "What brought about the idea to again try and finish up *Mathematics* was Cynic," says Jarzombek. "Their reunion album *Traced in Air* was a thirty-five-minute CD and it got me thinking of Watchtower. We've written a bunch of crap for *Mathematics*, but we have at least thirty-five minutes of good material, so why not release it?" Even with that mind-set, Watchtower's latest batch of new songs quickly neared the sixty-minute mark of releasable material.

So the final word on a third Watchtower album? In 2008 Jarzombek stated, "Don't hold your breath waiting for *Mathematics*. You'll die." The next year he said, "Do I really think it will come out? Yes. But that's what I thought in 2004 and 2000."

Watchtower and their peers brought "tech" into the metal lexicon in the 1980s after searching way beyond for something new and different. But, pushed into a corner of their own design, these bands found it hard to make a viable long-term career out of such difficult music. So they streamlined their sound, or they hit the peak of complexity, spun out, and crashed. Traditional prog metal bands such as Queensrÿche and Fates Warning found it much easier to navigate the 1990s. Yet the influence of tech-metal's earliest pioneers soon gave rise to a heavier, more intense strain of brain metal—as death metal bands began taking increasingly technical approaches.

Florida's Atheist, Death, and Cynic ratcheted their complexity upwards by the early '90s. By the end of the decade, bands like Gorguts, the Dillinger Escape Plan, and Meshuggah were ushering in more devastating brands of technicality, each of them owing some kind of debt to their tech metal forebears. And Watchtower's impact continues to be felt and their legacy insured. Their influence resonates even two decades after the release of their second album, but they would never gain the popularity of Queensrÿche or Fates Warning. Perhaps they were too difficult for any destiny but eternal cult status, and there they remain—a hallowed icon of tech metal's primordial era.

7. A CONSTANT MOTION

"We loved progressive, complex music—Rush, Yes, the Dixie Dregs, Frank Zappa—and also loved heavy music: Iron Maiden, Black Sabbath, Metallica, Queensrÿche. To us it wasn't some magical scientific formula that would change the world, it was just three college kids jamming for the fun of jamming. Trying to fill a void for ourselves as fans to create the kind of music we'd want to listen to." —Mike Portnoy, Dream Theater

D REAM THEATER'S ARRIVAL IN 1989 COMPLETED THE TRIFECTA of U.S. melodic progressive metal. The Long Island band showed up on the scene offering a torrent of metallic prog with enough finesse and keyboard presence to appeal to fans of '70s prog, and with the ample aggression and raw fire that reeled in metalheads. Thrash metal had "the Big Four"—Metallica, Megadeth, Slayer, and Anthrax—and the trio of influential progressive metal bands comprising Queensrÿche, Fates Warning, and Dream Theater would eventually be referred to as "the Big Three."

With stellar musicianship, a tireless work ethic, and endless support from a devoted, notoriously outspoken fan base, Dream Theater has successfully bridged the chasm between virtuosity and accessibility like no other band. As of 2010, Dream Theater had sold more than eight million albums worldwide—not to mention an enormous clutch of DVDs, live albums, and special fan club–only releases. They have secured an eternal legacy in the prog universe.

Dream Theater formed as Majesty in 1985, when Long Islanders Mike Portnoy, John Myung, and John Petrucci got together as music students at Boston's Berklee College of Music. Finding immediate chemistry, they forged a union that still shows no signs of relenting. The three quickly began writing songs of their own, filling out the lineup with keyboardist Kevin Moore and vocalist Chris Collins. Majesty's early material fused the approach of their prog and metal heroes with Collins's Geddy Lee–meets–Geoff Tate vocal approach.

From the beginning, the band publicly and enthusiastically hailed musical influences like Fates Warning. "I remember first hearing Fates Warning in 1984 at L'Amour," says drummer Mike Portnoy, recalling the legendary New York metal nightclub. "Anthrax was touring for their first album, and Fates Warning was the opening band. I was blown away by the heaviness, but at the same time, they were playing all these odd time signatures and tempo changes. They reminded me of Rush meets Iron Maiden, which at that point were two of my favorite bands, and a big part of Dream Theater's own blueprint."

Majesty demo cassette, 1986

Majesty recorded a demo tape in 1986, consisting of six tracks, including the eleven-minute "A Vision." Portnoy later wrote that Majesty's approach was about "a lot of notes, a lot of odd time signatures, heavy riffs, busy playing—the focus always being on the instrumentalists. This was what we were into." The music on the demo resembled other tapes floating around by bands such as Aslan and Heir Apparent—epic, ambitious, and bristling with youthful energy. Ultimately, the demo's impressive individual elements didn't equal a sum of much listening value—this was the work of kids who were completely blown away by themselves and wanted to show everybody else too. And the vocals were entirely too squeaky. But the seeds were sown.

The band parted ways with vocalist Collins, and Majesty changed its name to Dream Theater. (A Las Vegas lounge band claimed rights to the Majesty name and wasn't interested in sharing.) Dream Theater, coined by Portnoy's father, was an unusual name for a metal band, and less restrictively medieval-sounding. The name had an esoteric ring—it could have easily sufficed as the name of a new age group or an avant-garde dance troupe. The new moniker allowed the band to write music of any type, and over the next two decades they exercised plenty of creative free will.

Dream Theater found a new vocalist in Charlie Dominici, who was older than the others, and from a completely different musical background. Dominici was a former member of pop rockers Franke and the Knockouts, with whom he played guitar and provided background harmonies. Clearly odd man out in Dream Theater, Dominici hunkered down with the rest of the revitalized quintet in a basement rehearsal room

beneath a barbershop—a lovely irony—and there Dream Theater's early sound crystallized. Before long they caught the attention of major label MCA. Their Mechanic label imprint signed the band and announced the arrival of *When Dream and Day Unite* with plenty of advance hyperbole— pumping their find as "Metallica meets Rush." The hype was not for nothing. Popular conceptions about heavy metal—what it was and what it could encompass—were about to be transformed.

Influential British magazine *Metal Forces* gave the album a rave review: "an essential purchase for anyone whose tastes run from Rush to Queensrÿche"—a line the young band members must have read over and over with great pride.

Songs like "A Fortune in Lies," "The Ones Who Help to Set the Sun," and "Afterlife" united a variety of seperate elements. Warm, catchy vo-

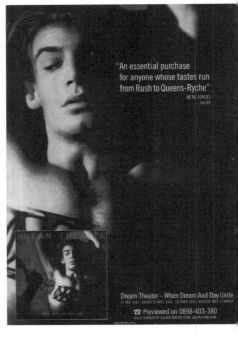

Print ad for Dream Theater's debut, 1989

cal refrains recalled an almost Journey-esque radio rock feel, slammed up against Portnoy's propulsive and precise drumming. Petrucci brought thrashlike palm-muted chords and a zillion lightning-fast solos, joined by Myung's equally fluid bass runs and Geddy-esque harmonics. For a metal band—and Dream Theater was certainly a metal band—Moore's keyboards were unusually dominant in the fray, a sonic page from the book of elders such as Deep Purple and Kansas. The debut worked wonderfully, despite a brittle, almost demo-quality recording that is hardly remembered as producer Terry Date's best work.

When Dream and Day Unite created a healthy buzz for Dream Theater across a diverse field of music fans. Another change in vocalists partly contributed to a three-year gap between the debut and album number two. The departure of Dominici slowed their momentum, and 1991 brought auditions for a new vocalist. Of great interest to progressive metal fans then and now, ex–Fates Warning vocalist John Arch tried out for the band but declined to join—another great *what if?* moment in metal history.

Arch had to walk away. He was deeply immersed in his personal life, committed to his family and a new career as a custom furniture craftsman. Perhaps that was for the best—Arch offered a style that was more arcane and mystical than the one Dream Theater were about to embrace. "I had the ambition and the drive," Arch says, "because I really love that band. I still do to this day—they're excellent. But in the interim between Fates Warning and the Dream Theater audition, I had gotten married and bought a house. I committed myself financially. I slept over at Mike's house during the audition. I'm lying there and I'm like, 'I miss my dog, I miss my wife.' I'm saying to myself, 'Do I really want to start this all over again?' I had just finished this with Fates Warning. I had to make a commonsense decision. I felt really responsible and I had to make the call, and I definitely made the right one."

As a longtime fan of all things Fates Warning, Dream Theater's Mike Portnoy agrees. "It was a blessing in disguise," he says. "I love and admire John Arch. *Awaken the Guardian* is one of my top metal albums of the '80s. But I think Dream Theater might have drifted into obscurity with somebody like John. His vocals are so incredibly unique. They're more of an acquired taste. When Dream Theater first started, we could've easily become this totally obscure progressive technical metal band, and maybe never have gotten out of the underground. But we always wanted to write songs that were melodic and catchy. We never wanted to be strictly a technical/acrobatic underground band. We wanted to have a little bit of everything for everyone."

Dream Theater finally settled on unknown Canadian singer James LaBrie. If the band wanted someone more musically compatible than Dominici—whom Portnoy has likened to "Billy Joel singing with Queensrÿche"—their choice of someone hundreds of miles away, from a glam metal band called Winter Rose, was curious. But LaBrie pushed the band into the stylistic center. His smooth, consistent, utterly personable vocals proved themselves over the long haul, defining Dream Theater's sound as much as the ridiculously talented musicians behind him.

"I think James ended up being a way more mainstream or commercially acceptable type of voice," Mike Portnoy says. "He helped make our sound a little more accessible. He really helped round things out." Other than a few changes in the keyboard department—filled for the past ten years by former Dixie Dregs member Jordan Rudess—the Dream Theater lineup has remained consistent for nearly two decades.

With new vocalist LaBrie out front, Dream Theater released its second album, *Images and Words*, on March 28, 1992. The band had signed with another major-label subsidiary, Atlantic's Atco Records, whose president at the time was none other than former Gentle Giant vocalist Derek Shulman. Three years after Dream Theater's debut album, their music had become slicker, grander, and more epic—a little less aggressive and a lot more melodic. If "Another Day" sounded wildly sugary—complete with Kenny G–like soprano sax—the band made up for it with epics like "Learning to Live" and "Metropolis—Part I: The Miracle and the Sleeper."

The band even scored a radio hit with "Pull Me Under." The song's success was unlikely, considering that Dream Theater's brand of music was unimaginably unhip in 1992, the era of Seattle and "grunge." The edited radio version—pared down from 8:12 to 5:54—ran longer than most radio hits. But "Pull Me Under" galvanized a wide variety of music fans, from veteran prog rockers to young 'heads raised on Metallica and Slayer, not to mention the everyday radio listener.

Images and Words and its 1994 follow-up, *Awake*, perhaps more than any other influences, kick-started a massive rush of similar progressive metal bands. *Awake* mirrored *Images and Words* in many ways, although it lacked a hit single. Setting itself apart from its predecessor, *Awake* featured denser, more frequent moments of overdriven shred, and seemed to come from a darker, more introspective place. Young musicians locked into the band's ability to balance accessibility and grandiosity while displaying mind-boggling chops. Even the artwork—stylized collages of dreamlike imagery—provided a look and atmosphere that hundreds of bands adapted to their own offerings in the coming years.

Most of the similar-sounding bands arriving in Dream Theater's wake didn't break much artistic ground, but their emulations led to long careers for a lucky few. As Jasun Tipton of Zero Hour observes: "Some bands labeled 'progressive metal' don't belong there. The term 'progressive metal' was used very loosely in the '90s to sell product to Dream Theater fans. This hurt the genre. And a lot of Dream Theater clones popped up. A lot of the newer acts didn't bring a new spark to the genre. I'm not saying there haven't been some great newer bands, but that's my take."

Says Glenn Harveston, organizer of the annual ProgPower USA festival in Atlanta: "It's the Dream Theater school of discovery. You start with the basics and work your way up. You scope out everything you can with a complex melody and then burn out on it. You want more out of your music, and this leads to finding bands that are indeed pushing the boundaries. Then you call every band with a Dream Theater influence a complete clone and dismiss them entirely—regardless of how good they are. But on the flip side, you have those that don't want the music to change; they just want it to vary a little bit. If they have a security blanket and enjoy it, why change? Give them *Images and Words Part 24* and leave them alone."

Not every musician influenced by Dream Theater settled into their template. Dan Swanö—of Swedish bands Edge of Sanity, Nightingale, and the bizarre Pan-Thy-Monium—took notice of Dream Theater in the early '90s, yet none of his bands sound remotely like the Long Island legends. "The best prog metal album is *Images and Words* and it will never be topped," he says. "It's got it all, the hooks and the complexity, hand in hand. *Images and Words* and *Awake* rule so hard it's spooky."

A noted producer/engineer with albums by Opeth, Novembre, Theatre of Tragedy, Millencolin, Dissection, and many others, Swanö uses *Awake* as a reference CD in the studio. "I must have heard it a zillion times, but I still love every second of it to bits."

By the mid-'90s, word had spread around the globe, and Dream Theater's momentum grew unstoppable. Pressure mounted for a follow-up to "Pull Me Under." Since *Awake* failed to produce a hit, maybe *Falling into Infinity* (1997) would do the trick—with a little arm-twisting from the record company suits. Instead, the fourth Dream Theater album garnered mixed reviews, and remains their most debated.

"The label was seriously trying to mold us into something that could be on the radio and compete with whatever was popular at the time," Mike Portnoy recalls

Dream Theater live at the Electric Factory in Philadelphia, 1998
(*Matt Johnsen*)

bitterly. "They tried to strip us down with that album. [Producer] Kevin Shirley came in and cracked the whip and rearranged a lot of the songs. Even [songwriter] Desmond Child stuck his nose into one of the songs."

Despite glaring weak spots, career highlights glimmered, such as the lush "Peruvian Skies." The textured instrumental "Hell's Kitchen" relied more on sound-track–like atmosphere than on drawn-out arpeggio exercises. "Lines in the Sand"—featuring guest vocalist Doug Pinnick of elite proggy pop/rock act King's X—remains a frequent live highlight. And "Trial of Tears" stands as one of Dream Theater's most enduring epics—complete with an opening that clearly references Rush's "Xanadu."

In the *Falling into Infinity* fallout, Dream Theater took complete creative control of their music. They never again allowed outside forces to dictate their creative moves. Picking up on a thread that started with *Images and Words* track "Metropolis," the band attempted an exemplar progressive metal album with 1999's *Metropolis Pt. 2: Scenes from a Memory*. The album offered an equal balance of over-the-top instrumental attack, accessible pop metal, and other Dream Theater hallmarks. From that point, Dream Theater progressed through less daring phases. They never lacked direction, but post–*Falling into Infinity*, fans would be treated to fewer surprises and more variations on familiar themes—naturally with consistently incredible musicianship and no lack of professionalism.

Ace of Bass: John Myung
of Dream Theater
(*Frank White*)

After Dream Theater's one-album clash with compromise and record company meddling, the band blazed a determined path with albums that straddled the line between relentless ambition and meeting fan expectations. Each has its particular place on the band's canvas. Some tilted toward a more accessible, song-oriented direction, such as 2005's *Octavarium*; some were more ambitious in scope and length, among them 2002's double-length *Six Degrees of Inner Turbulence* and 2009's *Black Clouds & Silver Linings*; while others focused on their heaviest aspects, as did 2003's *Train of Thought* and 2007's *Systematic Chaos*. *Octavarium* is probably the most diversified Dream Theater album since the early days, featuring the U2-esque "I Walk Beside You," the epic Floyd-ian title track, the crazed shred of "The Root of All Evil," and the propulsive metal blitz of "Panic Attack"—which inserts a section recalling arty modern rock band Muse into its almost tech-thrash main thread.

Starting with *Octavarium*, Dream Theater relied on Rush cover artist Hugh Syme to realize their visual concepts. Another Rush alum arrived when the band hired engineer Paul Northfield for *Systematic Chaos*. Northfield had worked on all the classic Rush albums alongside Terry Brown, something not lost on the Rush fans in the band. Dream Theater knows exactly what they are doing. If their choices sometimes appear calculated, the band's singular intent to remain at the top of the progressive metal heap is laudable.

Although Dream Theater never repeated the huge commercial success of *Images and Words*, their tireless recording and touring has spawned an insanely loyal following that remains glued to the band's prodigious output of studio and live albums, various DVDs, and globe-trotting tours. Dream Theater have become essentially the Grateful Dead of prog metal, with fans chatting online about the minutiae of each set list, customized each night by Portnoy; and savoring the huge variety of special releases and "official bootlegs" offered by the band's own YtseJam label. "Pull Me Under" is now considered a wonderful fluke for a band that no longer requires a hit single to survive. The band's sense of humor regarding their brief time in the mainstream was most excellently highlighted in the title of 2008's best-of collection *Greatest Hit (...and 21 Other Pretty Cool Songs)*.

Consistently writing and recording, Dream Theater also tours like mad. Figurehead Portnoy, in particular, deserves credit for handpicking great opening acts. "I've tried to use Dream Theater's success to help younger bands," he says, "whether it's Porcupine Tree, Pain of Salvation, Spock's Beard, or Symphony X. These are bands I admire and try to offer to Dream Theater's audience to help their careers grow. In some cases it has really helped. I feel like it's my job to be this kind of goodwill ambassador for progressive music, and try to use our success to help other bands."

Stepping up their crusade, Portnoy in 2008 organized the first annual Progressive Nation tour. That spring Dream Theater hit the American highways with an eclectic caravan including hybrid whiz kids 3, metalcore-in-bizarro-world band Between the Buried and Me, and Swedish progressive death metal legends Opeth.

Mikael Åkerfeldt of Opeth was flattered when Mike Portnoy reached out to him. "I got an e-mail from Mike one day saying that he loves the band, and it was a pretty big deal for me," says the Swede. "When I first heard Dream Theater, it helped me shape my own band. I wasn't super-interested in bands like Watchtower and Fates Warning at that time, but I thought Dream Theater took what they did to another level."

Dream Theater has also performed special live sets of classic albums by other artists in their entirety. The members are still music fans at heart, still awed by their heroes. On 1995 mini-album *A Change of Seasons*, they whipped tracks by Deep Purple and Led Zeppelin into shape. The same album's imaginatively titled "The Big Medley" joined songs by Pink Floyd, Kansas, Queen, and Genesis, among others.

At three different shows on the band's *Six Degrees of Inner Turbulence* tour in 2002, Dream Theater followed a full set of originals with an unannounced runthrough of Metallica's *Master of Puppets* in its entirety. They later gave Iron Maiden's *The Number of the Beast* the same treatment, played to the original specs except for "Gangland," which picked up a mirthful jazz swing. Pink Floyd's *The Dark Side of the Moon* and Deep Purple's live classic *Made in Japan*—which Dream Theater performed in its entirety in Japan, no less—have also been given the honors.

Dream Theater's John Myung, Mike Portnoy and John Petrucci (and projected ant) on the *Systematic Chaos* tour, 2007 (*Ann Marie B. Reilly*)

Apparently, this is not enough activity for Mike Portnoy. The restless drummer has racked up numerous live performances and more than twenty album appearances outside Dream Theater with other projects including Liquid Tension Experiment (featuring other D.T. personnel and King Crimson alumnus Tony Levin), Transatlantic (with members from prog rockers Marillion and Spock's Beard), Neal Morse (ex–Spock's Beard); OSI (led by ex-D.T. keyboardist Kevin Moore and Fates Warning guitiarst Jim Matheos), and John Arch's *A Twist of Fate* (a dream project for Portnoy, no doubt). Portnoy even played a full show as guest drummer with thrash legends Overkill in 2004.

The other Dream Theater members have also demonstrated an insatiable appetite for side projects. Everyone except Portnoy and Myung has recorded a solo album, including ex-keyboardists Kevin Moore and Derek Sherinian, plus former vocalist Charlie Dominici. Portnoy still dreams of collaborating with heroes such as Paul McCartney, Pete Townshend, and Roger Waters, although his more immediate prospects include a much-talked-about project with Opeth's Mikael Åkerfeldt and Porcupine Tree's Steven Wilson.

Dream Theater has provided a leading light to a generation of younger bands. Where Fates Warning was dark and difficult, Dream Theater was bright and accessible. When Queensrÿche went commercial and conservative, Dream Theater unloaded with behemoth forty-two-minute songs and heaps of shred. They effectively bridged the gap between the familiar and the obscure.

Former Dream Theater manager Jim Pitulski worked with the band before, during, and after their big break in 1992. He believed from the very early stages that the band would eventually take their place in a distinguished pantheon. "What happened was you had Rush, where every record from *2112* up to *Moving Pictures* was magnificent," he says. "Then, with the birth of thrash, there were bands doing really crazy, interesting things, like Metallica, Megadeth, and Watchtower. And then you had Fates Warning and Queensrÿche. When Dream Theater came out, they just pulled all that together and brought the whole thing into sharp focus."

The summer of 2003 brought a progressive metal dream tour to the U.S. with Dream Theater and Queensrÿche co-headlining—and Fates Warning providing "very special support." While it was arguable that one or two of the bands had seen better days, it was a kismet event—long meant to be. Fates Warning drummer Mark Zonder, grateful for the once-in-a-lifetime opportunity, summarized the occasion in the words of many fans: "Everybody was saying, 'Ten years before, it would've been the tour of the year,' and I agree with that. But it was still cool."

Fates Warning was rejoined for the tour by guitarist Frank Aresti. From Queensrÿche's original lineup, only Chris DeGarmo was missing. Each show was a treat for fans of progressive metal, drawing an enthusiastic and appreciative audience. Old-timers who had attended early Queensrÿche and Fates Warning shows came with their children in tow. Says Fates Warning's Jim Matheos: "In twenty-five years or however long I've been touring, it was probably one of my favorite tours ever. Perfect bill for us, and a perfect crowd. I had a blast."

Organized by Mike Portnoy, who had been in the audience watching Queensrÿche and Fates Warning play together seventeen years earlier, the tour further cemented the legacy of the Big Three, with each band publicly recognizing the others' important contributions to progressive metal's development. The camaraderie between the three bands was obvious, with Mike Portnoy joining Fates Warning on drums for one song each night. Although Portnoy also suggested that the tour was "probably about ten years too late," its historical importance was not lost on him. "It was the sort of tour that all our fan bases always talked about happening. It made so much sense on paper that it was inevitable."

PART III:
A Quantum Leap Forward

8. SUBLIMATION FROM UNDERGROUND I: VOIVOD & CELTIC FROST

"Tom G. Warrior of Celtic Frost is one of the strangest geniuses ever to walk the planet. He may not be the most agile musician on guitar, he's not known for his playing, but his mind is so twisted. Voivod too. The bass player would be playing these strange sequences of notes and their guitarist Piggy would be playing these other weird notes on top, and it worked. They created strange harmonies but had this punk rock attitude on top of it. Incredible artistry. I think those guys are full-on geniuses." —Jason McMaster, Watchtower

As much as the Big Three bands represented the arrival of prog metal after years of development, those bands were only the beginning of something much larger. The do-it-yourself ethic of the 1980s metal underground fostered independent labels, cut-and-paste fanzines, and homemade demo tapes. Some, with luck, talent, and hard work, grew out of the heavily populated underground and found homes at major labels. Queensrÿche and Dream Theater did just that, and although their music was radical compared to that of other big-label acts, their sounds were entirely accessible compared to those of the darker denizens of the underground.

A huge number of metal bands remained steadfastly loyal to the underground, with no intention of rising to the surface. Their subterranean home was a comfortable place where no one threatened their integrity, and fellow inhabitants understood their aims exactly. That freedom, and the influence of the fastest and heaviest bands of the time, brought into being the earliest emanations of thrash, black, and death metal.

Following forever uncompromising British heroes Venom and Motörhead, bands like Sweden's Bathory, Italy's Bulldozer, and Germany's Sodom dug deep underground and reveled in their primitive hollows. Taking the same influences—and many more from within and outside the metal sphere—a young band with the odd name of Voivod rose from an unremarkable factory town in Canada and completely rewrote metal's rules.

Born as crude punkish thrash metal, Voivod evolved remarkably in their first ten years, through seven compelling albums that influenced musicians throughout the metal spectrum and even ones outside it. Bands as varied as esoteric sludge artists Neurosis, ethereal goth-metal pioneers the Gathering, and epic metal lords Manilla Road have sung Voivod's praises. Canadian tech metallers Martyr covered "Brain Scan" in 2006—joined by an original member of Voivod—and Deceased, Order from Chaos, and Agoraphobic Nosebleed have also laid down their own tributes. Metal godfathers Lemmy and Bruce Dickinson have worn Voivod shirts; even alt-country hero Ryan Adams calls Voivod his favorite metal band. Bassist Jason Newsted was an enthusiastic supporter for many years, to the point that he eventually joined Voivod after quitting Metallica.

Says tech forefather Paul Masvidal of Cynic, "Voivod were doing something really fresh and original. It was so trippy and art-sensible. They looked different, and they felt different. They were just breaking the rules every which way."

Voivod was different from the start. Drummer Michel Langevin had been a daydreamer who couldn't get enough metal, prog rock, punk, or science fiction. Engaging his talents for drawing and drumming by spending lots of time doing both, he spent his childhood in a vibrant fantasy world. Though many boys pursue similar passions, his disposition was incredibly single-minded. Langevin inventions such as the character of Korgüll, his postapocalyptic domain, and his myriad adventures were firmly in place long before Voivod struck its first twisted chords. The drummer's creations provided a conceptual anchor for Voivod; the band's music morphed in tandem with the characters and worlds created in the mind of the imaginative drummer.

Voivod was born in Jonquière, Canada, a logging town 250 miles north of Quebec City. Despite the beauty of the surrounding area, the town's pulp, paper, and aluminum factories churned unceasingly, spewing smoke and generating a perpetual mechanical din. No surprise, then, that Jonquière's biggest heavy metal band emerged bearing an ugly, abrasive stamp. "It seemed we had to have a sound that was industrial and cold and heavy," Langevin explains. "And the lyrics would have to be about everything industrial and mechanical and cold. I learned to draw while listening to the sound of the factory, and I had nightmares because of these sounds. The sounds made me think of monsters and weird things, so it was connected visually."

The band drew from an enormous range of influences over the span of its first seven albums. Langevin's childhood fascination with Kiss led him to Deep Purple, Led Zeppelin, and fellow Canadians Rush. His curiosity drew him deeper into the realms of strange, heavy music, where lesser-known prog bands such as Nektar and Birth Control lurked. After he and his friends formed Voivod, guitarist Denis "Piggy" D'Amour shared his love for English rock innovators Gentle Giant with the others, and together the four members delved into various punk sounds, from the Sex Pistols and the Damned to crust punk pioneers Discharge and Broken Bones— even unique post-punk acts like Magazine and Joy Division. This huge melting pot informed Voivod's music.

Even while churning out the crude noise of their earliest original songs, Langevin knew the band would become more experimental. "We knew we were going to evolve and improve enough," he says, "so that eventually we would be able to emulate our heroes, like King Crimson and Van der Graaf Generator."

Voivod absorbed the lessons of Judas Priest and Motörhead, and padded their early live repertoire with songs by such small, fiercely independent bands as England's A-II-Z and Ireland's Sweet Savage. Langevin, D'Amour, and cohorts Denis "Snake" Belanger and Jean-Yves "Blacky" Theriault knocked out obscure cover songs in early rehearsals while sketching such originals as "Condemned to the Gallows," "Voivod" and "Blower" (The title of the latter quickly became the nickname of Theriault's super-distorted "blower" bass tone). During their first public performance in June 1983—at the band's high school—they tackled songs by Tank, Raven, Venom (lots of Venom), and oddball '70s rockers Budgie. The band later issued the performance on a tape titled *Anachronism*.

Voivod's first true demo recording, *To the Death*, from early 1984, was heavily traded in the underground. Word spread of this bizarre clan of noisemongers from the north. The demo previewed all of the songs recorded for their first album, and a couple that appeared on their second. Even Venom and Mercyful Fate songs were covered. The early demos introduced the band members, who had assumed aliases in the fashion of Venom: "Away" reflected Langevin's aloof nature and lack of punctuality; "Piggy" described D'Amour's stocky body; "Snake" captured Belanger's physical traits and slinky, writhing stage movements; and "Blacky" epitomized Theriault's jet-black hair and mischievous nature.

After launching the careers of Metallica and Slayer, Metal Blade Records president Brian Slagel was hungry to stake a bigger claim on the growing thrash movement. He offered the peculiar four-piece a spot on 1984's *Metal Massacre V* compilation, which found Voivod amidst other newcomers like Fates Warning, Hellhammer, Overkill, and Metal Church. Later that year, Metal Blade released Voivod's debut album, *War and Pain*. With that record, the four young Canucks had already come farther from their factory town than they'd ever dreamed.

War and Pain is a coal-black relic of early thrash, with an appropriately rough recording to match the lack of musical refinement. D'Amour's peculiar lead guitar was looser and more rock-inflected than that of string-scraping peers such as Venom's Mantas or lock-tight California bands Exodus and Metallica. The rhythm section of Langevin and Theriault was barely controlled chaos. Belanger screamed and bellowed over the din, achieving one of the most bizarre vocal performances heard on a metal album. Although the lyrics were in English, Belanger mangled the words unintelligibly, the result of a heavy French accent and youthful over-enthusiasm. *War and Pain* was abnormal metal noise, a strange-sounding album even in an underground brimming with otherworldly sounds. In a word, it was *different*—a description that continues to apply to everything Voivod has ever done.

The French-Canadians clearly stood out from other young thrash/death/black metal bands of the day. Their name alone was strange, and their artwork had an exotic look. Every Voivod album cover, T-shirt design, bumper sticker, and band logo was rendered by Langevin, drawing from his inexhaustible imagination. His signature jagged lettering, which adorned the lyric sheets and album covers, was stylized yet primitive, another defining element of the singular Voivod image.

After the band jumped to upstart German metal label Noise Records, the second Voivod album, *Rrröööaaarrr* (1986), brought a gripping assault of inaccessible thrash. The band's intent at that time was to play faster and heavier than all others—

they wanted to outpace Slayer and make Venom's mess sound orderly. Each of the album's nine songs is an out-of-control workout of disarrayed chaos metal. Songs like "Horror" and "To the Death!" are so disheveled they seem blurry and incomprehensible. Some moments sound like the collapse of an enormous factory building. A weird muffled production makes everything seem just out of reach.

Unlike other thrash albums of the day, *Rrröööaaarrr* sat alone and apart; too weird, too messy, too difficult. The band couldn't have sounded stranger to fans of conventional metal circa 1986. Compared to the party-rock attitude of the many L.A. glam-metal bands, and contrasted with the increasingly slick, digital productions Iron Maiden and Judas Priest were exploring, Voivod marked itself as a force apart.

Gasmask revival: Voivod's inimitable Snake
(Frank White)

Rrröööaaarrr's album cover, an imposing war machine on the death march, is still one of Langevin's most striking pieces of artwork. The disturbing image looks exactly as the album sounds: hell-bent on destruction and heavy enough to crush anything in its path. Maybe it wasn't the world's fastest or heaviest album in the final analysis, but its audacious primitive energy leaves *Rrröööaaarrr* the most daunting, uneasy listen in the Voivod discography. "We were trying to be a little heavier than we could achieve," Langevin admits.

Voivod didn't bother trying to outdo *Rrröööaaarrr* next time around. They left Korgüll's home of Morgöth and blasted off into the nether reaches of the cosmos—from a launchpad in West Berlin, where Voivod settled into Music Lab studio with producer Harris Johns.

Killing Technology (1987) was a stunning leap forward, confirming that Voivod could never be expected to repeat itself. With hugely improved playing, D'Amour's prog rock influences began to show. His dissonant and unusual chord shapes, open-finger chords, and chords utilizing all six strings—unorthodox for thrash guitarists—reflected his love of Yes, King Crimson, and Rush. His array of effects widened, and his chemistry with bassist Theriault intensified. Counterpoint between guitar and bass became more pronounced, with a variety of odd timings and unusual note sequences. Belanger's voice had also matured, introducing various robotic effects and a cleaner, more human tone amidst the panic attack. Langevin's barreling tank-tread approach to drumming was sharpened to a precision point while maintaining a crushing undertow.

Among the obvious and subtle influences that informed the sophisticated *Killing Technology*, Langevin reveals some considerably highbrow factors: "Piggy was the main writer, but Blacky brought a lot of ideas to the mix, because he was listening to a lot of contemporary music, and so was Piggy. But the two of them were huge fans of Béla Bartók and Dmitri Shostakovich, and actually took pieces from these composers and turned it into metal for Voivod. You can recognize bits if you know Bartók and Shostakovich and stuff like that."

The cluttered clatter of *Rrröööaaarrr* was considerably refined for *Killing Technology*. Dead-tight syncopation replaced chaotic calamity, the three instrumentalists locking into each other telepathically—and the individual parts were more complicated than before. Convoluted multitiered songs such as "Forgotten in Space" and "Killing Technology" showed tremendous maturity, taking giant leaps ahead that no one could have predicted based on their earlier work. "Cockroaches" and "Order of the Blackguards" combined machinelike precision and unstoppable velocity with thought-provoking lyrics and total musicality. Voivod's evolution from 1986 to 1987 was considerable; *Killing Technology* was a hulking epic of obtuse angularity and a majestic leap forward.

Killing Technology remained Langevin's favorite Voivod record for many years, partly because it established the unceasing exploration that became their trademark. The band had become a formidable cog in the thrash machine. A video was shot for "Ravenous Medicine," and although its low-budget limitations failed to convey its high-minded, well-meaning marriage of fictional medical-horror and protest against animal cruelty, it was an important step for a band that would use video very effectively in the coming years. Not even Metallica or Slayer were making videos yet, nor were most of their subterranean peers. As Voivod's easily identifiable T-shirts began to appear more frequently on fans and on other bands' members, and the band shouldered a heavy global tour schedule in 1987 and 1988, their cult and clout grew. They were leaving journalists dumbfounded and confused. Writer Dave Constable questioned in a 1987 issue of *Metal Forces*: "An art form or an unholy racket?" He also likened *Killing Technology* to "a picture painted by someone in a mental hospital."

What to do next? Widen the scope further, of course.

No longtime Voivod fan forgets hearing 1988's *Dimension Hatröss* for the first time. Voivod jumped radically beyond the previous album, and were now worlds away from *War and Pain*. Although created by the same four members, and again recorded at Music Lab in West Berlin with Harris Johns, everything else about *Hatröss* was unique and unfamiliar. The band struck a balance between order and disorder, creating metallic chaos in a highly composed setting. The bizarre dissonant guitar chords and oddball bass melodies were joined in harmonic polyphony at various points, while they had seemingly little relation to each other elsewhere—as on much of "Brain Scan" and "Chaosmongers." Langevin held radical time signatures and tempo shifts together with unwavering focus. The vocals were hardly as panicked or punk-influenced as before, and they joined with the cold laboratory music in their own melodic and robotic style. The earthy production remained raw, although the patented rough edges were smoothing out. Cosmic, psychedelic, and very heavy, *Dimension Hatröss* not only stands apart in the Voivod discography—there's nothing like it in any other musical genre, either.

The band ventured into the video realm again with two tracks, "Tribal Convictions" and "Psychic Vacuum," receiving generous airplay on MTV's *Headbangers Ball* throughout 1988. Both videos captured the surrealistic, cosmic psychedelia of *Dimension Hatröss*, and were more convincing excursions into multimedia than "Ravenous Medicine" had been.

Alongside Swiss eccentrics Celtic Frost, Voivod in the late '80s had become leaders of metal's avant-garde. More specifically, the Canadians were the first denizens of the extreme metal underground to adopt the spirit of the fiercely progressive

'70s. Though some thrash fans weren't ready for this, hungry prog rock enthusiasts set aside any qualms with the noisy music and became utterly hooked. The members of Voivod may not have been virtuosos on the level of Rush or Dream Theater, but the originality and scope of their ideas set them apart.

"I consider those guys early progressive metal pioneers," says Dream Theater drummer Mike Portnoy. "I loved Voivod's *Dimension Hatröss* and *Nothingface*. Those were big albums for me in terms of combining metal and prog."

Keyboardist Louis Panzer of Florida death metal band Nocturnus looked up to metal's Einstein-ian entity. "Voivod came up with some of the most unreal ideas," he says. "It's so bizarre—you can't even fathom thinking of how that music's created."

A card-carrying member of their Iron Gang fan club, Therion leader Christofer Johnsson calls Voivod "a great example of a band taking something completely different, like Pink Floyd influences, and incorporating them into what was, at the time, very extreme metal. Voivod is a band I can't listen to in the background. I simply must stop what I'm doing and get totally soaked into another world. Voivod is one of the most genius bands ever."

Opeth main man Mikael Åkerfeldt is another admirer. "With *Killing Technology* and especially *Dimension Hatröss*, I couldn't listen to anything else for weeks," he says. "It had some kind of psychedelic thing going on, which I didn't really realize at the time, but those albums clicked for me. To this day, I can still trace some of the stuff I write for Opeth back to Voivod."

Taking the template laid-down on *Dimension Hatröss*, Voivod's peculiar sci-fi tech metal was put through another few lab tests to create the cold, antiseptic *Nothingface*. Produced by Glen Robinson—who learned his craft at Morin Heights' Le Studio in Quebec, where Rush recorded various albums between 1979 and 1994—the band returned home to record their fifth album. Again progressing rapidly, Voivod made a remarkably clean album, largely due to the all-digital recording—still a novel approach in 1989.

Nothingface reveals the extreme confidence of a band comfortable with its music and surroundings but still testing itself with each song. The rapid time changes, the unpredictable key shifts, the seemingly hundreds-of-parts-per-song approach—Voivod pulled everything off with smooth liquidity on their fifth album. They made crazy compositional ideas sound natural. For such erratic music, the flow was total.

Most of the band's earlier rawness was shaved away by sheer, exacting precision. Only the grunting bass carried the raucousness of the early days, but its tone was sharper, less "blower" than before. While more involved than ever, the songs showed obtuse yet comprehensible design, and were remarkably mature. Key tracks including "Missing Sequences" and "The Unknown Knows" define the unique *Nothingface* approach—Voivod had mastered a completely original take on the metal form.

Before this major-label debut, Voivod albums had remained holistically pure, so it seemed suspicious that they included a cover of Pink Floyd's cosmic 1967 psych-out "Astronomy Domine." Cover songs are precarious for any established band—at worst, they reveal a dearth of new ideas, or seem like ploys for easy applause. The only cover song Voivod had officially released before was the campy '60s-era *Batman* show theme, tacked onto the CD version of *Dimension Hatröss*. "Batman" was an incentive "bonus track" on a format that was still a novelty to the metal-buying public in 1988. Yet "Astronomy Domine" managed to work toward the whole,

Top: Voivod teleports into the micro-galaxy of *Dimension Hatröss*, 1988; Bottom, the controversial and largely misunderstood *Angel Rat*, 1991

and it sounded like something of the band's own design. Plucked from Pink Floyd's *Piper at the Gates of Dawn* debut, the song paid tribute to the band's Syd Barrett era and the greater psychedelic movement that inspired Voivod—bands such as Floyd, the Soft Machine, Hawkwind, and Amon Düül II. Now *Nothingface* and "Astronomy Domine" announced Voivod's emergence as a band working in the spirit of the '60s and '70s psych/prog movements, even if forged from the now-discarded molds of former inspirations Venom and Motörhead.

Voivod's unorthodox prog metal grew more popular with each album. Major label MCA and its metal offshoot Mechanic—which also signed a young Dream Theater in 1989—gave Voivod a tremendous set of tools with which to reach that proverbial "next level." These included full-page color ads in such glossy magazines as *Rip* and *Hit Parader*; funds to shoot what turned out to be an acclaimed MTV-aired and Juno-nominated video for "Astronomy Domine"; and a co-headlining tour with two fellow upstarts whose music appealed to metal fans but could not properly be called metal, Seattle heroes Soundgarden and San Francisco hybridists Faith No More. Voivod even opened arena dates for their heroes Rush during the trio's Canadian *Presto* tour.

Major-label resources boosted Voivod's popularity enormously—and the label flexed financial muscle with the elaborate *Nothingface* CD package. Along with the band's music, Langevin's artistic talent had grown, evolved, and refined. *Nothingface* put his distinctive artwork on display, which was moving away from pen-and-paper and toward the computer. Within the CD's multipanel foldout design, each song was portrayed by a

Voivod circa 1991, L–R: Denis D'Amour (Piggy), Michael Langevin (Away), Denis Belanger (Snake) (*Mechanic Records*)

piece of artwork. "I took that from Emerson, Lake and Palmer," he says. "When I was young I remember sitting on my bed and listening to *Tarkus* and looking at the album. There was a drawing for each song. It gave a really good direction for the album."

Nothingface remains Voivod's best-known album, selling a quarter-million copies worldwide, at last count, with musicians of many stripes still inspired by it twenty years later. The album was a logical climax for the Voivod sound. Where could they go next?

Judging by the reaction to their following album, Voivod were now expected to ride the style of *Nothingface* for a few more years. Nobody expected Voivod to go back to their roots and unleash chaos-noise again. Expectations remained high as the band hired legendary Rush producer Terry Brown and began plotting a dark, subdued, highly textured album. Yet the result was hugely misunderstood. The band had accumulated fans in exponential numbers over the years, and *Angel Rat* cut that fan base clean in half.

While it seemed logical for Voivod to hire producer Terry Brown—as Fates Warning did that year for their streamlined and successful *Parallels*—the recording sessions for album number six were strained. Bassist Theriault, in particular, became disillusioned during the mix-down. After disagreeing constantly with Brown during the recording of *Angel Rat*, he drifted away from the other members. The highs and lows of ten tumultuous years together started taking a toll.

At the time, drummer Langevin shared an apartment with Theriault. "Blacky was more in an industrial music mode at the time, working with sequencers and samplers," says Langevin. "I was watching him slowly shift toward rave music. He became involved with dance troupes, and making music that was very rhythmic. He was slowly getting away from metal and prog rock."

Amidst various tensions—the differences of opinion; three-quarters of the members wanting to make a darker, moodier album; the changing musical climate— the new album was bound to be different, even for Voivod. They discarded their in- vented conceptual universe on *Angel Rat*, drawing lyrics instead from a variety of sources. "Nuage Fractal" was based on James Gleick's seminal book *Chaos*. Tales from Irish and Russian folklore inspired such tracks as "Angel Rat" and "The Outcast." The album included social/political commentary—"Best Regards" and "None of the Above"—while good old Voivod surrealism appeared with "Clouds in My House." "Panorama" and "Twin Dummy" were straightforward and relatively simple, the latter even playful and almost silly. On *Angel Rat*, Voivod straddled the line between simplic- ity and textural decoration; they honed and refined their approach while revealing an atmospheric depth learned from their prog rock heroes. The lush, cinematic produc- tion lent a layer of humanity to what were easily the band's most emotional songs. "The Prow" was probably the best example of 1991's Brave New Voivod: the catchy melodies, chimerical lyrics, and melancholy vocals relied less on brain and more on heart.

Predictably, not all fans were pleased. Says Langevin: "It's become some people's favorite, but other people really hate it and don't even consider it a Voivod album."

On the other hand, listeners who expected and even wanted the band to change were supportive. "It was scaled down but still just as amazing," says King

Fowley, of perennial death/thrash warriors Deceased. "*Angel Rat* is a very eerie record, with so much freaky rock and roll blending in. Even the happy songs sound melancholic. I loved it then and I love it now."

Another committed Voivod fan is John Mortimer, leader of NWOBHM band Holocaust—perhaps best known for composing "The Small Hours," which was made popular by Metallica. Holocaust's 1989 album, *The Sound of Souls*, revealed a Voivod influence. "In some ways [*Angel Rat* is] my favorite Voivod album," Mortimer says. "It's absolutely phenomenal. It has atmosphere that you won't find on any other album by any other band."

Sadly, this weirdly accessible album—with its melancholy gothic atmosphere, soft textures, and subtle beds of keyboards—brought the exit of their longtime bassist Theriault, breaking the bond of the boyhood friends. The bassist departed shortly after his tracks were completed, but before the album was released. Consequently, the band appears as a trio for all *Angel Rat*–era photos, with Theriault listed apart from the others in the album credits. His exit effectively killed off any touring that might have been planned on the back of the album's release.

After the dissolution of the original Voivod lineup, the remaining three members took time off before regrouping for album number seven. *The Outer Limits*, released in 1993, was in some ways simpler than anything on the previous album, particularly the punky "Wrong-Way Street" and crassly rocking opener "Fix My Heart." Regarding the bridge between *Angel Rat* and *The Outer Limits*, Langevin says, "The reaction to *Angel Rat* didn't discourage us from going further in that direction, because *The Outer Limits* is sort of similar."

But *The Outer Limits* wasn't *Son of Angel Rat*, either. The album's bright, airy production was worlds away from its dark predecessor. The creepy "Le Pont Noir" ("The Black Bridge") recalled *Angel Rat's* title track, while "Time Warp" and "The Lost Machine" might have been what some *Nothingface* fans wanted *Angel Rat* to be—but the sum total of *The Outer Limits* represented another walk on virgin terrain for the cosmic explorers.

Bassist Pierre St. Jean was recruited, but the band was reluctant to induct him officially. His playing fit well with the band's new material, although his superclean tone and subtle approach couldn't help but highlight Theriault's absence. Not

Away's 3D art pages from Voivod's *The Outer Limits* booklet, circa 1993.

surprisingly, St. Jean's hired-gun status found him seeking other avenues of expression. He went on to cofound Heaven's Cry, who released an ambitious debut, *Food for Thought Substitute*, four years later.

Voivod's prog rock personality peaked on *The Outer Limits*. They covered another Pink Floyd tune, 1969's "The Nile Song," and unveiled the gargantuan seventeen-minute "Jack Luminous." "In the early '80s," Langevin recalls, "doing long songs in prog rock was already over. The longest you'd get was eight or nine minutes. The days of a twenty-minute song were over. It was a challenge that we took on for *The Outer Limits*. We wanted to write a song reminiscent of 'A Plague of Lighthouse Keepers' by Van der Graaf Generator."

The Outer Limits was intended as Voivod's audio version of the television show of the same name. *The Outer Limits* series aired in the mid-'60s, clearly inspired by Rod Serling's *The Twilight Zone*. The CD package was designed like a '50s pulp sci-fi magazine, and, as on *Nothingface*, each song had its own visual representation, with Langevin's designs given 3-D treatment—glasses included! Only eerie Rod Serling–esque voice-overs were missing.

A young Michel Langevin devoured episodes of *The Outer Limits* and *The Twilight Zone* in his youth, and this was his tribute to them. "We wanted to do a soundtrack for so many years," says Langevin, "but never had the offer. So we decided to give the album a feeling of a soundtrack for an old sci-fi movie. It gave a total new direction to the album and to our music."

Even though the Voivod on *The Outer Limits* sounds like a completely different band compared to the young hellions who laid down the raucous *War and Pain*, it makes perfect sense considering their step-by-step mutations and continual absorption of new influences. Voivod's evolution remains one of the most fascinating in metal's vast history. Yet by 1994, much of the metal community seemed to lack the attention span for Voivod. Support dwindled. Labels, the media, and many fans moved on to easier, trendier sounds or heavier, more extreme death and black metal bands.

Feeling that Voivod had met a commercial and artistic wall and wrestling with what he calls "different habits"—not to mention exhaustion and disillusion with the music industry—vocalist Belanger exited in 1994. There was nothing else in the lives of the members for the band's first ten years: Burnout, on some level, was inevitable. In the fallout, members became involved in other musical projects. Langevin took on freelance art commissions for other bands (including hard-core hip-hop act Non Phixion, Dave Grohl's Probot, and belligerent rockers Danko Jones), and recorded with semi-legendary synth-pop band Men Without Hats and cofounded psych rock band Kosmos. Both he and guitarist D'Amour played in Montreal art rock act Aut'chose. For vocalist Belanger, however, leaving Voivod meant going cold turkey, from music and assorted poisons. "I just wanted to get away from everything," he says, "so I took a year off and was living in the woods. I wanted to be far away from the city and the habits and everything." Belanger's departure left Langevin and D'Amour to pick up the pieces of what had once been the ultimate "all for one, one for all" band.

During the same period that Voivod ascended, spiritual peers and onetime Noise Records labelmates Celtic Frost also evolved from raw Venom-esque noise to slick modern metal with some rock influence. In a handful of years, Celtic Frost spanned primitive proto–death metal, plodding doom, female vocal operettas, sound collage pieces, orchestral tracks, and even a ham-fisted attempt at glam. In Celtic

Frost, heavy metal's avant-garde arrived wearing bullet belts and battle helmets, carrying Roxy Music LPs under one arm and a box of moonwalk transmission tapes under the other.

Founded by Thomas Gabriel Fischer, aka Tom G. Warrior, the pre–Celtic Frost band Hellhammer comprised three headbanger pals fueled by such classic '70s bands as Deep Purple, Led Zeppelin, and Black Sabbath and an energy injection from NWOBHM bands such as Venom, Iron Maiden, and Tygers of Pan Tang. At an early stage, they covered the killer "Black Ice" by obscure British band Aragorn. Hellhammer's desire to be more over-the-top than Venom and faster than Motörhead long before they were musically capable resulted in a reckless, sloppy demo called *Triumph of Death* (1983). Shortly thereafter, friend and bassist Martin Ain was recruited, and the band—which included drummer Bruce Day—recorded the much improved but still primitive *Satanic Rites* demo. A deal with the fledgling Noise Records brought about the *Apocalyptic Raids* EP. Released in early 1984, the EP was received with some howls of rabid praise and scads of derision. *Metal Forces* magazine was particularly hard on the young band, likening the EP in one review to "Metallica's 'Whiplash' being played by a bunch of three-year-olds."

Even before the harsh condemnation, Fischer and Ain were well aware of Hellhammer's limitations. The duo disbanded Hellhammer and launched a new project intended to be more ambitious and professional. One night in May 1984, they drew up battle plans. With papers spread out before them, detailing the overall concept and lyric ideas, the pair decided to go with a two-word name for the new band. Ain threw out "Celtic," and Fischer offered "Fire," but Celtic Fire sounded, according to Fischer, "like a stupid cliché." Striving to be anything but cliché right from the beginning, they gazed at the copy of Cirith Ungol's *Frost and Fire* album, which was sitting amongst the papers, and Celtic Frost was born. Their long-term vision was mapped out from the earliest stages, with titles and concepts for their first several albums already conceived. They stuck to the plan for several years, with remarkable faithfulness (though some projects, such as *Necronomicon*, *Linebacker Three*, and *Under Apollyon's Sun*, never came to fruition).

Recruiting drummer Stephen Priestly, Celtic Frost recorded its debut, *Morbid Tales*, in 1984. With a tighter rhythmic foundation than Hellhammer and an incredibly fat guitar tone, the band delivered the primal essence of early death metal. *Morbid Tales* is dominated by songs that plow ahead with the grace of a bulldozer, slowing down long enough for the crawling doom of "Procreation (of the Wicked)."

Temporary truce: Celtic Frost lands on the cover of *Metal Forces*, 1985

Frost first visited unorthodox realms with "Return to the Eve," which featured a forlorn female-voiced narration. Following that, the curious experimental piece "Danse Macabre" was unlike anything attempted by a metal band before. It wasn't an intro or an outro, but a legitimate album track of ghostly voices and ritualistic chimes over three minutes and fifty-two seconds—which could have easily fit onto one of Goblin's horror movie soundtracks. Something strange had just surfaced on planet Metal.

Next, *To Mega Therion* was just as heavy as the debut, thanks to the thunderous approach of newcomer Reed St. Mark, previously a jazz drummer around New York City. Epic layers were draped over such tracks as "Dawn of Megiddo" and "Necromantical Screams," the latter using female vocals in a kind of apocalypse opera. Yet another experimental piece appeared: "Tears in a Prophet's Dream" was titled like a Marillion album and sounded like Tangerine Dream on acid—in hell.

Years later, Fischer remarked that Celtic Frost "wanted to provide the scene with new impulses and new frontiers."

After hinting at those impulses and frontiers in their first two albums, Celtic Frost made an ambitious leap forward with their third album that was simply unimaginable. *Into the Pandemonium* was recorded throughout 1987 amid stress and difficulty. Fischer detailed the long and protracted process in his 2000 autobiography, *Are You Morbid?* "Before long, the sessions for *Into the Pandemonium* turn into tough work," he wrote. "We have begun a difficult and complex album, a hard, unnerving pursuit which consumes hours on end, every day."

When Noise Records founder Karl Walterbach signed the young Hellhammer in 1984, he could have had no inkling of the giant stylistic leaps that would transpire in just a few short years. His signing strategy was instinctual: "I signed what appeared to be fresh and new, more looking at edgy and image-strong bands than at musical or technical perfection. Musically, I always considered Celtic Frost an awful band. What attracted me was their vision and image, how they were able to visualize things." But Walterbach's openness to originality had its limits, tested by this strange new Celtic Frost experiment.

Created at Horus Sound Studio—owned by Frank Bornemann of German prog band Eloy—*Into the Pandemonium* stunned and agitated Walterbach's staff. Though Noise had bravely taken on the nonconformist Voivod and proved their ability to sell them to the metal public, despite their difficult music, the sheer audacity of *Into the Pandemonium* was an entirely unwelcome challenge for the label. Noise's marketing department went into a panic. "The record company people came to the studio," Fischer remembers, "and they asked us 'Why don't you do albums like Exodus and Slayer? They're much easier to market.' At the same time, the classical musicians were sitting there in the studio."

Into the Pandemonium was misunderstood and heavily criticized upon its release in 1987, and it remains controversial today. The music wasn't just weird—it was wildly, inexplicably eccentric. The ambition that killed Hellhammer and birthed Celtic Frost exploded all over the album. Launching with a brazen confidence, the album opens with "Mexican Radio," originally recorded by Los Angeles new wave group Wall of Voodoo. You could easily visualize the denim-and-leather contingent jumping ship en masse. But that song was only the first of many bizarre turns throughout *Into the Pandemonium*. Never satisfied, old friend Bernard Doe at *Metal Forces* awarded the album a big fat o

Frost Bite: Tom G. Warrior (aka Thomas Gabriel Fischer) of Celtic Frost, 1986 (*Frank White*)

out of 100 in his review. Doe called the album "a mishmash of uneventful drivel that would be better suited for a pop or disco release" and opened the review by asking, "Avant-garde metal? Avant-a-clue metal, more like!"

Love or hate the album, *Into the Pandemonium* defied metal stereotypes. Only two songs recalled the Celtic Frost of old—"Inner Sanctum" and "Babylon Fell"—and the rest of the terrain was all new. Fischer introduced a disturbing, ultra-mournful moan, used on "Mesmerized" and the haunting "Caress into Oblivion." The core band members were swarmed by numerous guest players and singers. The operatic "Tristesses de la Lune" presaged future gothic doom pioneers Paradise Lost and My Dying Bride, with its female opera vocals and heavy reliance on classical instrumentation. Huge orchestral strokes enveloped "Rex Irae (Requiem)" and "Oriental Masquerade." The oddly titled "I Won't Dance" featured up-tempo hard rock beats, atonal "clean" vocals, a catchy chorus, and a ghostly female backup vocal that conjured disco and soul vibes. Then came "One in Their Pride," the oddest song on an album overflowing with odd songs. Underneath sampled radio chatter between Apollo astronauts and NASA ground control was a foundational track built on cheap beat-box thumping. The mixer manipulation and added effects made for interesting if completely alien listening for most of the Frost audience.

No one really knew what to make of *Into the Pandemonium*, then and now, and it hasn't even been imitated since. Intentionally retrogressive death metal bands like Obituary and Asphyx who cite Celtic Frost's early work as inspiration never dared to venture into the beyond the way Frost did. And while bands like gothic doom/death band Paradise Lost, symphonic prog-metal troupe Therion, and Norwegian avant-metal cosmonauts Arcturus later took its ideals and worked them into their own methodology, there is only one *Into the Pandemonium*.

Celtic Frost put one foot in highbrow artiness and the other in raw ugly death—a one-of-a-kind combination in the time of their reign. The Wall of Voodoo song was not their only unusual cover choice, either. Over the years they reworked material by David Bowie, Roxy Music's Bryan Ferry, and even Rat Packer Dean Martin. In 1993, Tom Fischer hinted to journalist Ula Gehret that the band was at work on new covers of songs by Prince, ELP, and Roxy Music. While the symphonic finery of Emerson, Lake and Palmer and the suave art rock of Roxy Music would seem to have no connection with the coarseness of metal, Frost's attempts to bring seemingly in-compatible sounds into alignment expanded the metal language and created a legacy no other band can claim.

Visually, Celtic Frost's ambition equaled the scope of their music. *To Mega Therion* featured the striking paintings *Satan I* and *Victory III* by the legendary H.R. Giger on the front cover and inside gatefold. Frost went deeper into art history on *Into the Pandemonium*. The cover features a detail from Hieronymus Bosch's *Garden of Delights*, while the gatefold shows an otherworldly scene of grayish-brown desolation titled *Ya—Tour of the Universe—Tombworld* by Les Edwards (whose work was already familiar to metal fans via Metallica's *Jump in the Fire* EP). The evolution of Celtic Frost's music and imagery achieved a feel of total continuity. They delivered not only music but an entire package—an entire world to explore. Their clever calculation and attention to detail were markedly different from what most other bands were doing at the time.

Upon *Into the Pandemonium*'s release, bassist Martin Ain defended their ex-perimental tendencies. "This band will always take risks," he said. "We are not content to be merely another thrash band. Thrash metal has become so conservative. Fans think they're acting in a free manner, whereas the truth is they're part of a strict social group, with its own code of behavior, dress, et cetera. They won't listen to anything outside of their field. These people are stuck in a room with four walls, no windows, and they keep the door firmly shut. Celtic Frost are putting cracks in the plaster, show-ing them that there is something else beyond their confines."

Strong words notwithstanding, that brinksmanship cost Celtic Frost the loy-alty of fans and the confidence of their label. Friendships soured within the band, and the essential Celtic Frost lineup broke apart in the wake of the strained recording ses-sions and hugely mixed reaction to *Into the Pandemonium*.

The outcome of the split was inexplicable: *Cold Lake*, one of the most de-rided albums in metal history. For the 1988 release, Fischer brought back Stephen Priestly on drums and added two new members. The Frost leader hinted in 1987 that the follow-up to *Into the Pandemonium* would be more "straight-ahead, contemporary, and modern," but *Cold Lake* didn't sound or even look like Celtic Frost. Clad in stone-washed denim, L.A. Guns T-shirts, and diamond jewelry, and sporting hair spray,

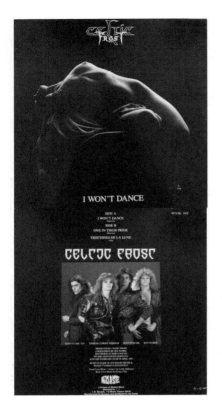

Art Metal: Celtic Frost's
I Won't Dance 12" single, 1987

the band offered songs titled "Seduce Me Tonight," "Dance Sleazy," and "Tease Me." *Cold Lake* was a gathering of onetime death metal musicians attempting to play cock rock in the ugliest, most ham-fisted manner, without any irony whatsoever. It was appalling.

With interview appearances and video play for "Cherry Orchards" on American MTV, and permed-and-hair-sprayed throngs cheering the band on in 1989's *Live at Hammersmith Odeon* video release, *Cold Lake* was given the cold shoulder by most hardcore Frost fans. The band's grand tour plans, which included a number of prestigious venues throughout Europe, aimed too high. Even with their most extensive stage set to date, most gigs were underattended; a show in Liverpool found the band pelted by Styrofoam cups and plastic bottles throughout the set. Ultimately, *Cold Lake* was a terribly misguided venture, an album Fischer has since called "utter crap." With an open, sympathetic ear, you can hear sturdy Frost-like guitar riffs in "(Once) They Were Eagles" and "Downtown Hanoi," but the essence of the band was obliterated in the haze of upheaval and disappointment that was *Into the Pandemonium*'s fallout.

After another lineup alteration, Celtic Frost returned to try and save face with 1990's *Vanity/Nemesis*. Hinting at the operatic and epic ambitions of the past, but retaining some of the carefree *Cold Lake* attitude, *Vanity/Nemesis* brought back the signature bloated guitar tone of the golden years, weirdly bridging the disparate values of *Cold Lake* and the exotic heaviness preceding it.

After the *Vanity/Nemesis* season wound down with a tour bearing the painfully prophetic title "Campaign Slow Freeze," Celtic Frost recorded new demos in 1992 with returning drummer Reed St. Mark. Frost intended to reestablish itself as a cutting-edge band, and its members had big ideas how to flesh out their vision in the studio. "We approach this next album as something like a successor to *Pandemonium*,"

Fischer envisioned. "We cannot do an album like that every day. We needed to rest for some years, but it's time again to do an album like that. We're going to use an orchestra, a lot of sampling, a lot of industrial sounds, male and female opera singers, acoustic tracks—a lot of experiments."

Unfortunately the stripped-down demo met with disinterest from a music industry whose sights were set on Seattle's "grunge rock" uprising. Suddenly, nothing Frost did seemed relevant. "Record companies just aren't risk-oriented," Fischer remarked at the time. "We would like to do an album that rivals the Beatles' 'White Album.' I mean, nobody can ever topple the Beatles, but we'd like to do something that rattles the '90s. Finding backing for that in a time like this is very hard. We're not going to compromise, though. If we cannot find backing for the project, it might spell the end of Frost." Sure enough, it did.

Celtic Frost's Martin Ain abuses his Rickenbacker in New York City, 1986
(*Frank White*)

They disassembled shortly thereafter—the proposed experimental sixth album but a dream, the band a broken reflection of Celtic Frost in its prime. Their brave approach, to go where no band had gone before, was both their triumph and their downfall. And just as Celtic Frost called it quits in 1993, Voivod released *The Outer Limits*, an album that closed the most important era of another metal innovator.

Voivod and Celtic Frost had uncannily matched each other step for step. Both bands offered a complete conceptual package and alternate worlds. Both reached far ahead—sometimes precariously far—with each new endeavor. And there was always mutual respect between the two, dating back to 1985, when they toured together. "Celtic Frost were totally avant-garde," Voivod's Michel Langevin says. "They tried to develop a new kind of thrash metal. Martin Ain called it 'avant-thrash.'"

To younger listeners, Voivod's and Celtic Frost's '80s albums might sound quaint, but without their adventurous trailblazing, the sound and shape of progressive and technical metal in the 2000s would be drastically different. Much of what the two bands introduced then is taken for granted today by thrash, death, and black metal renaissance bands—not to mention less genre-specific acts such as Tool and the Dillinger Escape Plan. Electronic percussion and drum machines are widespread in modern experimental metal, as are female vocals and operatic elements, all pointing back to Frost; and whenever someone uses robotic vocal effects, weird time signatures or fractured, dissonant, unorthodox guitar chords ("Piggy chords"), the Voivod name is sure to be invoked.

Voivod's jarring, angular technicality echoes today in a variety of bands that emerge fully formed as tech metal architects. Likewise, the oddball avant-garde weirdness of Celtic Frost's *Into the Pandemonium* has inspired an avant-metal subgenre, a daring approach to metal that is no longer an oddity sitting far apart in left field, but just one of many genre outgrowths. A battalion of forward-thinking bands who arose in the '90s—among them Therion, Opeth, Unexpect, and Maudlin of the Well—all owe a debt to Voivod and Celtic Frost.

In interviews conducted during the band's heyday, Tom Fischer frequently used the terms "modern," "contemporary," and "rock" when discussing Celtic Frost's music. While that sounded strange coming from a decidedly nonconformist artist, he was stating—and ultimately proved—that the metal genre was part of a larger musical stream, and that its form was eternally malleable. Anything could be done with metal that the mind could imagine.

BARRIERS & PASSAGES:
THE TRIUMPHS AND TRIALS
OF MIND OVER FOUR
AND THOUGHT INDUSTRY

THE LATE 1980S FOUND METAL'S GENRE-SPECIFIC BOXES in disintegration. Hybridization was the ruling zeitgeist for many varieties of heavy music. Post-punk, noise rock, and raw retro-rock bands on labels like Amphetamine Reptile and Sub Pop were no strangers to Slayer or Black Sabbath. Conversely, adventurous young musicians raised on Metallica and Judas Priest warmed to bands outside their comfort zone. Fans of Trouble and Saint Vitus soon felt the complicated crawl of Melvins' *Ozma*. Headbangers who found kinship in the blasting might of early Bad Brains and Black Flag went further and discovered early albums by musical mutts Faith No More and Jane's Addiction. By the end of the '80s, it was not unusual to find funk, noise, industrial, and goth seeping into metal.

Voivod's state-of-the-art *Nothingface* was a beacon in this new hybrid world. Their U.S. tour with Soundgarden and Faith No More caught the ear of musicians from a decidedly different world, such as Milwaukee post-hardcore shape-shifters Die Kreuzen and drummer Dave Grohl of Scream—later of Nirvana and the Foo Fighters. *Nothingface*'s barrier-crashing helped the struggles of two interesting young bands of the day—California's Mind Over Four and Michigan's Thought Industry.

Mind Over Four first appeared in 1983 with the self-released *Desperate Expression*, which didn't make the slightest ripple in the public consciousness. They reappeared four years later with *Out Here*, a title suggesting loneliness and alienation. That rang true, as there would never be a proper peg to hang them on. Mind Over Four mixed '70s art rock attitude with the bright but edgy vibe of alt rock heroes Jane's Addiction and the later, more atmospheric work of Die Kreuzen. The aggression of metal provided a constant but subtle thread on *Out Here*, heard loudest within the timing complications of "Pity" and various passages that presaged what Voivod did several years later on *Angel Rat* ("Sex with an Apparition," "God"). *Out Here* was alternative metal before the term "alternative" lost all meaning in the '90s.

A heavier band emerged on 1989's *Mind Over Four*. "Social Stature" wouldn't have been out of place on an early Soundgarden album, while "The Black Orgasm" and "The Mile Between the Molecule" might have appealed to fans of Mekong Delta and Voivod. The album's incredibly tiny Berlin-based label, Destiny, did next to nothing for the band.

Mind Over Four's visibility improved when Caroline Records stepped in for 1990's *The Goddess*. They were marketed as a very different metal band for the changing times— magazine ads featured *The Goddess* alongside other new albums by Bad Brains, Primus, and Pussy Galore. Yet even if the album arrived smack in the middle of the melting-pot expansion of heavy rock, it flew over many people's heads. The band remained unknown in plain sight, despite their record labels placing full-page ads in glossy metal magazines such as *Rip* and *Hit Parader*. English journalist Mike Exley called them "one of the most important happenings in the scene since Voivod or Faith No More." Phil Anselmo is even pictured wearing an MO4 shirt on Pantera's popular *Vulgar Display of Power* album.

Despite whatever person or group touted Mind Over Four as *the* band to usher metal into the '90s, major commercial breakthrough was elusive, and by the middle of the decade they were practically anonymous. But *The Goddess* delivered killer alt metal to those who would listen. Members of trash rockers Junkyard and semi-legendary hardcore band Dag Nasty appeared on rocking free-for-all "12 Days of Wind," while "Gemini" pressed layers of complication into a confounding four-minute tech maze. Quirky wailer Spike Xavier's vocals were empowering, soaring above an urgent metal melting pot. Relatively short compositions such as "Ice, Water, Steam" and "Hell's Bravest Song" exploded with energy and purpose. By the time of *The Goddess*, Mind Over Four was cramming more information into three-minute songs than many bands were putting into entire albums.

Xavier, who led Mind Over Four's twelve-year uphill battle, says, "The idea was to get four different guys from four different musical backgrounds and combine them into one style. Four guys combined into one mind equals one band—the idea behind the name. I can't stand Allan Holdsworth, Van Halen, and Journey, but our bassist loves it. He likes all Rush, and I only like one or two Rush albums. He can't stand the Melvins and stuff I get into."

Mind Over Four peaked with 1993's *Half Way Down*. Expanding the ideas forged on the previous two albums, and almost doubling the song lengths, *Half Way Down* was the ultimate MO4 statement—a gleaming fifty minutes of progressive metal that had no safe home even amongst the teched- and progged-out metal bands of the era. But the band always had as much in common with former Triple X labelmates Jane's Addiction as they did Voivod. Hints of punk, soul, and funk; stop-on-a-dime tempo shifts; an organic production crackling with electric energy—*Half Way Down* had no clear home, even in those hybrid-friendly times.

The demise of Mind Over Four was imminent, preceded by the ill-conceived *Empty Hands* in 1995. The album seemed to throw up a middle finger while the ship was going down—pointed at the industry, the listening public, or maybe even themselves. Seemingly slapdash, *Empty Hands* veered between groovy aggro-metal and punk, and dabbled in electronic music and junky garage rock. Not even the most hardcore MO4 fan could love the album. Accordingly, the band seems to be remembered only by a tiny scattered few—as much a relic of their time as they were ahead of it.

Michigan's Thought Industry met a similar fate. Metallica's Jason Newsted brought the band's 1990 demo to Metal Blade Records, who showed immediate interest. On the back of the heavily circulated demo—which included a cover of Rush's "Red Barchetta"—Thought Industry released its debut album in 1992. The cover and titles of *Songs for Insects* gave away the band's peculiar mind-set: Salvador Dalí's painting *Soft Construction with Boiled Beans: Premonition of Civil War* on the front, with strangely named songs like "Blistered Text and Bleeding Pens" and "Alexander vs. the Puzzle" on the back. "Experi-metal," "art thrash," "surrealist metal"—whatever the press called the album, *Songs for Insects* tested mental mettle with lengthy, erratic arrangements, obtuse riff constructions, and lyrics linked to a multitude of historical and literary references—all exuding a not-so-subtle eccentricity.

In 1993, Thought Industry moved forward with *Mods Carve the Pig: Assassins, Toads and God's Flesh*, more confounding and aggressive than the debut. The album's most memorable track was closer "To Build a Better Bulldozer," which joined tech metal with math rock, like the abrasion of Steve Albini's seminal Big Black wrestling with a metallic King Crimson–esque puzzle through seven instrumental minutes.

Says original Thought Industry drummer Dustin Donaldson, "We listened to, loved, and studied all forms of underground music, especially metal, as well as '60s, '70s, and '80s classic songwriting, including U.S. and British art rock/pop/prog stuff, and crammed it into a stylized Midwest new wave anxiety. Influence is everywhere when you're truly engaged in a creative endeavor. We really just used our own experiences in an attempt to sound like ourselves."

By 1993, Thought Industry were touring the U.S. using visuals to accompany their performances, predating the shows Tool and Neurosis performed at the end of the decade. Pink Floyd and Hawkwind had done multimedia concerts decades earlier, but the idea was certainly new to metal bands touring the club circuit (apart from the autopsy and vivisection films projected by death metal gods Carcass, anyway).

Donaldson left Thought Industry after *Mods*, moved to California, and joined gay pop/punk band Pansy Division for a brief time before hatching the experimental I Am Spoonbender. Spoonbender has drawn comparisons to Brian Eno, '70s German experimentalists Can, progressive post-punk/industrialists This Heat, Devo, and any number of synth-pop artists. While still a cult phenomenon, they have eclipsed Thought Industry in popularity and acclaim.

Without Donaldson, leader Brent Oberlin forged ahead with a revamped Thought Industry on *Outer Space is Just a Martini Away* and *Black Umbrella*. With *Black Umbrella*, the band had shed its metal plating and seemed to both embrace and parody the alternative rock sound that was commercially peaking in 1997. Along with Oberlin, guitarist Paul Enzio was the only remaining member from the band's early albums—and even he was gone by the time of the band's final album.

Thought Industry concluded in 2001 with mammoth seventy-one-minute, sixteen-song opus *Short Wave on a Cold Day*. By the release of *Short Wave*, Thought Industry had mutated into something akin to Radiohead's *OK Computer* or Failure's *Fantastic Planet*. The album is Thought Industry's magnum opus, though it didn't have much to do with the sound or lineup that caught Jason Newsted and other adventurous metal fans' attention in the early '90s. *Short Wave* was the only way the weird, wayward journey of Thought Industry could have culminated.

While Thought Industry and Mind Over Four had talent, chemistry, and vision in common with bands such as Voivod, they failed to secure the same kind of consistent label support. Similar cards were dealt to bands such as Wisconsin's eclectic Last Crack or the Beatles-infused Galactic Cowboys, all numbering among a host of late-'80s/early-'90s progressive acts too weird to be marketed to traditional metal audiences, and too alien to latch onto the post–Big Three wave.

9. SUBLIMATION FROM UNDERGROUND II: EUROPE

"Our music was never made for the big masses. We were ahead of our time by a few years; not only musically, but with all the graphic stuff, artwork, and photography. An artist who does not make progress from time to time will soon be musically dead." —Tommy T. Baron, Coroner

IN 1987, NOISE RECORDS WAS THRIVING. The Berlin-based label was formed in 1984 by Karl Walterbach—who had run punk label AGR in the early '80s—and in just a few years the label was enjoying the success of strong sellers like Helloween and Running Wild. The music press of the day—desperate to keep close tabs on mushrooming metal subgenres—dubbed these bands "power metal," the basis of a sound that carried the torch for traditional heavy metal into the '90s. But Noise wasn't content to specialize in just one area. The label also planted a strong foothold in the progressive end of the metal spectrum with Celtic Frost's *Into the Pandemonium* and Voivod's *Killing Technology*. They continued to sniff out a variety of left-of-center bands, along with dependable speed/thrash names like Kreator and Tankard.

Walterbach seemed interested in finding the best of each subgenre, from every corner of the globe. Notably, Noise was the first independent metal label to consistently bank on the genre's outsiders. Although Celtic Frost front man Tom Fischer had pushed tech metal pioneers Watchtower on Walterbach as early as 1985, the Texas band and German label finally joined forces in 1989 for the band's second album, *Control and Resistance.* "I wanted Watchtower's first album," remembers Walterbach, "but they had a true independent mind-set and couldn't be convinced otherwise." Closer to home, Walterbach put his money on a Swiss trio named Coroner.

Coroner came to the attention of the metal underground via 1986's *Death Cult*, a demo tape immediately noteworthy for its guest vocals by Celtic Frost's Tom Fischer. The members of Coroner had roadied for their fellow Swiss pals, and Frost's music had apparently rubbed off; the tape's four songs took a Celtic Frost–meets–Mercyful Fate approach, though not very successfully at that early stage. (No *Death Cult* songs made it to the band's later releases.) By 1987, Coroner claimed a more individual sound with their *R.I.P.* debut. The back cover showed the members' names engraved on cremation urns—and, along with the album title, the band made a peculiarly backwards introduction.

R.I.P. showed massive improvement from the demo, injecting classically tinged melodies into guitar lines of frenetic speed that always maintained flow. Still, *R.I.P.* was only a glimpse into what made this band so treasured to adventurous listeners in the thrash audience. Coroner's next albums really made heads spin.

The next year's *Punishment for Decadence* showed a deadlier, tighter, more technical Coroner. Their acrobatic four- and six-string scale-raping again pointed toward the symphonic influence of classical music, still a novel trait in that era of metal. "Absorbed" mixed difficult stop-start rhythms with an effortless fluidity that became Coroner's trademark. "Masked Jackal" was memorable yet unpredictable, balancing key and chord changes between sinister groove and instrumental prowess. "Arc-Lite" was a busy, eventful instrumental that featured as much melody as intensity. It was their equivalent of Rush's "La Villa Strangiato," in that the band displayed their ability to tell a musical story without vocals. The rest of the songs maintained a similarly high standard, winning praise and notoriety instantly from the kinds of metal fans that craved a more intellectual headbang.

The European cover of *Punishment for Decadence* featured *Porte de l'Enfer*, a sculpture by nineteenth-century French artist Auguste Rodin, best known for the iconic statue *The Thinker*. The black strip running along the right side of the album cover introduced what would be a visual constant for every Coroner release thereafter.

With an arty, shadowy picture of the band on the back cover and song titles such as "Arc-Lite" and "Shadow of a Lost Dream," it was all pretty highbrow stuff for a thrash band.

The U.S. office of Noise Records, however, felt the artwork would fly over the heads of the average fan. They replaced the original design with something deemed more "metal": a skeleton playing a bone with a violin bow. This was a compromise in Coroner's vision, something they would not bow to again. Drummer and conceptualist Marquis Marky, aka Markus Edelmann, stated that the record company "thought it wouldn't sell very well because the metal audience would think it's another kind

European cover of Coroner's *Punishment for Decadence*, 1988, deemed "not metal enough" by the U.S. Noise Records office

of music. That's pretty stupid. I think we should all be more open to other things. I would be much happier if thrash people also listened to other stuff. It's stupid to listen to one music direction. I'm into jazz music, and '60s and '70s stuff. I'm a big fan of the Doors." To be sure, Coroner's love of classic rock resulted in some unlikely cover choices for a thrash band, such as Jimi Hendrix's "Purple Haze" and the Beatles' "I Want You (She's So Heavy)".

Coroner's next two albums, *No More Color* (1989) and *Mental Vortex* (1991), took their basic blueprint and perfected it, cleaning up the production and tightening the overall attack to a finely honed tech-metal point. These albums etched Coroner's name onto the walls of the progressive metal hall of fame. *No More Color* kept the imagery arty and the thrash deadly, with the complexity of the riffs becoming the main focus. With vise-tight syncopation in the rhythm section, guitarist Tommy T. Baron climbed over piles of lesser thrash six-stringers with amazing fluidity.

No More Color suffered no lack of energy, but final track "Last Entertainment (T.V. Bizarre)" turned the corner away from hectic thrash metal. The song was mid-paced and sullen, a gray amalgam of orchestral flourishes, industrial atmosphere, and haunting narration by Marky. Curiously, Coroner chose to shoot a video for this unconventional track. Predictably, it did not set MTV on fire, and seemed to go over the heads of *Headbangers Ball* viewers.

Speed became a smaller part of the Coroner equation by 1991's *Mental Vortex*. During this time, many thrash bands were slowing and simplifying, or spinning their wheels in a generic malaise. Megadeth and Metallica became sleeker, as did Testament and Overkill. Even speed demons like Kreator, Dark Angel, and Slayer eased up on the gas pedal. Some, like Voivod, moved away from thrash entirely. Coroner maintained its vivid fire while moving ahead. The energy and dexterity of *Mental Vortex* was still pure Coroner, if decidedly more mature.

Mental Vortex's stylized package contained a chunkier, heavier trio. Baron added color by introducing a variety of interesting chords and cleaner tones. He relied less on arpeggios and harmonic minors, and more on shading and creative rhythmic ideas. "Pale Sister" recalled the jumpy, unpredictable nature of earlier Coroner, but "Sirens" and "Semtex Revolution" were more about rhythm and mood, not technical showmanship. The cover of the Beatles' "I Want You (She's So Heavy)" was an appropriately left-field way to close the album, even if their interpretation was relatively conservative.

Coroner leapt considerably far off from their signature approach with fifth and final album, *Grin*. As a variety of other bands were scaling the heights of technical mastery in 1993, Coroner instead made a significant departure, writing longer songs built on simpler—and fewer—riffs. Hypnotic repetition and huge expanses of groove-laden landscape produced an airtight atmosphere of unease throughout *Grin*. Marky had commented to *Metal Forces* two years earlier about coming changes in the band.

"We've left the classical influences of our past behind," he said. "That sort of metal no longer interests us. There is more of an industrial and psychedelic feel to our music."

Grin tested different waters, laying out a machinelike grayness that sometimes brought to mind the previous year's *Renewal* by contemporaries and former tour partners Kreator. The album shift saw another benefit, as guitarist Tommy T. Baron was given more room to breathe. He took advantage of the new environment by offering the lushest, most dramatic soloing of his career.

Coroner never capitalized on the direction explored on *Grin*. The band broke up in 1995, posthumously releasing the bits-and-pieces swan song *Coroner* that same year. The Swiss trio had brought stylish performance,

Coroner's Ron Royce in the early 1990s
(*Choon-Kang Walther*)

classical music complexity, and a wide array of outside influences to thrash metal, and were one of the first in the genre to bridge seemingly disparate worlds. Although popular with tech-heads, Coroner's approach to time signature was not as radical as many similarly-minded bands—most of their music was in basic 4/4 time; their stop-start rhythms were a well-integrated part of the machine, implemented with more subtlety than other tech metal bands managed. Coroner's main appeal to fans wanting complicated music was the spiraling, arpeggio-laden sequences fired off from the nimble fingers of Baron and bassist Ron Royce. Marky went on to cofound the ill-fated electro metal act Apollyon Sun with old pal Tom G. Fischer of Celtic Frost, while Baron joined a watered-down Kreator for 1997's *Outcast*—a completely inexplicable move, considering *Outcast* offered zero guitar solos, always Baron's deadliest weapons.

Not far from Switzerland in neighboring Germany, any radicalization of metal happened on the fringes—and at the risk of being deemed heretical. The country was a perennial hotbed of bands and ultra-loyal fans, but never a capital of metal innovation. Munich's Sieges Even was one of the first German bands to break tradition, and they hovered at cult status for their entire career. But the same time that Sieges Even broke ground, a few others arose from Germany's fertile thrash scene and took the path of the black sheep.

Mekong Delta appeared from nowhere with its self-titled debut in 1987, with no previous demo recordings, no known live shows, no band photos, and very little press coverage. The new band immediately had an air of mystery. From the beginning, they walked hand in hand with obscurity. Nobody even knew the identity of the members. Even later, in what few pictures appeared on their albums or in fanzine articles about them, the members appeared as indistinct shadows or photonegative images. They also used pseudonyms. And their albums were rather difficult to obtain. All of this obfuscation created an aura of intangibility. Mekong Delta became an untouchable oddity in the metal underground. They got people talking, although they never exactly sold records by the truckload.

In reality, Mekong Delta had been formed by bassist Ralph Hubert (early alias—Björn Eklund). He played his instrument with a sensitivity and dexterity usually shown by jazz bassists and classical violinists. In fact, Hubert was heavily influenced by classical music, especially modern twentieth-century composers, and he fused that with thrash, birthing a new metal hybrid that went beyond the classical dabbling heard on Deep Purple and Yngwie Malmsteen albums. Mekong's metal was aggressive and raw, but never primitive. Classical music was clearly the main outside influence, and was incorporated so tastefully that it never came across as a mere novelty. Searching for an appropriate peer comparison, Mekong Delta can be likened to a tech-centric mixture of Megadeth, early Rage, early Blind Guardian, Yngwie Malmsteen, and late-'80s Destruction put through a merciless classical meat grinder—but ultimately it's futile to look for similar-sounding bands. Mekong stood apart from the rest of the underground, forever the underdog, eternally uncool. What could they expect? They named themselves after a region in Vietnam; took inspiration from H.P. Lovecraft (*The Music of Erich Zann*); covered songs by modern classical composers

Obscure and obscured: early
Mekong Delta image, 1988

and mid'70s-era Genesis; hardly ever played live; and never revealed their identities. They were continually stuck on small labels with little distribution outside their native Germany. Theirs was hardly a formula for success, but inside their own bubble, their integrity was never threatened. And mystery sometimes works wonders—proven by the intrigue that bolstered the legends of Bathory and Opeth in their early phases.

Hubert took Mekong Delta's classical element to its logical extreme when the band covered Mussorgsky's *Pictures at an Exhibition* in 1997. While their album of the same name was ambitious and even impressive in spots, it failed to convince. Prog rock giants Emerson, Lake and Palmer had already done a superior version in the early '70s. But throughout its career, Mekong Delta continued to interpret pieces by a variety of modern classical composers, proving an ability to hammer thrash and classical into unusual and demanding new shapes.

The paths of many veteran German musicians weaved through the Mekong Delta lineup over the years, as members of Helloween, Rage, Living Death, and Grave Digger all made appearances in the band. Hubert put all their talents to the test with his exacting, demanding compositions. The band's first vocalist, Keil, aka Wolfgang Borgmann, was admittedly a weak link. His thin and reedy voice struggled against the band's power. He was more at home singing '70s symphonic prog, which he did away from Mekong, where his vocal cues from Yes's Jon Anderson and Genesis's Phil Collins were better utilized. Borgmann's third album with Mekong Delta, 1989's *The Principle of Doubt*, showed an increased confidence, but he would not get the chance to improve further, as he was soon replaced by Doug Lee, from Florida progressive/power metal band Siren. Lee sang in a similar style to Borgmann—though more convincingly—throughout the 1990s on *Dances of Death* (1990), *Kaleidoscope* (1992), and *Visions Fugitives* (1994).

After 1997's *Pictures at an Exhibition*, Mekong Delta went on hiatus. Hubert resurrected the band in 2006 with Mekong veteran and ex-Helloween drummer Uli

MEKONG'S
CLASSICAL GAS

MEKONG DELTA LEADER RALPH HUBERT IS, in spirit, a classical musician using the modern tools of metal to build his work. While he claims Genesis, Yes, ELP, and King Crimson as major inspirations, he is even further indebted to modern classical composers, especially those of Russian origin. In fact, Hubert seems far removed from the metal stream in many ways—when asked by *Hard & Heavy* online magazine what he thought of tech-metal bands such as Spastic Ink, Spiral Architect, and Cynic, the bassist replied: "I haven't heard any of those names."

Classical compositions reworked by Mekong Delta:

"The Hut of Baba Yaga," 1987 (Modest Mussorgsky)

"The Gnome," 1988 (Modest Mussorgsky)

"Toccata," 1989 (Alberto Ginastera)

"El Colibri," 1989 (Julio Sagreras)

"Night on a Bare Mountain," 1990 (Modest Mussorgsky)

"Sabre Dance," 1992 (Aram Khachaturian)

"Dance," 1994 (Christopher Young)

Pictures at an Exhibition, 1997 (Modest Mussorgsky)

"Allegro," 2007 (Dmitri Shostakovich)

Hubert also composed his own classically oriented tracks, such as "Interludium" (two parts), "Allegro Furioso," "Moderato," and "Suite for Group and Orchestra." These are original classical pieces performed via metal instrumentation—as opposed to the majority of Mekong Delta songs, which are thoroughly metallic in essence and utilize a classical influence around the edges.

Kusch, shredder Peter Lake from Swedish tech death band Theory in Practice, and the band's best vocalist yet—Leo Szpigiel, veteran of a variety of bands including Scanner, Wolf Spider, Duke, and Crows. The band's 2007 return album, *Lurking Fear*, found the patented Mekong Delta sound at the core of a ball of nervy, anxious tech thrash. With a brittle, trebly recording, the album sat apart from the many sterile-sounding albums of the modern era, for better or worse. Vocalist Szpigiel left the band in mid-2008 and was swiftly replaced by Tomorrow's Eve's Martin LeMar. By 2009, Hubert found himself surrounded by yet another lineup, occasionally interrupting rehearsals for the band's ninth album, *Wanderer on the Edge of Time*, to play the odd summer festival. Still one of metal's best-kept secrets, Hubert has much to be proud of, but would likely agree that crazy-ass classical-inspired tech thrash just doesn't pay the bills.

Among hordes of metal purists, a few German radicals ventured outside tradition and explored various complexities by the late '80s. Ralph Hubert may have inspired some countrymen to walk paths less traveled, and elements of Watchtower and Voivod could be heard in a variety of German bands. Even traditional thrash legends such as Destruction briefly landed on the tech metal map. Their 1988 album, *Release from Agony*, revealed a far more meticulous, mechanical Destruction than the one that produced such relentless thrash classics as *Infernal Overkill* and *Eternal Devastation*. The weird phrasing in the title track, the eerie, acoustic-based "Sign of Fear," and the hectic stop-start nature of several other songs showed Destruction taking small steps into the wild world of tech. Guitarist Vladimir Leiviman of Russian tech metallers Hieronymus Bosch cites this era of Destruction as a major influence: "Destruction's *Release from Agony* and *Cracked Brain* period—I've never heard more sophisticated and melodic yet extreme music than those albums."

Destruction guitarist Mike Sifringer was vocal about his adoration for Watchtower, but not everyone in the band was equally committed. The awkward rhythms and mind-bending riffs of *Release from Agony* and its follow-up, *Cracked Brain*, went only halfway to tech nirvana. Tellingly, the band's lineup fractured with each successive release, and Destruction ultimately reverted to a safer, more predictable sound.

An even more unlikely band soon threw its hat into the German tech metal ring. Düsseldorf's Deathrow, also from the Noise Records stable, had proved itself a good old violent German thrash band with its first two albums, but third outing *Deception Ignored* (1988) showed a completely different attitude. Three original members had been joined by newcomer Uwe Osterlehner on guitar, who soon was praised for the band's radical shift—or showered with blame, depending on the ear of the beholder. Taking an angular, left-field approach to riff writing, extending arrangements to include seven-, eight-, and nine-minute songs, and disorienting listeners with a time change every few measures, Deathrow took an amazing leap forward; incredible, after previously revealing no such ambitions. Taking cues from Noise labelmates Voivod and future Noise act Watchtower, guitarists Osterlehner and Sven Flugge skronked and squeaked, while bassist Milo cleaned up his vocal approach, which featured strange high-pitched squeals. The same lineup was responsible for the band's final album, *Life Beyond*—released four years later on impossibly obscure German label West Virginia Records—but by then Deathrow had scaled back on the blatant weirdness.

Uwe Osterlehner, the man who thrust Deathrow light-years forward with contributions to such songs as "Machinery," "Narcotic," and the weird-ass instrumental "Triocton," hooked up with Psychotic Waltz's Norm Leggio and Dan Rock in 1992 for the one-off End Amen project. Their sole album, *Your Last Orison*, was lost to the obscurity expected of a union of two cult-level bands. Less technical than Deathrow's *Deception Ignored* and much less melodic than Psychotic Waltz, the End Amen release did not seem to be what anyone was looking for. Despite a guest appearance by Frank Zappa's son Dweezil, *Your Last Orison* disappeared quickly.

Somewhere between the established German thrash sound and underground death metal, a young band named Atrocity started off simply with its 1989 single, "Blue Blood." Featuring one of the tackiest pieces of artwork ever—the British royal family apparently drawn by a fourth-grader with drippings of, yes, blue blood running down the front—the single found Atrocity tackling social issues, and betrayed the influence of political hardcore in the band's music and imagery. Instead of repeating themselves, Atrocity stepped up to the next level with its 1990 debut, *Hallucinations*. Graced with H.R. Giger cover artwork, the album presented oppressive and threatening music, made otherworldly with choking death rasps by Alex Krull and fractured riff structures that sped by at seemingly dozens per minute. *Hallucinations* was built of eight disorienting death metal excursions, staking a new claim on the heavier side of the tech metal spectrum.

Photos inside *Hallucinations* show guitarist Mathias Röderer and bassist Oliver Klasen sporting Watchtower shirts, and the Texas band's influence became glaringly obvious on Atrocity's second album, *Todessehnsucht* (1992). The bass playing was pushed out front, and the riffs became colder and more difficult. A few clean guitar tones appeared in songs like "Godless Years," and big booming layers of choral vocals dressed "Sky Turned Red"—a song that also molested a familiar theme by composer Richard Wagner. The overall momentum of *Todessehnsucht* was less frantic than *Hallucinations*, but the arrangements were more complicated. The guitars were just as heavy, but had a rounder texture. Krull's vocals were more varied, ranging from a gruff yell to his more deathly growl. The album caught the attention of a growing progressive/technical death metal audience, and its reissue in 2008 proved popular with younger fans of tech death too young to latch onto the album the first time around.

Unfortunately, Atrocity's tech promise would never be fulfilled, as the band took a complete 180-degree turn on its third album, *Blut* (1994). Entering a traditional heavy metal mode, the band relied on lots of groove, and only showed a few glimmers of their previous approach. The album played on vampire themes and other gothic elements, and incorporated female backing vocals long before doing so became a trendy device in extreme metal. Clearly Atrocity was a brave band—and certainly a stepping stone for the more developed tech death mutants that came years later. They ventured farther afield into the land of new wave and synth-pop with *Werk 80* in 1997, interpreting tracks by Tears for Fears, Frankie Goes to Hollywood, and Duran Duran. *Werk 80 II* reprised the idea ten years later. Many fans never forgave Atrocity for abandoning their tech death direction—and after the *Werk 80* cover albums, maybe they deserved a little excommunication.

The onus was on others to carry the torch for extreme technical metal. Peculiar Austrian trio Disharmonic Orchestra met the demands of listeners wanting to walk on the wild side of the burgeoning death metal and grindcore scenes (one of their T-shirts proudly proclaims "Weird Musick Since MCMLXXXVII"). Their cover art favored Dalí-esque motifs, and their earliest stuff is left-field grind-laden death of unbelievable rawness, with song titles and imagery pointing to one completely demented group. Titles such as "Disappeared with Hermaphrodite Choirs" and "Quintessentially Unnecessary Institution" revealed a lack of proficiency in English or a bizarre sense of humor—or most likely both.

Weird and getting weirder: Disharmonic Orchestra with furry friends, 1992

Even if it was totally progressive compared to Austrian peers such as Pungent Stench and Disastrous Murmur, early Disharmonic Orchestra was not the musical scale molestation of conservatory student exercises. Their angular, cluttered riffs sounded like crude Hellhammer trying to play Voivod's most complex material, with a healthy dose of nihilistic grindcore tossed in for extra disorientation. Like Atrocity's debut, Disharmonic's first full-length, *Expositionsprophylaxe*, was released in 1990 on the Nuclear Blast label—an oddity overlooked by most and treasured by a lucky few.

Compared to the basement-level production of the debut, the follow-up, *Not to Be Undimensional Conscious* (1992), seemed like the slick stuff of a sweet major-label deal. Of course it wasn't. With longer songs, improved recording, and a more emotional approach, the album was engaging if you could handle its obtuseness. Especially remarkable was "Addicted Seas with Missing Pleasure"—another wonderfully nonsensical title—which sounded like the band's surrealistic artwork looked. On the massive, melancholy groove of "Groove," Herwig Zamernik's bass sound was particularly deadly, jutting out of fractured guitar riffs like thorns on a vine, often taking the lead melody. Martin Messner's drumming bordered on collapse in the most involved moments, though he always kept within the framework, precarious as it was. Much of "Time Frame," a six-minute instrumental, sounded like Dead Can Dance bulked up with spacey Rush-like melodies and melancholy doom riffs. And if anyone took the rap vocal in the middle section of "The Return of the Living Beat" seriously, the joke was on them. These were three very white guys from Austria in an avant-garde death/ grind band, posing on the back cover with teddy bears wearing Deceased baseball caps. Little else could be expected.

Not to Be Undimensional Conscious was a fascinating cacophony that twisted metal into crazy new shapes, and appealed to hardly anyone. So what? Disharmonic Orchestra returned afresh in 1993 with *Pleasuredome*, another huge leap forward. Prior to the album's release, guitarist/vocalist Patrick Klopf acknowledged, "We're always in a state of progress. We're always pushing ourselves. It's always a development. Every new song, we try to go into the next border of our ability."

Klopf noted influences that ranged from Florida death metal lords Massacre and sci-fi metal gods Voivod to old rock music and even jazz. All these sounds coalesced wildly on *Pleasuredome*. Klopf's growls found a throatier, comparatively human monotone, and their once-dirty sound was cleaned up considerably. The songs themselves had a more buoyant, propulsive flow. The bass was still busy as ever, carrying melodies more often than the guitar, while song structures were sharpened to make them more memorable. If "Where Can I Park My Horse?" disturbed the flow with its pop-punk abandon, the rest of the songs blanked it out in their wild unpredictability. The instrumental title track is especially remarkable. With perhaps the sickest fuzz-bass tone since '70s Dutch eccentrics Supersister, "Pleasuredome" is possibly Disharmonic Orchestra's most memorable song, appropriately acting as the centerpiece for one of avant-metal's true treasures. The band dissolved shortly after the release of *Pleasuredome*, returning without much celebration for 2002's *Ahead*, another quirky album that pushed their sound forward but again appealed only to a scant few. Long may Disharmonic Orchestra alienate the masses....

Up north in Finland, bands such as Xysma and Amorphis displayed their adventurousness by undertaking rapid changes in a short span of time. Xysma began as a Napalm Death–inspired grind unit, swerved into Carcass mode for one EP, and then hit their stride with eclectic death metal oddity *Yeah* in 1991. Guitarist Olli Nurminen notes that around the time of *Yeah*, various members "started to buy all those progressive albums, like Yes, King Crimson, and Frank Zappa."

Nurminen himself was in a "Black Sabbath period" at the time, and that rocking groove and eclectic imagery carried over to Xysma's second album, *First and Magical* (1993). Next came *Deluxe*—built on concrete-stiff riffs and an equally simplistic rhythmic bludgeon—by which time the band's influences had moved on to American independent noise rockers such as Helmet, Sonic Youth, and Dinosaur Jr. Underrated rock masterpiece *Lotto* followed, which found Xysma's sound influenced by the even catchier strains of bands such as Danzig and the Stooges. Xysma's career ended on an appropriately baffling note with the '60s pop/surf-rock inflections of *Girl on the Beach* (1998). Amongst metal's true progressives, Xysma took perhaps the most unpredictable path of all.

Fellow Finns Amorphis were conventional by comparison, but no less remarkable. They began by playing ultra-raw brutal death metal, worked through prog- and psych-inspired albums *Elegy* (1996) and *Tuonela* (1999), and finally settled on a consistent dark/rock/gothic metal hybrid. Saxophonist/flutist Sakari Kukko, leader of Finnish jazz/folk band Piirpauke, played on *Tuonela* and *Am Universum* (2001), while Amorphis covered psych forefathers Hawkwind's "Leviation" in the *Elegy* era. Probably the band's pinnacle, in terms of bridging metal and an older prog aesthetic, *Elegy* put the synths of Kim Rantala up front with the band's doom-laden guitars. Tracks such as "Weeper on the Shore" and "Song of the Troubled One" unified an earthy '70s vibe with the brooding dark metal so popular in Europe in the mid-'90s.

As Amorphis guitarist Esa Holopainen said of *Elegy*: "We all dig very different forms of music. I love '70s progressive music that was made with good taste—Camel, Pink Floyd, Led Zeppelin, the Who, King Crimson, Jimi Hendrix, Hawkwind. Even southern stuff like Allman Brothers and Lynyrd Skynyrd. Kim likes funk and soul like Parliament/Funkadelic. I could give you a book of the bands we dig."

Despite all the lineup and stylistic shifts the band has endured since, not to mention consistent commercial success, the most lauded Amorphis album remains doom/death epic *Tales from the Thousand Lakes* (1994). *Tales* was one of the earliest albums in the extreme metal movement to combine clean vocals, folk music, and

Kids from the thousand lakes:
Amorphis in 1994

traditional metal melodies with subterranean growls and crushing downtuned riffs. As Jethro Tull were marrying folk, blues, and other traditional music with hard rock and proto-metal at the dawn of the '70s with *Benefit* and *Aqualung*, so too were Amorphis attempting a similar hybrid that set them apart from the death metal norm.

Obscure Finnish act Decoryah maintained a more consistent direction during its short life. Over the course of two demos, two EPs, and two albums, the band colored the emerging gothic/death hybrid of the mid-'90s with shades of post-rock and ambient/darkwave. Often hurt by recording sessions that did no justice to their grandiose aims, Decoryah could have brought so much more. Their attempts at expanding the gothic death/doom formula, years before it began taking a wider hold in the mid-'90s, are laudable and worthy of reinvestigation.

Another perennially overlooked band from the Finnish metal scene, Paraxism evolved rapidly through several demos between 1992 and 1998, inserting squishy Moog synth sounds by 1995 and generally upturning their gargantuan death-groove any number of ways. Strange and compelling from beginning to end, Paraxism was way too weird to secure a proper label deal, and the band eventually faded away.

Equally weird, but more successful than other strange Finns, was And Oceans. A.O. specialized in melodic black metal with committed left-field tendencies, aggressive music wrapped in difficult conceptual themes and arty album covers. They found a home for their first two of four albums on the Season of Mist label, while large indie Century Media picked up the latter two, *A.M.G.O.D.* (2001) and *Cypher* (2002). By the end, an industrial influence had crept into their music, and the band dissolved to eventually reform as avant-garde experimental industrial act Havoc Unit.

Demilich stood firmly in Finland's strong death metal tradition while setting themselves apart within it. Their one and only album, 1993's *Nespithe*, featured unpredictable riff patterns, incredibly low pig-grunt vocals, and absolutely amazing song titles, including "The Planet That Once Used to Absorb Flesh in Order to Achieve Divinity and Immortality (Suffocated to the Flesh That It Desired)" and "The Sixteenth Six-Tooth Son of Fourteen Four-Regional Dimensions (Still Unnamed)." Catchy. Even crude early Finnish black metal act Beherit dug into weird worlds at the end of its first phase, issuing two totally electronic soundscape albums in mid-'90s (*H418ov21.C* and *Electric Doom Synthesis*).

But of all that emerged from Finland's healthy avant-metal underground, one of the first remains one of the weirdest: the awesomely named Funcunt. Later morphing simply into F, Funcunt/F was too weird for words. Songs like the twenty-minute "Pronimo" and 1993's *I-III* album will forever wallow in the furthest corners of obscurity. Don't look for them. You probably won't find them, and if you do, you probably won't like them.

Finland's extreme progressive metal pioneers inevitably spawned a second generation of younger bands, among them Umbra Nihil, who mixed difficult, angular, dark prog rock with Voivod-esque metal and Sabbathy doom. A contemporary of Umbra Nihil, the entity known as Aarni must be heard to be believed, and can only hope to be understood. More bands emerge every day, and in a country whose biggest metal bands regularly reach the top of the national charts (Nightwish and Sentenced being the leaders of the pack), the sheer number of such bands, and the variety they offer, is remarkable, especially given that Finland's population is several million less than that of many major U.S. cities.

The European extreme metal scene in the late '80s and early '90s introduced many bands that attempted to push metal's barriers to the limit. Most of them evolved rapidly and died early, or settled on a more conventional style that would assure them careers more rewarding than those enjoyed by the Funcunts and Xysmas of the world. Some, like Coroner, left a lasting legacy. Many bands in Sweden and Norway that took their first baby steps during this time would later emerge as vanguards of cutting-edge extreme progressive metal. Simultaneously, a variety of bands across the Atlantic in North America collectively defined the very essence of tech-metal and brought the sound aboveground. They sublimated the thrash and death metal genres in a wave of remarkable enthusiasm, and created a strain of progressive metal that would have lasting influence.

10. SUBLIMATION FROM UNDERGROUND III: NORTH AMERICA

"Science and music are very similar, and I think this is why many scientists are musicians—Einstein, for instance, played violin. They both focus on the creative and collaborative process, and this is the reason I love them both. I'm fortunate that I can do both science and music. For me, they feed off one another."—Kurt Bachman, Believer

CALIFORNIA DURING THE 1980s WAS INSANELY PRODUCTIVE for all kinds of heavy metal, including traditional metal acts such as Armored Saint, Omen, and Cirith Ungol, and the hair spray–happy L.A. glam bands ranging from Ratt to Guns N' Roses. Important seeds of death metal were sown there, too, by Slayer, Dark Angel, Autopsy, and Possessed. By the end of the 1980s, San Francisco's prolific thrash metal surge had become influential on a global scale, with Metallica, Exodus, Death Angel, Testament, and others becoming household names across the world.

Every movement has its outcasts, and San Francisco's Blind Illusion had to be the blackest sheep of Bay Area thrash metal. Formed in 1979 by guitarist Marc Biedermann and bassist Les Claypool in Richmond, an industrial town northeast of San Francisco, Blind Illusion's earliest songs were spaced-out iron psych, like Hawkwind meeting Blue Öyster Cult. Partly due to Biedermann's restless disposition and varied musical tastes, and partly due to a revolving-door lineup, Blind Illusion evolved constantly throughout the '80s. They jettisoned their early keyboard-driven material and adopted a crunching metal style in the veins of old Judas Priest, Angel Witch, and early Fates Warning for an untitled 1983 demo and their 1985 demo *Trilogy of Terror*.

Too heavy for Haight-Ashbury: Psychedelic thrashers Blind Illusion in 1988
L-R: Mike Miner, Marc Biedermann, Larry LaLonde, Les Claypool

Where San Francisco trailblazers Anvil Chorus left off, Blind Illusion took charge and forged ahead. Two subsequent 1986 demo tapes saw Blind Illusion absorbing the influence of the thrash metal wave exploding around them. After nearly ten years of development, Biedermann finally assembled a seemingly stable lineup, bringing on guitarist Larry LaLonde, fresh out of the dissolved Possessed, while founding bassist Les Claypool returned, having gained recognition with local club sensation Primus in his time away from Blind Illusion. Along with drummer Mike Miner, the band unveiled *The Sane Asylum* in 1988.

Biedermann was raised on classic rock like Cream, Led Zeppelin, and Jimi Hendrix, then fell in love with the progressive rock of the '70s, citing Rush, King Crimson, and Jethro Tull as major influences. Fusing those origins with gritty thrash metal and a versatile band of kindred souls, *The Sane Asylum* stuck out like a sore thumb amid other thrash albums of the era. Beyond the prerequisite intensity, the album rode a loose, jammy vibe that sounded buoyant compared to Blind Illusion's peers. Even the most intense songs, "Vengeance Is Mine" and "Smash the Crystal," were swirled with the essence of pot smoke and incense.

Nearly alone among dozens of thrash metal acts from the Bay Area, Blind Illusion represented San Francisco the hippie haven, home of Haight-Ashbury and the Grateful Dead. One of the more unorthodox songs on *The Sane Asylum* was "Death Noise," which featured interesting muted-string scraping and strange sound effects amid nimble bass acrobatics and jazzy swinging drums.

"Metamorphosis of a Monster" was a multipart epic ode to Mother Earth in which Biedermann conducted a choir of children, shown wailing their little hearts out on the LP's inner sleeve. Ending an atypical album by an atypical band, the lyrics hauntingly narrated a scene set by hypnotic rhythm and snaky bass lines:

> *One day the whales will walk the earth;*
> *hunter will become hunted;*
> *mammoth will unearth itself from its tomb of hibernation;*
> *he will sprout wings and fly.*
> *Man will be consumed by fire then condemned to the sea;*
> *burning eternally with salty water in the lung.*
> *Reborn. Reformed.*
> *The humble will adorn a new way without treachery or scorn.*

Following a brief guest spot on Blue Öyster Cult's 1988 concept album, *Imaginos,* joining many other guest guitarists, including Joe Satriani and the Doors' Robby Krieger, Biedermann set to work on the second Blind Illusion album. *The Medicine Show* took aim at a peculiar subject: the medical industry. Biedermann appeared borderline paranoid (or just mad Christian Scientist) when discussing the project with *Anti-Poser* fanzine in 1988: "Instead of striking out at politicians it's going after doctors, because they have a license to kill. They have all the drugs—the pure shit. A lot of doctors are set up, they have their degrees in chemistry and their little factories."

Biedermann promised to further the weirdo quotient on the album, likening new track "For Me I Am" to psychedelia, and comparing "Healing" to Pink Floyd meeting Led Zeppelin. He even promised an album-side-length epic titled "Espionage in Hell" that would "blow your mind." Sandy Pearlman, a crucial behind-the-scenes cog in Blue Öyster Cult's unique mythos, planned to produce *The Medicine Show*. A 1989 demo of some songs exists, but that's as far as it got.

The promise of a grand future beyond *The Sane Asylum* never came to pass, as Blind Illusion disappeared after some scant touring behind the album. Two key members of the group left. Larry LaLonde joined Les Claypool in Primus, and the band soon went from popular Bay Area club oddity to huge concert hall draw. Primus's kinetic left-field classic, 1990's *Frizzle Fry*, kicked off a frenzied period of activity leading to international acclaim. By 1994, Primus were opening arena shows for Rush, while Marc Biedermann had all but disappeared in Syd Barrett–like fashion. After a sabbatical to China to further his martial arts training, Biedermann put together another Blind Illusion lineup, this time a power trio, and demoed material that was radically different than *The Sane Asylum*, bringing the band full circle to the psych rock sound they'd forged in 1979.

⦿ ∘ ⦿ ∘

Two debut albums surfaced in 1988 that challenged the by-the-numbers approach of the thrash metal mainstream. Metallica had shredded the metal rulebook, and their thousands of followers were content to work within their blueprint. Two exceptions, Anacrusis and Realm—both hailing from the American Midwest—rattled the cages of thrash orthodoxy and made sounds that still resonate.

On their *Suffering Hour* debut, Missouri's Anacrusis named influences from Pink Floyd to Chicago doom band Trouble in addition to Metallica and Slayer. The album featured incredibly intense spots; insane hawklike screeches from guitarist Kenn Nardi were tempered by a clean vocal approach that could have crept in from gothic or new wave music. Although *Suffering Hour* hinted at a band possessing serious originality, in their early form Anacrusis was still largely pedal-to-the-metal rawness.

Anacrusis's second album, *Reason* (1990), showed incredible maturity. *Reason* brought out Nardi's gentler vocal character, and memorable melodic guitar lines played a bigger role. But *Reason* seemed a mere transitional step once 1991's *Manic Impressions* hit the racks. The band's abrupt mood changes could already be anticipated, but their impact was heightened by impossibly sharp production that turned their raw metal to cold gleaming chrome. By now the band appealed more to Voivod fans than Slayer diehards. They looked outside of metal for inspiration, nestling "I Love the

Anacrusis on the set for the "Sound the Alarm" video, 1993
(*Michael Henricks*)

World" by influential English post-punk/gothic rock band New Model Army into the running order as naturally as if it were an Anacrusis original.

In 1992, guitarist Kevin Heidbreder hinted at more changes coming. "There's going to be a lot of really neat things on the next record, stuff we always wanted to do but never had the opportunity. We're moving in the same direction, but broadening the horizons a bit; some abrupt mood changes and some experimental things."

With the release of 1993's well-titled *Screams and Whispers*, Anacrusis offered their defining statement. Songs such as "Brotherhood?" and "Tools of Separation" were completely atypical for a metal band, merging a futuristic coldness with ominous gothic atmosphere. The music was technical and mostly midtempo, yet still intense, free-flowing, emotional, and melodic. A texturally dense production was crucial in creating the album's unique atmosphere, as were keyboards and other effects.

Key songwriter Kenn Nardi's influences came from both within and outside the metal sphere, but his keyboard adventures were inspired by another innovative metal band. "I thought the way Celtic Frost incorporated keyboards on *Into the Pandemonium* was very inventive and added a real gothic tone to the music," says Nardi. "I wanted to take that even further, and use them in a more melodic way."

Surprisingly, Anacrusis enjoyed some MTV airplay, as *Headbangers Ball* occasionally aired the clip for album opener "Sound the Alarm." Then all went quiet on the Anacrusis front. The band shut down, and the lights stayed off until for almost fifteen years. In 2009, Anacrusis announced that their original lineup was reuniting for one show at Germany's Keep It True festival in the summer of 2010.

Years after their demise, Nardi described his plans for a fifth Anacrusis album that would have out-progged everything before it. "I think it probably would have been a few steps further in the direction of *Screams and Whispers*," he says. "Our strong point was our more melodic songs. I would have incorporated more orchestration in the vein of 'Grateful' and 'Brotherhood?'.

"After we broke up, I spent some time recording five or six new songs, and rearranged versions of my favorite Anacrusis songs: 'Stop Me,' 'Afraid to Feel,' and 'Far Too Long.' All the songs were arranged for bass, drums, guitar, and acoustic guitar—combined with full orchestral arrangements. It could best be described as Slayer meets the Moody Blues."

Ahead of their time? The band thought so. As guitarist Heidbreder recalls, "A record company executive once said to us, in the fall of 1991, 'The world just isn't ready for Anacrusis yet.' That seed was planted in our heads. We needed to get used to it, to accept that we were on our own."

Also emerging in 1988, as Anacrusis was releasing its first album, Wisconsinites Realm debuted with *Endless War*. Notorious for a speed metal rendition of the Beatles' "Eleanor Rigby," the album also showed influence from Rush ("Eminence"), and featured the busy structures and fifteen-riffs-per-song ideals of bands like King Diamond. The piercing Geddy-Lee-on-acid wails and chilling mid-range of vocalist Mark Antoni separated the band from the speed/thrash norm, placing Realm more in line with bands like Toxik.

The Milwaukee band returned in 1990 with second and final album *Suiciety*. Improving the song arrangements and adopting a super-clean production, the album featured an ambitious title track and plenty of shorter, faster cuts that proved the musicians were technically some of the best in the progressive thrash metal field at the dawn of the new decade.

Although Realm played complex and tangled stuff, the "tech" or "progressive" designations were hardly premeditated. "If we have to be pegged in a genre, I guess it would be progressive music," guitarist Paul Laganowski explained. "To us, it's not necessarily progressive, it's just what parts we write are what the song calls for. People would *really* be blown away if we intentionally wrote progressively. Because we have to tone down, it's like 'No, wait, this is way too much.' We'd end up sounding like Watchtower. I think they're a great band, but man, those guys are way over my head."

Heady Metal: Metal Blade Records advert, 1992

Realm drifted after *Suiciety*, just as Anacrusis had done after their fourth album. Both bands had trouble fitting in anywhere. Their audience was small compared to the multitudes following thrash or death metal bands that were more direct, less cerebral, and easier to absorb. Realm suffered a fate much like that of Psychotic Waltz or Mekong Delta—their ambition and talent was appreciated enough that perennial cult status was assured, but most of the metal audience couldn't be bothered.

Realm's last gasp was a 1992 demo that featured a cover of King Crimson's "One More Red Nightmare." Afterward, the guitarists and bassist connected with vocalist Buddo of Madison, Wisconsin, alternative/metal hybrid Last Crack, creating the new group White Fear Chain. The relative obscurity of both Realm and Last Crack seemed to combine exponentially and curse White Fear Chain, who started obscure and remain even more unknown today. Their sole release, 1996's *Visceral Life*, met a largely muted response.

○ ○ ○ ○

Northwards and far to the east of Wisconsin, two Montreal-area bands appeared that took a page from Voivod's playbook and blasted out their own unusual takes on thrash. Dead Brain Cells, better known as DBC, didn't seem like a promising prog prospect with their self-titled debut of 1987. Its hardcore trappings and streetwise grit showed no real sign of what was to come on the band's 1989 follow-up, *Universe*. The influence of Voivod could be heard scattered all over *Universe*. The album centered on a ridiculously ambitious concept about the Big Bang, evolution, and the rise of man—all told in thirty-seven minutes.

Universe unfolded at an authoritative, mesmerizing mid-tempo pace, with robotic monotone voices narrating over the semi-technical soundtrack. All the songs were shot through with interesting ideas, but DBC didn't quite have the imagination of fellow Quebec natives Voivod, and by its second half the album feels redundant. Still, *Universe* is a remarkable and commendable effort of Canadian cosmic drama—and one not without impact. "*Universe* was huge for us," says Cynic's Paul Masvidal. "The whole concept of that record, we were like, 'Okay, this band is cool.' Cynic were huge DBC fans."

High-concept Canadian metal:
DBC's *Universe*, 1989

While DBC offered one noteworthy progressive metal album, another Quebec band, Obliveon, delivered at least twice as many. Originally known as Oblivion, the band altered their name after learning of another Oblivion in the U.S. (At present count, encyclopedic website Metal Archives cites twenty-six bands who have used the name!) Making huge waves in the underground with 1989's *Fiction of Veracity* demo, Obliveon's first album, 1990's *From This Day Forward*, sounded like a spacey, highly technical version of late-'80s Sepultura. Blurring the lines of thrash and death metal, seven songs threw the listener into constantly shifting rhythms and churning, cyclic riffs played by musicians with apparent attention-deficit disorder. Though the whole wasn't super-memorable, the individual parts were utterly fantastic.

In some ways, DBC and Obliveon picked up the thread left behind when the ever-changing Voivod traded ferocity for cleaner, more subdued sounds in the late '80s and early '90s. As do most of Canada's exploratory metal bands, Obliveon guitarist Pierre Rémillard acknowledges the impact and influence of his fellow Quebecois progressives. "Voivod had a huge influence on us, for their unique approach in all different aspects—music, lyrics, and artwork. The fact that they were from Quebec, like us, and were making an impact on the international metal scene was inspiring as well."

Obliveon's second album, *Nemesis*, offered leaner arrangements yet was stacked with layers of intriguing complexity. Psychedelic, spectral guitar-generated atmospheres permeated such songs as "The Thinker's Lair" and "Factory of Delusions." *Nemesis* was a masterpiece of deadly futuristic tech, but the band failed to secure any kind of record deal for the album. The label that released *From This Day Forward*, U.K.-based Active Records, had gone bankrupt by the time *Nemesis* was ready. Obliveon eventually released it themselves 1993, and it has since been lauded as a tech metal cornerstone. The band's own pressing sold out quickly, and the album didn't receive official release until Canada's Pro-disk label reissued it in 2007.

Obliveon bassist Stéphane Picard
(drummer Alain Demers, background)
(*Michel Roy*)

Nemesis was drier than Obliveon's debut, and more challenging despite the cleaner, more concise arrangements. Churning with mechanical precision, it abounded with nuanced rhythmic subtleties and a chilling guitar tone. If cold atmosphere is a conspicuous trait of tech metal, then *Nemesis* is positively freezing. Along with Voivod's *Dimension Hatröss* and DBC's *Universe*, *Nemesis* completes a cosmic triumvirate that forever made Quebec a glowing location on the tech metal map.

Canvas Solaris drummer Hunter Ginn, a scholar of '90s tech, places *Nemesis* on a pedestal. "If someone asks me 'What does tech metal sound like?' I tell them it sounds like Obliveon's *Nemesis*. That is the very essence of tech."

Obliveon brought in a new vocalist for 1996's *Cybervoid*. The album was a step toward the modern aggro-metal of the time—burly, groove-oriented bands such as Pantera and Machine Head—but being Obliveon, it felt as removed from that muscular scene as it was a part of it. Some fans of the more erratic, unpredictable Obliveon were put off by *Cybervoid*'s wealth of groove, but a variety of spaced-out moments remained from their early days. Boasting an atonal, rhythm-centered approach that brought comparisons to Swedish tech chuggers Meshuggah and L.A.'s Fear Factory, *Cybervoid* and 1999's beautifully recorded *Carnivore Mothermouth* concluded Obliveon's career on a confident, but not hugely acclaimed, note.

Though the band achieved only cult status, Obliveon's many years of activity made for a body of work that the members now look back upon with fondness. Having produced *Nemesis*, *Cybervoid*, and *Carnivore Mothermouth*, Obliveon guitarist Pierre Rémillard now runs his own Wild Studio and is one of the producers most sought after by Canadian metal bands. He's comfortable in his behind-the-scenes role: "Obliveon lasted for fifteen years, and after that great experience, we all tried some other projects here and there, but nothing we felt like investing as much time and energy in as Obliveon."

O o O o

Back in the U.S., Pennsylvania band Believer also emerged in the late '80s with a sound and spiritual ideal that many considered irreconcilable. Christian bands such as Stryper were understandable: Despite their flashy, audacious image, half their songs were ballads, and even their heaviest material seemed unlikely to offend their main man upstairs. But when the members of Believer named devilish bands like Kreator, Destruction, and Slayer as inspirations while proclaiming themselves a Christian band, it appeared to be a case of cross-purposes.

Indeed, Believer guitarist/vocalist Kurt Bachman confirms those influences, and names Swiss thrashers Coroner, too: "We also listened to a lot of jazz, classical music, Rush, Watchtower, and Mr. Bungle." Bachman also defends Believer's synthesis of beastly music and scriptural lyrics: "We've always tried to get our listeners to think for themselves and fit the lyrics into their own lives on a personal level. Sometimes this works better with lyrics that are not so blatant. We have never been out to spoon-feed a particular message to anyone."

Historically, Christian metal bands rarely measured up to their more worldly counterparts. Many of them were transparently using the trappings of metal as a conduit for evangelism. Nobody expected this new extreme Christian metal band to be any different. Not helping matters, Believer's first album was released on Christian label R.E.X. Records, which lacked the distribution and secular credibility of Metal Blade or Noise Records. Despite remarkably tight playing and a distinctive guitar tone, 1989's *Extraction from Mortality* drowned amidst hordes of many generic late-'80s thrash albums. Ultimately, it did nothing to reveal the band's grand visions.

Believer entered the secular metal world in 1990, appearing on Roadrunner Records' *At Death's Door* compilation. That comp and Earache Records' *Grindcrusher* collection of the same year did much to announce the exploding death metal genre. Appearing with "Not Even One" from their debut, Believer's thrash-leaning sound was intense enough to hang amidst the heavier, more brutal, and decidedly non-Christian (even fiercely anti-Christian, in the case of Deicide) bands on the compilation. Roadrunner signed Believer upon the release of the 1990 comp, and the energized members wasted no time handing in their second album, *Sanity Obscure*, later that year.

Kurt Bachman's dry, desperate vocals might have been the only conventional-sounding characteristic of *Sanity Obscure*. Dissonant guitar riffs, unusual start-stop rhythms, and complicated arrangements revealed the band's tremendous growth. Amidst the intensity and complexity, two tracks found Believer bravely stepping away from their thrash/death roots. The album-closer, a cover of U2's "Like a Song," was an odd choice, and Bachman's vocals didn't exactly force Bono off the stage and into a full-time career of world diplomacy. The tremendous original "Dies Irae (Day of Wrath)," however, was a commanding presence and formed *Sanity Obscure*'s climactic center. The song can even be considered a creative watershed in metal—other than Mekong Delta, who regularly delivered classical-entrenched compositions, no extreme metal band had merged the genre with classical music so seamlessly and convincingly.

Inspired by Mozart's Requiem Mass, according to Bachman, "Dies Irae" took characteristics of bands as disparate as Kansas, Celtic Frost, and Italian-Slovenian experimental theatrical rock act Devil Doll, and foreshadowed the operatic approach of future metal bands such as Therion and Nightwish. The first three minutes were comprised of Latin verses sung by soprano Julianne Laird over chilling orchestrated strings and dark, droning sustained-note synthesizer effects. At the halfway point, Believer kicks down the door to lay out a spectacular heavy riff sequence in tandem with Laird and the classical strings. Violin and guitars join together, then duel, then join

Believer in 1990, L-R:
Joey Daub, Kurt Bachman, Dave Baddorf, Wyatt Robertson
(*Tom Storm Photography*)

again, taking the main themes of the song to a mind-melting climax—like a young, hungry Metallica jamming on one of Kansas's most complex tracks. "Dies Irae" could have collapsed in a pile of melodrama, but the band, guests, and engineers involved in its composition and performance managed to create an authoritative chunk of chilling, believable opera metal.

At merely five minutes and fifty seconds, "Dies Irae" nonetheless feels as monumental as one of Rush's bygone twenty-minute behemoths. Explaining the work, Bachman says: "Violinist Scott Laird wrote an intro piece for 1989 song 'Extraction from Mortality,' and we wanted to work on a more extensive tune with him again on *Sanity Obscure*. Using his sister, who was an opera singer at the time, came about after discussions on how to make this piece something new in the metal genre and push things creatively a bit further. If done correctly, metal and classical fit quite well together. Classical and metal are probably the two genres that have the most in common when it comes to feel, texture, and creativity. The creative sky's the limit in these genres. Anything goes."

Three years after *Sanity Obscure*, the band returned with a revamped, expanded lineup, and upheld the standard of "Dies Irae" by delivering *Dimensions*, an entire third album that was equally ambitious in scope. As tech metal albums go, it is a masterpiece of frigid guitar tones, warped riffs, and constant tempo changes. Whereas lyrics on previous albums were based on specific Bible verses, *Dimensions* saw the band going a step further and drawing from a variety of other philosophical sources, even texts that stood in opposition to their own Christian beliefs. Works by Thomas Altizer, Jean-Paul Sartre, Sigmund Freud, and Stephen Hawking were referenced, and Julianne Laird and the violins and cellos returned for the ambitious twenty-minute "Trilogy of Knowledge." With *Dimensions*, Believer had borne a dense, challenging monolith of progressive metal that has few equals, even years later.

In typical tech-metal tradition, Believer's life span was short. They seemed to put every ounce of living energy into *Dimensions*, and needed their proverbial seventh day of rest—which extended into a fifteen-year hiatus. During the break, Kurt Bachman earned a PhD in molecular medicine, and he now oversees his own cancer research laboratory. But metal never left his blood.

Along with another original member, drummer Joey Daub, Bachman resurrected Believer in 2008 with a revamped lineup for their fourth album, *Gabriel*, which the band likened to "a sick, insane cross between Tool, Voivod, Nine Inch Nails, and Destruction." Of *Gabriel's* creation, Bachman notes how the band composed in a completely new way. "With *Gabriel*, we were absolutely conscious of not wanting to repeat what we did before," he says. "We decided *not* to throw out riffs or structures that might not reach the technicality of our past. We used to push ourselves in terms of composition and technicality. Using different time signatures just became part of our natural thinking process. So we have been trying to compose more straightforward material—this has now become a new creative challenge for us."

Legendary Chicago doom metal outfit Trouble shared Believer's Christian mind-set, though they were much less obvious about it. In fact, they went to great lengths to distance themselves from the unfortunate "white metal" tag that the Metal Blade label used to market their albums. Trouble's grief-stricken atmosphere and commanding riffs became the prime inspiration for one of the most unique metal bands of all time—Raleigh, North Carolina's Confessor. Mixing the turbulent doom of Trouble with extremely difficult rhythms and the pained cries of vocalist Scott Jeffreys, Confessor never fit squarely into the doom scene. They had even less in common with their Earache Records labelmates, and were simply too original to belong anywhere but in their own microcosm.

Confessor's Ivan Colon, live in 1992

After circulating three underground demos between 1987 and 1990, Confessor officially debuted in 1991 with *Condemned*. They found an unlikely home with pioneering grindcore/death metal label Earache Records, who were challenged to market Confessor properly. *Condemned* was a survey of the band's demo material, with only one truly new track, "The Stain," on offer. While the two guitarists and bassist provided gravity with twisted, difficult doom-laden riffs, drummer Steve Shelton flailed his seven arms. He flaunted a University of Mars degree in polyrhythmic mastery. If the guitars played a 4/4 riff, Shelton took the high road and met them many bars later after weaving through a variety of off-time, off-kilter rhythms. His unusual approach is heard best on the title track, which seemingly lacks any identifiable time signature. His disjointed drumming rolls over the guitar riffs, taking flights to la-la land that only Shelton can comprehend.

Despite alienating a large core of the metal audience, Confessor's nonconformist approach to doom and unique technicality was praised by many camps. Fans of technical metal and math rock were on board. Pantera's Phil Anselmo and the members of doom/death pioneers Paradise Lost loudly supported Confessor. The drone duo Sunn O))) have been longtime fans of Confessor. Many modern death metal drummers such as Vital Remains' multi-instrumentalist Dave Suzuki and Malignancy's Mike Heller are vocal admirers of Confessor's Steve Shelton—as is ex-Soundgarden and current Pearl Jam drummer Matt Cameron.

Although the band has garnered some measure of acclaim, Confessor remains the blackest of the black sheep. *Condemned* was the only album recorded in their prime. They toured Europe with Entombed, Carcass, Cathedral, and later Nocturnus, attempting to take their odd prog-doom to the world. After a self-titled four-song EP in 1992—including two Trouble covers—things went quiet. Yet another incredibly talented and technical metal band died too soon, as Confessor dissolved by

1993. Scott Jeffreys went on to the doom groove of Drench, following an unfruitful Watchtower audition earlier in 1992. Most of the other members formed the groove-laden Fly Machine. Drummer Steve Shelton hooked up with Pen Rollings of math rock legends Breadwinner, bashing out instrumental music as Loincloth, who sounded like a fusion of their previous bands.

Tragedy brought Confessor back together. On February 15, 2002, original guitarist Ivan Colon died suddenly of cardiac complications at the age of thirty-one. The remaining members of Confessor reunited for a benefit show in their hometown, to aid his widow with resulting medical expenses. The strength of the performance and the overwhelming positive crowd reaction brought the band back in earnest. They wrote and recorded new material that eventually became 2005's *Unraveled*. The album features subtler rhythmic complexities than their 1991 debut, and the vocals are a bit fuller and more palatable, yet it still sounds like no other band.

Confessor's return underscored how ahead of their time they were in 1991, yet fifteen years later the world *still* didn't have much use for progressive tech-doom. But they are a prime example of the ranks of searchers who sublimated extreme metal in the '80s and '90s. Throughout North America, not forgetting Europe, an entire subset of thrash and death metal bands were performing at a remarkably advanced level.

Were the likes of Blind Illusion and Realm pushing the absolute furthest limits of the genre? Not really. Beyond the intrinsic sonic escape, they offered a new way of experiencing metal, consciously sidestepping the rigid creative stasis of a genre sometimes too proud of its legacy to look forward. Obscure acts such as Anacrusis and Obliveon sacrificed long careers and commercial viability in exchange for short, bright flashes of awesome oddity. Most of these bands were considered ahead of their time in their prime, at best, and flat-out ignored by many, in the worst cases. Predictably, their initial record sales usually reflected their specialized appeal. But as a new generation of metal fans explores the genre's history, that renewed interest has been answered with reissues, reformations, nostalgia tours, and sometimes even new music.

Metal's younger fans weren't old enough to experience the genre's paradigm shifters the first time. Curiously, tech metal pioneers such as Atheist and Cynic found a more welcoming reception nearly fifteen years after they were first active in the early '90s. And it was the home of those two bands—sunny, tourist-infested Florida—that forever put extreme progressive metal on the map.

11. SUBLIMATION FROM UNDERGROUND IV: FLORIDA

"The idea of a formula in music is alien and ridiculous to me. You let the song tell you what it's going to sound like. You don't come in with any preconceptions; you go with the flow, let the material itself guide you, and the result is always going to sound different. It should amaze the creator, not just the fan. You don't write for the fans, you write for the song. I don't feel a band should owe anything to their fans. They owe it to the integrity of the creation of art. You do it for the sake of the art." —Louis Panzer, Nocturnus

IMAGINE HEAVY METAL AS A DARK PATH DOWN A PERILOUS LANDSCAPE. Most who walk the path, castaways from a brighter world, don't dare to veer outside the path on their journey through the darkness. These are the Motörheads, the Slayers, the Panteras of this world; the dependable, focused leaders. And they have many disciples. Then, for every cluster of straight-line walkers, there is one outlier that takes a less-traveled path. When traditional heavy metal bands ruled the land, Fates Warning went in search of something deeper; when thrash metal reared its head and bands arose in droves, Voivod monkey-wrenched the works; so did uncompromising death metal bands—brutal, unmelodic forces of inhumanity—eventually number in the many hundreds, and there too would be men in this strange world mad enough to drastically retool its hulking engine.

Death metal, seemingly unalterable, proved to be remarkably malleable in the hands of such innovators as Switzerland's Celtic Frost and Austria's Disharmonic Orchestra. But the music wasn't just a European phenomenon, and it sometimes took root in unlikely places. Death metal originating in Brooklyn or Detroit is entirely believable. But Florida's death metal explosion during the late '80s and early '90s was something else. According to Nielsen SoundScan reports, the top six best-selling death metal bands of all time are from Florida. Worldwide sales of Cannibal Corpse, Deicide, Morbid Angel, Six Feet Under, Obituary, and Death albums surpassed the five-million mark as of 2009.

While part of the local metal legacy belonged to earlier bands like Savatage, Crimson Glory, and Nasty Savage, death metal became the style forever associated with the Sunshine State. Something about such brutal music taking hold in the land of sun and fun is too peculiar to ignore. From genre-defining legends Cannibal Corpse and Morbid Angel, to such obscurities as Tallahassee's D.V.C. (Darth Vader's Church), Florida's attractive postcard exterior was forever blemished. Band after band and album after album cemented Florida as the U.S. equivalent of Sweden, home to an equally unlikely death surge.

From those deathly roots grew a few oddball branches, which considerably toughened the shell of progressive metal. In 1983, three young Orlando-area teenagers became hell-bent on forming the heaviest band in the world. First calling themselves Mantas, members Kam Lee, Rick Rozz, and Chuck Schuldiner eventually switched to one unbeatably extreme yet ridiculously simple moniker: Death.

In the formative years of Death, members came and members often went—including Lee and Rozz. Meanwhile, captain Schuldiner grew up in public through the band. Over a seven-album run of unceasing evolution, Schuldiner took Death's lyrical focus from horror fantasies toward horrors of a more personal nature. The music he wrote followed a similar course, morphing from primitive bludgeon to something more cerebral during the band's fifteen-year life span.

The global tape-trading circuit widely spread a series of developmental demos by Death between 1984 and 1986—twenty-five demo tapes all told, including rehearsal and live tapes. Then Death unveiled its *Scream Bloody Gore* debut in 1987. The album was as important in establishing the American death metal sound as Possessed's 1985 debut *Seven Churches*, and was perhaps the most brutal metal album the world had yet heard. Even at that stage, still chasing unforgiving heaviness, Schuldiner warned that Death would not be easily pigeonholed: "We don't want to be like every other death metal band," he said. "We want to be a musical death metal band, and people say you can't do that. That's bullshit."

Schuldiner tore through members at an alarming rate, blinded to anything but advancing the band's sound while broadening the language of the genre. His singular vision led to his reputation as a tyrant and a difficult person to work with. Former Death member Paul Masvidal befriended Schuldiner during the band's demo days. "Like any artist engaged in his work, Chuck was highly, extremely sensitive," Masvidal says. "Over time I saw Chuck closing up. The business was turning in on him, and he became more and more detached.

He was having a hard time with it, and Chuck had episodes of extreme shifts in personality. Sometimes he'd be the warmest, kindest, animal-loving, pot-smoking sweetheart, and then there'd be moments when anxiety was riding high and you'd get another person completely. This was Chuck. This is what made him an interesting, multifaceted person."

Hemorrhaging members at the same time Schuldiner was rapidly advancing his musical capabilities, Death offered *Leprosy* (1988) and *Spiritual Healing* (1990) while drawing ac-

Death's watershed moment: *Human*, 1991

claim as state-of-the-art death metal. Though pure and total death, *Spiritual Healing* embraced a variety of tempos and focused on memorable, even melodic guitar solos. Schuldiner's vocal performance on the band's third album was entirely remarkable. Perhaps for the first time in death metal, though his wrenching scream still came from way down in the gut, the lyrics were intelligible. "It was this dry growl that no one had done before," says Masvidal. "Everybody was doing this saturated, wet growl, and here was Chuck with such presence in his voice. He was really good at enunciation. He had such good control over that kind of vocal."

With the fourth Death album looming, Schuldiner's growing compositional abilities found a perfect match in three impressive new recruits: two members of Florida band Cynic—guitarist Masvidal and drummer Sean Reinert—and bassist Steve DiGiorgio from California's semi-technical death/thrash force Sadus. The release of *Human* in 1991 changed everything—not only for Death and not only for Florida, but for the entire metal constellation. No band had previously balanced brutality and nuanced complexity like the new Death lineup.

Drummer Reinert brought to Death his background of equal parts metal, prog rock, and jazz fusion. More likely to sport a Chick Corea T-shirt than a Morbid Angel one, Reinert brought jazzy inflection to death metal's hammering double-bass attack. His slippery polyrhythms and spicy cymbal work propelled Death into new realms, bending Schuldiner's matured but still fairly straightforward riffing into complex shapes unlike anything else in the genre before that time. There were other technically adept drummers in extreme metal at the time, but no one offered the kind of flowing, sensitive approach that Reinert brought to *Human*.

Reinert's Cynic bandmate, guitarist Masvidal, brought an equally cosmopolitan element to Death. He weaved a series of jazzy, celestial leads and intricate chord voicings around Schuldiner's more conventional scale-based leads and heavy-handed rhythm playing, each guitarist perfectly complementing the other.

One of *Human*'s highlights, "Cosmic Sea" features ethereal production textures, heavily effected thematic melodies, bizarre guitar lead trade-offs, and a bubbling fusionesque bass solo. The instrumental is a pivotal moment in the advancement of death metal music. Guitarist Masvidal recalls Schuldiner's single-minded drive to push the boundaries. "He really wanted to raise the bar," Masvidal says. "He wanted to make the bass player more featured and prominent. Sean was coming in and rhythmically reinterpreting Chuck's riffs. I was doing all the rhythm guitars with Chuck and adding harmony and colors. Chuck was opening up to more progressive music with that record. I think he realized that after *Spiritual Healing* there weren't a lot of places to go in that realm, and this was the next phase for Death. Basically, it was his 'statement' record."

Significantly more highbrow than other death metal artwork at the time, the *Human* album cover paralleled Death's musical changes. Artwork by Rene Miville recalled *Gray's Anatomy* mutated through a ghostly filter of psychedelic visages. While Death's name and logo fit the music and almost cartoonish Ed Repka paintings on their first three albums, that blunt ugliness did not seem appropriate for *Human*. Schuldiner did everything he could to make the Death logo less tacky and more streamlined. But even with the blood and cobwebs gone, the logo still looked blocky, like a throwback to a cruder metal era. Later, the flaming inverted crucifix "T" became less inverted, its flames were extinguished, and the cloaked zombie head over the "H" disappeared. Somehow, the scythe dissecting the "A" never got axed.

Death's name and logo became relics of a past that Schuldiner couldn't shake. "I have never wanted to be a category of a category," he stated in 1998. "I started in 1983 and thought, 'This is it, I'm forming a heavy metal band.' It's *extreme* heavy metal. I outgrew the band name a long time ago. I don't mean that in a bad way. The only reason I kept the name was because people identify with it. It's a name they know. But because of the name, we tend to get labeled in a category that I don't feel comfortable being in."

For all its musical virtuosity, *Human* did not lack power. Producer Scott Burns—then an in-demand death metal production guru—capably captured both the rawness and the finer nuances of *Human*. He helped focus the album, deftly balancing its overwhelming aggressive drive with the sleek, subtle elements put into play by Schuldiner, Reinert, Masvidal, and DiGiorgio.

But Burns's work was not perfect: Steve DiGiorgio's spidery fretless bass was a buried, subaudible tone. Going by what can be heard, in addition to his work on a variety of other recordings since, DiGiorgio is a master player, one of the most consistently dependable four-stringers in metal. Reinert and Masvidal exited Death after the ensuing *Human* tour to focus on recording Cynic's debut album—a debut that would be as hugely influential as *Human*, yet much further removed from death metal roots. DiGiorgio stayed with Death, and would have his four-string voice heard on the next album.

Schuldiner and Death pursued the sound and approach unveiled on *Human* throughout the following three albums, with changes occurring in smaller increments each time. The considerable leap forward from *Spiritual Healing* to *Human* was a distance the band never needed to jump again—Death had found its sound. With this trickier, more challenging version of Death, Schuldiner and his cohorts consistently pushed onto the front lines of forward-thinking metal.

Individual Thought Patterns in 1993 boasted the biggest names of any Death album. DiGiorgio and his unique fretless playing remained from *Human*, finally stronger in the mix. Ex–Dark Angel drummer Gene Hoglan per-

Only human:
The late Chuck Schuldiner
(*Mike Coles*)

formed beyond expectation. He was a harder hitter than Reinert, but played with the jazzy sensitivity so critical to Death's new approach. The addition of guitarist Andy LaRocque, King Diamond's perpetual left-hand man, seemed too good to be true. And indeed, LaRocque didn't last longer than many other members in Death's revolving door. He reeled off typically amazing leads throughout *Individual Thought Patterns*, but recorded no rhythm tracks.

Death followed up in 1995 with *Symbolic*, which saw DiGiorgio and LaRocque replaced by relatively unknown local Florida musicians Kelly Conlon and Bobby Koelble. The band's sound was brighter, less frantic, and probably more accessible—thanks to blunter, more straightforward songwriting. The album had a clean, punchy sound, and was the first Death album since 1988's *Leprosy* to feature a producer other than Scott Burns. Morrisound Recording owner Jim Morris stepped in to oversee the sessions, and his melodic sensibilities proved a perfect match. "I had respect for him from all the stuff he's done with Savatage and Crimson Glory," Schuldiner explained soon after.

A longtime fan of homegrown Florida acts Savatage and Crimson Glory, Schuldiner also looked up to Queensrÿche and Watchtower. The Death leader's growing love for highly textured, technical, and melodic metal helped him break out of the box where so many other extreme musicians had gotten comfortable. Even in 1995, after he'd repeatedly surpassed expectations, he was still fighting against death metal stereotypes. "I'm sincerely trying to break down barriers commonly associated with this style of music," Schuldiner said. "Death wants to reopen the idea of unlimited musical potential within a seemingly limited musical genre. That's what the '70s and to some degree the '80s were all about."

Perhaps to escape the categorization he despised, Schuldiner put Death on ice shortly after *Symbolic*'s release. He formed a new band called Control Denied, intending to expand into more classic metal sounds, including melodic vocals that never would have worked in Death. But before Control Denied was able to record an album, the legacy of Death came back to seduce Schuldiner one last time. In 1998 he put together an all-new lineup for Death's seventh and final album, *The Sound of Perseverance*, intending to revive Control Denied at the conclusion of the imminent tour.

With a hungry new crew of young players, *The Sound of Perseverance* revisited the energy and complexity of Death's early-'90s *Human* era. For the first time since Death's earliest days, Schuldiner constructed a lineup composed entirely of relative unknowns. He certainly picked the right guys—the trio of players collectively hailed bands such as Rush and King Crimson along with prog metal favorites Fates Warning, Watchtower, Cynic, and Symphony X—and they performed like seasoned pros.

Jim Morris returned to produce *The Sound of Perseverance*, and he saw the material as bridging an important gap. "There are some bands that are extreme for extreme's sake," he said during mixing. "That's not something I'm interested in. I love heavy stuff but I also like to hum the song. I doubt you're going to catch 'Scavenger of Human Sorrow' in the elevator, but you can sing these songs, you can sing the guitar parts. People into Queensrÿche will be able to get stuff off this record, as will people into Morbid Angel."

Despite the subsequent acclaim for *Perseverance*, Schuldiner soon put Death to rest once and for all. He brought along *Perseverance* players Richard Christy on drums and Shannon Hamm on guitar for the long-awaited debut by Control Denied, *The Fragile Art of Existence*, a strong first step onto a new musical path. Also featuring Tim Aymar's forceful and melodic vocals and Steve DiGiorgio's dependable bass work, Control Denied garnered the same voluminous praise that had been heaped upon Schuldiner's previous band.

Sadly, the title of the album hit too close to home. Before *The Fragile Art of Existence* was released in 1999, Schuldiner was diagnosed with a brain stem tumor. He battled through it fearlessly, keeping an unshakable positive outlook even in the darkest of times. During one of his last hospital stays, a friend asked about his health. Schuldiner steamrolled over the small talk and began detailing the music he was working on for Control Denied's second album, his ideas for the next phase of the band, and his current listening favorites. He never spoke a word about Death—or death—and instead glared stubbornly into his ideal future. For a man who had been so single-minded in his efforts to move metal above and beyond, his attitude was appropriate and unsurprising. Schuldiner ultimately succumbed to the disease on December 13, 2001—just over ten years after the release of the groundbreaking and revered *Human*.

As Death matured in the early '90s, other Florida bands experimented with the newborn death metal form. One oddity, going by the ridiculous name of Hellwitch, flooded the tape-trading underground with no fewer than five demos before unveiling their 1990 debut. Bearing the bizarre title *Syzygial Miscreancy*, the album offered such unusual material as "Sentient Transmography" and "Mordirivial Dissemination"; songs that sounded like Kreator and Morbid Angel sweating through Rush songs played backwards on water-damaged tape. Crazily intense and weird as hell, none of Hellwitch's other recordings display the daring of *Syzygial Miscreancy*. The follow-up *Terraasymmetry* EP of 1992 and *Omnipotent Convocation* full-length in 2009 only hint at the debut's left-field orientation.

Nocturnus, which started as an occult-oriented band, eventually took its death metal down a sci-fi path. Founded by original Morbid Angel drummer Mike Browning, Nocturnus operated between the bludgeoning heaviness of the patented Florida death metal sound and the more adventurous bands within and outside of the state. Centered on the lead guitar work of Mike Davis and Sean McNenney, the Tampa group steered the Morbid Angel style they plied on their early demos into an ungraceful cosmic clutter on 1991 debut *The Key*. The album's liberally applied keyboards garnered a lot of attention, lifting *The Key* up as a work of death metal innovation.

In the early '90s, a death metal band with a full-time keyboardist was a wild novelty—and an absurdly big deal was made of it. Keyboardist Louis Panzer was hardly a prodigy on the level of a Rick Wakeman or Keith Emerson, but his beds of synth layers brought a distinctly stellar atmosphere to tracks such as "Neolithic" and "Droid Sector." But it was the guitar team of Davis/McNenney that truly pushed Nocturnus into stranger realms, with artistic destruction of the whammy-bar, amazing sweep-picking fluidity, impossibly fractured riffs, and strange melodic choices.

A space oddity: Nocturnus's cold, cold, cold *Thresholds*

While the music of such Florida gods as Morbid Angel and Cannibal Corpse reveals moments of perplexing technical prowess, it would probably be a stretch to place them amongst Florida's progressive extremists. Where Morbid Angel sometimes offered organ segues and moments of arty diversion (as on their *Heretic* album), and Corpse albums such as *The Wretched Spawn* are technically exacting, both bands blasted and bludgeoned more than they experimented. Bands like Hellwitch and Nocturnus, however, reveled in left-of-center ideas. Their commitment to originality all but guaranteed obscurity.

By their second album, *Thresholds,* Nocturnus were much further outside of the box than Florida's death metal mainstays. A celestial, futuristic excursion, *Thresholds* represents the band at its technical outer limits. A muffled production adds to the alien vibe of the album, appropriately sounding as if it was recorded in a cosmic void and not, in fact, at the earthbound location of Tampa's Morrisound. Despite blocky drumming and generic death metal vocals, *Thresholds* gained respect from the tech metal crowd. Panzer's keyboards were more integrated throughout the album than they had been on *The Key*, even playing a commanding role in songs such as "Arctic Crypt" and the crystalline neoclassical-meets-*Star-Wars* instrumental "Nocturne in

Bm." For all its faults, *Thresholds* remains the ultimate in freezing anti-groove.

When the majority of Florida bands went one way—toward total brutality, acceptance amongst the *Headbangers Ball* demographic, and long careers—Nocturnus went the other. They were outcasts, to be certain. Keyboardist Louis Panzer compares his band to another group of misfits on the Earache roster—former touring partners Confessor. "We really respected that Confessor weren't afraid of breaking tradition," Panzer says, "because that's what we felt we were about: breaking new ground and setting new standards. We were never attracted to doing the same thing as everybody else. We were very much about the soloing guitars, the keyboards and themes that weren't going to pigeonhole us into any particular type of thing."

As did those of a multitude of other technically demanding acts, Nocturnus's career rapidly collapsed. The sacking of founding member Mike Browning led to a disappointing period. The band was dropped by Earache in the death metal–saturated mid-'90s, and other labels were not interested. But Nocturnus never regretted letting Browning go. When the band briefly regrouped a few years later, Browning wasn't contacted. "[Mike's playing] limited what we could do," recalls Panzer. "We had to tell him what to play, and that was holding us back. We wanted somebody who could jump in and add something, somebody who was powerful and tricky, who could make use of the space and not just be a pounding machine."

Nocturnus returned in 2000 with appropriately named new drummer Rick Bizarro and released the *Ethereal Tomb* album, but its more subtle character and rigid rhythmic churn failed to capture the excitement of some old fans. They made no attempt to outdo *Thresholds*. The band was apparently not interested in exponential forward evolution, but the album had positive qualities regardless.

As for the dudes in a Sarasota, Florida, band clumsily dubbed R.A.V.A.G.E., a rush forward with every single endeavor was the only way to go—emphasis on the Rush. After a couple demos, R.A.V.A.G.E. became Atheist and released *Piece of Time*. That debut—released in 1989 in Europe and nearly a year later in the U.S.—was just as intense as comparable efforts by such semi-technical death/thrash bands as Hellwitch or Sadus, but Atheist showed a more controlled, refined approach. Drummer Steve Flynn openly named Neil Peart as his number-one influence, and Atheist's guitarists snaked around his busy drumming like jazz adepts possessed to kill.

Part of Atheist's off-kilter style was due to guitarist Rand Burkey's unusual approach. Both he and guitarist/vocalist Kelly Shaefer were left-handed, and Shaefer had learned to play using a custom-made left-hand guitar. But Burkey, a self-taught player, simply picked up a right-handed guitar and learned everything upside down.

Only high-caliber players could hang with the unorthodox guitarists in Atheist, and bassist Roger Patterson was a prodigy on the level of Metallica's Cliff Burton. Fluid as hell, even at dangerous velocities, Patterson was perfect for the band's psychedelic Slayer-esque death/thrash. Tragically—his demise eerily similar to that of Burton—Patterson was killed in a van accident in 1991 as the band was driving home from a cross-country U.S. tour.

After mourning and some heavy reevaluation, the remaining members fleshed out the last songs they had written with Patterson and set to work on album number two. They attempted to reel in Watchtower bassist Doug Keyser and, failing that, brought aboard Cynic bassist Tony Choy, with whom they recorded tech-metal monument *Unquestionable Presence*.

Exhibiting more jazz and prog rock influences, *Unquestionable Presence* merged scathing intensity, thoughtful lyrics, constantly shifting tempos, and highly skilled playing. A worthy tribute to the lasting influence of Patterson—who cowrote a handful of riffs and helped shape the direction of this particular Atheist era—*Unquestionable Presence* is yet another ahead-of-its-time landmark in the progressive music sphere. Ignored by much of the death metal fan base and the metal press upon its release in 1991, over the years the album gained stature as a tech metal cornerstone.

In the liner notes to the 2005 reissue of the album, Shaefer explained one of Atheist's favorite creative catalysts: "We smoked a lot of weed. It opened up our arrangements and led us to our style. I am a firm believer that some of the best music ever written was done under the influence of substances, be it alcohol, weed, or something else. Unfortunately, it has also led to the demise of some of the greatest artists of our time. But man, did we get some great music out of it! We loved to smoke and write the craziest shit we could think of and then practice for hours."

Atheist in 1992, L-R: Steve Flynn, Kelly Shaefer, Rand Burkey, Darren McFarland
(*Michael J. Mulley*)

Shortly after recording *Unquestionable Presence*, Choy bailed for the Dutch band Pestilence. The three core members of Atheist located yet another impressive bassist in Darren McFarland. They did some more touring—including a U.S. jaunt with Cannibal Corpse and Canadian newcomer Gorguts—and were heckled by narrow-minded death metal audiences on several occasions.

More internal disruption occurred when drummer Steve Flynn took leave of Atheist, leaving guitarists Shaefer and Burkey to pick up the pieces. But in a late 1992 interview with *Symposium* fanzine, Atheist seemed to be falling out of focus for the duo. Instead, they talked enthusiastically of their side projects—the Alice in Chains–esque Neurotica for Shaefer, who went on to a small degree of success, and stoner rock group Euphoria for Burkey. They sang the praises of marijuana—always a favorite Atheist topic—professed their continued love for the Beatles, Rush, and King Crimson; and discussed their interest in the emerging Seattle sound. They even commented on the weather in Florida—any topic but new Atheist music. But when their record label pressured the band in 1993 to fulfill their contract, the duo had to scramble. Shaefer freed himself from the guitar to concentrate solely on vocals, and they coaxed Tony Choy back into the fold. With a new drummer and second guitarist in tow, the third Atheist album, *Elements*, was written, recorded, and mixed in a fortyday binge in the spring of 1993.

While the peculiar *Elements* does sound hurried, the album is still a work of great depth, informed by Rush and jazz fusion bands as much as by Slayer and Possessed. The eight longer songs—titled "Air," "Earth," "Fire," "Water," and so on—were easier to comprehend, flowing with momentum very unlike the panicked vibe of *Unquestionable Presence*. Atheist seemed to be attempting a more listenable strain of complexity, giving strange melodies and numerous mood shifts more space to let the music breathe. Four shorter songs featured compositions by each instrumentalist, à la Yes's *Fragile* album, the most remarkable being Tony Choy's left-field "Samba Briza." The two minutes of Caribbean jazz placed nine minutes into *Elements* underscored how driven Atheist was to be completely and utterly different.

"*Unquestionable Presence* flew right the fuck over everyone's head," Kelly Shaefer said in 1992. "Everybody's into Obituary and stuff now, and I love all that. That's fine. Unfortunately we're caught in that same scene, where they see us as being wimpy. Music is music, but we're in an entirely different league. We spend lots of hours working on tiny things that probably no one will ever notice, subtleties that you hear but don't realize you hear them. With other bands you tend to not get that. Once you hear it one time, you've heard it and that's it. I like to listen to something and hear different things every time."

Elements capably closed Atheist's legacy of technical/progressive intensity. Relapse Records reissued the three Atheist albums in 2005, and the response from a new generation of metal fans proved Atheist had grown much more popular long after their demise than when they were active. Time had finally caught up with Atheist; by 2006, Shaefer, Flynn, and Choy began making appearances on the European and American festival circuits with members of Atlanta band Gnostic filling out the lineup. Their shows culminated in a live album, with a comeback studio album due for release in 2010.

Nocturnus's *Thresholds* and Atheist's *Unquestionable Presence* and *Elements* are lasting, important works of progressive death metal. The last several Death albums are equally revered. But *Focus*, by the incomparable Cynic, is the only Florida-spawned

Rush's Geddy Lee in the limelight–
Moving Pictures tour, 1981
(*Frank White*)

From top: Fates Warning circa 1989 (*Mark Weiss*);
Jim Matheos leads Fates Warning at
ProgPower USA, 2009 (*Christina Ricciardi*)

Prog metal royalty: Queensrÿche's Geoff Tate,
live in 2006 (*Cristel Brouwer*)

From top: Dream Theater's John Myung and
John Petrucci in 1989 (*Frank White*);
The goodwill ambassador of prog metal, Mike Portnoy of
Dream Theater (*Ann Marie B. Reilly*)

"Marty Friedman and I asked Allan Holdsworth about his music theory, and he whipped out this chart and started to explain it to us. Marty and I had no freaking idea whatsoever what he was talking about!"
–Ron Jarzombek

!!!

From top: Watchtower's Ron Jarzombek (kneepads) and Doug Keyser (the other one) stun a German festival crowd in 2000 (*Gerrie Lemmens*); Jazz/fusion luminary Allan Holdsworth flips out guitarist Ron Jarzombek of Watchtower/Spastic Ink/Blotted Science at the World Guitar Congress in 2004 (*Marty Friedman*); Dan Rock of Psychotic Waltz (*Danielle Gallanti*)

Top: Voivod summons tornadoes in 1987 (Frank White);
Bottom: Magazine ad for Voivod's *Nothingface*, 1989

Top: Pain of Salvation's revered Daniel Gildenlöw (*Todd Brown*);
Bottom: Atheist's Kelly Shaefer in 2007 (*Mike Coles*)

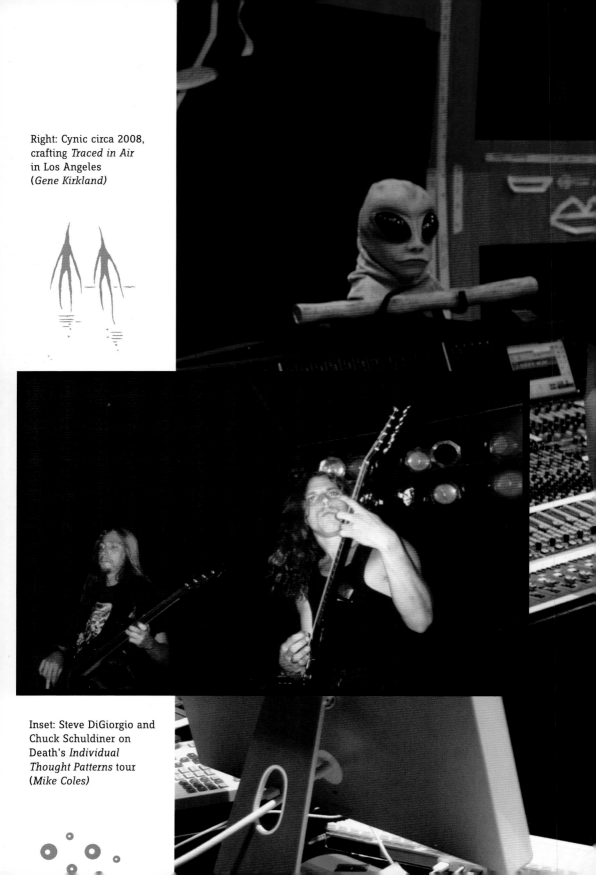

Right: Cynic circa 2008,
crafting *Traced in Air*
in Los Angeles
(*Gene Kirkland*)

Inset: Steve DiGiorgio and
Chuck Schuldiner on
Death's *Individual
Thought Patterns* tour
(*Mike Coles*)

Clockwise from top:
Evergrey and string quartet, 2006 (*Todd Brown*);
Angra live, 2005 (*Todd Brown*);
Michael Romeo of Symphony X (*Cristel Brouwer*)

ockwise from top:
ero Hour lets rip (*Kristina Malzahn*);
oog metal: Canvas Solaris (*Esa Ahola*);
goist's Stanisław Wołonciej
Wojciech Szadorski)

Background: Rune Eriksen (aka Blasphemer) of Mayhem (*Andreas Torneberg*);
Inset: Norwegian shape-shifters Ulver (The End Records)

From top: Shipwrecked frontier pioneers Arcturus in 2005 (*Kim Sølve*);
Cosmic heirs Enslaved, 2008 (*Karoline Bruland Moen*)

Clockwise from facing page top: Meshuggah (*Micke Sandström*); San Francisco's Hammers of Misfortune in 2008 (*Profound Lore*); Prog-death artists from Russia, Hieronymous Bosch; Mikael Åkerfeldt of Opeth (*Frank White*)

Clockwise from lef
Therion's Christofer Johnsso.
(*Cristel Brouwer*)
Maudlin of the Well, liv
(*Ted Tringo*)
Between the Buried and Me, 200
(*Frank Whit*)

album that equals Death's tech-heavy and groundbreaking *Human*. Chuck Schuldiner spotlighted the talented band when he recruited two Cynic members to play on *Human*; but Cynic's recorded work up to that point—four demos between 1988 and 1991—gave little indication of the creative strides and eventual lasting influence of their 1993 debut.

Cynic in the demo days, 1989. L–R: Sean Reinert, Jason Gobel, Tony Choy, Paul Masvidal (*Michael J. Mulley*)

After touring for Death's *Human* album was complete, drummer Sean Reinert and guitarist Paul Masvidal regrouped with guitarist Jason Gobel and set to work on the long-anticipated first Cynic album. The band had one year earlier recorded a three-song demo for Roadrunner Records, consisting of complex, difficult death metal comparable to Atheist's second album. The songs on the Roadrunner demo—"Uroboric Forms," "The Eagle Nature," and "Pleading for Preservation"—were more fluid and memorable than previous demos, with earlier thrash metal tendencies fading from view.

Cynic's heavily traded early tapes were interesting slices of complicated, gnarled death/thrash, but the erratic song structures and lack of repeating parts only effectively blew minds on a stiff, cerebral level. The early material lacked cohesion, as Masvidal later acknowledged. "We used to have songs with a beginning, middle, and end—they would rarely repeat ideas," he says. "With those songs we had a whole bunch of different moods within a song, whereas now we're trying to have a song with one strong feeling."

Even the 1991 Roadrunner demo, a taste of the direction of their imminent debut, hardly embraced a less-is-more approach. By 1993, however, when the lush, expansive, innovative *Focus* album finally appeared, Cynic had evolved by a few enormous steps. On a continual quest to become better players, the members had been taking lessons from jazz fusion instructors. The members' interest in forms outside of metal music—jazz subgenres such as be-bop and fusion, classical composers like Debussy, even synth-pop like Missing Persons—contributed in part to the maturation displayed on *Focus*. But an unpredictable, destructive act of nature proved to be a more significant catalyst.

Hurricane Andrew ravaged southern Florida in August 1992. Despite the resulting havoc, Masvidal calls the calamity "a blessing in disguise."

"It literally wiped out southern Florida," he says. "Leveled it, including Jason's whole home. We were watching trees fly by. It was just totally surreal, like out of a movie. Everything was destroyed, including our rehearsal studio. We had to start over. But it was so great, because I locked myself back up in my room and got to work and focused on what needed to be done. We all made leaps and bounds as musicians, and I got to the core of the Cynic language. It was in that year that we refined *everything*."

The results bore little resemblance to the Florida death metal scene that nurtured the band. Like Cynic's demos, *Focus* was complex and technically proficient, but the comparisons ended there. *Focus* carried a sense of elevation, of sublime musical journey. Eight songs followed an airy and accessible flow that belied the music's many complexities. Technicality was no longer the be-all and end-all—now virtuosity was simply the means to an end, first and foremost serving the songs. The gauzy guitars sounded softer than previous recordings, even somewhat distant. The propulsive rhythms and contrapuntal guitar layering shared as much with intense jazz fusion as with metal. The material's only literal link to death metal was the occasional raw vocal passage, performed by briefly enrolled Cynic member Tony Teegarden. Other vocals included Masvidal's processed robotic voice, and guest Sonia Otey offering a spoken mantra for "Sentiment." New bassist Sean Malone—a music teacher and author of bass theory books—was a clean-cut outsider, even among outsiders. His jumpy, active explorations on the bass added to the liquid movement of the material.

Instrumentation on *Focus* was more varied than on the Cynic demo tapes, including guitar synths, electronic drums, keyboards, and the Chapman Stick—a ten-stringed oddity designed to be played solely via two-handed tapping. Masvidal's growing interest in yoga, meditation, philosophy, and spirituality inspired the lyrics, an alternative to the gore and violence embedded in the music of the band's Florida

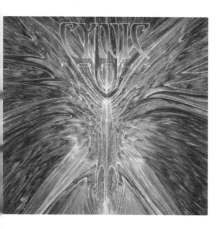
Perhaps the only good outcome of Hurricane Andrew: Cynic's *Focus*

peers. Cynic's message was more hopeful than the scathing political/social critiques of Atheist, or the vitriolic accusations in Chuck Schuldiner's lyrics for Death. Put simply, *Focus* didn't fit anywhere. The album was highly criticized at the time of its release in June 1993, flatly dismissed by death metal diehards who had a tough time with its colorful approach. *Focus* was so progressive that it nearly shot Cynic out of the metal genre the band had grown up in.

Focus was misunderstood before it was even released. Producer Scott Burns had worked on Cynic's demos and countless albums by other death metal bands, yet Masvidal recalls how the producer couldn't connect with *Focus*. "He did not understand what we were doing," says Masvidal. "Scott isn't a musician—he's a scientist, a computer guy—and he didn't really understand where we were coming from. There was so much tension and discomfort in the studio. Scott was saying, 'Wait till [Roadrunner Records'] Monte [Conner] hears this, he's gonna freak out! And now there's this computer vocal!' We had to go with our gut instincts and believe in what we were doing."

Touring to promote *Focus* was bound to be a trip down a thorny trail, considering the album's highly unorthodox nature. Canvassing Europe with death-turned-tech band Pestilence proved to be a highlight—though the gigs were hampered by the cold reception Pestilence received for their own progressive departure, *Spheres*.

A totally mismatched U.S. tour with Cannibal Corpse and Dutch death metal purists Sinister did nothing to place Cynic in front of the proper crowd. Being heckled by shouts of "You suck!" night after night was a deflating experience for Cynic's peaceable, sensitive members. For many Cannibal fans, the sight of headless Steinberger guitars, a growling female vocalist playing keyboards, and deeply tranced-out musicians playing in shut-eyed serenity was just too much.

"We didn't get a lot of love on that tour," Masvidal remembers. "Not being mean, but it's meatheaded. It's that kind of primal fan that doesn't want to think too much. We love the guys in Cannibal Corpse and they were cool, but their music is so visceral and more about something else."

Their frustration with touring compounded by never-ending music business hassles, Cynic collectively decided there had to be better ways to release their creative energies. "In the end, it killed us," says Masvidal. "Here we were by '96—done, essentially."

The core of Cynic—Masvidal, Reinert, and Gobel—shifted their attention to Portal, a post-rock project with a new agey feel. Featuring the caressing vocals of Aruna Abrams, Portal would have been at home on goth/darkwave labels such as Projekt or 4AD, but the band failed to gain label backing. Only completist Cynic fans picked up on the Portal demo, and as a result, the music was spread through mostly inappropriate channels.

After Portal, Jason Gobel laid low, reappearing years later on Gordian Knot's second album, *Emergent*. Spearheaded by former Cynic bassist Sean Malone, Gordian Knot was an amalgam of metal, jazz, prog rock, and new age music. The band produced a debut album in 1998 and another in 2002. Completely instrumental and very composition-based, Gordian Knot was where the worlds of prog rock and prog metal met. An all-star cast including Trey Gunn of King Crimson, Bill Bruford of Yes and King Crimson, Steve Hackett of Genesis; Jim Matheos of Fates Warning, John Myung of Dream Theater, and Ron Jarzombek of Watchtower all helped flesh out Malone's vision. Ever so briefly, Cynic's *Focus* lineup reconvened for the *Emergent* track "A Shaman's Whisper," though none of the participating members consider it a Cynic song.

Masvidal and Reinert moved to Los Angeles and found session work in film and television. Any viewer of *Third Rock from the Sun*, *That '70s Show*, *The Price Is Right*, *Queer as Folk*, and any number of other random television programs has probably stumbled across Cynic's core members without even knowing it. But the session work was not a final resting place. Despite good paychecks and regular work, the duo burned out. "We realized that the world of TV is disposable," states Masvidal. "Film music is a little cooler. But it's not a great source of communication as an artist. It's just turnover, turnover, turnover, generate income, next gig, next gig, and it becomes very humdrum for people like us who have something to say as artists."

So through the Coldplay-gone-shoegaze project Aeon Spoke, Masvidal and Reinert reacquainted with their muse, quietly releasing a couple albums in the 2000s.

The second one, *Aeon Spoke*, came out through the SPV label in 2007, and, according to Masvidal, was "dead in the water." Whatever the pedigree of the players, a hard rock and heavy metal label could not do much for a band of Aeon Spoke's nature.

A funny thing happened while Aeon Spoke and session gigs consumed the attention of Masvidal and Reinert: Cynic's *Focus* continued attract new fans each year. In fact, few metal bands besides Cynic have amassed such a rabid cult following with just one album. Momentum continued building behind Cynic during the first decade of the 2000s. Roadrunner Records saw the interest and satisfied demand by reissuing *Focus* in 2004, adding Portal songs as a bonus.

Focused: Paul Masvidal recording Cynic's 2008 comeback, *Traced in Air* (*Gene Kirkland*)

On the continued interest in and the impact of *Focus*, Masvidal admits, "I'm completely floored. It's a testimony to trusting your instinct and going against all odds."

Cynic's friends in Atheist reaped the same posthumous acclaim when their catalog was reissued in 2005, and they seized the moment to play European and American shows. Being linked closely to Atheist since the early days of both bands, Cynic's Masvidal says: "I got a call from Atheist's Kelly Shaefer saying, 'Do you understand? You gotta get out there, you don't even know the demand that's happening for the band and the love that's there for you guys.' I'm grateful. I feel fortunate."

In what Masvidal calls "a combination of curious synchronicities," a reformed, new-look Cynic eventually made its way to Europe for festival appearances in 2007. In addition to familiar *Focus* selections, they debuted a new song, "Evolutionary Sleeper," and performed Mahavishnu Orchestra's "Meeting of the Spirits"—an old favorite they sometimes performed in the *Focus* era. The band's announcement that they would record a new album sparked a bidding war among indie metal labels, with France's Season of Mist coming out on top.

The release of Cynic's *Traced in Air* in October 2008 was met with great fanfare, and even sounded like the rightful answer to *Focus* many listeners had expected during the mid-'90s. Like its predecessor, the band's second album offered a take on metal that wasn't there before. Very little music is truly original, but in the case of *Focus*, Cynic brought something completely new into the world. *Traced in Air* is clearly kin to *Focus* but is very much its own entity, with its own demands and rewards. The album's flurry of color and variety of celestial melodies and melodic vocals revealed the growth of Masvidal and Reinert in the years between Cynic albums. Their work in film, TV, and the Aeon Spoke project informs *Traced in Air* as much as, if not more than, their origins in the Florida death metal underground. *Traced in Air* is a rounded, heavy, delicate, cosmic, and powerful effort—only time will tell if it will have the same impact as *Focus*, but even that album took plenty of time to catch on.

After completing *Traced in Air*, Paul Masvidal said, "I feel it's the duty of the artist to push the envelope, to do something new, to create and invent. We have this gift of being musicians; we might as well try and do something special, make it interesting to people, and make something that no one else has made before. Why not?"

12. SUBLIMATION FROM UNDERGROUND V: FROM 2112 TO 1993

"Death metal petered out by 1993. It got so saturated—labels flooded the market with the same old stuff. But there was this weird offshoot of death metal bands that grew sick of playing death metal and started listening to other kinds of music. Instead of giving up on metal, they found a way to integrate those influences. And you wound up with Atheist, Cynic, Believer, Pestilence—stretching out from where they had been before, and Gorguts growing exponentially. It was a trend across the board in general, not just in death metal. There was this overall spirit of experimentation that happened with Coroner and Anacrusis and all sorts of bands. For me, 1993 represents this pastiche and dialogue between past and future." —Hunter Ginn, Canvas Solaris

DEATH METAL'S BURST OF CREATIVITY IN THE LATE '80s and early '90s quickly led to near-stasis. The sickest sound on the planet reached a nadir. Most bands had no interest in evolving or exploring—they just pushed and shoved at the limits of brutality. Plenty of solid albums appeared, though very few said anything new. Around that time, thrash metal also bounced against a wall, as hundreds of bandwagon jumpers leeched the ideas and vitality of the genre's best bands and albums. Nineteen ninety-three spelled the end of death metal's productive first phase, a year when thrash metal could also with confidence be declared creatively dead.

But a small clique of bands pushed these genres to their ultimate creative ends in exemplary fashion in 1993; at the same time, a new strain of progressive metal found its genesis at the opposite end of the spectrum from extreme metal. Steering into a more advanced realm, a small clutch of thrash/death bands sculpted crude foundations to the fullest extent of their abilities. They made daring leaps into the unknown, fueled by influences from within and outside of the metal sphere. Parallel to that, more melodic bands began forming by the dozens, influenced by the Big Three of Queensrÿche, Fates Warning, and Dream Theater, staking their own ambitious claims in the vast and growing metal universe.

On September 14, 1993, tech metal's greatest period reached its zenith when Roadrunner Records released Believer's *Dimensions* and Cynic's *Focus*. Two weeks earlier, Dutch death metal pioneers Pestilence took a surprisingly spacey turn with the release of fourth album *Spheres*. The three albums *Dimensions*, *Focus*, and *Spheres* flew together in magazine ads under the banner "Forging New Metal." Each of these albums ended the first stage of the three bands' careers. (They all went into hibernation, and curiously all returned to address unfinished business fifteen years later).

Listening to these albums, it seems Believer and Cynic were just getting started. But metal bands had a tough time during the stripped-down Seattle grunge era. Additionally, both bands stumbled under the weight of various demons, combinations of personal and industry struggles that proved too great to overcome. Poor Pestilence just sputtered and died after the cold reception to *Spheres*. Nobody saw that curveball coming; the band reached its logical artistic conclusion and split.

Pestilence's early material was raw death metal accented with dry, choking vocal rasps—songs about dehydration, suffocation, infection, all manner of fun life-threatening situations. Respectable musical chops sliced away under the surface, and orchestral track "Proliferous Souls," from 1990's *Consuming Impulse*, seemed to foreshadow things to come. With the band's third album, *Testimony of the Ancients*, Pestilence revealed seriously ambitious aims. *Testimony* presented eight proper tracks of crushing death, but the production was cleaner, and the band's experimental tendencies flourished during eight between-song interludes. Employing Florida bassist Tony Choy—already known from Cynic and Atheist—Pestilence cemented their prog cred, but as was his pattern, Choy stayed only briefly. The band replaced Choy with Jeroen Paul Thesseling and moved forward. Pulling hair back in ponytails and committing the unpardonable metal sin of wearing collared shirts, they released *Spheres* in 1993. The album's opening track, "Mind Reflections," immediately affirmed that Pestilence had reoriented significantly from their savage early sound.

The booklet accompanying *Spheres* made this emphatic claim: "There are no keyboards on this album." It echoed Queen, Iron Maiden, and hosts of manly hard rockers before them. Queen flaunted its "no synthesizers" approach to highlight that Brian May's guitar was actually generating all those lush orchestral layers. Iron Maiden's disclaimer on 1983's *Piece of Mind*—"no synthesizers or ulterior motives"—showed their commitment to metallic purity...at least until 1986's *Somewhere in Time*, which relied heavily on guitar synths. Pestilence, however, were only honest on a technicality—the liner notes in *Spheres* boast that

Pestilence's foray into "fusion metal":
1993's *Spheres*

the band used no fewer than twenty-four effects gizmos, including a Teletronix LA-2A vintage soft-knee tube limiter, an Eventide H3000 Ultra-Harmonizer, and an Atari 1040 ST computer. The guitarists' main axes included Roland GR-50 MIDI guitar synths. But no keyboards!

The alien, effects-laden atmosphere of *Spheres* was supported by blocky stop-start rhythms and fluid six-string bass lines. Shorter instrumentals such as "Aurian Eyes," "Voices from Within," and "Phileas" dotted the chilly landscape with extra color. Pestilence guitarist and leader Patrick Mameli called *Spheres* "fusion-metal," although drummer Marco Foddis let the material down if jazz was really the aim. His playing was hardly nuanced enough to keep up with that of the accomplished string players.

Changes began when Pestilence traversed Europe as support act on Death's *Human* tour in late 1991. Cynic members Paul Masvidal and Sean Reinert were part of Death's ranks then, and their taste rubbed off on Mameli and the other Dutch deathsters in Pestilence. "It really opened our ears and minds," says Mameli. "We were influenced by Tribal Tech, Allan Holdsworth, and Chick Corea. We wanted to make a fusion of metal and contemporary jazz. We tried to go where no one had gone before, using a non-typical metal guitar sound and changing how the songs were structured. The death metal market was flooded with too many insignificant bands. Everybody was jumping on the death metal wagon, and we needed to go another direction."

While Believer's *Dimensions* and Cynic's *Focus* were greeted enthusiastically by a small but eager number of open-minded metal fans, the response to *Spheres* was more muted. "We wanted to progress as musicians," says Mameli, "but we should have done it under another name, not as Pestilence. We didn't see the problem at the time, but later on this became our demise. The album was not very well received by the fans, and we were just burned out. And then we were dropped by Roadrunner."

Unlike Believer and Atheist, whose 1993 releases were *expected* to be eclectic, based on their exponential growth in the preceding years, a surprising number of bands advanced themselves suddenly in 1993. France's Loudblast had previously impressed few with their derivative death/thrash, but something remarkable happened with their third album, *Sublime Dementia*. Recorded at the infamous Morrisound in Florida under the watchful eye of Scott Burns, *Sublime Dementia* sounded like the European alternative to Quebec's Obliveon. Even the rigid cosmic rhythms of D.B.C. worked their way into Loudblast's style. Unpredictable tempo changes abounded, and a female lead vocal was featured throughout "About Solitude," which explored Celtic Frost or Paradise Lost terrain. "About Solitude" was perhaps influenced by Believer's "Dies Irae (Day of Wrath)," though less overtly grandiose, at only a fraction of its length. Throughout the album, throaty roars met a clean, almost melodic, robotic voice that recalled Voivod. *Sublime Dementia* may as well be an honorary Canadian tech metal album. Loudblast took five years to follow it up, and, much as Obliveon did, they went in a simpler, more modern direction, for 1998's *Fragments*. As with Obliveon's *Cybervoid*, the material on *Fragments* betrayed aggro-groove elements akin to Machine Head and Fear Factory. Indeed, Pestilence was not the only band to take a strange and heady turn in 1993.

Another French band, Supuration, shed humble death metal origins in 1993 in favor of a more innovative shape. *The Cube* was the band's first full-length after a clutch of demos, EPs, and seven-inches, and Voivod influences blared loud and clear throughout its ten songs. Thematically, Supuration abandoned its early predilection for medical/gore imagery and went in for a concept that could have been inspired by sci-fi writer Isaac Asimov. "Through the Transparent Partitions" and "The Accomplishment" were full of robotic riffs and vocals, as the band supplanted its deathly past with a more cerebral sci-fi approach.

While building a strong following in France, Supuration struggled to find a foothold in the global metal community. So it was that 1994's *Jacques le Fataliste*, a soundtrack to the French film of the same name, was released in very limited quantity—and only on cassette, no less. Supuration shortened their name to Sup with 1995's *Anomaly* album, and released several more albums with that odd moniker before changing back to Supuration for the release of 2003's *Incubation* (a nine-part concept album, each song representing a month of a pregnant woman's gestation period—the story itself a complicated, bizarre psychological horror tale, revisiting ideas explored on *The Cube*). Now moving between both names as they see fit, Supuration/ Sup have streamlined their music greatly since 1993, tempering a monochromatic drone with a sci-fi edge. None of their later albums masters the balance between complexity, originality, and intensity that *The Cube* achieved, although the band's sense of focus remains sharp. The magic year 1993 also brought Italian progressive/tech metal band Sadist. Their *Above the*

Voivodian Cubists: France's Supuration in 1993

Light debut is a worthwhile contribution to progressive thrash/death metal, consisting of unpredictable changes and a variety of textures drawn from classical, gothic, prog rock, and soundtrack music. *Tribe* (1996), *Crust* (1997), and 2007's self-titled comeback album boosted Sadist's tech cred, even if 2000's *Lego* threatened to tear it all down with seventy minutes of Korn-y nu-metal groove.

Younger Italian bands, such as Gory Blister and Illogicist, do their best to confound with their own brands of tech death, but so far remain in the shadow of their teachers. It's fair to note that onetime Illogicist member Marco Minnemann; the sought-after German-born drummer (who currently lives in Southern California) has also lent his talents to German tech-death band Necrophagist, Italian avant-garde metal act Ephel Duath, neoclassical metal guitarist Marco Ferrigno, and plenty of artists outside the genre, such as Nina Hagen, Eddie Jobson and Mike Keneally.

The rather different Eldritch, whose first demo material surfaced in 1993, should also be noted. Stating influences such as Metallica, Fates Warning, Annihilator, Coroner, Watchtower and Queensrÿche, Eldritch pumps their own thrash/power metal fuel through an engine of unpredictability. Many full-lengths and one live album later, they churn on with their signature sound.

One formerly unremarkable death metal band from Canada surpassed all others in 1993 by marrying dizzying complexity with unmatched brutality. Quebec's Gorguts were essentially a Death clone in their early days, but the band's second album, *The Erosion of Sanity*, rewrote the book on technical death metal. Released in January 1993, the album merged the skilled ferocity of New York band Suffocation with the mold-breaking labyrinths of early Atrocity, welding strange lyrical topics to a dexterous, deadly musical approach. Gorguts paused for five years before their next album, and once released, 1998's *Obscura* landed with a resounding, immediate impact. With its dry sound and thick musical complexities, the hour-long album is an exhausting test of endurance and patience; anti-melodic riffs and strange rhythms ooze through the tracks with a chilling unease. Somehow, this unlikely, unwieldy work became mandatory listening for just about anyone into extreme metal of any kind, and is still praised loudly in many quarters of the underground.

Gorguts spurred other Canadian death dealers, such as the hyperblasting Kataklysm and Cryptopsy, and the more traditionally technical Martyr—whose Daniel Mongrain played in Gorguts, and has joined Voivod in their post-Piggy years. Gorguts' musical excellence, innovation, and unpredictability, in combination with an ever-present component of brutality, proved inspiring to a variety of future tech death bands around the world, including Germany's Necrophagist, Sweden's Spawn of Possession, South Carolina's epic deathsters Nile, California's ridiculously shred-drenched Brain Drill, and Florida weirdos Gigan. Even intentionally difficult grind-meets-noise-rock acts such as Car Bomb, the Dillinger Escape Plan, and Psyopus owe some kind of debt to Gorguts. The band's influence is even clearly noted in the name of German technical death band Obscura—a modern day entry featuring Jeroen Paul Thesseling, veteran of Pestilence's 1993 opus *Spheres*, on fretless six-string bass.

After reaching the end of the tour trail for their fourth album, *From Wisdom to Hate*, Gorguts sputtered then dissolved altogether by 2005. Shortly thereafter, guitarist Luc Lemay rejoined with former Gorguts member—and major *Obscura* contributor—Steeve Hurdle in Negativa. The band's 2006 debut, a self-titled three-song EP, sounded much like the previous two Gorguts albums—but it also marked a new beginning. The band added vocalist Roxanne Constantin in late 2007, and Hurdle announced on Negativa's website: "With her emotional voice, and her love and knowledge of music, Roxanne will add a fresh color to our sound. We felt it was time to explore new avenues, so we've made significant changes to our musical approach. The four musicians are now involved in the writing process, which brings more diversity to our sound. Our music is therefore becoming more experimental, progressive, and ambient. This natural evolution will broaden our horizons, sound-wise."

But Constantin didn't stay with Negativa long enough to appear on an official recording, and by late 2009, the band had boiled down to just Hurdle and drummer Etienne Gallo. The duo's shared and/or individual influences include Dead Can Dance, Voivod, Death, Tool, Meshuggah, Rush, Pearl Jam, and Johann Sebastian Bach, among many others, and with a melting pot like that providing inspiration, who knows what's around the corner for Negativa? Meanwhile, Luc Lemay put his loyalty and full energies back into Gorguts. Reviving the band in 2009, Lemay is joined by Kevin Hufnagel of Dysrhythmia on second guitar and busy, formidable bass innovator Colin Marston—known for his work in Behold the Arctopus, Dysrhythmia, Krallice, and Indricothere. Lemay's new Gorguts promises music even farther out there than previous accomplishments.

Lemay, the only constant throughout Gorguts' life span, defies the metal stereotype. He notes that the intellectual illumination of meditation played a major role in the creation of *Obscura* (hence the floating, cross-legged elder on the album cover); he has studied classical music formally and composes his own classical pieces. His pursuits in classical music have expanded his metal vocabulary. "Since *Obscura* we've been on our own planet," says Lemay, "and that's time. It takes time to find your own

Gorguts' Luc Lemay and Steeve Hurdle blast out the difficult strains of *Obscura*, September 1998 (*Frank White*)

speech. It's the same thing in classical music. The first things Beethoven was writing sounded like Haydn, and then he found his own way. It's just time and devotion to songwriting. When you learn a language, you use the same words all the time, but then you get to know more words and you get good enough to invent your own."

Together with earlier, more melodic tech metal such as that created by Watchtower, Psychotic Waltz, and Sieges Even, the early '90s wave of extreme tech provided a huge impetus for young bands to create their own variations. One of 1993's cornerstones, Cynic, influenced a variety of modern prog metal bands. Meshuggah, Dysrhythmia, Canvas Solaris, and the Dillinger Escape Plan, among many others, have hailed Cynic as a major influence. Some bands even seemed to exist exclusively to fill the gap left by the band during their hiatus—Dutch band Exivious is a doppelgänger for Cynic, while Italians Esicastic released three demos between 1996 and 2001 that owed a major debt to *Focus*. One member of Exivious, Tymon Kruidenier, saw his dreams come true when he joined the revitalized Cynic in 2007 and played on their acclaimed 2008 return, *Traced in Air*. His Exivious bandmate bassist Robin Zielhorst also joined Cynic for live performances.

Two bands from Norway rekindled the spirit of 1993 long after tech metal's most eventful year had passed. Formed in 1994, Extol pointed to Believer as their number-one influence—not surprising, as they shared the same Christian beliefs.

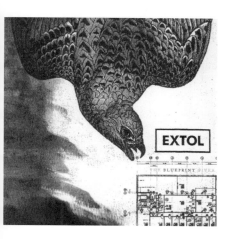

Extol's early albums were fairly complex takes on death/thrash, but by 2003's *Synergy* they had started to find their own sound. *Synergy* more deeply explored the band's melodic and technical tendencies, with cover artwork drawn by longtime Rush artist Hugh Syme. In 2005, *The Blueprint Dives* distanced Extol from their former work, alienating many fans and bringing their ten-year career to a screeching halt. With more melody and flow—and curious leanings toward emo and indie rock—*The Blueprint Dives* was both eccentric and accessible. The ghost of Believer still lurked nearby, although the material straddled a precarious line between tech circa 1993, modern art rock, and blatant emo

Not without worshippers or detractors: Extol's *The Blueprint Dives*

influence. With an extended array of guest musicians playing synths, piano, Rhodes organ, and even upright bass, the sound canvas on *The Blueprint Dives* is exceptionally wide. The album deserves more acclaim than it received, but perhaps Extol was just another band ahead of its time.

Oslo, Norway's Spiral Architect popped up in 1993, the name clearly nabbed from Black Sabbath's *Sabbath Bloody Sabbath*, but the sound straight from the Fates Warning and Watchtower playbook. Shortly after their 1995 demo, the band brought in vocalist Øyvind Hægeland from neighboring Fates Warning worshippers Manitou. Hægeland's style was a clever and convincing meld of Fates Warning vocalists John Arch and Ray Alder, with distinct shades of Psychotic Waltz's Buddy Lackey.

Spiral Architect's sole album, *A Sceptic's Universe* (2000), displayed students who had almost surpassed their teachers. Containing a barrage of difficult note sequences and disorienting rhythmic trickery, the album succeeded thanks to the vocal choices of Hægeland. Where vocalists in Watchtower, Confessor, and Sieges Even had problems navigating the fog of instrumental complexity, Hægeland managed viable vocal lines amid the swirling kinetics. As a piece of tech metal art, *A Sceptic's Universe* proved nearly as commanding as such cornerstones as Watchtower's *Control and Resistance* and Fates Warning's *Perfect Symmetry*. Spiral Architect happily embraced what they called "true Norwegian technical metal"—a nod to their eternally "true" black metal countrymen. A couple members later performed session work with black metal legends Satyricon and Mayhem, and drummer Asgeir Mickelson proved his versatility in Borknagar, Ihsahn, and Vintersorg.

Spiral Architect's Lars Norberg
(*Matt Johnsen*)

Disappointingly, the fire of brilliance in Spiral Architect burned out quickly. Massively letting down every tech metal fan, the new millennium's answer to Watchtower came and went even quicker than Watchtower had. Ken Golden, who released *A Sceptic's Universe* on his Sensory label in 2000 after a five-year friendship with the band, thinks the members aren't all that motivated to record a follow-up. "The guys got involved in so many different things," Golden says, "and frankly it was probably more profitable for them. Then when you don't do something for a long time and the album takes on a life of its own, it reaches a point where the guys say, 'Why should we do this?' It's got this mythic status. There's nothing that could live up to that first album, even if they could make a better record."

Several veterans of Spiral Architect and Extol joined forces in Twisted into Form, who released the impressive *Then Comes Affliction to Awaken the Dreamer* in 2006 on Sensory. Some tech metal enthusiasts expected the album to fill the void left by Spiral Architect, and the most judgmental fans deemed it a failed substitute. The expectations were unfair, no doubt, but label chief Golden saw them coming: "I let the guys in Twisted into Form know that from the start: 'You're always going to be compared to Spiral Architect, so get used to it.' I tried really hard to play up that this is not Spiral Architect, that this is a different band. And people could not accept that."

Tech year 1993 also birthed a monster called Spastic Ink, the invention of guitarist Ron Jarzombek. Frustrated with the simpler material Watchtower had written for its ill-fated third album, *Mathematics*, the talented Jarzombek reeled in his equally gifted brother Bobby on drums, along with Bobby's rhythm partner in Riot, Pete Perez, on bass. Under Ron's direction, Spastic Ink's first album, *Ink Complete*— finally released in 1997—found the trio detonating a series of madcap fireworks that were clearly the design of a lunatic, a genius, or both. Each instrumental track had a particular theoretical theme intentionally set up as a challenge to the musicians.

"See, and Its Sharp" uses only two notes—C and C sharp—played in straight-forward 4/4 time. A tricky middle section that appears to alternate 7 and 5 time is actually triplet eighth notes played over 4/4—also a favorite time manipulation of Swedish tech thrashers Meshuggah, who often play in 4/4 but disguise the signature as something more complicated by employing dropped hits or illogically alternating accents. Ron's "no drum toms" rule for "See, and Its Sharp" further challenged his drummer brother. (Ex-Genesis vocalist Peter Gabriel laid down a similar maxim in 1980 on his third solo album, where cymbal use was forbidden.)

Other musical challenges on *Ink Complete* are revealed in titles such as "Suspended on All Fours" and "To Counter and Groove in E Minor." But the album's centerpiece has to be "A Wild Hare." Ron's "musical interpretation of an animation classic released in 1942"— described as such in the liner notes to avoid copyright infringement—is loopy cartoon music poured into the mold of mad metal. Ron spent "countless hours" on the transcription, even transcribing the pitch and timing of the famous rabbit's dialogue, including laughs, sniffs, gulps, and throat clearings.

Before the second Spastic Ink album in 2004, Ron released two solo albums that further highlighted his bizarre thinking process. *Phhhp!* offered fourteen exercises in oddity, all played entirely by Ron. Besides guitar, he incorporated drum programming, tape manipulation, noises, effects, beeps, white noise, cat meows, and the sound of cricket legs rubbing. A more widely distributed endeavor from Jarzombek came four years later. *Solitarily Speaking of Theoretical Confinement* contained no fewer than forty-five tracks of twisted theory, once again conceived and performed solely by the wizard of weird himself. Each track melted into the next so that the album flowed like one long, ever-changing song. Ron's time in Watchtower obviously influenced the album, either through inside-joke titles such as "Rigidude" or stuff like "Snuff" and "Yum-Yum Tree," which were inspired by odd creative discoveries during Watchtower rehearsals. "Frank Can Get Drunk and Eat Beer" displayed the guitarist's trademark wordplay and the unusual conceptual approach that had become his calling card. Jarzombek described the song title as a "mnemonic device used to learn the order of sharps in major keys (F, C, G, D, A, E, B). Workouts such as "A Headache and a Sixty-Fourth," "Dramatic Chromatic," "Tri, Tri Again," and the fourteen-second "Watchtower" indicate a tireless creative mind, even if the album itself threatens to tire listeners after the thirty-fifth track or so of such difficult, demanding nonsense.

After his exceedingly insular solo exercises, Jarzombek unveiled two albums that worked not just as bizarre guitar demonstrations but as actual listenable music. Spastic Ink's second album, *Ink Compatible*, was a song-oriented affair that explored the darkly humorous side of humanity's relationship with the personal computer. Adding Watchtower vocalist Jason McMaster to the original Spastic trio, the album gained further depth through guest performances by vocalist Daniel Gildenlöw of Pain of Salvation, renowned jazz bassist Michael Manring, Watchtower bassist Doug Keyser, Cynic bassist Sean Malone, and ex-Megadeth guitarist Marty

The wacky world of Spastic Ink,
L-R: Bobby Jarzombek, Ron Jarzombek, Pete Perez
(*Jennifer Jarzombek*)

Friedman. Some listeners were wary of McMaster's gruffer vocals—he hadn't even been heard on a prog metal album since Watchtower's *Energetic Disassembly* two decades earlier, and his voice had changed considerably since that auspicious debut. *Ink Compatible* wasn't exactly a replacement for the doomed third Watchtower album, but with so few albums being released in a similar mold, Spastic Ink satiated audience hunger for tech.

Moving back to an instrumental format, Jarzombek outdid himself with the Blotted Science project. Conceived with Cannibal Corpse bassist Alex Webster, the unlikely union resulted in perhaps the most devastating tech-metal workout of all time. The 2007 album *The Machinations of Dementia* throbbed and pulsed with a brutality not heard in Spastic Ink, while Behold the Arctopus drummer Charlie Zeleny added a layer of trickiness to the dizzying damage worked by Jarzombek and Webster. Between full-time teaching during the week, producing his own instructional DVDs, guest appearances on various albums, and the revived sessions for Watchtower's *Mathematics*, Jarzombek has already begun plotting the second Blotted Science album.

The impact of the tech metal surge of 1993 and its wake inspired a young generation of ambitious bands in the late 1990s. Georgia's Canvas Solaris began as an adventurous death metal band before dropping vocals and embarking on an entirely instrumental path. They eventually became Sensory labelmates with such heroes as Spiral Architect and Gordian Knot, recording a string of albums that defy tech metal's tradition of short life spans. With impressive regularity, Canvas Solaris bends the borders of the form, bringing in influences from more traditional metal bands and eclectic influences from across the prog universe and beyond.

Drummer Hunter Ginn considers tech metal merely a stepping-off point for Canvas Solaris. About their 2010 album, *Irradiance*, he says, "All the songs have four or five parts apiece. We're building things up more vertically rather than having these elaborate horizontal narratives. I don't think we've been a true tech-metal band since 2003's *Spatial/Design*. Tech metal has always played a big part in our music, but the sounds got too adulterated. And that's largely because, as listeners, we're interested in so many other things."

The cycle of innovation continues, as California's Scale the Summit and Washington, D.C.'s Animals as Leaders play music too involved to bother with vocals, joining Canvas Solaris in the growing instrumental branch of tech metal. With or without vocals, the allure of tech metal spans the globe. Spanish instrumental trio Continuo Renacer are entirely committed to tech, while Russian quintet Hieronymus Bosch took influence from Pestilence, Death, and Voivod, and from the more melodic Rush, Fates Warning, and Sieges Even. With harsh vocals a part of their sound, Hieronymus Bosch sculpted modern tech metal monuments in 2005's *Artificial Emotions* and 2008's *Equivoke* before their premature demise in 2010.

Technical, demanding modern metal bands, from Canvas Solaris to Obscura, have a better shot at capturing the metal public's ear than pioneers such as Cynic and Pestilence did when they turned the genre upside down in the early '90s. Almost two decades of tech metal evolution have readied listeners for the challenge. While Cynic's *Focus*, Atheist's *Elements*, and Obliveon's *Nemesis* are now held in high regard, they were largely considered strange, left-field oddities upon their release in 1993. Even Pestilence's oft-reviled *Spheres* finally found its niche. Patrick Mameli is probably accurate when he says "most people still don't like *Spheres* that much," but the album has never been duplicated, and its influence persists in certain corners of the modern metal world. Polish musician Stanisław Wołonciej of progressive band Newbreed and experimental project Egoist says, "*Spheres* was my number one album for years and years. It changed my musical point of view significantly. It was something completely different and fresh."

Wołonciej was approached in 2007 by Patrick Mameli to play drums in the Pestilence leader's other band, C-187. Due to logistical issues, he had to bow out, and his seat was filled by the more-than-capable Sean Reinert of Cynic. But Wołonciej finally collaborated with his hero on Egoist's 2009 album, *Ultra-Selfish Revolution*, where Mameli contributed wild guitar leads on two tracks. Mameli says, "I like the songs and structure a lot; I like the fact that Stan is trying to do something different." But then Mameli underscores the fact that, as innovative as a band like Egoist might be, many metal fans will never be up for that level of mind-bending challenge: "Stan told me the Egoist album isn't doing too well, and again it's proof that such musical combinations are not for the masses."

1993: YEAR OF THE EGGHEADBANGER

ONE OF THE MOST PROLIFIC 365-DAY CYCLES IN PROG METAL HISTORY, 1993 was a time of paradigm shifts, career peaks, and creative abandon. Witness the evidence:

Anacrusis: *Screams and Whispers*
Atheist: *Elements*
Believer: *Dimensions*
Carbonized: *Disharmonization*
Coroner: *Grin*
Cynic: *Focus*
Death: *Individual Thought Patterns*
Disharmonic Orchestra: *Pleasuredome*
Gorguts: *The Erosion of Sanity*

Loudblast: *Sublime Dementia*
Obliveon: *Nemesis*
Pan-Thy-Monium: *Khaooohs*
Pestilence: *Spheres*
Psychotic Waltz: *Into the Everflow*
Sadist: *Above the Light*
Supuration: *The Cube*
Voivod: *The Outer Limits*

While tech purveyors confounded and amazed during the movement's zenith in 1993, the year also marked the arrival of a different breed of progressive metal. Inspired by Rush and the Big Three, with nods to prog rock, neoclassical wizard Yngwie Malmsteen, and Savatage's theater, the wheels started turning for Pain of Salvation, Ayreon, and Symphony X. By the mid-'90s, the influence of Fates Warning and Queensrÿche was deeply ingrained in thousands of young musicians worldwide, and after the enormous impact Dream Theater made with *Images and Words* and *Awake*, the stage was set for hundreds of new-breed prog metal bands to emerge. Labels sprouted from nowhere, offering talent like Digital Ruin, Mind's Eye, Ion Vein, and Vanden Plas. It was an exciting, prolific time for those wanting more of what Dream Theater and the others pioneered. And it should be noted that Ron Jarzombek's left hand was successfully operated on in 1993, ensuring that one of tech metal's early pioneers could continue leading the way.

PART IV:
Genetic Blends

13. DEVIATION OR DERIVATION?

"Dream Theater spawned this whole 'recipe genre' of prog metal. I remember their first album, in 1989, being something nobody had really heard before. A magazine compared it to a mixture of Crimson Glory, Pink Floyd, and Metallica. We were all intrigued by that. Up to that point, progressive metal was more open, a bit more alternative. Now I can't listen to Dream Theater anymore, because instead of hearing Dream Theater in all the bands that are trying to imitate them, I hear all of those really bad bands in Dream Theater when I listen to Dream Theater." —Daniel Gildenlöw, Pain of Salvation

"There is no better tribute to a creative influence than being creative." —Patrick T. Daly, liner notes of Refused's *The Shape of Punk to Come*

N o wonder Dream Theater made such an impact in 1992. Progressive rock was dead—or might as well have been. Innovators such as King Crimson, Gentle Giant, and Van der Graaf Generator were nowhere to be found. Yes and Jethro Tull were long past their prime, and Genesis and Pink Floyd were winding down for good. ELP sputtered to their third death with albums no one remembers, including *Black Moon* and *In the Hot Seat*. Even Rush was releasing ultra-streamlined, less complex albums such as *Presto* and *Roll the Bones*.

Meanwhile, the extreme metal underground was branching out exponentially, offering a variety of wild, interesting and truly progressive bands—yet listeners wanting a more melodic element in their prog metal were ready for something completely different. Watchtower had fizzled by 1992, while Queensrÿche and Fates

Painted Norwegian of a different stripe:
Jørn Lande of Ark, ProgPower USA festival,
November 2001, Atlanta, GA
(*Matt Johnsen*)

Warning's albums had become less exploratory and more infrequent. So when Dream Theater truly arrived in 1992 with second album *Images and Words* and its surprise hit "Pull Me Under," they provided a candle in the dark for fans of progressive rock and heavy metal.

ProgPower USA festival organizer Glenn Harveston traces his enthusiasm for progressive metal back to one moment in 1992, when he was transformed by the prog metal equivalent of seeing the Beatles on the *Ed Sullivan Show*. "I was watching MTV *Headbangers Ball* on a Saturday night and saw the video for Dream Theater's 'Pull Me Under,'" he recalls. "That was like getting hit across the jaw with a brick. I loved what I heard and wanted more."

Partly because of Dream Theater's success, a new breed of progressive metal band emerged in the early '90s. Inspired by the same bands as Dream Theater, and to a great extent by Dream Theater itself, noisemakers in a similar vein seeped up from the underground and set off one of the most prolific movements in metal history.

Looking back, the anti-virtuosic grunge/alternative/neo-punk climate that dominated the 1990s demanded a musical answer. Though not often celebrated, many bands and even national movements stepped up to defend the honor of rock music with unlimited chops. The clutch of groups taking cues from Dream Theater applied lessons learned from Rush, Fates Warning, and Queensrÿche, and blurred the lines by adding elements of European power metal. Soon, a new strain of progressive metal was born. The movement was global, kicking off as early as the late '80s when a few bands—among them Conception and Royal Hunt in Europe, and Mystic Force and Shadow Gallery in the U.S.—began recording demos, playing live, and carrying the torch for their inspirations.

By the mid-'90s an incredible number of new bands joined the cause. Denmark was an unlikely hotspot, offering Manticora, Wuthering Heights, and Beyond Twilight in addition to Royal Hunt. The rest of Scandinavia kept pace with Pain of Salvation, Mayadome, Manitou, and Ark. Far-flung territories offered new hopes, such as Angra from Brazil and Vigilante from Japan. New record labels eagerly capitalized on all the activity, including Inside Out, Sensory, Massacre, and Rising Sun.

Upstarts Ayreon, Evergrey, and Symphony X eventually blossomed into big sellers, while Dreamscape, Ivanhoe, and Lanfear took positions on the second tier of this prog metal renaissance. And this is only skimming the surface. Fans of this new breed were hungry, demanding more and more, and they were getting it. Another significant branch of the progressive metal tree rapidly gained strength and size.

In short time, this onslaught of bands represented a style that became known globally as "progressive metal." Curiously, much of it wouldn't have held up as truly *progressive* if a strict dictionary definition was applied.

The first bands to play a progressive form of rock in the late '60s—Pink Floyd, the Moody Blues, Yes, Genesis, Jethro Tull, the Nice—drew influence from a wide variety of sources. They unwittingly created a progressive rock scene from scratch. By the mid-1980s, those classic prog bands were either defunct, on hiatus, or making "less is more" music. Along came a new creative eruption in the heavy metal genre to fill the gap, as Fates Warning, Watchtower, and Voivod forged their own strains of innovative, adventurous music.

The 1980s also brought Marillion, Twelfth Night, IQ, and Pendragon—the U.K.'s "neo-prog" movement—who took inspiration directly from the old prog masters and created something new using familiar templates. Their approach was something that might be called "pseudo-progressive." The circumstances leading to the 1990s progressive metal movement were almost the same. A multitude of bands came in the wake of Dream Theater's success that drew from a narrow field of influence—instead of building from scratch, prog metal could now nourish itself by cannibalizing itself. Perhaps that stunted the growth of what, in its true spirit, should have been an uncompromisingly forward-reaching movement.

In their best moments, Rush, Fates Warning, Watchtower, Voivod, and Cynic swerved around the norm to arrive at something unique and individualistic.

They integrated a wide variety of influences, but then leapt off into the unknown. Somehow, most of the '90s new-breed prog metal bands avoided experimentation and risk taking while maintaining "progressive" credentials. In the view of some media, labels, fans, and musicians, simply imitating a well-worn sound or having amazing instrumental chops qualified as "progressive." As these new bands grew in number across the globe, the definition of "progressive" became looser and more liberally applied. Good music is good music—everybody knows it doesn't necessarily have to be ultra-original to be great. But there seemed to be some doubt in the rapidly blossoming post–Dream Theater world whether writing a blueprint, as the Long Island band certainly did, was any more laudable than tracing over one.

Dream Theater built a model of prog metal perfection with lengthy multi-part songs, high-pitched vocals, dominant keyboards, chops-intensive musicianship, memorable melodies, and heavy rhythmic attack. They gladly wore their influences on their sleeves, and went several steps beyond. What they developed as their own became the primary blueprint for hundreds more. This is all to their credit—why damn them for jumpstarting a musical surge that continues twenty years later and has inspired younger musicians to play to the peak of their abilities and given fans of their patented sound hundreds of other bands to choose from? Like those of King Crimson and Black Sabbath before them, Dream Theater's legacy encompasses not only their own music but the mass of talent and ambition that followed.

Many bands in this new breed of progressive metal had grandiose aims and undeniable skills. A few great ones recorded a few great albums using Dream Theater's template. Fewer still, like Sweden's Pain of Salvation, followed their own muse. Instead of deviating from the norm, this movement established a new norm—progressive in appearance but not in practice. That doesn't mean some great music wasn't recorded, because Symphony X's *Twilight in Olympus* is impressive stuff, no matter what subgenre it does or doesn't belong to. But ironically, many in the new "progressive" movement faithfully adhered to familiar methods.

The same thing happened in the '70s prog rock scene. French band Artcane took a specific page from King Crimson's *Larks' Tongues in Aspic* and built the fantastic *Odyssee* album. Similarly, Dutch band Kayak's early albums are basically extensions of classic Genesis and Yes. Decades later, Sweden's Änglagård and Norway's Wobbler paid exclusive tribute to the '70s era, constructing such solid albums as *Hybris* and *Hinterland*, respectively, that shouldn't be overlooked despite their derivative nature.

So in the early 1990s, what became known as "Dream Theater clones" appeared in indomitable waves. Andromeda and Dreamscape were two new bands that proved themselves with formidable playing, strong writing, and an output of not-truly-progressive progressive metal. Twilight Kingdom, Mayadome, Lemur Voice, and others also went through at least a short period of Dream Theater cloning, if not entire careers.

Dream Theater's Mike Portnoy finds the cloning of his band "very flattering"— but only in a limited respect. "We're honored by the impact we've had on other musicians," he says, "but most bands that sound like Dream Theater I can't stand to listen to. The progressive bands that I like—Spock's Beard, the Flower Kings, Beardfish, Pain of Salvation—those are the bands I truly admire. Back in the early days of progressive music, Yes, Genesis, and ELP were taking rock and classical and jazz and putting it in a giant melting pot. And then when bands like us, Fates Warning, and Queensrÿche came, we took metal and progressive rock and put that into a melting pot. The bands doing it best these days are the ones drawing from lots of different areas of progressive music."

Besides the Dream Theater copyists, the same period also saw the arrival of Fates Warning imitators, Queensrÿche revivalists, and obvious Rush wanna-bes. Casting a skeptical eye toward imitators, Jim Matheos of Fates Warning points the finger, good-naturedly, in Dream Theater's direction. "There are a lot of bands doing things that are really derivative, and they're called 'progressive,'" Matheos observes. "Sure, you can say Queensrÿche and Fates Warning were also influential, but 90 percent of the kinds of bands we're referring to are Dream Theater clones. So I always tell Mike Portnoy that he's to blame."

Matheos also admonishes listeners for inventing boundaries to surround what should be boundless music. "A lot of it is the fans," he says. "All of a sudden this great progressive category has become this little box with really high walls. You've got to play really long songs, in odd time signatures and really fast, and then you're progressive. Before all this it was more of an all-encompassing category—different instruments, different song structures, slow, fast—it was quite experimental."

Opinions vary passionately when it comes to applying the "progressive" definition to the heavily populated and popular Big Three–derived scene. Ken Golden of The Laser's Edge label references Paul Stump's *The Music's All That Matters*. "In that book," Golden says, "Stump clearly delineated the difference between Progressive with a capital 'P' and progressive with a little 'p.' Progressive with a capital 'P' meaning a style, a formula. Progressive with a little 'p' being an adjective, describing music that's trying to progress, trying to do something innovative and challenging and break down barriers."

The capital-"P" Progressive tag is not even necessarily pejorative, according to Golden: "They're content to work within clearly defined boundaries, and some of these bands do it really, really well."

The turning point from where Progressive metal really blasted off as a movement came in 1994, in the wake of Dream Theater's *Awake*. Before that, it was a small underground wave, represented by only a few bands with a modest fan base. After *Awake*, Progressive metal proliferated at an incredible rate. Support from fans spread the music across the globe, and, thanks to a new computer-based networking technology known as the Internet, it spread the wildfire further and faster. Those who couldn't get enough of the big bands sought out more obscure ones in the same vein and were met with an overwhelming number of choices.

With the intensity of this growing movement came enterprising new record labels. Major labels were content to stick with cash cows Dream Theater and Queensrÿche. Metal indie Metal Blade was happy to pump most of its prog metal dollars into Fates Warning—also stepping in briefly to help Symphony X and the Quiet Room. The new breed were left to find homes on smaller labels, and companies such as Italy's Lucretia and the U.S.'s Magna Carta and Nightmare sprouted quickly. So did band-run labels including Siegen Records, started by Keith Menser of Mystic Force, which released Mystic Force albums while helping others like Sweden's Mayadome and East Coast pals Digital Ruin.

One particularly influential label was formed by prog guru Ken Golden. While his flagship company, The Laser's Edge, was formed in 1990, first as a mail-order service and then as a bona fide prog rock label, Golden founded Sensory Records to meet growing demands on the metallic side of the prog tracks. A longtime progressive rock enthusiast, Golden kept track of the parallel metal movement over the decades with a discerning but wary ear. A fan of early Scorpions and a variety of '70s hard rock acts, he attempted to find a new fascination in the NWOBHM and America's various metal uprisings in the early 1980s, but he felt a majority of what he heard sounded "kind of juvenile." He wasn't impressed with NWOBHM leaders Iron Maiden or more obscure acts such as Ethel the Frog and Praying Mantis. "Most of them were lunkheaded," he says.

Even pioneering U.S. metal band Fates Warning failed to wow him. He lent an ear to Fates' *Awaken the Guardian* upon its release in 1986 and was less than impressed. "I recognize the importance of that record, but that's in hindsight. That was a very transitional period, and it's kind of like the beginning of Progressive metal." Golden found a little bit more to like about Queensrÿche and Dream Theater. "Queensrÿche's prog angle was something that developed. I was aware of them from the beginning, but they came back on my radar with 'Silent Lucidity,' which was clearly influenced by Pink Floyd. But they were never a huge band for me. I bought *Promised Land* and found it a bit ponderous. My respect for them developed retroactively when I explored their albums later in the '90s. With Dream Theater, I bought *Images and Words* when it came out and had a hard time getting past some of the formulaic metal trappings, but I had respect for the musicianship and also recognized that there was an innate intelligence to their music that put them on a different level than the other bands that were being churned out at the time. I guess this would be the spark of my interest in Progressive metal."

While remaining heavily involved in progressive rock, in 1995 Golden finally found a metal movement to suit his tastes. Along with traditional prog, his mail order customers began requesting all kinds of new metal imports—of both the progressive and Progressive variety. Names such as Time Machine and Superior were unfamiliar to Golden at the time, but in an effort to satisfy demand, he brought in albums by these and many other new bands. After he heard Dutch act Ayreon's *The Final Experiment*, a lightbulb illuminated in his head. It was a significant moment for Golden as a music fan and as an eventual player in the growth of the new Progressive metal movement. "I got that first Ayreon album," Golden says. "I remember it had the original keyboard player from '70s prog rock band Finch on it. It was metal, but it was really interesting. It married elements of old-school prog rock with this younger, hipper infusion of metal. I was looking for something different at that point, and it was just the right blend. Prog rock was moribund at the time, whereas the metal bands were doing just as complex music, maybe more so, and it was heavy. I really started to get into this stuff."

That same year, a demo by obscure Norwegian band Spiral Architect landed in Golden's tape deck. Impressed with their super-technical metal, Golden went in pursuit of the band, and Sensory Records was born.

The imminent Spiral Architect album would take five years to see completion, so an inspired Golden pursued other acts in the interim, releasing albums by short-lived but influential super-trio Ark, Swedish band Mind's Eye, obscure U.S. act Clockwork, Norway's unusual Divided Multitude, and a couple from the productive Danish scene—Behind the Curtain and Wuthering Heights. Sensory reached a new plateau when it secured a deal with veteran Cynic bassist Sean Malone for his Gordian Knot project. Shortly thereafter, Spiral Architect released what would be their first and only album, *A Sceptic's Universe*, in 2000. After the release of *A Sceptic's Universe*, the band slowly dissolved, but not before reaching America for an appearance in Atlanta at the 2001 installment of the ProgPower festival.

Golden continued to make smart signings, discovering Poland's Riverside—who sounded essentially like an amalgam of U.K. bands Anathema and Porcupine Tree—along with challenging instrumental band Canvas Solaris from Georgia, and California acts Zero Hour and Redemption. The latter gained attention immediately thanks to their vocalist, Ray Alder, already well known from Fates Warning.

Amidst Sensory's flagship bands, Golden signed a handful of acts that fit into the '90s-era mold of Progressive metal—stuff dubbed "progressive" that wasn't really deviating much from the norm. Suspyre, Pantommind, and Circus Maximus delivered the goods to fans who expected a certain level of quality and comfort. All were worthy—Circus Maximus amassed a considerable cult following in a short period of time—but Golden knew the score and never pushed these bands as radicals: "There's a formula, a sound, a style, and they're not interested in doing something necessarily different. The ones that stand the test of time are the ones looking to break down barriers. People are going to talk about Spiral Architect twenty years from now—nobody's gonna remember Ivanhoe."

Another industry figure, Jim Pitulski, came to prog metal much the same way as Ken Golden, beginning as a fan of the '70s prog rock scene. Befriending Dream Theater and becoming the band's manager during their upswing in popularity in the early '90s, Pitulski worked his way through the music industry, was employed by a variety of major labels, and finally found his true calling as the head of Inside Out America. Started by Germans Thomas Waber and Michael Schmitz in 1994, the Inside Out label catered to fans of progressive music with such early signings as Spock's Beard and Enchant (the

Symphony X's *Twilight in Olympus*, 1998

very first Inside Out release was *Test to Destruction* by ex–King Crimson violinist David Cross). By 1999, U.S. demand for Inside Out releases grew to such a degree that a stateside office was launched. Pitulski headed the branch and took an active role in signing bands.

Inside Out quickly became the label of first choice for adventurous modern rock and metal bands looking for a deal. With artists including Symphony X, Pain of Salvation, Ayreon, Devin Townsend, Threshold, Evergrey, Vanden Plas, and one-time Sensory bands Riverside and Redemption on its roster, Inside Out lorded over the progressive metal empire—according to Pitulski, an empire truly built by Dream Theater. "Progressive metal, as a movement, didn't really exist until Dream Theater came along," he says. "They were in the right place at the right time. The advent of the Internet was happening, and fans were finding each other and scenes were developing. People realized that they were not alone in this sphere of music which kind of went away for awhile."

This groundswell of activity and interest was a huge benefit to a little band out of New Jersey called Symphony X, who quickly became a staple of the Inside Out roster. Formed in 1994, Symphony X mixed influence from prog rock bands

Kansas, Rush, and ELP; traditional metallers Iron Maiden, Black Sabbath, and Judas Priest; and a healthy dose of classical and soundtrack music. A song like 1998's "Church of the Machine" epitomizes the Symphony X experience: dynamic buoyancy and melodic mastery in the best Kansas tradition merged with the darkness of Dio-era Black Sabbath—a rush of power with a touch of grace. At its best, Symphony X is killer symphonic prog firing on all cylinders with what sounds like an army of Yngwie Malmsteens and Randy Rhoadses enlisted on the front line. At its worst, the band sounds like a more theatrical, classical-drenched Dream Theater. But at their worst they are still formidable—the performance levels of all five members are something most other musicians can only hope to attain. And they've proven themselves on touring jaunts with Dream Theater, Blind Guardian, and Stratovarius—even holding their own on the 2005 Gigantour bill alongside dissimilar bands Megadeth, Dillinger Escape Plan, and Fear Factory.

Is Symphony X truly "progressive"? If they are, they're not the most radical of the bunch. They rarely veer into illuminating new areas; some albums, such as 1998's *Twilight in Olympus*, focus more on the classical side while others, such as 2007's *Paradise Lost*, go for the metallic jugular. They do what they do extremely well and don't necessarily concern themselves with breaking new ground or reinventing the genre. Guitarist Michael Romeo has stated in interviews that he doesn't even have a preference for the "prog metal," "Euro-metal," or "neoclassical" tags continually put on them. Comparing his band with that perennial benchmark, Dream Theater, he states, "We are more of a metal band, and we have some progressive influence here and there. Dream Theater are more like a progressive rock band."

Jim Pitulski, who signed Symphony X to Inside Out, feels that branding the band as "progressive" is misleading. "It's by association with Inside Out. I love Symphony X, but I don't really consider them progressive. They're closer to the whole European power metal scene—Helloween, Yngwie Malmsteen. But they have the same fan base as many progressive bands. You do have to split hairs sometimes. What is truly progressive, and what is just following something you like where you insert yourself into that mold?"

Ultimately, the emerging face of Progressive metal was shaped by a handful of remarkable bands. Beyond Symphony X, highly regarded examples such as

Zero Hour's *The Towers of Avarice*, Angra's *Holy Land*, Evergrey's *Solitude • Dominance • Tragedy*, Threshold's *Hypothetical*, and Shadow Gallery's *Room V* cannot be easily discounted—and those are only a few of many.

Perhaps the quandary of not-exactly-progressive Progressive metal had become one of success and oversaturation—there was now enough of the music available that Progressive musicians could draw from a vacuum of influences. The Big Three, however, like Rush before them, built their early music on a deeper foundation of diverse influences. And, at least in the cases of Rush, Fates Warning, and Queensrÿche, they continued to artistically evolve beyond their most celebrated, influential phases. Their main writers remained interested in all kinds of modern music, much of it outside the metal/rock spheres, something that significantly informed their musical direction. By contrast, the well of inspiration for many '90s new-breed Progressive metal bands didn't seem to run as deep—starting at the Big Three and Rush, and ranging about as far afield as ELP, Kansas, and maybe classical music in some cases. There were always outliers, of course: Seemingly incompatible styles, from singer/songwriter pop and movie soundtracks to alternative rock and glam, informed Pain of Salvation's brand of metal—but the band is one whose progressiveness has never been in question.

Chris Roy grew up during the thrash metal wave of the 1980s, and he later became a key member of underground U.S. prog metal band Reading Zero, which fused thrash influences with clear inspiration from Fates Warning and Queensrÿche. Far from a clone, Reading Zero wore their influences on their sleeves while going for something deeper than the typical Progressive metal offering. "If those sorts of bands were really good songwriters, I would have welcomed any other band that sounded like Dream Theater or Queensrÿche," Roy says, "but sadly most were a much weaker or watered-down version of the bands they most wanted to emulate."

Roy stresses his support for bands from the late-'90s heyday who "never got their shot, but were quite good," including Power of Omens (whose vocalist now sings with modern heroes Zero Hour), Digital Ruin, Divine Regale, and the impossibly obscure Auditory Imagery. As for Reading Zero, Roy believes they avoided the clone wars by keeping their ears and minds open. "I felt we encompassed closer to fifteen influences instead of just one or two."

POWER MEETS PROG

JUST AS MERCYFUL FATE AND METALLICA INSPIRED a wilder, darker, more extreme strain of progressive and technical metal during the 1980s, European "power metal" trailblazers Helloween and Blind Guardian influenced many musicians and fans who worshipped Dream Theater and Rush. Germany's speed/thrash scene in the '80s was one of the biggest of its time. Two early participants, Helloween and Blind Guardian, quickly outgrew their origins and transformed into classic-sounding traditional metal bands. Emphasizing fast double-bass drumming, classical-influenced melodies, twin guitar interplay, and huge sing-along choruses, they crossed the line dividing Iron Maiden and Tchaikovsky, defining the European power metal sound. Helloween and Blind Guardian even deviated from the norm at times, but ultimately reeled themselves back to the comfortable realms of Euro-metal tradition.

Long songs do not automatically equal progressive music, but Helloween got their prog rocks off with two lengthy late-'80s epics, "Halloween" and "Keeper of The Seven Keys," each clocking in at over thirteen minutes. The band's increasingly melodic sound led to a pair of peculiar albums in the early '90s. Embracing Hipgnosis-like imagery and goofy pop elements on 1991's *Pink Bubbles Go Ape*, the band discarded their signature sound on 1993's *Chameleon*, bringing in brass, über-cheesy ballads, and songs about cats and windmills. These albums took daring turns away from metallic convention, but the two-part *Keeper of the Seven Keys* cycle (1987/1988), and follow-ups *The Time of the Oath* (1996) and *Better than Raw* (1998), left the deepest influence on many young Progressive and power metal musicians.

While Helloween strayed from their signature sound in the early '90s, the European power metal blueprint was reinstated and expanded by Blind Guardian on 1990's *Tales from the Twilight World* and 1992's *Somewhere Far Beyond*. To call the albums "progressive" would be a stretch, although their epic atmospheres, neoclassical elements, and Tolkien-esque imagery were seductive to many a prog metal fan. Peaking with 1995 genre classic, *Imaginations from the Other Side*, they then embarked on their most adventurous period. *Nightfall in Middle-Earth* (1998) didn't differ drastically from the previous albums; it was the growing symphonic influence in the arrangements—choirs, thick multitracking—and a variety of shorter segues that tempted the prog tag. Then, in 2002, they ripped off a Queen title for *A Night at the Opera*, which found Blind Guardian at the height of their ambition. Complex arrangements, layers of keyboards, stacks and stacks of overdubs, a four-man vocal choir, many months in the studio—*A Night at the Opera* was a very conscious attempt to out-bombast their English art rock heroes. The band later admitted that there seemed no way to push that approach further, so they U-turned toward more comfortable realms on their next album, *A Twist in the Myth*.

The symphonic Euro-metal approach of Helloween and Blind Guardian was supported both by traditional and Progressive metal audiences. What became known as "power metal" and the new Progressive metal movement became intertwined, and U.S. bands such as Crimson Glory and Savatage greatly contributed to this intersection. Crimson Glory's *Transcendence* may not have pioneered anything truly new, but it was so well written and performed that it remains a prog metal monument decades later. At the time of *Transcendence*'s release in 1988, fellow Floridians Savatage were morphing from tradition-bound headbangers to Broadway-ready prog metal avatars. Their reinvention in the '90s acted as a major catalyst for Progressive metal bands the world over.

Vauxdvihl's *To Dimension Logic*, 1994

The answer to the question "What is truly progressive?" is more like Australia's Vauxdvihl. And their reward was cult status, at best, and a one-way trip to obscurity before total demise. Vauxdvihl released the lasting cult favorite *To Dimension Logic* in 1994. Although influenced by Queensrÿche and Fates Warning's trickiest work, the Australians put an exotic spin on their material that only became weirder with successive releases. *Vog*, from 1998, and *Siberian Church Recordings*, from 2001, displayed music built of perplexing shapes that moved far from *To Dimension Logic* into an unfamiliar, almost irreconcilable melting pot of ideas. Vauxdvihl were so original that they painted themselves into the most obscure corners of the genre.

Germany's Secrecy, while more firmly rooted in tradition, released two albums in the early '90s of angular, challenging metal. They successfully merged technical post-thrash power metal with unpredictable rhythmic changes and acquired-taste vocals. Dig even deeper and you'll find such peculiarities as Carisma and Fatal Opera, two bands that met the same obscure fate as Vauxdvihl and Secrecy—the price of originality.

Yet the story is not as simple as "progressive" versus "Progressive." A select few bands emerged during the overpopulated 1990s and found success, building large discographies while bringing much-needed individuality and character to the scene. Chief among those stand-outs: Dutch act Ayreon, led by mastermind Arjen Lucassen; Sweden's incredibly ambitious Pain of Salvation, whose Daniel Gildenlöw is the prime creative engine; and one Devin Townsend, an eccentric Canadian who has shared labels, stages and fans with many in the Progressive metal movement but remains a square peg in the round hole of its orthodoxy. Each of these artists represents a rejection of herd mentality—Townsend could even be considered a pariah.

The towering body of work by Ayreon simply speaks for itself. Beginning with Dutch traditional metal band Bodine at the dawn of the 1980s, and then moving onto the more popular Vengeance in 1984, Arjen Lucassen eventually left conventional metal behind in 1994 to form Ayreon, a band of his own design. "I was tired of touring and making concessions for others," he says with relief. "I'm somewhat of a recluse. I don't like to work with people very much. It's fantastic not having to compromise anymore and to be my own boss—at least for this egomaniac."

Lucassen has certainly been accused of having an ego, freely manifested not only in his music but in his enthusiasm for his music. In the liner notes for the reissue of Ayreon's *Into the Electric Castle,* he writes: "Recently I listened to the album, after not having heard it for quite some time. A feeling of joy came over me; it sounds so impressive and almost flawless...a damned classic album."

Whether the result of ego, confidence, genius, or mere megalomania, the majority of fans agree that *Into the Electric Castle* is Ayreon's pinnacle, referring to it in online reviews as "the greatest album ever made," or simply as "mind-blowing."

One of many Ayreon guest musicians, Gary Wehrkamp of Shadow Gallery has only found Lucassen to be a generous, unselfish friend. "He's probably the nicest guy I have met in the music business, and that's saying a lot, because I've met a lot of nice people. He's also been the most helpful, and the guy seems to be devoid of any ego of who he is or what he does. Just the help he's given me—I can call him and ask for anything and he would not hesitate to help in any way."

Each Ayreon album is entirely written by Lucassen, and while the spine of the material is clearly more in the progressive rock vein, he thickens it with mammoth slabs of guitar and pounding, simplistic rhythms. To achieve the fine balance between rock and metal, Lucassen has employed Symphony X guitarist Michael Romeo, Gorefest drummer Ed Warby, Rocket Scientists member and solo artist Erik Norlander on synths, and Uriah Heep keyboardist Ken Hensley. Add these to the long list of literally scores of other performers, guest vocalists and ever-dominant conceptual threads over the project's fifteen-year run, and Lucassen's own keyboard and guitar work almost get lost in the pageantry.

At first listen, Ayreon seems insanely overwrought, even for fans of melodramatic, theatrical rock and metal. The albums are extremely long; only one clocks in at under an hour, and most are double-albums with playing times of well over two hours. Ayreon's debut, *The Final Experiment*, featured a mostly Dutch lineup, yet still cast a wide net that caught members of bands as varied as '70s prog band Finch to death metal lords Gorefest. Later efforts amassed an enormous list of guest musicians, including the Gathering's Anneke van Giersbergen and Within Temptation's Sharon den Adel; '70s prog rock icons Ton Scherpenzeel of Kayak and Thijs van Leer of Fo-

cus; and major prog metal figures like Opeth's Mikael Åkerfeldt and Dream Theater's James LaBrie. Even Iron Maiden vocalist Bruce Dickinson lent his pipes to the ten-minute "Into the Black Hole" for 2000's *Flight of the Migrator*.

Ayreon's bombastic music is smothered with vocals and lyrics that convey Lucassen's ambitious story lines. He notes that *Into the Electric Castle* is intentionally "over-the-top," a "tongue-in-cheek science fiction story with exaggerated cliché characters." None of this for its own sake, as Lucassen explains: "I didn't want it to be complicated. I wanted everyone to easily become one with the story. No obtrusive messages, just plain escapism."

Lucassen's sense of drama and storytelling quite obviously comes from the '70s prog rock ethic. His material is the modern equivalent of the big rock operas of the Who,

Ayreon mastermind Arjen Lucassen
(*Cristel Brouwe*

Jeff Wayne's *The War of the Worlds*, the deep conceptual works of Pink Floyd, and the rock/classical fusion pioneered by Procol Harum and Deep Purple. He also credits the Beatles, whose influence can be heard very clearly throughout his albums, especially 1996's *Actual Fantasy*. Queen, Rainbow, Jethro Tull, Led Zeppelin, and relatively obscure Canadian band Klaatu also figure into the inspirational mix. Growing up in the middle of the Netherlands' healthy '70s prog scene, Lucassen also names Kayak, the "wacky" Supersister, and Trace's first album as major influences.

Ayreon albums demand a long attention span and a large chunk of time—snacking on a song here or there doesn't work. To create something more than "just music," Lucassen designs his albums to be cinematic, multidimensional experiences. He hopes people focus on the larger scope of Ayreon's detailed 140-minute journeys. "I don't have the attention span to listen to just music for over an hour," he says. "I am, however, able to watch a movie for two hours. So with my music, I try to combine the two, and add an extra dimension to the music. I couldn't listen to just the first record of Pink Floyd's *The Wall*. I have to hear the whole double album. So I hope people experience my albums as an adventure and have the patience to sit the whole thing out."

Recalling Dream Theater's hyperactive Mike Portnoy, Lucassen doesn't find his demanding main gig to be enough. Outside the time-consuming Ayreon writing and recording schedule, Lucassen developed Star One in 2002, a project focusing solely on the metal character of Ayreon. On the opposite side, he recorded a one-off project as the lush, atmospheric Ambeon—"ambient" plus Ayreon. And he helped kick off the career of gothic metal band Stream of Passion. He also inverted roles by acting as guest performer on various albums by Within Temptation, obscure prog metal bands Space Mirrors and Galexia, and projects by vocalist Ian Parry and keyboardist Erik Norlander.

In 2009, Lucassen launched Guilt Machine, whose debut, *On This Perfect Day*, aimed in a more modern direction than Ayreon and bore some resemblance to Porcupine Tree or English art rockers Muse. Incidentally, ex–Porcupine Tree drummer Chris Maitland laid down the drum tracks.

As of 2008, Ayreon went on hiatus, leaving Lucassen plenty of time for his other ambitions. But his main project is hardly on ice due to poor sales or other wavering business circumstances. In fact, Ayreon has consistently been a top-selling act for the Inside Out label. Perhaps the band just did all it could do. Considering the effort it requires to assemble extended lineups and compose music of such density and conceptual weight over eight more-than-full-length albums, Lucassen has a right to be exhausted. But resting isn't exactly on the agenda. "I will be recording some side projects, and I want to see what happens after that," he says. "If I ever do an Ayreon album again, it would have to be quite different from the previous albums."

In 1994, as Arjen Lucassen first launched the Ayreon ship in the Netherlands, Pain of Salvation was coming to life in Sweden. Yet while Ayreon was about bombastic sci-fi escapism, Pain of Salvation's concerns were worldly and immediate—and the Swedes grew to be an underground phenomenon of the 2000s.

The restless and creative Daniel Gildenlöw had written the phrase "pain of salvation" on a school notebook long before he formed the band. Gildenlöw felt from a young age he would one day play music for a living. A multi-instrumentalist and constant seeker of knowledge, Gildenlöw has taken Pain of Salvation through a variety of concept albums, constantly retooling his musical direction. One of the most unpredictable acts in the modern progressive metal sphere, Pain of Salvation's perpetual drive forward has left behind nearly as many listeners as each successive album has gained. In the words of Inside Out Records vet Jim Pitulski: "Even their own fans can't keep up with them."

Gildenlöw was raised on a steady diet of Simon & Garfunkel, the Beatles, and Kiss. Later came fascinations with Queensrÿche and San Francisco hybrid pioneers Faith No More, an influence still heard in Pain of Salvation's music. But he never stuck with most bands for long. "I get fed up very easily," Gildenlöw admits. "I usually say, 'I change, therefore I am.' Just as I started to explore my inner Geoff Tate, I suddenly said 'nah, I want to go this way now.' Plus, I've always been more of a song fan than a band fan." For instance, David Bowie's "Life on Mars?" is one of Gildenlöw's all-time favorite songs. "Only 5 percent of what Bowie does is interesting," he says. "It's just that when he's good, he's really good."

Unlike nearly all of his contemporaries, Gildenlöw never latched onto early metal classics such as Black Sabbath and Rush, or legendary proggers Yes and Genesis. "At one point I have to catch up with all that music," he says. "I just don't have a history with that stuff, but I appreciate it every time I hear it."

Small wonder, with such an unorthodox set of influences—and the lack of more obvious ones—that Pain of Salvation would itself be unorthodox and anything but obvious. The band's first two albums—*Entropia* and *One Hour by the Concrete*

Lake—offered a dynamic, dramatic kind of metal. Released in 1997 and 1998, respectively, the albums were only loosely products of their time. For every song like "Inside" that could be paralleled to Dream Theater and the new breed, there were ten more that couldn't be easily pinned down, such as "Handful of Nothing" with its Meshuggah-like drum patterns, or "People Passing By," rife with funky slap-bass.

"At that point we would gladly have been described as 'progressive metal,'" says Gildenlöw, "although I've never considered us one of those bands."

Much of Pain of Salvation's material is thickly layered, textured stuff that moves in a cinematic fashion: full of drama, changing scenes, varied in color. As Gildenlöw continued to absorb new influences and shed old ones, Pain of Salvation's music also changed. Following the highly regarded *One Hour by the Concrete Lake*, Gildenlöw broke the mold and distanced the band from easy Progressive metal affiliations with *The Perfect Element* and *Remedy Lane*, albums of remarkable depth that demanded time and focus from the listener.

In perpetual motion: Pain Of Salvation's Daniel Gildenlöw, 2002 *(Matt Johnsen)*

With a growing body of work, various online chat rooms and discussion boards became abuzz with all things Pain of Salvation. By 1999, new progressive metal discussion board Perpetual Motion had gathered opinionated enthusiasts by the dozens. Gildenlöw remembers a thread "about how progressive metal was for the 'thinking man,' and how stupid all other music was. Someone said that a song with only three chords could not be a good song. It pissed me off because that's the exact kind of narrow-mindedness they're also complaining about."

Already thick into the writing of the band's third album, *The Perfect Element*, Gildenlöw responded by penning "Ashes," completely bursting the complexity bubble. "It's just three chords over and over again," he says with a chuckle, "the same three chords for the verse, for the bridge, the chorus, and the solo."

Gildenlöw got the last laugh: "'Ashes' was voted Song of the Year on the Perpetual Motion board in 2000. A lot of them probably didn't realize it was only three chords, because it's all in what you put onto those three chords. It was my victory."

After stealthily challenging the attitudes of his own fans with "Ashes," Gildenlöw invited them to actively participate in the band's next endeavor. The fifteen-part epic *Be* (2004) confounded even their most devout followers with abrupt shifts in sonic scenery. *Be* was an erratic adventure that spun a variety of twists and turns throughout seventy minutes. One highlight was "Vocari Dei," a series of real voice-mail recordings by fans who were encouraged to leave personal telephone messages for God. The raw emotions heard in the array of responses provided a compelling centerpiece and an easily grasped anchor on an album of conceptual convolutions. An accompanying DVD helped make clearer the album's myriad layers, allowing people who didn't "get" *Be* the first time to evaluate it in a new light. Gildenlöw hopes to dabble further in the world of musical multimedia, in order to transcend the career cycle of album/DVD/tour that binds most bands.

As much as lyrics and concepts play a role in Pain of Salvation, Gildenlöw is careful to not let them overtake the music. "I really care for that balance," he says, pointing to Simon & Garfunkel. "They always sang about things that matter. I remember listening to 'The Sounds of Silence' and 'The Boxer,' and I'd be completely devoured by both the music and the lyrics. That's been with me ever since. Sometimes I write lyrics that I really like, but I find no way of combining that with music. Then I know better than to try. But when you can find that combination, it's really good."

Response to *Be* was varied, and its follow-up, 2007's *Scarsick*, further subdivided the band's audience. Where *Be* was sprawling, *Scarsick* was brazenly provocative. The first half of the album was like a sampling of the past several decades of popular music run through the Gildenlöw filter. The title track incorporated simplistic nu-metal in its vocal and rhythmic syntax, marrying fat grooves to the kind of ethereal melodies expected from the band. "Spitfall" took that a step further, with hip-hop verses and a chorus that sounded more hardcore than metal. "Cribcaged" swayed like a heavy lullaby, lyrically clever despite, or perhaps because of, its excessive "fuck this, fuck that" text. "America" was a burning condemnation of Bush-era U.S. politics, set to the tone of metallic pop punk meeting '70s art rock. "Disco Queen" added levity with dumb dance beats and double-entendre lyrics. Those who stayed with *Scarsick*'s schizophrenic opening barrage found an anchor in the second half, with "Kingdom of Loss," "Mrs. Modern Mother Mary," and "Enter Rain" sounding more characteristic of the band's older, more beloved work.

Scarsick's mishmash of styles felt a lot closer to Faith No More than the Queensrÿche and Dream Theater tones of earlier Pain of Salvation material. The album distanced the band definitively from the more predictable groups in the Progressive metal pack. Fans holding out for a return-to-prog-metal album had little encouragement from Gildenlöw in 2009 when, working on their seventh album, he likened the new material to "Jeff Buckley meets Foo Fighters with a little Led Zeppelin and Black Sabbath."

"The only band or artist from those that I actually listen to is Jeff Buckley," he added.

The result was 2010's *Road Salt One*, an entirely earthy and rocking thing, lacking no passion but hardly looking back to the band's previous work. The band was careful to warn that *Road Salt One* "will not beg for your liking, it will not make excuses, it will not carry you safely across dangerous waters. If you don't pick up its pace it will leave you stranded at the curb of the road." Talk about forward thinking. By the time you read this, Gildenlöw and his band will have likely taken yet another change of direction.

Though he seems to shirk his own legacy, Gildenlöw's perpetual forward movement and the intimacy of his lyrics have gained the admiration and loyalty of fans who lionize him and the band. For a brief time in October 2008, a fan and Wikipedia monkey-wrencher altered the band's listing on that site to read: "Pain of Salvation is a Swedish progressive metal band featuring Daniel Gildenlöw (known in a few other countries by the name of God)... Another trademark of the band is that each album is a concept and are the best albums made by mankind, ever, in forever."

Gildenlöw finds that level of adoration and accompanying gargantuan slices of hyperbole "both flattering and a bit scary. The music we do is a bit different from what's out there. And the lyrics deal with topics people can relate to on an emotional level, so they get drawn in close. They feel connected. They become very convinced by all that is Pain of Salvation."

Pain Of Salvation at the 2004 ProgPower USA festival,
L-R: Daniel Gildenlöw, Johan Langell, Johan Hallgren
(Esa Ahola)

Wisely, Pain of Salvation ripped up the Progressive metal rulebook early in their career. Gildenlöw acknowledges the irony of non-progressive Progressive metal: "It's like the Britpop wave. Britpop bands imitated the Beatles, but the whole thing with the Beatles was that they did not imitate. They were breaking boundaries, trying to find new ways. The Britpop bands get the clothes, the style, the accent, all of the surface bits, but they don't push the boundaries. The Beatles were about having odd time signatures when needed, trying different instrumentation when needed, screaming when you want to, singing very softly when you want to. So, for 'Progressive metal,' maybe we should invent a new name."

Say what you like about him, but Devin Townsend does not have a problem coming up with a new name. "How about calling me industrial trance pop progressive hard rock?" he says. "Most people aren't going to like it anyway, so fuck it."

But since his arrival in 1993, enough people have grown to love the Canadian musician to form a dedicated core audience for his vast musical outpourings. Townsend's public introduction came at the age of twenty-one on Steve Vai's 1993 album, *Sex and Religion*. After flirting with the mainstream in this short-lived, major-label, lead vocalist role, the young Townsend completely sidestepped all that with his Strapping Young Lad and Ocean Machine projects. Strapping Young Lad is where he put his excess anger and frustration, while Ocean Machine's wide-open cosmic atmosphere offered the introspective, chilled side of Townsend. Ocean Machine eventually found a home on the Inside Out label, which continued to release most of Townsend's endeavors. Even amidst a roster of unique acts, his ever-changing artistic nature and continual musical evolution gave him black sheep status in a scene he refuses to call home.

Searching for lattes and deconstructing cheeseburgers: Devin Townsend in 2001 (*Frank White*)

"There's an archetype that has been established for what is and isn't progressive," Townsend says, "and that just seems ironic. It's this idea that progressive music has to be about fourteen-minute-long directionless epics. It seems hilarious that if something was groundbreaking, like [1974 Genesis album] *The Lamb Lies Down on Broadway*, people hold on to the archetype of what it was that broke the ground in perpetuity. Here we are thirty-five years later and people are still holding on.

"When Dream Theater first came out, I thought they were great. And Mike, their drummer, he's a good dude. And the keyboard player, Jordan, that guy's fucking brilliant. But a lot of the clones of Dream Theater, it's just kind of glued together under the guise of being 'progressive' strictly by the fact that they're taking twenty-minute-long journeys up their own asses."

As much as Devin Townsend is apart from the Progressive metal stream, he is, in some ways, a part of it. His extensive catalog has endeared him to a wide variety of music enthusiasts (like Daniel Gildenlöw, Townsend has his share of obsessed fans), although some who appreciate colorful, textured albums *Synchestra* or *Terria* probably found his abrasive Strapping Young Lad alter ego hard to swallow.

Just as he doesn't fit into the typical Progressive metal archetype, neither did Townsend gain membership to the "Rush club," as he calls it, after contributing a cover of "Natural Science" to Rush tribute album *Working Man* in 1996. His quirky, liberal interpretation was widely lambasted. "Rush is revered in such a way that people are super-hostile over anything that's not by the book with that band."

Acknowledging Rush's impact—"they mean ten thousand times more than I'll ever mean"—he admits he was never fond of the band, which nearly constitutes an act of heresy for a forward-thinking Canadian musician, especially in the heavy music field. Townsend names less predictable sources of inspiration: traditional metal bands Judas Priest and W.A.S.P., as well as composers Igor Stravinsky and Andrew Lloyd Webber. "Andrew Lloyd Webber was how I learned about music. It was a great way to teach somebody how to be emotional in music, because it's stuff with such heaving, broad strokes of emotion. Like, this is what 'happy' looks like, and this is what 'happy' sounds like. This is 'sad,' this is *so* 'sad.' This is 'angry'! Big, broad strokes."

In 1997, his aggro/industrial metal band Strapping Young Lad released the highly acclaimed *City*. The album seethed with an unbelievable intensity, then went a few steps further. *City* and its fallout took a toll on Townsend. A diagnosed bipolar personality, he entered a mental hospital to retrieve the sanity that was hanging by a thread. With some stability regained, Townsend set to work on less artery-bursting material through his solo work, though S.Y.L. later reformed and recorded three more albums before going back on hiatus. "I spent so many years screaming my head off about shit that really didn't matter too much to me," Townsend admits.

Together with drummer Gene Hoglan—companion in Strapping Young Lad and veteran of heavy hitters Dark Angel and Death—Townsend has recorded a stream of interesting solo albums, from the abrasive *Physicist* to the more approachable *Terria*, all of them huge in scope and atmosphere. Later projects such as *Devlab* and *Hummer* even traveled in the world of experimental music. "[Real] progressive music, to me," he says, "is more like ambient music, like soundscapes—letting things morph from one thing to another."

With every move Townsend defies convention, and together with his erratic personality, it has led some to describe him as crazy, or a genius, or "a crazy genius." He maintains that he is none of those things. "I'm actually a really basic human," he

Devin Townsend's right-hand man:
Indomitable drum god Gene Hoglan
(*Mike Coles*)

says. "I like being warm, I like eating, I like sleeping, I don't like moving. I like to think about bullshit that I'm never gonna figure out. 'Crazy,' to me, is Nickelback."

In addition to his own work, steady gigs as a producer have ensured that Townsend enjoys a life surrounded and supported by nothing but music. His studio work with Gwar, Soilwork, and Lamb of God—not to mention Strapping Young Lad—won him acclaim in aggro-oriented circles. And whether he likes it or not, the material recorded under his own name has etched its way into the modern Progressive metal consciousness.

His 2007 album, *Ziltoid the Omniscient*, was based around the wacky concept of Ziltoid, a fourth-dimensional alien who came to Earth in search of the best coffee in the universe—coffee that would fuel the alien's time machine, aiding him in achieving legendary coolness by being the greatest guitar player to ever have lived. Somewhere between profound and ridiculous, the concept is typical Townsend. "I love that record," he claims proudly. "The metaphor behind that record is what was interesting about it, yet a lot of people were like, 'That's just really stupid.'"

Townsend's music can be taken on a variety of levels, sometimes evoking great meaning as metaphor, sometimes functioning as pure entertainment, or sometimes, as he readily admits, meaning "absolutely fucking nothing." Beneath the jokey rubbery exterior, however, is a will of steel, as Townsend vows to "never compromise artistic value or musicality in favor of commercial success or image."

Chasing the meaningful nonsense, he toyed with writing an album called *The Deconstruction of a Cheeseburger*. "I like the idea of deconstructing things down to their source. Anything—a rubber duck, gum boots, or a cheeseburger. Anything."

Instead, his next release was 2009's *Ki*, the first of four releases under the Devin Townsend Project banner. He describes *Ki* as "a subtle, severe album. The point of the music is that the whisper is louder than the roar in many ways."

The follow-up by the Devin Townsend Project, *Addicted,* is a relatively straight-forward work of energetic, electronic pop metal. The world may have to wait a while longer for *The Deconstruction of a Cheeseburger.*

Playing at Atlanta's ProgPower festival in 2002, Townsend raged at and even poked fun at the crowd while tearing through a set that pleased a few and maddened most others. Chris Roy, stage manager of the festival since its inception, fondly re-members Townsend's appearance: "Devin was one of the best moments of the festival, for me, because he was almost too progressive in attitude and presentation for most to 'get.' I was already a fan of his, so I knew what we were in for. Glenn [Harveston, festival organizer] decided to have an 'oddball' band each year, and Devin fit that per-fectly. From the moment the curtain opened, some of the crowd was completely lost by his sense of humor, and it was only downhill for them after that. The rest heralded him as the hero of weekend."

While adventurous listeners grappled with Ayreon, Pain of Salvation, and Devin Townsend's assorted projects, a growing contingency happily consumed a steady diet of Symphony X, Shadow Gallery, Evergrey, Manticora, and the many other core artists of the more conventional Progressive metal movement. Lance King formed Nightmare Records to meet the demands of the quickly expanding global scene in the early '90s. For King—who doubles as a vocalist and has fronted a number of bands, including Balance of Power, Pyramaze, and, most recently, Avian—"'progressive' doesn't necessarily have to mean something that hasn't been done before."

Apparently it all depends how high you set the bar for "progressive" and what that actually defines. "'Progressive' is a term that indicates a specific element in the music," says King. "It's not your three-chord songwriting style—it's more technical in nature, generally more over-the-top. I think of it as 'musician's music' or 'intellec-tual's music,' or to coin a phrase that was used to promote Queensrÿche's early music, 'thinking man's metal.'"

King points out that "technical" does not necessarily equal "progressive," or vice versa. As many others have noted, progressive music doesn't have to be technical to be forward-thinking. "Pink Floyd and Talking Heads were progressive," he says, "but surely Talking Heads weren't technically proficient on any level."

In fact, Devin Townsend sees the overabundance of technical skills today as having little to do with progressive music. "When I was fifteen," he says, "there were basically eight guitar players that were amazing and no one could touch them. Now everybody is amazing. Everybody knows how to sweep pick. Everybody knows how to do forty-five-finger tap-ons. Everybody's got everything, and with Pro Tools you can polish a turd until it shines. So the idea of technique being 'progressive' is ridiculous to me."

Zero Hour guitarist Jasun Tipton understands and embraces both sides of the "technical = progressive" debate. He defines "progressive metal" as "dark, heavy music that incorporates odd time signatures, tempo changes, key modulations, and polyrhythms with beautiful clean-tone passages. Progressive metal is music without limits. You can incorporate classical, jazz, new age, fusion, and many other styles of music into the mix. It's the freest type of metal music to play."

Tipton also believes bands can throw technique out the window and still be progressive. "Some say Pink Floyd's music is easy to play," he says. "But that's not the point. Pink Floyd is so creative and dynamic. David Gilmour's phrasing can put you into another world. Creating a masterpiece like *Dark Side of the Moon* is no easy task. If you don't have creative vision, you have nothing."

The consensus seems to be that impressive technique, something anyone can learn, can never compare with creative vision, something you're born with. Artists that sit on both sides of the line are rare. In the end, a musician's set of natural, inborn tools—crafty songwriting and incredible imagination—are probably most valuable. Mistaking the mechanics for the art is probably a key division between Progressive metal, the style, and truly *progressive* metal.

Russian artist Wassily Kandinsky famously declared, "There is no 'must' in art, because art is free." So with the art of music, Pain of Salvation is no more "right" than Symphony X. Some bands subvert the progressive metal ideal of total creative freedom, while others embody its very essence. Once all possible combinations of the twelve-tone musical scale have been combined, it becomes vastly more difficult to put a new spin on metal.

"It's truly rare to find a band that breaks the boundaries of what has been done musically," says Lance King. "There really is nothing that hasn't been played, no chord progression or chain of notes in any particular order—it's all been played before."

Yet in the mid-1990s, bands began popping up all over Sweden and Norway that challenged and destroyed that very assertion, proving yet again that reports of the death of progress were vastly premature.

PROGRESSIVE BY NUMBERS

HERE'S A BRIEF LOOK AT TEN IMPORTANT VOICES in the modern Progressive metal stream. A couple were there at the very beginning; some arose in the thick of the '90s explosion; several are newer permutations of its continuing evolution. This is not a complete list and is not meant to marginalize anyone. This enormous sector of the greater prog metal world almost deserves its own thousand-page book.

ANDROMEDA (formed 1999, Sweden)

Obvious influence from the Big Three and Rush, pushed in a chunkier, more modern direction; melodic, controlled, power metal–ish vocals somewhere between mid- and high range. Torrents of guitar/keyboard melodies, some Dream Theater–ish shred while staying song-based. Celestial/spacey atmosphere; even some AOR catchiness in tracks such as "In the End"; full-time keyboardist. **Key albums:** *Extension of the Wish* (2001), *II=I* (2003) **Members also played in:** FKÜ, Nonexist, Opus Atlantica, Space Odyssey

Quote: Guitarist Johan Reinholdz was asked what he was listening to in 2003: "I've been listening to Soilwork, *Figure Number Five*. Great album! The 3rd and the Mortal, *Tears Laid in Earth*; Propellerheads; the *Twin Peaks* soundtrack; Tori Amos, as always. Refused, *The Shape of Punk to Come*, also some orchestral stuff like Stravinsky and [Antonín] Dvořák."

ANGRA (formed 1992, Brazil)

Began with a European power metal sound obviously derived from Helloween; quickly established a more individualistic style by the mid-'90s; theatrical, lots of melody, dense layering, multitiered arrangements, vocals in the higher range, virtuosic guitar

Angra's Kiko Loureiro
(*Christina Ricciardi*)

playing; lots of keyboards as atmosphere, but no full-time keyboardist; occasionally draws from vastly different kinds of music, like samba or bossa nova, giving their music an ethnic/exotic touch; later works have revealed a variety of influences beyond the usual names; one of the most important and successful bands to come from the '90s Progressive/power metal wave. **Key albums:** *Holy Land* (1996), *Temple of Shadows* (2004) **Members also played in:** Almah, Looking Glass Self, Shaman, Tribuzy, Viper

Quote: "We had the same inspirations that [European power metal bands] did, but the difference is that we are very much in contact with many other styles, rhythms, harmonies, and melodies. So we combine our Brazilian way of music into metal." —guitarist Rafael Bittencourt

ARK (formed 1990, Norway/U.S.)

A union of lauded musicians, Ark burned brightly, although briefly. While the idea was hatched by guitarist Tore Østby and drummer John Macaluso at the dawn of the '90s, their first album didn't arrive until 1999, and by 2003 they were finished. A breath of fresh air in the clone-dominated post–Dream Theater microcosm of the late '90s/early 2000s, Ark's music drew from hard rock, prog rock, and classic metal, filtered through the adventurous inclinations of the membership. Ark's unique, refreshing sound was clearly the product of its ridiculously talented lineup: Østby, Macaluso, bassist Randy Coven, keyboardist Mats Olausson, and vocalist Jørn Lande.

Key albums: *Ark* (1999), *Burn the Sun* (2001) **Members also played in:** Conception, MCM, Yngwie Malmsteen, Jorn, Silver Mountain, Kamelot, Starbreaker, TNT, Mullmuzzler, Riot, Powermad, Masterplan, Allen/Lande, Beyond Twilight

Quote: "The meaning of Ark comes from Noah's ark. We are not a religious band, but we took the reference from the Bible because we have our ark, too. Our ark takes all musical styles, all musical elements. It's about freedom: Nothing is too stupid, nothing is too serious, any style is welcomed as long as it fits in well with the music we want to create." —guitarist Tore Østby

CONCEPTION (formed 1989, Norway)

One of the first bands to combine European power metal with a more progressive mind-set; dynamic and unpredictable mood changes, a few tricky rhythms, rock-solid rhythmic grooves, excellent guitar work by Tore Østby (later of Ark); down-to-earth vocals by Roy Khan, who would move onto enormously popular epic power metal band Kamelot; an important player in the welding together of power and progressive metals, and far from a clone. Conception reunited to play ProgPower USA in 2005, which organizer Glenn Harveston claims as "a personal high. I don't think I will ever come close to the personal satisfaction of seeing Tore and Roy back onstage together."

Key albums: *Parallel Minds* (1993), *In Your Multitude* (1995) **Members also played in:** Ark, Crest of Darkness, Kamelot, Satyricon

Quote: "The two most important bands or artists for me are a-ha and Geoff Tate from Queensrÿche. The first one was the one that made me see that I like those kinds of high shining vocals and melancholy lyrics and melodies. And Queensrÿche's *Rage for Order* in 1986 was great, and they were great up until 1990. Of course, a lot of other artists from pop and jazz. And I had my classical period." —vocalist Roy Khan

EVERGREY (formed 1995, Sweden)

Another band with a foundation in European power metal who deepen the sound with the occasional ambitious idea; emphasis on dramatic, gothic, dark atmosphere. Later work has become catchier, paired with chunky aggro- and groove-metal rhythms; full-time keyboardist.

Key albums: *Solitude • Dominance • Tragedy* (1999), *Recreation Day* (2003)

Evergrey delights the faithful
(*Todd Brown*)

Members also played in: Crystal Age, Kotipelto, Nightrage, Stratovarius, Warmen

Quote: "My musical inspiration is very wide. I like everything from jazz and hip-hop to death and black metal. My favorite artists are Kiss, Pantera, Nine Inch Nails, and Richie Kotzen, but I don't use them in any way when I write music for Evergrey. When I write Evergrey songs, I only think Evergrey. I try to get into an 'Evergrey mode' and just play." —Drummer Jonas Ekdahl

Redemption's Bernie Versailles (left) and Nick Van Dyk
(*Esa Ahola*)

REDEMPTION (formed 2001, U.S.)

Aggressive, driving rhythms and thick guitar tones; earthy mid-range vocals; catchy chorus melodies; multiple tempo changes; top-notch musicianship; power metal energy level; features vocalist Ray Alder of Fates Warning, a full-time member; guest performers have included Mark Zonder (Fates Warning), members of Reading Zero, and Symphony X guitarist Michael Romeo; full-time keyboardist.

Key albums: *The Fullness of Time* (2005), *The Origins of Ruin* (2007) **Members also played in:** Agent Steel, Fates Warning, Magnitude 9, Prymary, Steel Prophet

Quote: "I want to try and get away from clichés as far as possible. On *The Fullness of Time* I had a bunch of stuff that was kind of thematic. I wanted to present [the four-part title track] in a slightly connected way. A lot of people interpreted it as one twenty-minute-long song, which was not what I intended. However, I thought that the four songs also stood on their own, rather than just having to be listened to as part of the suite. I just think it's so clichéd and expected for every prog metal band to have their concept album. I wanted to take a step away from that. There is a thematic relationship in a loose way between the songs, but each one is left to stand on its own." —guitarist/leader Nick van Dyk

RIVERSIDE (formed 2001, Poland)

Heavily layered, contemplative, and introspective; less virtuosic and more focused on emotional content and atmosphere; solid playing all around, especially drummer Piotr "Mittloff" Kozieradzki; somewhere between prog rock and metal; obvious elements of Anathema and Porcupine Tree; full-time keyboardist. **Key albums:** *Out of Myself* (2003), *Anno Domini High Definition* (2009) **Members also played in:** Hate, Indukti, Xanadu

Quote: "When we first started this band, we were interested in Porcupine Tree and Anathema, and they were an influence, but our main influence is everything—not only music, but books and everything that is artistic. Our main goal is to create and build our own style, the Riverside style. In the future, no matter which direction bands like Porcupine Tree or Opeth choose to follow, we're going to go our own way. One thing I heard recently was that Riverside's music on *Second Life Syndrome* is too metal to be art rock, and too art rock to be metal. That was meant to be negative, but for me it's a great compliment because it means our music isn't easy to label and that we have our own style." —bassist/vocalist Mariusz Duda

ROYAL HUNT (formed 1989, Denmark)

Like Conception, an early player in the melding of melodic power metal and more ambitious ideas; some catchy elements that border on AOR territory; neoclassical guitar work mixed with a sharper '80s metal shred approach; keyboards played in the studio by leader André Andersen; lauded vocalists such as D.C. Cooper and Mark Boals have been members. **Key albums:** *Paradox* (1997), *The Mission* (2001) **Members also played in:** Cornerstone, Pretty Maids, Silent Force, Yngwie Malmsteen

Quote: "There's not many I've idolized, because once you start studying a particular singer you start sounding like them. But in terms of vocals, Rob Halford, Robert Plant, Aaron Neville, George Michael, and Bruce Dickinson have influenced me a lot over the years. In terms of bands, each of us is into different bands, but we all like Deep Purple, Yes, Rush, and Dream Theater." —ex-vocalist D.C. Cooper

SHADOW GALLERY (formed 1990, U.S.)

Dramatic neoclassical/symphonic elements, especially in guitar and keyboard melodies; very dynamic, with plenty of soft, quieter moments. Since their first album in 1992, Shadow Gallery have been accused of being Dream Theater clones, while others have lauded them for their professionalism; inspirations reach back into the '70s prog scene, recalling Kansas and Pink Floyd on such songs as "Destination Unknown," and neoclassical metal in the vein of Yngwie Malmsteen and the more epic side of Judas Priest. Their first-ever live performance finally took place in 2010, twenty years after their formation. **Key albums:** *Tyranny* (1998), *Room V* (2005) **Members also played in:** Amaran's Plight, Ayreon, Explorers Club, Star One

Quote: "I've spent my time being detailed, creative, challenged, and disciplined with the instruments I play. I've practiced hard because I wanted to be able to play better, find more ways to express my creativity. I worked at my skills and learned from the discipline of pushing myself to become a better player. So for me to flip on the radio and hear two-chord rock, where the guitars aren't in tune, the drums are sloppy and boring, and the content is so unoriginal and mundane, I just feel that none of my needs are expressed. The music business is 5 percent music and 95 percent business in the United States. It's not that I can't appreciate a simple song—I surely can—but when it's done by design and for the needs of the industry machine, it's so fake and unappealing." —guitarist/keyboardist Gary Wehrkamp

ZERO HOUR (formed 1993, U.S.)

On the more technical side of Progressive metal, while not quite true "tech"; obvious Fates Warning influence on early material, later stuff is more rhythm-based and aggressive, bordering on Meshuggah-esque complication; dynamically vast; wailing, high-ish vocals with great control; lots of shredding and angular time shifts; super-energetic; guitarist Jasun Tipton also plays keyboards. **Key albums:** *The Towers of Avarice* (2001), *Specs of Pictures Burnt Beyond* (2006) **Members also played in:** Death Machine, Power of Omens, Z-Lot-Z

Quote: Jasun Tipton's approach to seven-string guitar is featured on the *Progressive Shredoholic* instructional video. In his words, the DVD features "sweeping techniques;

Seven strings and 127 tricks up his sleeve:
Zero Hour's Jasun Tipton
(*Todd Brown*)

modal, exotic, and wide interval string-skipping ideas; two- and three-note-per-string wide-stretch segments; groupings of fives; progressive riffing ideas that add chromatics, exotics and arpeggios; Zero Hour solo sequences; and much more." Of bands that influenced their wide-ranging sound, he says: "We're fans of so many bands. We're inspired by Rainbow, Pink Floyd, King Crimson, the Pat Metheny Group, Tool, Dream Theater, Cynic, Meshuggah, Killswitch Engage, this list can go on forever. Zero Hour's focus is to create dark, heavy, technical, dynamic music. We never said, 'Let's be more like this band or that band.' We wanted to make our own mark."

"One thing I'm really proud of is that we're building bridges over generations. I was embarrassed the first few times that fans told me, 'My mom loves your record!' but now I hear it all the time. We have a much older fan base, compared to other bands from our generation, because we build a bridge to the past."—Christofer Johnsson, Therion

S INCE THE EARLY 1990s, IT SEEMED QUITE POSSIBLE that half of Sweden's population of roughly ten million were metalheads playing in at least three different bands each. Sweden's enormous metal boom seemed an unlikely phenomenon, and the main subgenre it exported—death metal—even more strange. Here is a country of great natural beauty—its people included—yet its main contributions to metal exuded ugliness and filth. Sweden is typically nonaligned during peacetime and neutral in times of war, yet the breed of metal that put Sweden on the map has been nothing if not extraordinarily nihilistic.

Author Daniel Ekeroth addressed this phenomenon in his book *Swedish Death Metal*. The short explanation is that the country's thriving underground was born of boredom with small-town Sweden, the inevitable energy of youth, and a national culture that encourages and even pays for music programs in and outside of the schools.

The popularity of grisly, violent metal from Sweden couldn't have been predicted. In the 1980s, the country offered classical music-influenced metal bands Silver Mountain and Yngwie Malmsteen's Rising Force; melodic hard rock/metal such as Europe and Treat; and harmless generic thrash such as Mezzrow and Tribulation.

ABSTRAKT ALGEBRA

Not terribly mathematical: Abstrakt Algebra's one and only album, 1995

Only late in the decade did the kids of Nihilist, Treblinka, and Carnage begin making harsher noises—eventually making history. That scene spawned hundreds of death metal imitators, and also ushered in Tiamat, Edge of Sanity, Meshuggah, and Opeth, bands that became manipulators and leaders. These bands loosened all ties to tradition and found something to call their own, something decidedly beyond the norm.

Death metal in Sweden wouldn't have been possible, Ekeroth believes, if not for groundbreaking black metal entity Bathory and revered doom-mongers Candlemass. In *Swedish Death Metal*, he writes: "The unexpected success of these two groups galvanized youngsters in Sweden to be more dedicated to their own bands. They were living proof that extreme music of superior quality could be produced in Sweden. They provided an example that Swedish metal could also be successful."

One could argue that Bathory were "progressive" with a small "p"—their initial six-album run was one of continual forward evolution. The contrast between the band's sixth album, 1991's *Twilight of the Gods*, and their self-titled debut of 1984 is remarkable. Credited with single-handedly creating the "Viking metal" genre, band leader Quorthon—born Tomas Forsberg—pointed to composer Richard Wagner and the most epic Manowar material as major catalysts for Bathory's pioneering "Viking metal" sound. So maybe Bathory can be considered progressive, though probably not "prog metal." The same can be said of other metal bands that went through a series of drastic growth spurts—England's Carcass and lesser-known Germans Pyogenesis, for example— while the usually tradition-bound Candlemass briefly threw their hat in the prog ring.

By 1994, Candlemass bassist, founder, and songwriter Leif Edling was left without a band, a legacy of classic doom metal albums behind him in the distant '80s. He put the band on ice and created the more adventurous Abstrakt Algebra. Their one and only album, released in 1995, found Edling's Sabbath-inspired doom taking on a '70s-era mentality. It was old prog in theory, but still quite modern in practice. While Edling admitted his Dream Theater fandom at the time of the album's creation, *Abstrakt Algebra* failed to go all the way, ending up a too-careful, compromised work.

While Edling was creating the second Abstrakt Algebra album in 1997, the band's label, Music for Nations, requested that he revive the Candlemass name. Having written the new material with a more advanced A.A. in mind, it's no wonder the music on the resulting *Dactylis Glomerata* had little to do with the Candlemass people had come to know. Even if plodding, ultra-heavy doom formed its foundation, the approach was a strange, experimental one with no obvious reference points save Black Sabbath's more psychedelic moments. Yet it wasn't Dream Theater, either. It was spacey and psychedelic—a unique Candlemass by any standard.

Dactylis Glomerata showed Edling had no interest in writing to formula, even if it brought him a healthier paycheck. He then moved the band forward and backward simultaneously with follow-up *From the 13th Sun*. The 1999 album was a trippy sci-fi take on early Black Sabbath, merging something tried and tested with something fresh—including an obtuse in-studio drum solo inside "Cyclo-F" and hazy layers of guitar effects everywhere else. "Rather than saying, 'Why should we have this in here?'" Edling explains, "I'd rather say, 'Why not?' I dislike things that are cliché and standard and mainstream." This curious seventh Candlemass work spelled the end of the band's progressive era. Edling returned to Candlemass's more recognizable style for future albums, and to more familiar lineups.

Johan Edlund's band Tiamat emerged early from the Swedish death metal scene, initially bearing the controversial moniker Treblinka. An important player in the Swedish uprising, Tiamat worked in a more occult-/black metal–influenced area than did most of their peers. Edlund's array of influences ranged from gothic rock to metal cult Mercyful Fate to '70s legends Pink Floyd, and the non-metal input informed his writing progressively until later albums bore little similarity to Tiamat's crude early material. On fourth album *Wildhoney* (1994), hypnotic goth and psychedelia were grafted onto the band's mid-paced occult metal frame. Acoustic guitar leads, synths, sound effects, and a lush, textured production lent the album an exotic quality. The throaty vocals, chunky mid-tempo riffs, and overall dark atmosphere of Tiamat's past meshed with the new elements for a curiously subdued work—one that proved incredibly successful. *Wildhoney* was the Century Media label's biggest seller in the years immediately following its 1994 release, topping previous best-sellers Unleashed and Grave (both more loyal participants in the Swedish death scene).

"I was just a very young guy [who] wanted to sound like his favorite band, Pink Floyd," says Edlund about *Wildhoney*. That influence came through even stronger on the follow-up three years later, *A Deeper Kind of Slumber*. The album took the dreamy qualities of *Wildhoney* ten steps further into esoteric coma-rock that was steeped in the influence of Pink Floyd's most chilled material and married to Edlund's pervasively depressive touch. *A Deeper Kind of Slumber* was a highly contentious album that left its metal past behind almost entirely, and was disliked even by some who embraced *Wildhoney*. Thereafter, Edlund took the band into realms that had more to do with Sisters of Mercy than with Pink Floyd. In the realm of dark gothic metal, Tiamat became well loved, and there they have stayed.

Another of the earliest underground Swedish death metal bands was Therion, founded and guided by guitarist/songwriter Christofer Johnsson. Symphonic and bombastic to the extreme, the Therion ensemble has come a long way since their cave-dark, ultra-heavy emanations of the early '90s. Their debut EP, *Time Shall Tell*, was standard Swedish death: crushing riffs, fat guitar tone, guttural vocals, and raw recording. While 1991 follow-up *Of Darkness* wasn't much different, an ambitious thread connected its eight songs. Several riffs utilized major chords—a distinct no-no in death metal's minor-scale orthodoxy—and keyboards were already creeping into the music.

As Johnsson told *Swedish Death Metal* author Daniel Ekeroth, "For *Of Darkness*, guitarist Peter Hansson got the idea that we should use keyboards on two songs; mainly as an effect on 'The Return,' but also for a melody at the end of 'Genocidal Raids.' I think Nocturnus was the only death metal band that had done that before."

From these baby steps, Therion soon crossed into a weird world. By 1992, when the band released *Beyond Sanctorum*, Johnsson had become fully immersed in Voivod's classic period and Celtic Frost's *To Mega Therion* and *Into the Pandemonium*. *Beyond Sanctorum* toyed with the abrupt time changes and unusual chord shapes inspired by the Canadian space cadets in Voivod. "Symphony of the Dead" and "Paths" foreshadowed Therion's future direction, while giving a nod to Frost with choral vocals and "orchestration"—symphonic keyboards rather than live musicians, due to a tiny budget.

"*Into the Pandemonium* is responsible for making me aware of what you can do with metal," Johnsson says, "how you could incorporate all these different elements. I have to give that album most of the credit for inspiring Therion, but on the other hand, without Uli Jon Roth and also Voivod, we wouldn't have begun doing what we do."

Therion's Christofer Johnsson makes an offering to the gods of prog (*Cristel Brouwer*)

Therion still had the unrefined charm of a minor death metal oddity. They were not yet anywhere near being in the league of Voivod or Celtic Frost. Yet Johnsson ambitiously expanded Therion's arrangements to create eleven-minute songs inspired by such '70s prog heroes as Kansas and King Crimson. Johnsson likens this period of Therion's growth to that of the earthier '70s prog bands. "It wasn't always so important that you had to be the tightest band back then," he says. "It was more about having great imagination."

Though Therion's earliest material might have been odd by typical death metal standards, in the early 1990s Johnsson journeyed even deeper into progressive and avant-garde interests, exorcising his weirdest musical demons in a bizarre metal trio called Carbonized. Founded by bassist Lars Rosenberg, who went on to play in Entombed and later Therion, Carbonized also included fellow Therion alum Piotr Wawrzeniuk on drums. The trio recorded three albums between 1991 and 1993 that ranged from psychedelic death/grind on *For the Security* to the posthumously released *Screaming Machines*, which found the band far removed from its origins.

Johnsson likens *Screaming Machines* to "the most psychedelic and weird-sounding elements of Voivod, Sonic Youth, Primus, and Black Flag," while noting the influence of Frank Zappa & the Mothers of Invention's 1966 debut, *Freak Out!* Angular, dissonant, inaccessible, and strange, *Screaming Machines* was an album no one could possibly love—and it was a total flop. Issuing label Foundation 2000 initially shipped three thousand copies, only to receive a third of them back in returns just one month later.

Loved by no one: Carbonized's
Screaming Machines

Between *For the Security* and *Screaming Machines* came 1993's *Disharmonization,* combining early death metal and grind influences with traits of Voivod and Sonic Youth. As Joakim Sterner—drummer for Swedish death metal band Necrophobic—described it: "You don't need to drink when you listen to this music—you get drunk from listening to it anyway."

Also in 1993, the next Therion release, *Symphony Masses: Ho Drakon Ho Megas,* continued to stretch into different territories, with a rocking groove inside "Powerdance" and "A Black Rose." Songs such as "Symphoni Drakonis Inferni," "The Ritualdance of the Yezidis," and "Dark Princess Naamah" moved into the dark, symphonic opera-metal realms that eventually engulfed Therion's sound. *Symphony Masses* found an entirely new lineup behind Johnsson, and from then on it would clearly be his band, with a talented array of musicians and vocalists coming and going with each album.

Two years later, *Lepaca Kliffoth* further explored the vein of *Symphony Masses,* albeit with markedly improved production thanks to the larger budget afforded by new label Nuclear Blast. Covering Celtic Frost's "Sorrows of the Moon" and keeping the gothic/opera flame alive with such tracks as "The Beauty in Black" and "Evocation of Vovin," Therion slowly carved its own niche. The band recruited guest vocalist Claudia-Maria Mokri—the same Claudia-Maria who sang on Celtic Frost's *Into the Pandemonium.* But for Johnsson, that small victory was overshadowed by public disinterest. Already in 1995, his hopes for Therion were beginning to fade. His band was looked upon as a peculiarity at best.

Though Therion's early albums were considered progressive, the later growth and diversification of ambitious occult/dark/death metal bands lessened their impact, if not their importance. *Beyond Sanctorum* sounds unsophisticated in light of such modern bands as Opeth and Orphaned Land. Johnsson understands. "We were kind of progressive or innovative with what we were doing within death metal," he says, "but today it's not very spectacular, because death metal has branched out in so many ways. Somebody could listen to an old Therion record today and think, 'This was innovative?' But you have to see everything in its own perspective, in its own time."

The same can be said of a band like Fear Factory, which emerged in the early '90s mixing the inhuman rage of death metal, the rhythmic stiffness of industrial, and the simplicity and brevity of hardcore, adding futuristic sci-fi imagery and a dual extreme/clean vocal approach. They were considered progressive, but so many other bands grafted similarly disparate worlds in the ensuing years that the innovation became the norm. This also holds true for Dream Theater and their influence, as the opportunities to hear their patented prog metal blueprint are now endless. Eventually, an innovation becomes something commonplace.

On the musical fringe and perhaps ahead of his time, Christofer Johnsson could have succumbed to the lure of a trendier path in hopes of capturing success. But his musical inspirations—'70s art rock such as Klaatu and Pavlov's Dog, prog and hard rock staples Eloy and Uriah Heep, and metal heroes Voivod and Celtic Frost—steered him always along a forward-thinking path. Still, perpetual cult status seemed to be Therion's fate. "I was disappointed that nobody was getting what we were doing," says Johnsson. "Not that I wanted to be famous, but I wanted to be recognized for our music, and it's frustrating to see all the reviews saying, 'This is the best thing we've ever heard,' while the records weren't selling."

Johnsson soon came to accept the price of originality. Therion was finding it harder and harder to match themselves with suitable bands to tour with. Worse, their record sales weren't encouraging, and they seemed to have painted themselves into a corner careerwise. Assuming the band was doomed to obscurity, Therion's leader decided their next album would be their last. He would go out big. Johnsson squeezed as much money from the label as possible and recorded the elaborate, over-the-top album he'd promised for years.

The Therion troupe at work
(Cristel Brouwer)

The band and their label undertook an enormous financial gamble in the name of progress. In laying everything on the line, Johnsson was unconsciously following the steps of his Swiss heroes. "Celtic Frost totally risked their career by doing *Into the Pandemonium*," he rightly notes.

But 1996's *Theli*, the album intended as commercial suicide, in fact granted Therion a brand-new life. *Theli* instantly sold twenty thousand copies in Europe— doubling what *Lepaca Kliffoth* had barely managed in a span of two years. Johnsson was shocked and the record label was extremely happy. "I was absolutely sure it would be our good-bye record," he insists, "a big 'fuck you' to the world. Nobody would buy it and it would be the last thing we'd do."

Theli's dark, mid-paced metal makes a bombastic dive into esotericism and exotica using opera and choral vocals and lyrics drawn from a variety of occult sources. This intentionally overblown, melodramatic Therion seemed to find three new fans for every old one that was turned off. Therion have since become one of Nuclear Blast's best-selling artists. They are allowed sizeable budgets to record albums thick with atmosphere and full of guest performers, and they enjoy the luxury of taking an extended cast of musicians on the road. A Therion show features so many people onstage that it's more like Cirque du Soleil than a metal gig. Ultimately, both the band

and Nuclear Blast benefit from a dedicated worldwide base of tens of thousands of fans who have embraced this unlikely and unusual band, which somehow found life after death.

While the modern Therion story merely starts with *Theli*, the band's rate of progress has since moved across a more lateral plane. They've found a comfortable area to inhabit. They maintain their successful sound by tinkering only with the microelements—a darker work here (*Secret of the Runes*), a bombastic double album there (*Lemuria/Sirius B*). *Gothic Kabbalah* showed that forward progress was still a part of Therion's modus operandi, achieved in a somewhat backward fashion—it peeled off more layers than it piled on. "It has fewer orchestral and operatic influences than our records normally do, so it's a bit of an odd Therion album," says the bandleader.

Maybe there is less surprise on the surface these days, but Johnsson still throws the occasional curveball—it's just harder to notice, because Therion have covered so much ground and because weird, hybrid metal styles are accepted more enthusiastically in the 2000s. "On the *Lemuria* album, on 'The Dreams of Swedenborg,' there's some Jimi Hendrix–influenced stuff, and some Madchester pop in some of the riffs—totally different from what we normally do," Johnsson says, "but no fans reacted like, 'Hey, this is completely different!' It just melted into what we do. So there's still innovation there, but it's not as easily recognized as something truly different. People are just more tolerant of change now."

Arriving in the late 1980s, Edge of Sanity clung to the Swedish death metal archetype only briefly. By their third album, 1993's *The Spectral Sorrows*, they were covering Manowar songs and writing Sisters of Mercy–inspired tracks such as "Sacrificed." Shortly after that, they recorded a version of the Police's "Invisible Sun" for the *Until Eternity Ends* EP. "We wanted to do a sort of Voivod thing with the song," says bandleader Dan Swanö, "with the strange twin vocal harmony. Together with Celtic Frost, Voivod are one of the bands that completely floored me during my thrash/death awakening. They were completely unique and even invented their own guitar chords. There were many Voivod moments in Edge of Sanity."

THERION'S SYMPHONIES
OF THE DEAD

LIKE MEKONG DELTA LEADER RALPH HUBERT, Therion's Christofer Johnsson has spent as much time studying classical composers as banging his head to the metal classics. Johnsson's critics say he's failing in his attempts to be a bona fide classical composer, but they may be failing to see the bigger picture. "Of course it's not classical music," Johnsson maintains. "That's not what we do. It's a blend. It only has elements of classical."

Other metal bands took the classical bull by the horns before Therion. Rock bands Procol Harum and Deep Purple went symphonic as far back as the late '6os. It was innovative then, and its increase in popularity in the '7os was an integral component of the classic prog sound. By the end of the 1990s, the idea was being exploited by a variety of different artists across various genres, second only to the popular acoustic/unplugged scenario.

A fan of both metal and classical, Johnsson has attempted a variety of metal-meets-classical projects. "If you listen to Metallica's *S&M*, you can tell they don't understand the classical part, and conductor Michael Kamen doesn't understand rock and roll," he says, preferring instead Yngwie Malmsteen's *Concerto Suite for Electric Guitar and Orchestra in E Flat Minor Opus 1* and Scorpions' collaboration with the Berlin Philharmonic. Johnsson also appreciates more symphonic, bombastic songs by tried-and-true metal gods Manowar ("Battle Hymn," "Mountains") and Ozzy Osbourne ("Revelation [Mother Earth]," "Diary of a Madman").

"I'm huge into classical and opera," he says, "but not much modern stuff. Nicholas Lens would be one of few exceptions. His way of working with rhythms on 'Flamma Flamma' affected me. I like 'old modern' composers to a certain extent. Stravinsky is brilliant, and influenced Therion's 'Via Nocturna' on the *Deggial* album. But my biggest passion is Richard Wagner. Without him it's hard to imagine how Therion would sound. He's by far my biggest musical hero. Beethoven never had any direct influence on a composition of mine, but he should be mentioned, as Beethoven's Fifth was the first music I ever picked to listen to myself, when I was around three years old. I'd press the button on our fully automatic vinyl player and play the A side over and over again until my mom would put headphones on me."

In 2009, Johnsson and Therion put all their classical cards on the table with *The Miskolc Experience*. The double-CD features one disc of Therion originals, and another disc of Therion-ized Dvořák, Verdi, Mozart, Saint-Saëns, and Wagner compositions, all recorded live with a full orchestra at Hungary's International Opera Festival of Miskolc.

The fourth Edge of Sanity album, 1994's *Purgatory Afterglow*, introduced an-other goth-rock track in "Black Tears," while opener "Twilight" was an epic multipart adventure that opened the door a few inches for upcoming diverse Swedish death metal bands such as Opeth and Mourning Sign.

Swanö is rightly proud of Edge of Sanity's defiance against the norm. "I hope the coming generations will find Edge of Sanity and be inspired by our diversity," he says. "So many death metal bands sounded the same, and they disappeared. We wanted to show that every band coming from this genre doesn't have to be narrow-minded. Just look at other forms of music. I'm always drawing comparisons to Kiss.

Whatever gets the job done: Left-handed Dan Swanö playing upside down right-handed guitar, 2001
(*Matt Johnsen*)

They were doing different stuff all the time, but you could still hear it was Kiss. They could do rock, disco, metal, whatever. So we just thought, 'Why can't we do a goth-ic rock song?'"

Under Swanö's leader-ship, Edge of Sanity quickly suc-cumbed to his wide palette of in-fluences and talents. The growler introduced pitched singing as early as their second album, *Un-orthodox*—before it was common practice in extreme metal sub-genres. In 1996, he directed the creation of the monumental *Crimson* opus. Featuring guest vocals by young Opeth leader Mikael Åkerfeldt, *Crimson* was comprised of one single titular track, with a run-ning time of exactly forty minutes. The song moved from epic death metal to melan-choly goth to '70s prog–inspired passages, all arranged in tighter and more digestible fashion than could be expected of any forty-minute song. *Crimson* stands as Edge of Sanity's towering achievement, cementing their place in progressive metal history.

While Edge of Sanity was Dan Swanö's main musical focus throughout the 1990s, he should also be remembered as leader of the groundbreaking Pan-Thy-Monium during the same period. In the midst of Sweden's death metal boom, this obscurity delivered albums that blew genre paradigms right off their hinges.

Wrapped in enigma and shrouded in mystery, there was seemingly no precedent for a band like Pan-Thy-Monium. Their 1990 *Dawn* demo and following *Dream II* EP introduced a band that did everything contrary to orthodoxy. Their odd music was arty in presentation. They rarely took photos, and when they did, they went the Mekong Delta route of intentional obfuscation. They used words and language of their own invention, à la French band Magma.

Pan-Thy-Monium began as a project between Swanö, Edge of Sanity bandmate Benny Larsson, and guitarist Robert Ivarsson. In the tradition of Hellhammer and Voivod, the band took on alter egos; Swanö as Day DiSyraah, Larsson as Winter, and Ivarsson as

Sinister footwear: Pan-Thy-Monium dwelling in shadowy realms
(*Dag Swanö*)

Mourning. "Benny always liked Hellhammer," says Swanö, "and he wanted to do this weird doomish stuff with keyboards. The basic idea was to do all that Edge of Sanity didn't do. We did a demo and it got spread through the underground."

Reaction was excellent, so they ran with it, the band eventually morphing into something far more bizarre than they had envisioned. "We'd just get strange ideas, like, 'Let's do brutal grindcore with hand claps.' And it worked. We've done stuff like total blast beats with a nice acoustic guitar and all this weird stuff that doesn't fit together—somehow we twist it around and it works. It's not the kind of work where you sit at home making the riffs. It's created in a moment of total inspiration."

The band's name was inspired by Celtic Frost's *Into the Pandemonium*, which Swanö calls: "one of the most progressive albums ever. Their evolution was completely insane, and at the time we wanted to do something equally weird and confusing."

The early P-T-M material sounds as if warmongering English death metallers Bolt Thrower swallowed acid tabs by the dozens and recorded the resulting jams. On debut *Dawn of Dreams*, the Swedish oddballs offered seven untitled songs, weeding out the uncommitted with a demanding first track that swallowed twenty-two of the album's forty-five minutes. *Dawn of Dreams* leapt toward the outer reaches of the bizarre. Traditional metal instruments were joined by saxophone and synths, while the guitar leads had rock-inflected warmth, clearly more '70s than '90s. These ingredients were eons distant from death metal at the time of the album's release in 1992.

The experimental approach of *Dawn of Dreams* grew exponentially on 1993's *Khaooohs*—still probably the weirdest thing ever released by the largely black metal–focused French label Osmose Productions. With a variety of strange sound effects and an expansion of their '70s prog and hard rock influences, as well as an uncomfortable atonality reminiscent of such offshoot prog movements as Zeuhl and RIO,* the band carved out a permanent niche in the left field of metal's avant-garde with *Khaooohs*.

After a brief hiatus, Pan-Thy-Monium returned in 1996 for the final sonic emanations of their god Raagoonshinnaah, for whom, according to their invented legend, they were mere conduits. The *Khaooohs and Kon-fus-ion* EP offered a bizarre marriage of '70s prog rock, avant-garde experimental music, and devastating, doom-laden death. Opening track "The Battle of Geeheeb" is the perfect distillation of everything P-T-M offered—otherworldly doom, inhuman vocals, panicked screams, groovy '70s rock guitar leads, skronking saxophone, ticking clocks, other strange sound effects, psychedelic atmosphere, abrupt mood shifts, dreamlike melodies, dissonance, and icy keyboards—all tumbling out of the speakers with frightful, mystifying authority.

* MAGMA MAIN MAN CHRISTIAN VANDER named his music "Zeuhl" in the language he created for Magma's lyrics (Kobaïan). It has since come to describe bands that share traits with Magma—dissonance, marching/martial beats, brass instrumentation, and a fractured hybrid of fusion jazz, symphonic rock, and neoclassical; Zeuhl's cousin subgenre, "RIO," or Rock In Opposition, identified a group of bands from the late '70s who stood opposed to the music industry that seemingly failed to recognize their music. Coined by Henry Cow, the term has also been used to describe U.S. band Thinking Plague, Belgium's Present, and the U.K.'s Guapo, among others. "Zeuhl" and "RIO" are essentially interchangeable descriptors.

Nightingale 2007, L-R: Dag Swanö, Erik Oskarsson, Dan Swanö, Tom Björn
(*Erik Ohlsson*)

A veil obscured the exact identities of Pan-Thy-Monium's members for most of the band's life span. Initially this was due to contractual ties, but they quickly discovered the power of mystique, and kept up the ruse as long as possible—something more easily achieved in pre-Internet days. By the time of their final recording it was widely known that the main drivers were two members of death metal band Edge of Sanity—Swanö and Larsson—plus Dag Swanö (Dan's brother, and source of the Robin Trower–/Ace Frehley–esque guitar leads) and Robban Karlsson, keeper of various otherworldly voices.

Both Swanös also appear in Nightingale, the prog polar opposite of Pan-Thy-Monium. Nightingale's 1995 debut, *The Breathing Shadow*, reveled in goth rock. The album became a surprise best-seller for the Black Mark label. Intending Nightingale to be a one-off solo project, Swanö was caught off-guard when Black Mark asked him to make a follow-up. "By that time my lust for goth—the main catalyst for the Nightingale project—was gone," Dan Swanö says. "I had already gone back to my musical roots and rediscovered pomp rock, and couldn't write a goth song to save my life."

Eventually older brother Dag—the Swanö responsible for introducing young Dan to hard rock, prog, and pomp bands such as Moxy, Gentle Giant, and Magnum— joined the fold. Together the Swanö brothers began working on ideas for a second

Nightingale album. "From the moment we started writing 'Deep Inside of Nowhere,' I knew we had something going, and it proved to be a good match," says Dan.

The younger, most notorious Swanö has long admitted to a heavy influence from British neo-prog legends Marillion, an inspiration that informs much of later Nightingale albums *Alive Again* and *White Darkness*. For a project meant as a one-off, Nightingale has grown considerably, earning a coveted spot on the Atlanta ProgPower festival stage in 2001 and racking up a total of six full-length albums as of 2009.

While Nightingale, Pan-Thy-Monium, and Edge of Sanity are Dan Swanö's main contributions to progressive metal, his work in countless other projects has earned him a reputation as one of the more prolific metal musicians of all time. Along with a huge variety of production and guest appearance credits, bands such as pomp/prog act Unicorn, eclectic post-P-T-M solo project Karaboudjan, and traditional Swede-death brutalizers Bloodbath are additional highlights of his lengthy résumé. His work as a musician with Katatonia, Godsend, Diabolical Masquerade, Route Nine, and Frameshift only further endeared him to a wide sampling of the metal audience, and his behind-the-board studio credits with Opeth, Dissection, Theatre of Tragedy, Marduk, and Hail of Bullets (among many others) deepen his considerable legacy.

O   o   O   o

During the Swedish death metal explosion of the early '90s, innumerable bands chased the sheer horrifying brutality of such genre pioneers as Entombed, Dismember, and Carnage. A majority of them fit into a narrowly defined template, and that was the whole idea. Swedish death was about oppressive atmosphere, guttural vocals, and fat guitar tones—the famed "Sunlight sound," named after the studio where many bands recorded. While soundalike scenester bands numbered in the hundreds, a few, such as Afflicted and At the Gates, briefly strayed from the pack and made some ambitious music before settling into a more straightforward approach.

Afflicted's 1992 album, *Prodigal Sun,* was a psychedelic wreck of brutality mixed with Eastern/Indian melodies, cosmic atmosphere, and passages of triumphant traditional metal. They completely embraced the denim-and-leather approach for their second album, 1995's *Dawn of Glory,* and then faded away.

At the Gates, on the other hand, immortalized themselves with 1996's *Slaughter of the Soul*, yet their early albums were more unorthodox. Their unusually titled debut, *The Red in the Sky Is Ours*, credited one of the members, Jesper Jarold,

Sidereal Svensson:
Alf of Oxiplegatz
(courtesy Season Of Mist)

with violin. The only other notable band incorporating violin into metal at that time was U.K. avant-garde doom/death act My Dying Bride. For At the Gates, unlike the Englishmen, violin dabbling proved to be a brief phase.

"*The Red in the Sky Is Ours* was almost entirely Alf Svensson," says At the Gates guitarist Anders Björler. "He mixed Swedish sadness with an almost classical atmosphere—like a soundtrack. We came from different backgrounds, and everybody wanted to prove they had musical ability. But I still don't understand what made us sound like we did. It's a mess of folk music, death metal, and classical music."

Svensson moved to the background and became a writing-only member, and At the Gates' second album, 1993's *With Fear I Kiss the Burning Darkness*, dropped the violin and wrestled with busy, haphazard arrangements. Thereafter the band cut out all progressive pretense, sharpened its songwriting, and recorded 1996's enormously influential *Slaughter of the Soul*, an album that has gained legendary stature in extreme music in the years since its release.

While At the Gates stormed into metal glory, founder and initial creative catalyst Alf Svensson continued to build his strange machine in the Swedish underground. His Oxiplegatz creation released three albums between 1994 and 1998—each a far cry from his work with At the Gates. As sole instrumentalist, Svensson used Oxiplegatz as a sci-fi themed vehicle that moved in cinematic fashion and embraced an array of styles from within and outside the metal genre. *Sidereal Journey* was a particularly ambitious piece of work consisting of one long song segmented into thirty-three parts.

Funded by the Season of Mist label—a supporter of other deviants such as Cynic, Confessor, Mayhem, Atheist, the Dillinger Escape Plan, and Goninish—*Sidereal Journey* is a metal opera of cosmic proportions with no easily comparable peers. Svensson was clearly driven to create something original, and he paid the price in obscurity. "My music will never appeal to the masses," he says, "but judging from the amount of e-mail I get with positive criticism, there are at least some freethinkers out there. Most metal bands seem to follow certain patterns, where everyone wants to be just like the other—the same sound, same lyrics, same looks, same attitude. Isn't anyone thinking for themselves anymore?"

Sweden has long been a country rich in metallic elements. From melodic, accessible '80s metal to the incredible death metal movement, there is no end to the talent coming out the country. Its progressive representatives number among the most renowned in the world, from Pain of Salvation and Therion to Meshuggah and Opeth. But in terms of sheer numbers, the genre-busting metal avant-garde due west in Norway remains king.

15. THE 'WEIRDING' OF NORWAY

"Back when we and a lot of other bands started—Emperor, Immortal, Dark-throne, Mayhem—everybody was listening a lot to other types of music as well. Classical music, psychedelic music, rock and roll... We listened to a whole collage of stuff. None of us listened only to black metal. The purists claim we are 'untrue' now, or are spitting on our roots, but they tend to forget that everything started somewhere. What inspired the first black metal music? It was not black metal, was it? Some of the older bands, like us, have developed in totally different directions. Some of us have become more progressive."
— Grutle Kjellson, Enslaved

RIFE WITH '70S HARD ROCK, PSYCHEDELIC, AND PROG ROCK INFLUENCES, Enslaved is the most successful but hardly the first band to develop a progressive path from the traditional Norwegian black metal scene. Also formed in the heady days of the early 1990s, Norwegian bands Arcturus, Ulver, In the Woods, and Solefald unleashed storms of incredible creativity. Some traditional prog fans might find the bands a bit unwieldy, and some black metal purists claim these bands have wandered too far off the beaten path. Yet Norwegian extreme progressive metal—or post–black metal—is a sound and philosophy united only by its will to suspend rules, borders, and expectations. It was dubbed "The Weirding of Norway" by onetime *Terrorizer* editor Nick Terry; a better name for the phenomenon has yet to found.

The tech thrash styles of Coroner, Obliveon, and Meshuggah never really took hold in Norway—semi-technical obscurity Equinox is a Norwegian band most listeners can and do live without, and the slightly more familiar Scariot evolved in a more streamlined, melodic direction. As for death metal, early-'90s Norwegian bands Molested, Cadaver, and Fester owed quite a bit to their Swedish neighbors. Cadaver's 1992 album, *In Pains*, is one of few Norwegian death metal albums that stretched into a more experimental area. The album is a rare, isolated example, yet still a shadow of a band such as Atheist, which took a similar turn and did it ten times better. Not even melodic/traditional Progressive metal caught fire there—Trivial Act and Manitou were exceptional but died early; Circus Maximus and Communic, plus a few other modern peers, sparsely dot the map and maintain a healthy degree of respect; Norwegian Dream Theater clones are, thankfully, very rare.

Black metal is Norway's prime contribution to the metal genre, and quite a few bands perverted it considerably, keeping the music fresh, challenging, and free from stagnation. "Norway has had good potential for a long time," said Covenant/the Kovenant guitarist Blackheart (aka Psy Coma, aka Amund Svensson) in 1998. "Finally there are bands starting to search for their own individuality. It's a complete change of mentality. You have all these black metal bands and the attention has been on Norway for a long time, and as a reaction to that, Norway is starting to be a breeding ground for original metal."

Early-'90s Norwegian black metal was extraordinary enough in its original state. But as the scathing speed, inhuman screaming, shrill bone-dry guitar sounds, super-raw "necro" recording ethics, and hypnotic minimalism became the defining foundation of hundreds of younger bands in and far outside the country, its original creative essence led ironically to an almost militant loyalty to conformity. Many black metal fans seemed to forget that each of the original Norwegian purveyors had distinct personalities. The movement's forerunners were easy to distinguish from one another. Early Darkthrone was primitive and simplistic, influenced by Hellhammer and early Celtic Frost. Burzum was even more minimal than Darkthrone, taking those same influences along with a healthy page from the early Bathory playbook. Eventually even Tangerine Dream–like ambient soundscapes worked into Burzum's sound. The earliest black metal band in Norway, Mayhem was always bizarre, even at its most direct, mixing a Venom-esque aesthetic with the quirks of various prog and avant-garde bands. Meanwhile, Emperor was probably the most musically advanced, adding keyboards and a wide variety of classical influences to its caustic brew.

During the early 1990s, these bands and other important early hordes Immortal, Dimmu Borgir, and Enslaved carved out individual niches. They have all become influential, each owning a particular piece of the country's claim to the genre.

"The ideal was to have a scene in which each band created their own genre with their albums," says Enslaved guitarist and chief songwriting catalyst Ivar Bjørnson. "I think that ideal is very much alive still. But at some point the newer bands had this idea that being a proper Norwegian black metal band was about repetition and maintaining status quo—yet the initial idea was the opposite: Tear down your ideals and just totally fuck up every possible rule."

While breaking the rules of metal tradition, various members of Burzum, Emperor, and other bands were also breaking Norwegian law—and once the media took hold of that, the perception of "Norwegian black metal" changed forever. The press's focus on a few band members' aberrant actions—arson and murder among them—made a media circus of the scene. And, in their rush to tell a sensational story, reporters failed to note anyone's musical integrity, casting a long shadow over many artists who never partook of the extramusical madness.

Perhaps as a reaction to this, to create distance from the controversy, some Norwegian bands pushed themselves into more challenging musical spaces, and some veered out of the genre entirely. Others, such as Darkthrone and Immortal, continued on a stricter regimen. As each of the elder bands evolved, a second generation emerged with new takes on the sound. Many started out playing raw black metal and stayed there, while a few others used the genre only as a launching pad. Soon a huge variety of Norwegian bands were incorporating prog rock, electronica, indie rock, classical, tech metal, traditional metal, hard rock, and ambient elements into their raw core sound. Names such as Ved Buens Ende, Dødheimsgard, Fleurety, and Solefald significantly expanded the black metal scope—some left it behind altogether.

Norwegian black metal, a thing weird enough to begin with, became even weirder in the hands of the country's most creative metal minds. "I think it's more a natural consequence of the black metal scene than a reaction to it," says Bjørnson.

Guitarist Torstein Nipe of new-generation Norwegian band Ansur analyzes the strange musical growth of his peers simply: "If individualism is an important component of black metal, why sound like all the other black metal bands?"

Mayhem's Jan Axel Blomberg (aka Hellhammer)
onstage with The Kovenant, one of his several bands
(*Mike Coles*)

Retracing the origins of Norwegian black metal reveals that a mind-bending quirkiness was present from the beginning. Over the past twenty-five years, genre originators Mayhem survived tragedy, instability, and controversy while managing to produce two remarkably experimental albums. Founded by guitarist Øystein Aarseth, aka Euronymous, Mayhem had a predilection for experimentation that was manifest from the start. The 1987 *Deathcrush* EP opened with "Silvester Anfang," composed especially for Mayhem by German experimental musician Conrad Schnitzler of Tangerine Dream and Kluster.

Seven years later Mayhem finally released their debut album, *De Mysteriis Dom Sathanas*, an eight-song blizzard rife with peculiarities and subtle progressive elements. "What Mayhem did in the beginning was total heresy to what black metal was before that," says Enslaved guitarist Ivar Bjørnson. "Black metal was Venom and Bathory, and Mayhem were the opposite—going for hi-fi, recording the drums in a big concert hall, all their major and minor chords, sevenths and ninths and all these theories, and how to use two guitars—it mixed the pompous, ambitious, create-a-universe-in-a-song prog aesthetic from the '70s with the rawness of punk and Venom. So it was a radical, heretical thing to do. At some point I think people forgot that and started thinking black metal was always [primitive] like Darkthrone in 1992."

Mayhem drummer Jan Axel Blomberg (aka Hellhammer) sees the parallels between prog rock and metal. "I'm a huge fan of early prog rock," he says. "I think the link between prog and metal is, among other things, that in these music forms you have the possibility to do everything. There are no rules, like in certain other music forms. The reason for that, I guess, is that both prog and black metal are relatively new forms of music."

Members of Mayhem and their hell-raising friends were particularly taken by Swedish prog rock revivalists Änglagård. Influenced by Genesis, King Crimson and Van der Graaf Generator, Änglagård's lush, earthy prog may have been miles away from Mayhem, but the metalheads no doubt admired the music's transportive qualities. When Änglagård made a live appearance in Mayhem's hometown of Oslo, metalheads outnumbered proggers. According to legend, the prog metal crowd stayed home, afraid of Mayhem's black metal mafia, who apparently donned capes and corpse paint for a night on the town.

By the time their landmark album *De Mysteriis Dom Sathanas* was released in 1994, Mayhem was in limbo. Aarseth had been murdered by Varg Vikernes of Burzum, and drummer Blomberg was left to pick up the pieces. Continuing without its departed founder, Mayhem saw the return of members from earlier lineups. Sven Erik Kristiansen, aka Maniac, was reinstated on vocals, and Jørn Stubberud, better known as Necrobutcher, came back on bass. Virtual unknown Rune Eriksen, aka Blasphemer, filled the guitar position. The choice of Eriksen turned out to be pivotal to the band's musical development. The late Aarseth had been not only a central figure in Norway's black metal scene, but someone absolutely lionized by fans across the globe. Yet Eriksen stepped in, marched forward, and quickly became the driver of Mayhem's musical direction.

While the *Wolf's Lair Abyss* EP in 1997 announced Mayhem's return and offered a logical step forward, *Grand Declaration of War* in 2000 was like nothing Mayhem had done in the past. Eriksen had continued using Aarseth's unusual chord shapes on the EP, but his six-string work throughout *Grand Declaration* was entirely his own. Incredibly, for a black metal musician, he was teching out on the level of Watchtower's Ron Jarzombek and Voivod's Denis D'Amour, playing a virtual catalog of impossibly angular chords and fractured riffs. Eriksen's tone was cold, per genre dictate, but also sleek and futuristic. Long phrases and longer buildups tested the listener's attention span—earning pockets of acclaim amongst a huge backlash from many longtime fans who despised Eriksen only because he wasn't Aarseth.

Elbow solo? Mayhem's Sven-Erik Kristiansen (aka Maniac) on tour for the controversial *Grand Declaration of War* album (*Mike Coles*)

Vocalist Kristiansen offered a variety of vocal shadings to match the multi-layered music. His progression was remarkable, considering that his work with Mayhem before and after *Grand Declaration* was decidedly monochromatic. "A Time to Die" was one minute and forty-eight seconds of black calculus. "A Bloodsword and a Colder Sun" offered squishy electronic groove, so close to trip-hop that it instantly became the album's most controversial track—"a disgrace," in the words of one review. "Completion in Science of Agony" was a mesmerizing ten-minute sprawling landscape of doom, elevated with vocals by guest performer Øyvind Hægeland of Spiral Architect.

Even the album's sonic clarity stunned listeners. For a band that defined the scuzzy "necro" approach with early recordings, this was a complete 180-degree turn. Said drummer Blomberg, "A lot of musicians hide behind that crappy sound and their musicality doesn't shine through. If you're a lousy drummer and you have a muddy sounding album, your mistakes won't go through as clearly. On a clearly defined album, everything is audible to the listener, and that's the way to go, absolutely."

Grand Declaration of War was Mayhem's own *Into the Pandemonium,* an album that perverted and turned inside out the black metal genre as Celtic Frost's *Pandemonium* had done to thrash metal. The album laid down a gauntlet to other experimental metal bands, and few have yet risen to the challenge. Few bands, it seems, are willing to explore their creativity on the level of *Into the Pandemonium* or *Grand Declaration of War*. To do so could split a band's previously loyal fan base in half—as it did for Celtic Frost—or make a pariah of a once legendary name. While Mayhem's abrupt turn was immensely controversial, worldwide sales of the album reached an impressive seventy-five thousand copies by 2009. Even if the album has naysayers, and has only sold half as much as Mayhem's debut, there clearly exists an audience ready to take on such a challenge.

Black metal purists remain disgruntled, but Blomberg wholeheartedly believes the band's late founder, Aarseth, would have been pleased with *Grand Declaration of War*: "I think he would have been very much into it. It's an intelligent record."

Mayhem followed their paradigm-shifting second album with the vicious and relatively straightforward *Chimera* in 2004. Soon afterward, Kristiansen left the band, prompting Mayhem to reinstate vocalist Attila Csihar. He had turned in a notoriously bizarre performance as guest vocalist on *De Mysteriis Dom Sathanas* fifteen years earlier, and his second coming in 2007, *Ordo Ad Chao*, was no less bizarre.

Draped in a gauzy, muffled, claustrophobic production—contradicting Blomberg's previous endorsement of "clearly defined" recordings—*Ordo Ad Chao* was a completely inaccessible barrage of blurry riffs and rhythms. The otherworldly emanations from Csihar's throat boosted the weirdo-quotient of the album, one that proved durably challenging even after repeated listens. Marrying the disjointed elements of *Grand Declaration* with the foggy evil of *De Mysteriis*, the album moved Mayhem's music forward and backward simultaneously. *Ordo Ad Chao* showed that the band wasn't yet done twisting minds on the fringes of black metal.

Mayhem's satanic noise has avoided the cartoonlike pitfalls some other black metal bands can't seem to miss. Perhaps the band's commitment to their subject matter, a drive to push philosophical boundaries along with musical ones, imbues their material with an intellectual integrity missing from the work of early black metal pioneers such as Venom. Mayhem's deep exploration of all facets of their art shares a bond with such challenging, progressive-minded French entities as Blut Aus Nord and Deathspell Omega. Intensely committed to themes of mysticism, esotericism, and various orthodox theologies—not to mention music of incredible depth and complexity—they and others around the globe are a testament to the creative possibilities of metal's darkest offshoot.

Mayhem's drummer is one of the most prolific metal musicians in all of Norway, and his versatility has been in great demand. Through session work he has tackled classic heavy metal with Jorn and Carnivora, melodic progressive metal with Tritonus, and even "Christian black metal" (or "un-black metal") with Antestor. His considerable skills have also been utilized by a variety of cutting-edge and avant-garde bands, including The Kovenant, Winds, Age of Silence, and the immensely important Arcturus.

Though Arcturus broke up in 2007 after nearly two decades together, they were perhaps the central figure in Norway's prog/avant-metal surge, and one of the first to appear. Others have been more prolific and even more experimental, but Arcturus's body of work has earned a high degree of respect.

From the ashes of primitive death metal band Mortem, Blomberg and guitarist Steinar Johnsen, aka Sverd, formed Arcturus in 1987 to do something more ambitious. Sverd switched from guitar to play keyboards exclusively, the axis point from which the band's music sprang. A demo in 1990 and then the *My Angel* seven-inch a year later barely spread their name—they were next to impossible to obtain, and Arcturus didn't really sound like a fully developed band, yet the music's bleak atmosphere and slow churn were already coming from a weird place, and certainly avoided easy categorization.

Arcturus truly became established with the *Constellation* EP in 1994, a work with obvious parallels to black metal. The four songs followed a similar escapist route of screamed vocals and wide swaths of non-barred guitar chords, but the general feel was far more expansive than the music of most of their peers. Johnsen's classical melodies—influenced mainly by composer Johann Sebastian Bach—were crystalline and cosmic, conveying a sound that was rich, regal, and gothic. He might have been coming from a creative point of origin similar to that of such '70s synth gods as Rick Wakeman or Tony Banks, but he bypassed the purist prog ethic by using modern equipment, rendering his sound cold and digital in comparison to the warmer old-school vibe.

Besides Johnsen's keyboard work, the vocals and drumming also set Arcturus apart. Vocalist Kristoffer Rygg, aka Garm, alternated between clean and harsh singing, a contrast that was still fairly new in metal. Although Fear Factory, Edge of Sanity,

Amorphis, Opeth, and others were experimenting with the dual approach by 1994, the technique was hardly common. In Rygg's harsher moments he screamed in harrowing desperation, while his multitracked clean vocals were deep and booming, possessing an operatic quality. Drummer Blomberg had yet to become a prolific session man, and Arcturus was his first experimental forum outside of Mayhem—years prior to the radically progressive *Grand Declaration of War*.

By the time Arcturus released 1996 full-length *Aspera Hiems Symfonia*, they'd recruited guitarist Carl August Tidemann. His sweep picking was impeccably fluid, adding a heightened melodic element to the sound. As though trying to corner the Norwegian market on talent, Arcturus included bassist Hugh Stephen James Mingay, aka Skoll, also a key member of Rygg's other band, Ulver. More often than not, Mingay's playing took the melodic path less traveled—even if his work on *Aspera* was drowned by ghostly keyboard layers and a weirdly squishy guitar sound.

While *Aspera Hiems Symfonia* is a benchmark in Norway's wave of the weird, its successor totally epitomizes the country's post–black metal happenings. Shooting Arcturus's spacey sound into more theatrical realms, *La Masquerade Infernale* proved to be eccentricity incarnate, a Dante drama brought to life by a quintet of Norwegian jesters. Released in 1997, the album brought real attention to the country's post–black metal scene, flying the flag high for strange and adventurous metal. Rygg's vocals were pushed far up front, his bellowing totally drenched in melodrama—none of the eight songs featured even a trace of harsh vocals.

Behind him, a gauzy web of symphonic sound, keyboards, and synthetic strings vied for space amid thick beds of sound effects. Guest musicians provided other sounds, such as coronet and flute, while new guitarist Knut Valle somehow managed to incorporate his work into the busy compositional mire.

La Masquerade Infernale was so flamboyant and grandiose that it bordered on the absurd. The whole thing had more to do with outsider Italian avant-garde outfit Devil Doll or a Cirque

A cornerstone in the weirding of Norway: Arcturus's *La Masquerade Infernale*, 1997

du Soleil soundtrack than the black metal underground from which Arcturus had sprung.

Blomberg holds the album up as one of his proudest moments. "I still like *La Masquerade* very much. That album was liked by both metal and prog fans. We weren't purposely trying to go for something completely different—I guess it was just the lineup and all of us as individuals with strong musical ideas that really made the difference. And those ideas worked together."

The following two Arcturus albums, though entirely noteworthy, were doomed to bask in the shadow of *La Masquerade Infernale*. Rygg sang in a slightly higher register on 2002's *The Sham Mirrors*, adding a soulful falsetto to his bag of tricks. He communicated a more down-to-earth tone than before. Guest vocalist Ihsahn of Emperor contributed the album's only harsh vocal on "Radical Cut." Still utterly cosmic, Johnsen's keyboards and compositions were of a more streamlined nature.

Rygg exited after the album's release to concentrate on Ulver, and after some inaugural live work in 2003 with Spiral Architect's Øyvind Hægeland out front, Simen Hestnæs arrived to fill Rygg's big shoes. A veteran of Borknagar, and later a key member in Dimmu Borgir, Hestnæs already had recorded session vocals on *La Masquerade Infernale* before taking the spotlight as vocalist on the fourth and final Arcturus album.

Sideshow Symphonies wasn't greeted as enthusiastically as previous Arcturus albums, but it was harder to stand out in the world of Norwegian weird metal in 2005 than it had been ten years earlier. The lukewarm reception the album received probably had little to do with Hestnæs, who upheld the eccentric Arcturus tradition. The band simply seemed to have little left to discover. "It's a different album from what I thought it would be," says Blomberg. "I honestly don't know what I feel about it. I feel this record is for Arcturus what *Chimera* was for Mayhem: it could have been brilliant, but something went wrong."

Yet during the *Sideshow Symphonies* period Arcturus suddenly emerged as a formidable performing entity. The band's live performances within Scandinavia and even as far away as Australia found their eccentricities spring to visual life via elaborate clothing, masks, makeup, strange headgear, and costumed female dancers. Rygg was never fond of live performance, so Arcturus remained a studio-only entity for most of the band's career. But with Hægeland and then Hestnæs, Arcturus found new life onstage, playing as the various musicians' schedules permitted. The band officially documented its live persona on the 2006 DVD release *Shipwrecked in Oslo*.

But, live or otherwise, their days as a band were numbered. Hestnæs opened a Melbourne concert saying, "Welcome to the last Arcturus show ever." Then, in April 2007, Norway's beloved space cadets released a public statement: "This is a decision we made some time ago. We all have a lot of things going on in our careers and lives, and therefore cannot find the time to continue working with this band. We are humble and grateful to all the people that have supported and loved us over the years." So ended the influential, genre-defying career of Arcturus.

Comparing Arcturus with other bands is difficult. Beyond Johnsen's classical influence, the band drew from a remarkably wide palette, as each member brought his own personality, inspiration, and talent to the table. While parts of *La Masquerade Infernale* sound as if that table is about to collapse under the weight of ideas, somehow Arcturus kept everything focused, even in their most elaborate moments.

Particles of Arcturus have resurfaced in other projects—Tore Moren, guitarist on *Sideshow Symphonies*, enjoys a stable career playing with former Ark vocalist Jorn. Early guitarist Carl August Tidemann formed Tritonus and plays a major part in neoclassical proggers Winds. Blomberg, who also plays in Winds, obviously has his pounding hands full, notably with Mayhem, but also as an in-demand session player. Mastermind Steinar Sverd Johnsen, however, has been content merely to enjoy his free time and let his mind wander.

Meanwhile, former Arcturus vocalist Kristoffer Rygg's band Ulver remains active as a continually fascinating group of searchers and shape-shifters. Ulver—"wolves" in Norwegian—is the most experimental band to arise from Norway's '90s metal underground. Ulver's career arc has been built solely on abrupt change and brave eclecticism. What started as earthy black metal embracing folklore, nature, and mysticism eventually moved into pure folk, industrial-gothic metal, electronica/trip-hop, dark ambient, and the bewilderingly unclassifiable music heard on 2005's *Blood*

Inside and 2007's *Shadows of the Sun*. They haven't released an album even remotely in the metal realm since 1998.

An early Ulver rehearsal demo includes a cover of Celtic Frost's "Babylon Fell," from the paradigm-shifting *Into the Pandemonium*, which seemed an intentional hint of the iconoclasm to come from the young Norwegians. "Celtic Frost's *Into the Pandemonium* and Voivod's *Dimension Hatröss* are albums I hold in high regard," says Ulver main man Rygg. "It's curious how many times I picked up on bands when others dropped off. Take Kiss's *Music from 'The Elder'* for instance. Everyone hates it, but I think it's perhaps their best one. Maybe it wouldn't be so good without the context of the other albums, but still, I don't understand why people want their favorite bands in repeat mode. I always appreciated bands that made an effort to reinvent themselves."

Ulver's 1993 demo *Vargnatt* ("Wolfnight") was a raw beehive buzz of black metal riffs, some straightforward and others obtuse, with an ambitious streak already peeking through. Multidimensional vocals went from gravelly growls to weeping moans to a high King Diamond–esque wail. Lyrics were written and sung in the band's native Norwegian—forging a key trait of the '90s black metal aesthetic. All in all, it was an auspicious start to a wildly diverse career.

By Ulver's debut album, 1995's *Bergtatt*, the fogginess of the demo was replaced with earthy clarity, though the sound was far from polished. Providing as many clean vocals as harsh ones, Rygg's voice remained a focal point. Though Rygg's young melodic voice was not yet as forceful or deep here as it was on his later work in Arcturus, it had a distinctive thinness, which was paired with flutes, acoustic guitars, and scathing storms of searing, raw, forest-tramping metal in a forlorn expulsion of melancholy. *Bergtatt* continues to sell in great numbers today, remaining one of the most influential folk/pagan-geared black metal albums.

Although many hoped for a return to that sound on Ulver's second album, the band did not repeat itself—then, or ever again. Second album *Kveldssanger* surprised with thirteen tracks of earthy acoustic folk music. While the *Vargnatt* demo had featured the all-acoustic "Trollskogen," *Kveldssanger* brought similar ideas to a long-form conclusion. The album is spare and stripped-down, its aura is purely emotional and hugely captivating—impressive stuff, considering the simplicity of the material.

Sidestepping all metal trappings entirely, the band used no electric instruments any-where. Two members of the quintet even sat out entirely so that *Kveldssanger* could convey what it needed to.

One of the ultimate deep winter listens, the album was the second of a tril-ogy that began with *Bergtatt*. For sure, *Kveldssanger* captured the interest of fans and musicians playing everything from neo-folk to gothic metal. And while English band Skyclad and Norwegian supergroup Storm—including members of Darkthrone and Satyricon—were instrumental in shaping folk metal, *Kveldssanger* brought pure folk music to the consciousness of many metal fans.

Ulver's first two albums encouraged a wave of folk-influenced metal albums. Tuomas Holopainen, leader of Finnish superstars Nightwish, initially formed his band as an all-acoustic project. While writing the first songs for Nightwish, he was enraptured by Ulver and another folk-steeped Norwegian band, the 3rd and the Mor-tal, who, like Nightwish, were fronted by a female vocalist. "I listened to *Kveldssanger* a lot," Holopainen says, "and thought maybe I should try to do that stuff even better."

Ever unpredictable, Ulver followed the gentle strains of *Kveldssanger* in 1997 with *Nattens Madrigal*, an album of screeching, impossibly lo-fi black metal. Its eight examples of scathing primitivism were subtitled "Eight Hymns to the Wolf in Man," the music as viciously lycanthropic as billed. By then, Century Media Records had signed Ulver for both Europe and North America. The label was dumbfounded by the final product. "It's safe to say when Century Media heard the record they didn't know how to handle it," says longtime Century Media staffer Ula Gehret. "Coming off *Bergtatt* and *Kveldssanger*, it was quite a shock."

Further confusing matters, Ulver released an unusual press photo to coincide with the album's release. Instead of portraying the band lurking in a forest or look-ing forlornly over cliffs into the fjords, the five members were adorned in Armani suits, hustling around a sleek sports car. The image was very *Reservoir Dogs*—a defi-ant middle finger to the black metal rulebook. But such was Ulver's way. As stated on their official website, "Ulver has always been in radical opposition to all forms of restriction and habit."

According to popular legend, *Nattens Madrigal* was recorded in the forest us-ing a generator, though the band would never confirm that. As Gehret recalls, "There were some issues during the recording of the album. The band weren't entirely happy with how the album was coming out, which led to the story of them not thinking the album sounded raw enough, thus lugging their equipment out and rerecording it in the forest—which I guess only Garm could confirm."

For his part Garm—née Rygg—has simply fueled the rumor, insisting that the band used most of the recording budget not for the album, but to fund the members' "expensive tastes."

Certainly, the remarkable melodicism inside the album's harsh, buzzing songs was easy to miss—even for Century Media. After funding the recording and marketing of what seemed like forty-four unapproachable minutes of beehive field recordings, the label was initially disappointed, but consistent sales have kept the album in print. "It's probably sold as many copies in the last five years as it did in its first five years of release," says Gehret. "The album definitely had a longer life cycle than almost anyone could or would have predicted."

The entire *Bergtatt/Kveldssanger/Nattens Madrigal* cycle was released by Century Media in an elaborate vinyl box set in 1997. Titled *The Trilogie: Three Journeyes Through the Norwegian Netherworlde*, it effectively closed the book on Ulver's brief liaison with the label.

The subversive Norwegian wolves then followed a loner's path, with plenty more radical shifts in store. Fourth album *Themes from William Blake's The Marriage of Heaven and Hell* was a double-studio album centered around twenty-seven "plates" from Blake's eighteenth-century work. A sprawling amalgam of metal, industrial, electronic, gothic, and darkwave elements, it was many things, but it sure wasn't black metal. Readings by members of Darkthrone, Satyricon, and Emperor within "A Song of Liberty Plates 25-27" was as close as it would get.

After *Themes*, Ulver's lineup fragmented into a smaller unit. Shedding the garments of classic literature, Norse mythology, folk music, and naturalistic themes, the *Metamorphosis* EP presented a new urban Ulver. The band's new electronic/techno sound radically divided their fan base and effectively put them in front of a new audience. This new Ulver offered sonic sculptures with appeal to a huge cross-section of music aficionados, from the rarefied elite of electronica and drum-and-bass deep-listeners to the open-minded, headphone-equipped segment of the metal audience.

"An early perception of black metal was that it was more of a principle than a set form," says Rygg. "Obviously it had to be metal, which we were, but our interests were expanding. Our first external influence was folk music, which is evident on the first two releases. But we were delving into a lot of other stuff as well. At first it was things with a dark gist, as we were still pretty fastened in the black metal zeitgeist—bands or artists with connections to Satanism, magick, or subversive subject matters, like NON, SPK, Laibach, Whitehouse, Coil, Psychic TV. We also liked certain goth bands and progressive rock with an occult leaning, like Magma or Univers Zero. Diamanda Galas, too, with her emphasis on topics such as suffering and death, was a huge obsession. We soon felt black metal was becoming too rigid."

Springing ahead from *Metamorphosis*, Ulver unveiled *Perdition City* in 2000—a convincing work of adulterated, Ulver-ized trip-hop. Subtitled "Music to an Interior Film," the album showcased the band's skill to shape-shift wherever their creative minds urged them to go. Fans of artists as varied as electronic icon Squarepusher and broad-spectrum experimentalists Coil embraced this new Ulver while having no inkling of the band's metallic past.

Pastoral era behind them, Ulver basks in the action and lights of urbanity: 2000's *Perdition City.*

The 2000s remained busy and artistically erratic for Ulver. A two-part EP series, *Silence Teaches You How to Sing* and *Silencing the Singing* (both 2001), delved into dark ambient experimentation. Two soundtracks—*Lyckantropen Themes* (2002) and *Svidd Neger* (2003)—tested Ulver's compositional mettle. Then the wolves gathered thirteen eclectic artists to rework songs from their entire catalog: Reputable names such as Stars of the Lid, Christian Fennesz, Jazzkammer, and Merzbow helped the band realize *1993–2003: 1st Decade in the Machines.*

Rygg barely sang on these latter-day efforts, dismaying more than a few long-time fans. But his voice returned with power and confidence on 2003's *A Quick Fix of Melancholy* EP and the Kiss cover song "Strange Ways," which appeared in 2005 on a Norwegian tribute to the masked rockers.

Finally, after years of EPs, cover songs, and soundtracks, as fans wondered if Ulver would ever release another proper full-length, 2005's *Blood Inside* answered those doubts with a vibrant explosion. A jarring forty-five-minute work, the album contains nine songs that whirl erratically in a genre-less pool somewhere between chaos and composure. Like mad scientists run amok, the members used anything and everything at their disposal, retaining the electronics of their prior period while reuniting with more traditional instrumentation, such as drums and guitar. Guest musicians came from within and outside the Norwegian underworld, including early Ulver member Carl-Michael Eide (aka Czral, also of weird metal pioneers Ved Buens Ende) and Frank Zappa alum Mike Keneally, who rips apart his guitar with abandon on "Christmas" and "Operator."

The tense *Blood Inside* left listeners breathless, and the chiller *Shadows of the Sun* brought welcome relief in 2007. Atmospherically stable, patient in momentum, and lush in texture, its forty hushed minutes featured Rygg's half-whispered singing throughout. Alongside compelling original compositions, Ulver's cover of Black Sabbath's "Solitude" certainly steals some fire.

Ulver is progressive, absolutely, but perhaps "transient" is a better word for the band's utterly unpredictable nature. "The start of Ulver going left-field came from the desire to incorporate electronic beats and weird sounds into the music," declares Rygg, "but how we ended up as what we are today is a mystery even to me."

On the very edges of Norwegian black metal, In the Woods's relatively brief existence between 1992 and 2000 brought an impressive body of work that consciously married the atmosphere of their '70s prog rock mentors with primal Norwegian black metal. Like Ulver, In the Woods drew heavily from nature for their imagery. And like a handful of high-minded bands before them—including Mekong Delta, Pan-Thy-Monium, and, at one point, Opeth—In the Woods avoided the camera lens in order to put the focus on the music and cast a shroud of mystery over the band.

Released in 1993, In the Woods's *Isle of Men* demo sold an impressive 2,200 copies, creating a healthy buzz to support their 1995 debut full-length, *Heart of the*

Ages. Released on Misanthropy, the debut was spiritually akin to what Ulver were doing, but sounded nothing like them. In the Woods fused varied traditions in their elemental music—raw aggression and screeching vocals were only part of the story.

From the start and ever after, In the Woods were resolutely "epic." Huge expanses of sound filled out the main metal material, some passages symphonic in nature, others moving toward ambient territory. Slow builds and crashing climaxes made "Yearning the Seeds of a New Dimension" and "Wotan's Return" throttling experiences.

In 1995, vocalist Jan Kenneth Transeth, known by a variety of names over the band's career, promised, "We will never do the same thing twice, a certain development will always be present."

Ad for In the Woods's *Omnio* promising "a voyage through melodious melancholia in a most exquisite form"

Sure enough, 1996 brought the first in a series of three seven-inch singles that shifted gears and paid tribute to the band's late-'60s psych and prog influences. The A sides offered covers of Jefferson Airplane ("White Rabbit"), King Crimson ("Epitaph"), and Pink Floyd ("Let There Be More Light"), while the flip sides featured an In the Woods original.

As In the Woods developed in fast-forward mode, *Omnio*, released in 1997, shaved off the harsh vocals and rough musical elements to create a metal-gilded equivalent of Pink Floyd's most atmospheric work. *Terrorizer*'s Nick Terry described the album as "little short of genius... Arguably, this is where a whole line of metal's development since *Into the Pandemonium* culminates."

The hour-long *Omnio* is like a great piece of architecture as much as it is all-absorbing music. The construction is majestic, made from all-natural material with a rounded, organic production that does justice to the band's compositional gifts. Guitars are heavily layered and lushly orchestrated. Transeth's vocals come in rich waves on the level of onetime Japan front man David Sylvian or Van der Graaf Generator's Peter Hammill.

"A lot of people would call this album, not necessarily a sell-out, but they would say it's more commercially viable because there are more melodic vocals on it," said Transeth at the time of *Omnio*'s release. "But if we wanted to sell out, we'd make a total black metal album. We could sell heaps more records if we did, but that's not what we want to do."

While indeed metal, thanks in large part to its foreboding walls of distorted guitar, *Omnio* is adulterated metal, a band taking off into the vast unknown and caring not where they sit in the genre—only that they're communicating something deep. *Omnio* definitely sounds like a band aiming for something big and important, without coming off as being too intentionally pompous. The album's title track presents the band at their best, combining the nature/pagan ideals of their early days with something far-reaching and cosmic, sounding universal in both a physical and metaphorical sense. Transeth titled *Omnio* after a word of his own invention—or so he thought. "I looked up the word 'omnio' later in an encyclopedia, and it's Latin for 'an entirety,' for 'everything.' And for the ideas I had for the lyrics, it fit perfectly."

In the Woods forged further on with *Strange in Stereo* in 1999. The eleven-song album was a modern, depressive, sometimes stark take on the In the Woods style. Heightened synths and greater focus on beats and rhythm in songs such as "Closing In" and "Cell" signaled their ongoing push forward, while the lush six-string layers so abundant throughout *Omnio* led key tracks "Generally More Worried Than Married" and "Path of the Righteous." The leap in style was not as dramatic as the one the album's predecessor had shown, but a looser grip and more synthetic elements distinguish it from the band's previous work.

In the Woods dissolved in 2000, playing farewell concerts in Los Angeles and their hometown of Kristiansand, Norway. The Kristiansand show was released posthumously three years later as the double CD *Live at the Caledonian Hall*, a long set of over two hours, representing each era of the band's development. The live recording betrays In the Woods's strength as a studio band. The epic scope of their albums didn't translate well to the rawer, more immediate environment of small clubs—and they didn't look very epic either.

"We had a lot of different reactions," recalls Transeth. "When people saw all these different people on stage, they were like, 'What the hell is this, a substitute for the band or something?' I think that's probably why the sound is as individual as it is, because we're so completely different to each other."

Before bowing out forever in 2000, the band offered odds-and-ends release *Three Times Seven on a Pilgrimage*, which compiled the seven-inch trilogy, rerecordings of older tracks, a new cover of Syd Barrett's "If It's in You," and several new songs, including "Empty Room" and "Soundtrax for Cycoz – 1st Ed." With these final originals, one could envision In the Woods evolving after Ulver or even Radiohead—highly experimental, focused less on guitars and more on electronics and associated devices.

The youngest band in the first wave of Norway's avant-garde metal surge, the Solefald duo of Lars "Lazare" Nedland and Cornelius Jakhelln emerged in 1995 with *Jernlov* ("Iron Law"). The demo tape merged seething, screeching black metal with a variety of influences from outside its main metal frame, an approach that remains the very essence of Norwegian avant-garde metal. Drummer/keyboardist Nedland—also a veteran of Borknagar and Age of Silence—welcomes the term. "We are avant-garde," he says. "'Avant-garde' means that you do something new. So if people want to call us 'avant-garde metal,' then fine by me."

Solefald's prolific career was officially launched with debut album *The Linear Scaffold* in 1997, a remarkably sophisticated take on black metal. Whether quoting British romantic poet Lord Byron in "When the Moon is on the Wave" or digging into the intellects of famous philosophers in "Philosophical Revolt," Solefald seemed to be more about red wine and reflection than blood and battle-axes, though the shrieking vocals and abrasive white-noise guitar still mainlined their root black metal sound.

Second album *Neonism* blasted Solefald off into the outer reaches of the genre in 1999, offering a satirical look at the world of fashion and pop culture. "*Neonism* was, in a way, our big sexual experiment where we tried all the forbidden things we have dreamt about," Jakhelln says. "This experiment can be regarded as our objection against what we consider steady, boring, and prejudicing within heavy metal."

A more to-the-point musical thread ran through 2001 concept album *Pills Against the Ageless Ills*. The story compared and contrasted the life-searching of Pornographer Cain and Philosopher Fuck, both more complex and nuanced characters than their provocative names suggest. With Solefald's fourth album, 2003's *In Harmonia Universali*, it was quite clear the duo would rather dissolve than remain complacent in sound and subject matter. The album included unorthodox instrumentation and an ambitious lyrical scope: Hammond organ, Spanish guitar, saxophone, and grand piano were thrust forward in the sound spectrum, while the lyrics were sung in a variety of languages, including German, French, Norwegian, and English.

By the mid-2000s, the duo had embarked on other projects outside of Solefald. Nedland kept busy with Borknagar, Age of Silence, and other bands, and began working for Norwegian television channel TVNorge as a reporter and researcher. Jakhelln formed the Sturmgeist and G.U.T. projects, and published books of philosophy and poetry, which garnered the young author several literary awards. In late 2009 he published his first crime noir novel, *Voguesville*.

Solefald's Cornelius and Lazare in 2005
(*Kim Sølve*)

Solefald remained a key priority for the duo, and they embarked upon the writing for what became a two-part "Icelandic Odyssey" in 2003. With funding from Norwegian music initiative Tekstforfatterfondet ("copywriter fund"), Jakhelln and Nedland traveled to Reykjavík, Iceland, to compose *Red for Fire*, which was released in 2005, and *Black for Death*, which appeared a year later. In an official statement from the period, Jakhelln offered, "Solefald was experimenting when everybody was being true. Now that things are changing and we've pushed the experiment quite far already, we wanted *Red for Fire* and *Black for Death* to be our attempts at being true. This will be a true Nordic Viking metal album."

With a total of six albums released since 1997, each more than intriguing, Solefald are the epitome of the metal avant-garde they helped create. "Critics have called us fruitcakes and eggheadbangers," Jakhelln wrote in the liner notes to demo/remix collection *The Circular Drain*. "We agree. We think of our songs as Baroque paintings with several layers of meaning. The apparent chaos of rivaling layers is what constitutes the Solefald sound. We have named it: Red Music with Black Edges. Radical Designer Rock'n'Roll. Extreme Epic Metal."

"The thing about Norway is that we kind of started the whole black metal movement in the late '80s, and we've grown quite tired of it," says Solefald's Nedland. "You have tens of thousands of bands playing straightforward black-as-you-can-get-it metal, and it seems Norway's at the front of the avant-garde when it comes to reinventing the genre."

Though Norway's avant-garde legacy remains strong, with Solefald and many others engaged in a continual cycle of creation and invention, in practical terms Enslaved continues to lead the country's progressive metal push almost by default; Ulver is leagues distant from their metal phase, and Arcturus and In the Woods have completely dissolved. And even though black metal godfathers Mayhem recorded the experimental *Grand Declaration of War* and the utterly bizarre *Ordo Ad Chao*, they haven't exactly been prolific. Meanwhile, Enslaved has been the most recognizable face of Norwegian extreme progressive metal for more than two decades—on every front.

As but one example, Enslaved's seventh album, 2003's *Below the Lights*, begins with twenty-five seconds of sampled Mellotron. The sustained weeping waves of reedy faux-strings, so characteristic of that odd instrument, bear an uncanny resemblance to the opening of Genesis's *Foxtrot* album, the supreme real Mellotron moments of "Watcher of the Skies." In those twenty-five seconds, Enslaved makes a direct link from modern hypnotic metal churn to prog rock's distant past. And like their forebears in Genesis and the other English prog bands, Enslaved is on a continual quest for new and different ways to stay compelled by their own music. When they succeed, deep listening becomes an otherworldly adventure.

Enslaved did not shift radically from one album to the other, but rather progressed in measured increments. The band's core of guitarist Ivar Bjørnson and bassist/vocalist Grutle Kjellson met in 1989 at a show by Norwegian thrash band Witchhammer. Kjellson crash-landed onto Bjørnson in a fit of stage-diving mania, momentarily knocking the younger lad out cold. A concerned Kjellson was on the spot when Bjørnson regained consciousness. A friendship was formed, and thus began one of the most interesting evolutions in Norwegian metal's rich history.

Bjørnson and Kjellson started death metal band Phobia in 1990, but the duo quickly changed course, broke up the band, and formed Enslaved. Phobia's 1990 demo had featured the song "The Last Settlement of Ragnarok," which pointed the way forward. Enslaved embraced the history of their homeland and made its mythology an integral part of their overall concept.

Early Enslaved albums *Vikingligr Veldi* (1994), *Frost* (1994), and *Eld* (1997) defined "Viking metal," filled with folkish melodies, tumbling battle-ready drumming, chaotic riff storms, and lyrics regarding pre-Christian Norway. The band struck a balance between fluid smears of atmospheric guitar and raw, bestial intensity. Kjellson's vocals came from deep in a cavern, and the guitars carried a similar resonance. Yet Enslaved used synthesizers even then. On their earliest recordings, keyboards lent an epic, orchestral hand to the swirling chaos, their role a bit more obvious and less integrated than on later albums.

Enslaved could have made a career pumping out *Frost* and *Eld* repeatedly, but they had no interest in becoming a caricature. They drew a line in the sand and left behind most of their familiar Viking metal traits with 2000's *Mardraum: Beyond the Within*. "I have great respect for the fans and I hope they have great respect for what we do," Kjellson says. "But it's about making challenges for yourself, not to think about whether people will appreciate it or not. That's the worst limitation you can have, making music for someone else. That's not music. That's not art at all. You have to make music for yourself. I think Enslaved fans love to be shocked. They're expecting the unexpected."

Nevertheless, some fans of Enslaved's black metal material had trouble acknowledging their later, more progressive work. "There are people that want us to write *Frost* twenty times over," says Kjellson. "I just tell them, 'Why torture yourself by listening to the new stuff? Listen to those old albums and shut up.'"

With 1999's *Blodhemn*, fresh blood arrived in the form of drummer Dirge Rep and second guitarist Roy Kronheim, who made the band a four-piece for the first time in its career. With this lineup, Enslaved was ready to make a great leap forward. The period after *Blodhemn* represents the only time in their career that the band made a premeditated

Enslaved live in 1998
(*Matt Johnsen*)

decision with respect to their direction. Bjørnson recalls, "We actually had a talk where we said, 'Should we proceed, should we do this? It could get ugly.' It ended up killing the band a couple years later, in terms of losing half the lineup, but on the other hand, it made way for a rebirth and put us where we are now."

With *Mardraum* (2000), and then the particularly psychedelic *Monumension* (2001), the band shed its old skin for something fresh. The lineup soon shifted again, with second guitarist Ice Dale replacing Kronheim, drummer Cato Bekkevold replacing Dirge Rep, and yet another member expanding the band into a quintet with the addition of full-time synth/organ player Herbrand Larsen.

Enslaved's radical period exploded in varied directions with *Monumension* and then renewed itself on *Below the Lights*, which can be seen as the foundation for everything that has come after it. Once "As Fire Swept Clean the Earth" revs up with its eerie Mellotron intro, *Below the Lights* reveals a crystallized manifestation of the transitional albums before it. Largely built on repetitive riffs that cycle through a series of subtle alterations, the album is enhanced by strong sung vocals by Kjellson, a wider variety of harsh vocals, synthesizers, hypnotic King Crimson–esque guitar patterns, and even a prominent flute in "Queen of Night."

Hopefully *Below the Lights* listeners wanting more Viking metal were satiated with the multitracked vocal chants of "Havenless," because afterward Enslaved left that style behind entirely. Later Enslaved albums *Isa* (2004) and *Vertebrae* (2008) are packed with unique riffs, Pink Floyd–esque atmospheres, lots of vocal variety, and moments of intensity that prove the band never totally left black metal behind—just expanded on its possibilities—but "Viking metal" seemed relegated to their past. Others in Europe, like Finland's Moonsorrow, the Netherlands' Månegarm, and Germany's Falkenbach were happy to further explore the heathen pulse of Viking metal.

The 2004 outing *Isa* tidied up the Enslaved sound further with smoother production that did not sacrifice ferocity or depth. Shades of Rush and Voivod lingered in its margins, and the sustained, purely emotional guitar leads throughout the twelve-minute "Neogenesis" were a clear tribute to Pink Floyd's David Gilmour. Instrumental track "Secrets of the Flesh" offered several tricky, techy rhythmic shifts.

The five-piece lineup that revamped Enslaved's sound on *Isa* followed up with *Ruun* in 2006 and then *Vertebrae* in 2008, while still holding up the exploratory ethic of the *Mardraum* and *Monumension* albums. "If some of my guitar riffs had continued to be developed as I initiated them, it would become very bizarre," says Bjørnson. "But then Herbrand comes along and adds a classical vocal line to it, or, if something's really psychedelic black metal, maybe Grutle would get some ideas in reference to old classic prog or something. So there's always somebody pulling it in a different direction, and that turns it into Enslaved."

As *Monumension*, *Isa*, and *Vertebrae* each placed Enslaved on new plateaus, the members continued to challenge themselves. Ice Dale and founders Bjørnson and Kjellson teamed up with members of Norwegian noise band Fe-Mail in the experimental Trinacria, releasing *Travel Now, Journey Infinitely* in 2008. Not just another face of Enslaved, Trinacria delivered harsher, dissonant tones that reverberated in common with such post-hardcore progressives as Neurosis and Isis.

In 2007, Enslaved joined a package tour with experimental Norwegian rock/jazz act Shining and other countrymen Keep of Kalessin. When they hit Munich, Germany, the three bands collaborated on a devastating cover of King Crimson's "21st Century Schizoid Man." (Kjellson later contributed vocals to a studio version that appeared on Shining's 2010 album, *Blackjazz*.) Inspired by this intersection of black metal, prog rock, and jazz, Shining's Jørgen Munkeby described the musical union as something to "freeze your heart, boil your blood, and make your brain shake hands with your soul."

During the extremely busy year of 2008, Enslaved teamed up with Shining for a ninety-minute collaboration at Norway's Molde International Jazz Festival. The commissioned piece "Nine Nights in Nothingness—Glimpses of Downfall" saw Bjørnson composing with Shining leader Munkeby. Bjørnson called the results "prog, doom, jazz, extreme metal, northern mythology, and science fiction," while Munkeby described it as "Ligeti meets Dillinger Es-

Enslaved enters the Norwegian Weird-Metal Hall of Fame: *Monumension*, 2001. Cover artwork by Truls Espedal

cape Plan meets Sunn O))) meets Pharoah Sanders at the day of Ragnarok."

"It was really interesting, like two worlds that collided," says Kjellson. "They're not used to the strict structure that we have in our songs, and we're not used to improvisation. The actual gig was total magic."

In the midst of their ongoing evolution, Enslaved have garnered recognition not only from an enthusiastic metal public, but from listeners and watchers outside the genre. As of 2010, the band had won three Norwegian Grammy awards for Best Album. Additional media attention was received when, in 2007, Bjørnson and Kjellson stole a sheep belonging to Norwegian politician Lars Sponheim. The stunt, televised in cooperation with the Norwegian Piracy Kills Music coalition, rallied against Sponheim's advocacy of legalized free music downloading. For Enslaved, it was an eye-for-an-eye response to something that threatens their art and livelihood. The sheep was unharmed and eventually set free.

Clearly a band on a mission, Enslaved have never seen their creative drive stall and have never retreated backwards. They blast ahead with bravery. The reception they have been given from the metal audience, the opportunities they have had to record and tour the world, the bands they have influenced, and the mainstream media attention prove there are sometimes rewards to be reaped for trekking off the well-worn trail.

Maybe the most interesting thing about Norwegian extreme progressive metal is that its origins lay in black metal, a genre commonly considered determinedly unprogressive. Many question whether black metal can become adulterated and still be black metal, yet the genre's popularity gave each band a springboard, a confidence and a sense of freedom—a base that was sometimes the only uniting factor in what can only loosely be called a "movement."

Scene unity is often something of an illusion, and this was no different in Norway. In fact, as of 1999, Enslaved didn't even know who countrymen In the Woods were. All they shared were common influences, but what Enslaved did with their Pink Floyd inspiration was much different than what In the Woods did with it.

The reach of Norway's progressive post–black metal wave is vast. North American bands Agalloch and Sculptured are no doubt akin to it and probably share many of the same influences. Similar attitudes to those that arose in 1990s Norway can be heard in the forward-thinking music of Chicago's Nachtmystium, or diabolic offbeat French bands Blut Aus Nord and the paradigm-shifting Deathspell Omega. And back inside Norway, younger bands Ansur, Angst Skvadron, and Drottnar are carrying on the trailblazing nontraditional traditions forged by their pioneering countrymen.

PHILOSOPHICAL REVOLT

THE FOLLOWING IS A LONG (BUT NOT EVEN COMPLETE) glossary of additional bands that contributed to Norway's prolific progressive metal surge:

Age of Silence

Very much a "supergroup," Age of Silence boasts members from a variety of notably weird and progressive metal bands. Keyboardist and leader Andy Winter, currently residing in British Columbia, is a Norwegian native. His work in Winds and Washington State's avant-metal band Sculptured fills out his resume. Solefald's Lars Nedland sings—using a style he refers to as "Duran Duran–type vocals"—and ubiquitous skinsman Hellhammer weirds up the drums. Sprawling, sometimes delicate, always dark, and with plenty of wicked organ, Age of Silence isn't even close to black metal. The *Complications* EP is based around the delicious concept of a shopping mall in Hell, or perhaps Hell itself as one infinite mall—all completely metaphorical, of course.

Ansur

One of the newer sprouts in the Norwegian left field, like most Norwegian prog/avant-metal bands Ansur started out playing black metal and evolved quickly. Their second album, 2008's *Warring Factions*, features almost no trace of the early sound, and that's good. What they're doing—musically and conceptually—is incredibly ambitious and even original in many ways. While in no way a retro-prog band of any kind, Ansur still looks back to Rush and Pink Floyd for inspiration. "Like any decent prog rock–inspired band," says guitarist Torstein Nipe, "there are a few Rush things here and there. But Pink Floyd is the ultimate. You never stop discovering more layers in their music, even after listening to it all your life. The musical quality of David Gilmour's guitar playing is truly one of a kind, perhaps the best example that technique is not important compared to quality of tone and melody." Nipe's own guitar work not only brings in elements of Gilmour, Alex Lifeson, and several others, but he has already carved out his own instantly recognizable style. And the cover art of *Warring Factions* is gorgeous. Hopefully their vocals will improve.

Atrox

Featuring members of Manes, Atrox plays self-described "schizo metal." It's exotic for sure, steeped in the grandeur of gothic metal, with some power/heavy metal elements, a few indie/emo moments, lots of keyboards, and clean male and female vocals. Atraox would probably appeal to fans of artists as wide-ranging as Type O Negative or Kate Bush. *Contentum* (2000) is a great place to start, especially if Arcturus's *La Masquerade Infernale* is your cup of strangeness. They really should be much bigger.

Beyond Dawn

This is one of the most unique bands in Norway, which says a lot. Their early demo material is sick and raw death/doom that already showed glimpses of evolution to come. The 1994 EP *Longing for Scarlet Days* revealed Voivod and Celtic Frost influences, while 1995's *Pity Love* album was drenched in gothic melancholy and huge inspiration from New York band Swans, especially in the deep, drugged Michael Gira–like vocals. In this era, the band gained much attention for featuring a full-time trombonist, Dag Midbrod. They carried their love for brass all the way to 1999's *Electric Sulking Machine*. Even by 1998's *Revelry*, metal was totally behind them. From earthy prog/goth/darkwave, they evolved into a synthetic, electronically based art pop sound—or as they called it, "traumatic electro rock." By the time of 2003's *Frysh*, Beyond Dawn's evolution hit a wall and the band went on hold. *Frysh* features an utterly mangled, unrecognizable cover of Autopsy's "Severed Survival."

Borknagar

Similar to Emperor's semi-progressive melodic/symphonic black metal, Borknagar never gets too wacky, although *Quintessence* certainly fits the Norwegian prog metal ideal. Lately the band has become less prolific. After their sixth album—2004's *Epic*—they released an all-acoustic album, *Origin*, and then a "best of" package. They finally offered new material in 2010 with *Universal*. Borknagar has a who's-who lineup history that includes past vocalists Kristoffer Rygg and Simen Hestnæs, as well as current vocalist Vintersorg (who still resides in Sweden). Leader Øystein G. Brun has filled out the rest of his lineup, past and present, with members of Enslaved, Emperor, Solefald, Spiral Architect, Immortal, and Gorgoroth (who briefly went weird themselves on 2000's

Bassist/vocalist Simen Hestnæs, performing with Borknagar during the *Archaic Course* era, 1998 (*Matt Johnsen*)

Incipit Satan album). Brun also partners with Vintersorg in Cronian, which sounds enough like Borknagar that it can be seen as an extension office of the home base. *Quintessence*, *The Archaic Course*, and *The Olden Domain* are highly recommended.

Covenant/the Kovenant

This Norwegian industrial/electro-metal conglomerate is not exactly experimental or avant-garde, but their contributions should be noted simply because their lineup has featured members of Mayhem, Arcturus, Dimmu Borgir, Troll, and Ram-Zet. They don't fall into easy subgenre holes, so their role in the weirding of Norway is duly noted. The band became the Kovenant in 1998, due to a rights conflict with a Swedish synth pop act. At that time, guitarist Blackheart (who soon became Psy Coma), commented: "We're at that stage where we're breaking up traditional forms and starting to put other elements in the music. We even have some stuff that resembles cabaret, and in the future you'll see much more of that. Metal has been so unexplored."

Dødheimsgard

Beginning life with a stock, by-the-book Norwegian black metal sound, Dødheimsgard began throwing unusual imagery ("Bluebell Heart") and hesitantly strange music into their thrashing black mix on second album, *Monumental Possession*. By the time of 1998's *Satanic Art* EP, the band were among the progressive elite with a sound that incorporated eerie noise, dissonance, challenging arrangements, keyboards, and awesome violin work ("Traces of Reality"). They completely changed their look and outlook with third full-length, *666 International*. Few vestiges of their black metal past remained, and while indeed a huge forward leap, the blaring, intentionally confusing approach lent the album a stiff, uncomfortable sound. After an eight-year gap, main man Vicotnik (also of Ved Buens Ende) and a mostly new cast of characters unleashed *Supervillain Outcast* in 2007. The album wasn't any easier to digest than its predecessor, but was a more cohesive reinvention. Highly artificial and futuristic sounding, insanely intense and erratic, the album is a listening experience with many conundrums and complications. The artwork accompanying *Supervillain Outcast* is almost better than the music itself. They tried to shift away from associations with their early days by changing the name to DHG, but most people didn't buy into it.

Drawn

Formed by In the Woods member Christer Cederberg, the similar-sounding Drawn are described by Christer himself as incorporating elements of psychedelic, progressive rock, metal, and ambient—metal being merely one component. "My inspiration and interest comes from a lot of different directions within music," he says. "Metal is not my first priority, but an interesting expression among others." Their one and only album, 1999's *A New World?*, shares a lot in common with In the Woods, Cure-ish melancholy, and pre–*Dark Side of the Moon* Pink Floyd. The hypnotic dark metal uses a variety of vocal approaches. A few ideas sound unfinished, but Drawn still touched greatness more often than most.

Drottnar

Curious, these Drottnar guys. Their lyrics come from a Christian angle and they play what has been called "un-black metal." With 2006 full-length *Welterwerk*, they began shooting photos and performing dressed in early-twentieth-century military regalia, mocking notorious Nazi and Communist regimes. And their musical scope broadened too—*Welterwerk* is intensely technical, aiming somewhere between Atheist, Extol, and the most complex Mayhem material and almost hitting the mark. As idiosyncratic as they come.

Emancer

Sometimes a dead ringer for later Enslaved, this band may not be the most original out there, but they have clout, if five full albums are anything to judge by. Loads of ability and an interesting sound. They even have moments where they find their own direction, and then it's really something. One of few Norwegian bands in this vein that does not share members with a ton of other bands. Recommended album: *Twilight and Randomness*—has a pair of green dice on the cover, with wings!

Emperor/Ihsahn

Emperor's place at the top of the Norwegian pantheon is not to be marginalized. But in terms of their progressiveness, they were never as eccentric or far-reaching as their peers in Mayhem, Enslaved ,and Ulver, and never went schizo like the more obscure bands populating the country. Their contribution as a progressive band is based on the symphonic/classical interests of guitarist/vocalist/songwriter Ihsahn. They were good at keeping their experimental tendencies in check, although fourth and final album, *Prometheus: The Discipline of Fire and Demise* (2001), was not only a mouthful, but easily their most adventurous. For a view into what Emperor likely would have sounded like had they continued, Ihsahn solo albums *The Adversary*, *Angl*, and the especially far-reaching *After* keep the flame of proggy symphonic black metal alive. With 2010's *After*, Ihsahn wrote the best album he's been involved with in over a decade, within which he proves himself as one of metal's most formidable and recognizable lead guitarists. Ihsahn lists Iron Maiden, Judas Priest, King Diamond, Bathory, Diamanda Galas, and Radiohead as influences on his solo work. His albums have featured performances from Ulver's Kristoffer Rygg, Opeth's Mikael Åkerfeldt, Spiral Architect members Asgeir Mickelson and Lars Norberg, and Shining leader Jørgen Munkeby. Ihsahn's backing band for solo shows functions as a separate entity called Leprous, who bear some resemblance to countrymen Frantic Bleep in their amorphous genre-blending; Leprous released *Tall Poppy Syndrome* on the Sensory label in 2009. See also: Peccatum

Fleurety

Fleurety's early material was infamous for its shrieking hawk vocals done by a kid just entering his teens. Their black riffs were somewhere between Mayhem and Voivod's fractured structures. The recording of 1993's *Black Snow* demo was ridiculously lo-fi. With 1995's *Min Tid Skall Komme* album, they had advanced on every level, adding psychedelic, experimental, and folk characteristics. Four years later, the *Last Minute Lies* EP made the kind of abrupt shift that Beyond Dawn and Ulver would make careers of, and the following album, *Department of Apocalyptic Affairs*, carried on the EP's angular, eclectic, unpredictable mixture of metal, gothic, new wave, indie rock, and prog. The album succeeds with the kind of approach that Sweden's Carbonized failed at on *Screaming Machines*. *Department of Apocalyptic Affairs* finds saxophones, synthesizers, and guest musicians from Mayhem, Ulver, Arcturus, and Dødheimsgard joining the perennial core duo of Svein Egil Hatlevik and Alexander Nordgaren. Hatlevik now heads experimental electronic unit Zweizz, who are just about unlistenable.

Frantic Bleep

Featuring members of Madder Mortem, Frantic Bleep have perhaps one of the best band names ever, even if it sounds more appropriate for an insane-BPM techno act. The band's only album so far, 2005's *The Sense Apparatus*, sits somewhere between fellow Norwegians Age of Silence and Twisted into Form—more interesting and technical than the former, not nearly as tricky as the latter. Some elements of Faith No More, too—and only distant allusions to black metal. Eclectic yet approachable, they're even melodic enough that some fans of the Inside Out stable of Progressive metal bands have picked up on it. Let's hope they offer a second album someday.

Green Carnation

Green Carnation was a pre–In the Woods band formed by Terje Vik Schei (aka Tchort) in 1990. When he left to join Emperor in 1993, the remaining members of the fledging Green Carnation morphed into In the Woods. After Schei's departure from Emperor, he revived Green Carnation using various members from within and outside the In the Woods family tree. Debut album *Journey to the End of the Night* (2000) was long and sprawling stuff in the epic gothic/doom mode, but it didn't signal the brilliance that would come on follow-up *Light of Day, Day of Darkness* (2001). One hour-long song, *Light of Day* is remarkably well written and entirely listenable. The album shows Green Carnation's epic doom foundation spiced with prog and art rock elements. In its wake came the formation of the band's key lineup, with most members contributing to songwriting. *A Blessing in Disguise* and *The Quiet Offspring* are the result of this lineup, yet despite moments of pure brilliance, neither is as consistently impressive as *Light of Day*. The mellow *Acoustic Verses* (2006) spotlighted the band's folk, prog, and singer-songwriter influences, but touring and business hassles fragmented the band in 2007, leaving main man Schei to pick up the pieces after five wonderful and diverse albums. Maybe things would be totally different now had the band become Coldplay-huge with the-hit-that-never-was, 2006's "The Burden is Mine...Alone."

Madder Mortem

Releasing consistently high-quality albums since 2001, this band has earned a dedicated cult following. Theirs is a sound comparable to fellow Norwegians Atrox, the 3rd and the Mortal, Frantic Bleep, and Leprous...maybe. Dark melody lines, moments of shimmering brightness, gothic atmosphere, eccentric diversions, and attention to sonic detail have attracted fans from a variety of musical backgrounds. In the band's own words, "Our only rule to creating music is that there are no rules." *Deadlands* (2002) and *Eight Ways* (2009) are especially remarkable and recommended.

Manes

Manes is somewhat comparable to Ulver, in that they have evolved in similar stages. Manes began releasing demos in 1993 and somehow didn't catch fire like many of their peers; their first album took until 1999 to arrive. Early Manes material is cold, symphonic, raw black metal, somewhere between early Emperor, Limbonic Art, and early Dimmu Borgir with an eclectic edge. Five years later came *Vilosophe*, a dizzying amalgam of avant-metal, electronica, and trip-hop. Manes's black metal origins were completely absent, as they were on 2007 follow-up *How the World Came to an End*. Even if already expecting weirdness, listeners were surprised by the hip-hop/nu-metal moments in opener "Deeprooted." Later promo pictures recall early-'90s Mr. Bungle, and, on second thought, they probably shouldn't be compared to Ulver; Manes was much less prolific, more abrupt, and less interesting. They have since broken up to reassemble as Kkoagulaa, who play, in the band's own words, "electroacoustic/emo-tronic" music. Members of Manes also played in Atrox and the 3rd and the Mortal.

Minas Tirith

A favorite of erstwhile Mayhem guitarist Rune Erikssen and maybe three or four other people. Impossibly obscure and terribly underrated, Minas Tirith has had the same trio lineup since 1989, producing one EP and three full-length albums. The members are probably more well known for their work in other bands (Old Man's Child, Thorns, Funeral, Tulus, Antestor). While not exactly prolific, and not at all black metal, the band deals in prog metal that is rooted firmly in classic doom, thrash, and death metal bands of the '70s and '80s, with a unique flavor that is exceptionally hard to nail down, but quite easy to like. Not terribly "out there," but certainly as unique and original as any of their more messed-up Norwegian brethren. The band's website pledges: "There are no limits. Heavy or soft. Progressive or mainstream. Everything is allowed in Minas Tirith." Maybe their song titles tell the story best: "Mad Alpha (Lunatic-tac)," "Brain and the Bee," "Wisdom's Saberteeth," "God of God's God."

Peccatum

Comprised of Ihsahn of Emperor, his wife, Heidi (also known from Star of Ash and Hardingrock, the latter which also features Ihsahn), and, on their first albums, Source of Tide's Lord PZ. All over the place, stylistically, their three albums and two EPs incorporated a wide variety of influences that can only place them under the "avant-metal" umbrella. Cool cover of Judas Priest's "Blood Red Skies" on the *Oh, My Regrets* EP and a turn toward darkwave/gothic territory on final release, 2005's *The Moribund People* EP.

The 3rd and the Mortal

The 3rd and the Mortal were an odd band out when they first emerged on the scene in 1993 with a three-song demo, but word of mouth spread quickly once members of the country's black metal community started singing the band's praises. Their profile was raised even further when original vocalist and now solo artist Kari Rueslåtten joined members of Darkthrone and Satyricon for the Storm project. The 3rd and the Mortal began somewhere between goth rock, doom metal, and whatever Enya does. *Tears Laid in Earth* (1994) is timeless; it also makes a mockery of various female-fronted "goth metal" novelty bands that have come since. Rueslåtten left after its release, and the band found the equally, perhaps even more capable Ann-Mari Edvardsen. With *Painting on Glass* and *In This Room* albums, the band delved headlong into experimentation. The result was something incomparable to the work of any other artist, but residing in an area not unlike a more metal- or rock-based Dead Can Dance or Kate Bush. Wonderful stuff, but most fans were caught off guard by final album, *Memoirs* (2002), which found the core of the band dismissing Edvardsen and turning an abrupt corner toward an avant-pop/electronic sound, full of samples, loops, and guitar treatments. Edvardsen went on to weird-pop/ambient band Tactile Gemma, which featured members of Atrox, while drummer Rune Hoemsnes ended up in Manes. Hoemsnes also helped out another 3rd member, Trond Engum, in the Soundbyte, which has so far released two albums of avant-garde metal/rock.

Ved Buens Ende

Released in 1995, Ved Buens Ende's *Written in Waters* was one of the earliest proclamations that something strange was afoot in Norway. It remains the band's sole album, but still sells thanks to a 2003 reissue. Noted metal writer and musician Chris Black (aka Professor Black) once described *Written in Waters* as "Enslaved meets Jane's Addiction"—very much in the pejorative, to his ears. Despite derision in some corners, *Written in Waters* is a paradigm-shifting progressive black metal album that was still finding listeners many years after its release. Their 1994 demo, *Those Who Caress the Pale*, was rawer and merely presaged the

Ved Buens Ende pioneers post-black metal: *Written in Waters*, 1995

Winds and guests in the studio during the *Prominence and Demise* sessions.
L-R: Carl August Tidemann, Andre Orvik, Øystein Moe, Jan Axel Blomberg,
Dorthe Dreyer, Vegard Johnsen, Hans Josef Groh, Andy Winter, Lars Eric Si
(*Misty Greer*)

album's coming. Despite a 2006 reunion demo, nothing really took off, and the members reverted back to Virus, an outgrowth of Ved Buens Ende (the name means "at the end of the bow," as in the Bifrost rainbow bridge of Norse mythology). Members of V.B.E. have also played major roles in Ulver, Dødheimsgard, and Beyond Dawn.

Virus

"Talking Heads meets Voivod" has become a popular description of Virus. Main man Carl-Michael Eide (aka Czral) formed the band after the dissolution of Ved Buens Ende. Virus pretty much extracts the black metal from Ved Buens Ende and replaces it with a kind of Sonic Youth mentality—another band achieving a more convincing take on what Sweden's Carbonized was aiming for on their final album. Eide is joined in Virus by Ved Buens Ende alumni Einar Sjurso (also of Beyond Dawn) and Petter Berntsen (also of Audiopain). They have released two albums: *Carheart* (2003) and *The Black Flux* (2008).

Winds

Neoclassical, melodic prog metal having nothing to do with black metal, but featuring veterans of that scene. The band revolves around keyboardist Andy Winter (Age of Silence, Sculptured), drummer Jan Axel Blomberg (Mayhem, Arcturus, and zillions of others), guitarist Carl August Tidemann (Arcturus, Tritonus), and vocalist Lars Eric Si (Age of Silence, Khold, Tulus, Eikind). Mellow in tone, bountiful in color, smooth in texture—yet still somehow metal. Must be Tidemann's awesome leads.

PART V:

Into Data Overload...

16. THE EXPANDING UNIVERSE

"In an expanding universe, time is on the side of the outcast. Those who once inhabited the suburbs of human contempt find that without changing their address they eventually live in the metropolis." —Quentin Crisp

ENSLAVED'S DILIGENT HARD WORK ASIDE, the band was not alone in experiencing healthy success at the turn of the century. There was a sea change around 2000, as the success of such adventurous pioneers as Dream Theater and soon Meshuggah and Opeth proved that challenging music could worm its way into the public stream. This kind of groundwork needed to be laid so that avant-garde bands such as Japan's Sigh and the U.S.'s Kayo Dot could flourish in the 2000s. As Rush had accomplished in the 1970s, this music had appeal to a broad base of listeners, and, despite its challenges, it was possible for musicians to make a decent living from their art. For Rush, Dream Theater, and various others, total musical freedom and uncompromising attitude paid off handsomely. But for many similarly adventurous artists, those same attitudes had previously guaranteed obscurity.

The groundwork for progressive metal was finally firmly in place as metal entered the 2000s with mutant hybrids and strange offspring zooming all over. "Everybody's so used to bands mixing anything these days, I don't know what you need to do to be different," says Christofer Johnsson of Therion. "Play in clown clothes and with one hand cut off, I guess!" The metal genre fragmented into a hundred different sub-sub-subgenres, almost to the point of ridiculousness. Gothic death, death doom, stoner doom, symphonic power metal, symphonic black metal, post-thrash, half-thrash, metalcore, and mallcore were just a few of the new descriptors—some more useful than others. For the ever-diversifying progressive quadrant of the genre, the words "progressive metal" could apply to a myriad of different sounds and ideals and not one particular style. Lowercase progressive metal was a principal, even as uppercase Progressive metal remained a more static style.

There was no lack of inspiration for "new millennium"–era bands to draw from. The previous decade saw the rise of Progressive metal borne by the Big Three, with an even more daring route taken by Canada and Florida's tech metal leaders. Texas offered jazz fusion metal bands, and Sweden burped up prog-death mammoths and unpopular left-field freaks. Norway gave the world prog rock–inspired Satanists and onetime black metal bands more comfortable in the world of trip-hop, ambient, techno, and experimental music.

Single songs such as Edge of Sanity's "Crimson" in 1996 and Fates Warning's "A Pleasant Shade of Gray" in 1997 clocked in at forty and fifty-four minutes, respectively—and were soon topped in 2001 by Green Carnation's sixty-minute song/album "Light of Day, Day of Darkness." Into the "anything goes" new decade came guitarists releasing exhausting forty-five-song albums crammed with bizarre musical theory and head-spinning playing, strange bands with strange names like Blue Coconut, and kids raised on death metal rubbing shoulders with avant-garde saxophonists.

Overall, as the clock struck 2000, even metal of the weirdest mutation finally found reward.

Compared to its death metal uprising, Sweden's thrash metal scene was microscopic. Generic bands modeled themselves on the American sound—particularly the San Francisco thrash of Exodus, Testament, and Forbidden. Swedish thrashers Hexenhaus, Tribulation, and Mezzrow were second-rate in those days, and efforts such as Mezzrow's *Then Came the Killing* have even less purpose today.

In 1989, a band named Midas Touch attempted to thwart the generic thrash around them with the fairly technical *Presage of Disaster,* released on the prog-friendly Noise Records. Midas Touch merged a Megadeth speed approach with colder Watchtower/Voivod designs, but they lacked the imagination and technical ability to craft a bona fide classic.

That same year, an obscure new band named Meshuggah created very little interest with an EP on the even more obscure Garageland label. The *Psykisk Testbild* EP—Swedish for "psychological test pattern"—bore similarity to Midas Touch, who were, incidentally, the only band Meshuggah name-checked on the EP's thanks list. Plenty of Metallica and Testament influences could be heard, but even at that early stage Meshuggah showed promising technical ability and vision. Still, the debut was no classic.

Before their first full-length, 1991's *Contradictions Collapse*, Meshuggah brought aboard new drummer Tomas Haake, an addition that set the band on a perpetually complex course. Though the band was mostly overlooked amidst the peaking death metal wave in 1991, some members of the media got behind them. *Metal Forces* commended the band for their "complex techno-thrash," likening it to "Bay Area–thrash cruncherama" meets "eerie, sometimes Voivod ambience." The spacey break in "Qualms of Reality" found guitarist Fredrik Thordendal going off into Allan Holdsworth la-la land, revealing the English guitar innovator's major influence on the Swedes. Thordendal's jazzy touch, laid over the band's aggressive and complex rhythms, became a Meshuggah trademark.

Each of those elements was ratcheted up tenfold for their next album, and without a doubt 1995's *Destroy Erase Improve* put Meshuggah on the map. With two further EPs (*None* and *Selfcaged*) acting as warm-ups in the four years since the debut, Meshuggah had plenty of time to tear down and rebuild their devastating machine. Thordendal's clean, cosmic lead approach provided *Destroy*'s sole melodic element, whereas the quirky, jagged rhythms had an almost dehumanizing effect.

With the following album, 1998's *Chaosphere*, Meshuggah did the impossible and churned out their brutality in an even blunter manner—still twisting and turning through challenging rhythmic exercises. Vocalist Jens Kidman did little but bark through every song and every album, but musically the band was busy establishing a confounding rhythm-based sensory attack. With no real melodic anchor, Meshuggah offered as its main selling point machinelike rhythmic abrasion, something that drew a reaction of either total boredom or utter fascination. And for sure, some big people were listening. The band benefited enormously from the ongoing endorsement of modern proggers Tool, who used their enormous popularity to take Meshuggah on the road for several U.S. tours. While the Swedes' bionic bludgeon didn't appeal to every Tool fan, the band was thrust in front of an audience that could at least respect their ambition. U.S. tours with Slayer and a spot on Ozzfest 2002 continued to put this difficult experimental metal band into some big arenas.

Once Tool and Robb Flynn of post-thrash aggro-mongers Machine Head endorsed Meshuggah, people started taking notice. Acclaim rose higher, as Meshuggah was touted in a rare metal-centric *Rolling Stone* feature in 1999 as "one of the ten

Meshuggah's Mårten Hagström (front) and Gustaf Hielm (back) on the *Chaosphere* tour, 1999 (*Michael J. Mulley*)

most important hard and heavy bands," joining mathcore leaders the Dillinger Escape Plan—who themselves showed respect for the Swedes. While they come from distinctly different backgrounds— Meshuggah's Bay Area thrash influence versus Dillinger Escape Plan's hardcore and math-rock roots—the bands eventually toured together. "I understand why the bands are compared," Dillinger guitarist Ben Weinman said. "I don't think we sound anything alike, but we certainly wouldn't exist if it wasn't for them. I don't

think people would really give a shit about us if it wasn't for a band like Meshuggah paving the way. But we think in the same terms as far as not really thinking conventionally, just having an open palate when making music."

Save for the basic Bay Area thrash influences, Meshuggah seems like a band without precedent, yet they have their heroes. Thordendal has credited Allan Holdsworth often for his spidery lead style and unusual phrasing. And second guitarist Mårten Hagström says, "When I was twelve, growing up as a guitar player, I listened to so much Rush. The way they did stuff like 'YYZ' and 'Jacob's Ladder' was really amazing. When I write, I might write a song and think it's cool, then six months later I go, 'I know where that came from' and it's almost always Rush."

Meshuggah's circle of admirers extends beyond Tool and influential peers such as Dillinger Escape Plan. "We played Berlin," remembers Hagström, "and afterward this opera singer from the Berlin opera walked up to Fredrik and said, 'I drove down here to catch you guys, I heard one of your records—I think you're awesome!'"

Meshuggah's trademark rhythm patterns have puzzled fans and critics to an incredible degree, yet despite all appearances, the band claims they don't consciously go for total mindfuck. Though many passages are seemingly mathematically complex in their patterns, sometimes the tricky-sounding stuff is simply a matter of placing accents in different places within the same 4/4 riff cycle. Meshuggah admit that many of their riffs are deceptively simple. "We don't actually change time that much," says Hagström. "The time signature is straight 4/4 about 85 percent of the time, but we work around the 4/4 pattern. Sometimes it seems like we're using a 7/4 or 9/4 time signature but we're not. We make it sound like another time signature—maybe we're not playing the first beat, or playing against Tomas. We don't try to make it hard or complex; we just want to make it intriguing."

New technologies have always been a trait of progressive rock music. King Crimson used Mellotrons and some of the earliest synthesizers (such as the VCS3 unit), while less popular but no less innovative late-'60s band United States of America are widely credited as one of the first rock bands to exploit electronic gizmos— such as engineer Richard Durrett's electronic music synthesizer and ring modulator. So too has Meshuggah widened its scope with newfangled toys. Thordendal and Hagström play custom seven- and eight-string guitars made by Nevborn and Ibanez, while Thordendal uses a "breath controller"—a MIDI device that allows him to blow out a guitar solo through a mouthpiece, something heard within the "Future Breed Machine" track, among others.

On 2002's *Nothing*, the band introduced groovier rhythms marked by long sustaining notes and a remarkably bass-heavy drone. Thordendal had proposed using only bass guitars, but eventually chose instead a more versatile guitar to achieve the fat drone they were seeking. The guitarists worked with eight-string models made by small guitar manufacturer Nevborn, but when the prototypes failed in the studio, Hagström and Thordendal resorted to detuning their Ibanez seven-stringers. After the album's release, the guitarists were given an Ibanez endorsement deal for the company's own eight-string guitars. Unsatisfied with the outcome of the original guitar tracks, they rerecorded their parts using the new Ibanez eight-stringers, and

Seven-stringed technical turbulence:
Meshuggah's Fredrik Thordendal
(*Matt Johnsen*)

a revamped version of *Nothing* was released in 2006.

The rerecordings of *Nothing* saw Meshuggah drummer Tomas Haake innovate in step with the guitarists. Working on the development team for drum sample program Drumkit From Hell, or DFH—developed by the Toontrack company—Haake beefed up *Nothing*'s original drum tracks using the DFH technology. In fact, a year earlier the band used DFH in the making of *Catch Thirtythree*, an album based entirely on sampled drum tracks. The virtual drum kit has since become remarkably popular, in use by a wide array of drummers for writing and recording work.

Meshuggah helped a super-aggressive strain of prog metal commercially—making the jobs of later bands Dillinger Escape Plan, Gigan, Behold the Arctopus, and Spawn of Possession much easier. Ears have now become open to unusual and tangled complexities. The once-tiny field of technical, experimental metal finally inhabits a world of its own. Complex metal bands could now find listeners welcoming their dedicated efforts with enthusiasm, as opposed to the huge question marks that used to greet bands of this nature.

All across Europe, the 1990s saw a huge variety of bands expanding the black and death metal language. U.K. bands Paradise Lost, My Dying Bride, and Anathema united death and doom metal with elaborate female vocal parts, gothic chord patterns, Latin lyrics, and layered symphonic arrangements. In Finland, Xysma and Amorphis dug into indie and prog rock influences after evolving away from their death/grind origins. Sweden's Therion wove classical and opera into dark occult metal. Göteborg,

Sweden's At the Gates briefly featured a full-time violinist, while In Flames and Dark Tranquillity brought an Iron Maiden influence into death metal—a decidedly radical step in 1994. Fellow Swedes Mourning Sign widened the death metal playing field with elements of jazz, alternative rock, and psychedelia. And nutty Norwegians such as Arcturus and Ulver, and other shape-shifters such as Sentenced and Katatonia each evolved in myriad directions. But the one single band that best represents the adventurous spirit of '90s-era European metal is certainly Opeth.

Opeth began in the dawn of the '90s as Opet. In Wilbur Smith's 1972 novel, *The Sunbird*, Opet was an ancient empire, a "city of the moon." The obscure name gave the young pioneers a fitting identity, although at the very beginning their aims were stricter. Founders David Isberg and Mikael Åkerfeldt wanted Opeth to be, in Åkerfeldt's words, "the most evil band in the world."

Influenced by the twisted death metal of Morbid Angel and Death, early songs "Requiem of Lost Souls" and "Mystique of the Baphomet" were intended solely to provoke with ultra-heavy riffs and satanic imagery. Opeth played a few less-than-monumental gigs with early incarnations of Therion and At the Gates, while shuffling its lineup often. Isberg soon lost interest; he joined chaos-death outfit Liers in Wait briefly, then faded into obscurity. Peter Lindgren entered the band, and after a brief spell as bassist—a position also previously held by Åkerfeldt—Lindgren became Opeth's second guitarist. A committed bassist was finally found in Johan DeFarfalla.

Meanwhile, Åkerfeldt honed the songwriting capabilities that would determine his band's future course. When he finished "Poise into Celeano" in late 1991, it was clear he had stumbled upon a new and unique direction. The song was remarkably different from earlier material. "There were no blast beasts, no ultra-doomy parts," Åkerfeldt says. "It had acoustic parts, harmonies, and lots of double-bass drumming."

As fate would have it, Åkerfeldt discovered Dream Theater just a few months later. "When I first saw and heard the 'Pull Me Under' video," he says, "I was like, 'Wow, this is what I've been looking for.' They had the double-bass drumming, they had more technical parts, great solos, long songs, lots of dynamics, and that's what I wanted to do. But obviously I wanted to stay with one foot in the whole extreme death and black metal thing—which was what I really loved at the time—but also take it into something more unique by incorporating different influences like Dream Theater and whatever else I was into at the time."

Åkerfeldt's fascination with '70s hard rock and prog soon merged with his Bathory, Voivod, Celtic Frost, Morbid Angel, and Death roots. The band still lacked any kind of official demo recording, and very few people had actually laid ears on what would become Opeth's groundbreaking style: epic-length songs, multiple mood shifts, dynamic shading between light and dark, tortured vocals offset with melancholy crooning and fluid musicianship. Even such early tracks as "Into the Frost of Winter" and "Eternal Soul Torture," though unrefined compared to the material that surfaced on Opeth's debut, carried a sophistication that belied the band's young age. Scarce few metal cognoscenti had heard Opeth before the debut was released. Their name was known, but nobody had actually heard the band.

Heightening the aura of mystery, Opeth rarely appeared in photos. When they did, the photos were grainy and shadowy. As with Bathory, Mekong Delta, Pan-Thy-Monium and In the Woods, this not only created allure, but brought sharp focus to the music itself and not the personalities playing it. "It was more or less a conscious move," Åkerfeldt says about the non-image image, "but it also happened a little by accident. When we shot the pictures for the sleeve of the first album, the silhouette ones were the best by far. Having been a big fan of Bathory and the mystique that surrounded them in the beginning, I kind of liked that we were kept somewhat anonymous. A few years later, along came the Internet and spoiled all that."

Signed to Candlelight Records solely on the strength of a rehearsal recording, Opeth debuted with *Orchid* in 1995. Produced by Dan Swanö, the album looked and felt different than anything else that had come before. The cover was in the '70s prog tradition—a blooming orchid bursting with color on a black background, no logo or writing anywhere—and so was the shadowy band photo on the back. The song titles had a poetic, nature-oriented slant—"The Twilight Is My Robe," "In Mist She Was Standing," "Forest of October." The music itself balanced subdued, low-key melancholy odes with kinetic dual-guitar harmonies and a lead style that recalled the emotional approach of such '70s greats as Uli Jon Roth and Robin Trower. The songs' emotional span was immense, recalling the ethereal, folkloric qualities of '70s bands Renaissance and Comus with a metallic essence that bridged the genre's history, hitting upon Black Sabbath, early Scorpions, and Iron Maiden as well as obvious alignment with Opeth's death and black metal contemporaries. Songs were lengthy and arrangements flowed smoothly despite a variety of mazelike shifts. Åkerfeldt's vocals shifted between agonized growling and gentle lament. The rhythmic momentum balanced harrowing turbulence and deep calm.

Nobody really knew what to make of this new band, but the excitement in the metal underground was palpable. An instant degree of respect marked Opeth as a highly regarded entity from the beginning. Some were making comparisons to peers like Dark Tranquillity, Amorphis, and In the Woods—not that the band actually sounded like any of them, but the spirit was similar. Ultimately they defied easy comparisons; Opeth was truly something new and different.

In the band's early years, as *Morningrise* and *My Arms, Your Hearse* built upon the sound introduced on *Orchid*, Åkerfeldt enthusiastically shared his love of '70s prog rock with any interviewer who would listen. When he cited weird names such as Gracious, P.F.M., Trettioåriga Kriget, Camel, and Culpeper's Orchard, it piqued people's curiosity. For many metal diehards, the discovery of a radical band that no one else in your circle knows is like a badge of honor; Opeth fans who also held arcane knowledge of Mefisto and Furbowl were intrigued by these obscure names of the past. If Åkerfeldt was extolling Gracious and P.F.M. along with Bathory and Morbid Angel, they had to be worth investigation.

Opeth's seminal *Morningrise*, 1996

Åkerfeldt was virtually a one-man publicity department for Camel in the mid- to late '90s. His continual praise of Camel and in particular the guitar work of Andy Latimer helped bridge a divide between the proggy past and the deathly modern age. The liner notes of *My Arms, Your Hearse* noted that it was the band's "third observation," which seemed to borrow from King Crimson's *In the Court of the Crimson King*, touted as "an observation by King Crimson." Even Opeth's album titles seemed a tribute to that bygone era: *Still Life* and *Blackwater Park* were also the names of '70s hard rock/prog acts, and the title *My Arms, Your Hearse* was taken from a line in Comus's diabolical "Drip Drip" of 1971: "As I carry you to your grave, my arms your hearse."

For all the references to the past, Opeth was plenty innovative. The band's rate of progression was measured and never drastic, yet significant enough to discern with each album. *My Arms, Your Hearse* marked one of Opeth's most significant evolutionary shifts. After *Morningrise*, the spidery fretless work and jazzy sensibility of bassist DeFarfalla left along with him; Åkerfeldt and Lindgren took the opportunity to deepen and darken their sound. Says Åkerfeldt, "In a perfect world, every album we did would be a fantastic progression from the one before—mind-boggling genius—but it simply doesn't work like that. You can't force progression. You have to be natural."

With 1999's *Still Life*, which featured a rhythm section of transplanted Uruguayans Martin Lopez and Martin Mendez, Opeth's sound crystallized into formidable shape. No one in death metal was as intricate, involved, dynamic, or ambitious as the mighty Swedes. The band felt like the best-kept secret of fans who had either discovered them on *Still Life* or had been following them since *Orchid*. The band never toured, having only played some fifty shows by 1999, and they had yet to cross over to the prog rock scene that would soon welcome them.

Blackwater Park changed everything for Opeth. The album, released in March 2001, brought the band to the world stage. Switching labels from Peaceville to Music for Nations—the latter having superior U.S. distribution at the time—allowed the band to capitalize on the momentum created by their previous albums. Opeth was beginning to break through the protective layer of the underground. They were also lifting the veil of mystique. They took more traditional band photos and embarked on real tours for the first time ever. The involvement of one Steven Wilson didn't hurt much either.

By the time of *Blackwater Park*, Steven Wilson had led his own band, Porcupine Tree, through a series of albums that hammered the '70s prog/psych sound into modern shape. Starting life with obvious Pink Floyd and Hawkwind influences on cassette-only releases *Tarquin's Seaweed Farm* (1989) and *The Nostalgia Factory* (1991) and progressing to later albums *Up the Downstair* and *The Sky Moves Sideways*, Wilson and band firmly established their own sound by the time of 1996's *Signify*. A few smart-pop curveballs were thrown into following albums *Stupid Dream* and *Lightbulb Sun*, and by the early 2000s Porcupine Tree had become leaders in the modern prog sphere. Ever aware of a variety of musical movements, Wilson was initially drawn to metal via the New Wave of British Heavy Metal, but soon lost interest in favor of other, more experimental musical happenings. So when the Porcupine Tree leader was given a copy of Opeth's *Still Life* by a French journalist who had interviewed Åkerfeldt just days earlier—a scheme hatched by Åkerfeldt himself—Wilson reluctantly took it. "I get given a lot of CDs when I'm on tour, and usually they don't particularly blow me away. But this one completely blew me away to the extent that I dropped Mikael a line and said, 'I was given your CD and I really love what you're doing.'"

In no time Wilson was hired to produce the fifth Opeth album. Although the band hadn't radically moved their songwriting style forward, save for perhaps "Bleak"—featuring mesmerizing EBow work and a vocal duet with Wilson—*Blackwater Park* is most notable for its firm statement of intent and depth of sound. Wilson, as talented an engineer and producer as he is a writer and performer, achieved a broader, deeper tone for *Blackwater Park* that hadn't been heard on the band's previous efforts. Suddenly they were highly visible, with acclaim coming at them in waves. Ten years after forming, Opeth was finally receiving its due.

Even elder prog metal statesmen were taking notice of Opeth; guys like Dream Theater's Mike Portnoy and Fates Warning's Jim Matheos were listening. Says Matheos, "Opeth are pushing the envelope and doing something new. They're out there doing something different. They're adding to what's been there before. I can't say they're derivative of anybody specifically, and that's what progressive is about—they're a great example of what progressive should be."

Portnoy used his considerable muscle to offer Opeth a slot on Dream Theater's first annual U.S. Progressive Nation tour in 2008, a bill that also included the compelling hybrid sound of 3 and ambitious post-metalcore act Between the Buried and Me. But the Dream Theater drummer had his eye on the Swedes long before that. "I originally wrote Opeth off as just some death metal band," Portnoy admits. "I didn't realize the progressive and psychedelic elements they had until I actually sat down and listened to them. Steven Wilson turned me onto *Blackwater Park*, and that's when I realized, 'Holy shit, these guys are intense, they're not just a death metal band, they're playing this music that's kind of Pink Floyd–ish at times, and really moody and dynamic.' Then when they put out *Damnation*, that was just a confirmation. As time goes on they're embracing these other elements more and more, and I think they're getting a lot more recognition because of that."

Riding a seemingly unstoppable wave, Opeth went from strength to strength starting in the late '90s. Åkerfeldt promised the band's heaviest album ever with sixth opus *Deliverance*, also produced by Wilson. Excepting "A Fair Judgement" and "For Absent Friends"—not the Genesis song of the same name—the album delivered the darkest, heaviest Opeth yet. Åkerfeldt's vocals were deepening, evolving in a similar fashion to those of his Morbid Angel hero David Vincent, and the guitar riffs were absolutely monolithic. The arrangements were as intricate as ever, and the drumming of Lopez was subtly jazz-inflected as it hadn't been before.

Offsetting the oppressiveness of *Deliverance*, Opeth followed in 2003 with *Damnation*. Another Steven Wilson–produced effort—recorded at the same time as *Deliverance*—*Damnation* was the album Opeth had been threatening for years. As haunting as it was sedate, *Damnation* featured melodic vocals exclusively and a much greater keyboard presence than ever before. More than any other Opeth album, it brought prog fans aboard who couldn't tolerate the guttural growls of

Opeth's Martin Lopez works the
(*Mike Col*

their heavier material. "Death vocals are an acquired taste," Åkerfeldt admits, "but I think we've helped a lot of people get into that type of vocal. If they hear *Damnation*, maybe they'll give the other stuff a chance, and once they do maybe they'll start to understand that brutality and aggressiveness are a big part in how we use dynamics. There are a lot of people telling me, 'I'm not into metal, let alone death metal, but I like you guys.'"

That kind of openness mirrors something Åkerfeldt told *Metal Maniacs* magazine in 1998: "People into progressive music, even if they're not into death metal, might understand our music. That's what progressive music is to me—music without boundaries. When you do music just because you love it, when you can incorporate any parts you want and don't care what music style it is, just play whatever you feel—that's progressive music. To me, progressive music is the ultimate form of music, and that doesn't mean it's pretentious. It opens your mind."

In great demand on the tour trail, Opeth documented the *Deliverance/Damnation* era with the *Lamentations* concert DVD, recorded at London's prestigious Shepherd's Bush Empire theater. By now they were media darlings, no longer anyone's secret pet band—and they hadn't compromised one bit. Opeth had become one of metal's most unlikely successes.

After three albums of successful partnership, Åkerfeldt and Wilson ceased working on Opeth albums together, but not before Åkerfeldt lent vocals to 2005 Porcupine Tree track "Arriving Somewhere But Not Here." Wilson has since considered producing other metal bands, but he was spoiled by Opeth. "Since I did Opeth," says Wilson, "I get invited probably once a week to work with a metal band of some variety. There are quite a few bands I've been approached by that I would have loved to work with, but there aren't many bands with the quality of Opeth. Once you've worked with Opeth, there's only a few other bands in that league." By late 2008, Wilson had finally found one of those bands to produce—eclectic Israeli metal act Orphaned Land and their fourth album, *The Never Ending Way of ORwarriOR*.

In early 2005 it was announced that Opeth had signed to massive independent label Roadrunner Records. By the late '90s, Roadrunner had completely rid itself of the many death and progressive metal bands it had made its name on earlier in the decade. The label interests had shifted from Cynic and Believer to trendier, more marketable sounds such as nu-metal extremists Slipknot and post-grunge sensations Nickelback. But Roadrunner's wide net swung back around to metal by 2005, bringing aboard not only Opeth but fellow prog legends Dream Theater. Opeth's first album for the label, *Ghost Reveries*, perfected the ultra-dense approach of *Deliverance*, but it would be the final album to feature drummer Martin Lopez and longtime guitarist Peter Lindgren. Lopez departed due to illness and anxiety attacks; Lindgren, weary of the road and the increasing demands made on the band, left after a decade of service—a noble move, considering the numbers Opeth were amassing, both in terms of record sales and concert attendance.

Mikael Åkerfeldt (left) and freshly-
instated Opeth guitarist Fredrik
Åkesson, February 2008
(*Frank White*)

Åkerfeldt stayed strong in the fallout. With keyboardist Per Wiberg now a fulltime member, Åkerfeldt and bassist Martin Mendez welcomed drummer Martin Axenrot and guitarist Fredrik Åkesson to the fold. Having experienced the most drastic lineup alteration of their career, Opeth rebounded in 2008 with an invigorated sound on the appropriately titled *Watershed*.

If Opeth has any kind of weakness, it's that some of their riffs seem interchangeable, and even if a few moments on the new album harkened back to older records, Åkerfeldt was clearly writing *Watershed* with the intent that it would be a considerable step forward. And it was. Keyboards—warm, vintage-sounding organs and synths—were more prominent than ever, while Åkesson's guitar work brought a sharper, more disciplined technique into the picture, comple-

menting Åkerfeldt's looser, '70s-oriented lead style. Åkerfeldt's clean vocals were warmer and remarkably more soulful than before.

Holding *Watershed* up to the *Orchid* album of thirteen years earlier, it becomes apparent just how far Opeth has come. Comparing their new material to the early stuff, Åkerfeldt states, "The main ingredients remain intact. It's dynamic, which I thought the first album was. There's still a lot of switching going on between the heavy parts and the acoustic guitars and the clean and screaming vocals. We still have long songs. So there's a lot of stuff that's the same, but that said, there's probably more that has changed."

Through a variety of cover songs, Opeth's leader has paid respect to such heroes as David Coverdale (via Deep Purple's "Soldier of Fortune") and Robin Trower (a reworking of "Bridge of Sighs"). On these tracks, and *Watershed* original "Burden," Åkerfeldt's vocals proved as rich and commanding as those of the elder gods he worships. *Watershed* found Opeth moving forward as significantly as they had in years.

There were perhaps as many soft vocals as deadly growls, and with the added colors introduced throughout the album, the band had indeed come a long way from where it started. In many cases, Opeth is now more like an extreme progressive rock band than a death metal band influenced by progressive rock.

Åkerfeldt has recently been linked to Mike Portnoy and Steven Wilson as part of a proposed side project. Aligning the schedules of three of progressive music's busiest characters is the only thing keeping the trio from recording what would undoubtedly be one of the most anticipated albums in modern prog circles. But the Opeth leader seems even more enthusiastic about doing a solo album, as a sort of challenge to himself. "Just an experiment, to see if I could do it. I'd like to produce an album's worth of material completely on my own—write, perform, record, produce, engineer, even master it. Do everything." For now, Åkerfeldt is content working in Opeth and enjoying what little time he has off.

Opeth has never compromised. They are still brutally heavy in spots, their songs still long and involved. They make plenty of demands on the listener, yet continue to draw enormous crowds and sell huge amounts of albums every time one is released. *Watershed* even landed at number twenty-three on *Billboard*'s Top 200 album chart upon its 2008 release. Åkerfeldt is as pleasantly surprised by Opeth's incredible popularity as are people who picked up a strange-looking album called *Orchid* by a mysterious Swedish band in 1995. "A couple years back I would've said we couldn't take this further, but now I'm not so sure. Because there's been a jump—there's a lot of people coming to see us now. I see all kinds of people at our shows—old guys, young guys, metal fans, non-metal fans, entire families. I'm not really sure we've reached our peak, but I don't know how big we can become. I guess it could die down—I don't think it'll ever get Metallica-big—but there's a lot of interest in the band right now."

While countrymen Meshuggah, Therion, and Opeth have enjoyed widespread acclaim and enormous crowds in a variety of territories, the band and man known as Vintersorg quietly built a legacy via his early Viking/folk metal albums and, later, more ambitious excursions such as *Visions from the Spiral Generator* (2001) and *The Focusing Blur* (2004). Also known as Andreas Hedlund, Vintersorg is as interested in nature, the cosmos, and old prog rock as he is in classic metal and hanging out in Old William's Pub in his hometown of Skellefteå. Vintersorg is a mesh of classic heavy metal, black metal, folk music, and '70s hard rock and prog; Hedlund has tied an array of interests and disciplines together through a series of deep and dynamic albums.

At the band's outset, Hedlund intended to mix clean vocals with black metal music—a novel idea in the early '90s. He points to fellow Swedes Edge of Sanity as particularly inspiring. "I think the first time I ever heard this done was by Edge of Sanity on the *Unorthodox* album, on 'Enigma.' But I hadn't heard an entire album with this kind of approach." Implementing the idea on his early releases, Hedlund soon took the band beyond those modest ambitions. Leaving the longships behind, he shifted from pagan/historical subjects to ruminations on metaphysics and the cosmos. *Cosmic Genesis*—appropriately released in 2001—marked that shift. Upbeat, bright, drenched in keyboards, and spiced with inspired lead guitar work from partner Mattias Marklund, the album is unapologetically grandiose. Hedlund's prog fascination was revealed in a cover of Uriah Heep's "Rainbow Demon," and his songwriting acumen was proven through a string of songs as memorable as they are heavily layered. With 2000's *Cosmic Genesis*, Vintersorg's imagery became engulfed by astronomy and all things sidereal; their music was no longer a simple black/pagan metal construct, but one of myriad facets.

Vintersorg's sci-fact era climaxed with *Visions from the Spiral Generator* and *The Focusing Blur*. Lyrical influences ranged from the writings and ideas of popular scientists such as Carl Sagan and Stephen Hawking to nineteenth-century physicists such as James Clerk Maxwell. With the recruitment of former Death bassist Steve DiGiorgio and Spiral Architect drummer Asgeir Mickelson, *Visions* was the first true "band" album from the onetime duo; the successful approach was carried over to *The Focusing Blur*. By this point, Vintersorg's multitiered vocals, increased reliance on melody, layered productions, complex arrangements, expanded lineup, and elements of prog, jazz, and folk all helped attract a wide variety of listeners.

While Hedlund was venturing off the beaten path, neighboring Norwegian musician Øystein G. Brun was watching and listening. One of many progressive bands in metal-rich Norway, Brun's Borknagar had caught Hedlund's attention with 2000 album *Quintessence*, and the admiration was mutual. There was no arm-pulling necessary when Brun offered Hedlund the job of Borknagar lead vocalist. The union between the two has resulted in three "proper" Borknagar albums, plus all-acoustic album *Origin*, and the Cronian project, which explores the mellower textures of both Borknagar and Vintersorg. The very busy Hedlund has gone on to record Vintersorg albums in between Borknagar and Cronian, even branching out further with Waterclime, which finds the Swede embracing his '70s jazz and prog rock influences to an even greater degree.

Bridging the gap between Sweden's well-known and "traditional" progressive metal bands—with Evergrey and Pain of Salvation leading the way—and its boundary-breaking death/thrash acts, Loch Vostok and Bokor are create yet newer sounds. Their *Reveal No Secrets* (2009) and *Vermin Soul* (2008) albums, respectively, are undoubtedly interesting, if stuck in the gelling stage. The bands borrow from a vast field of influences and end up with a Frankenstein's monster of melting-pot metal. Only time will tell if yet another revolutionary Swedish metal wave is bound to break.

The breed of strange progressive metal bands emerging in the late 1990s had one major advantage over those from the earlier part of the decade: metal-friendly record labels that traveled exclusively in the weirdest regions of the genre. While the Inside Out label's tentacles extended worldwide to snare a variety of modern prog rock and Big Three–oriented Progressive metal acts, various labels operated similarly in the edgier, heavier underground.

English label Misanthropy Records were clearly enthusiastic about Norwegian avant-metal. Until Misanthropy's closing in 2000, owner Tiziana Stupia released music by Arcturus, In the Woods, Ved Buens Ende, Fleurety, Madder Mortem, Mayhem, and Beyond Dawn. All too briefly, the legendary grind/death label Earache Records supported its short-lived Elitist Records imprint, signing Italy's leading avant-metal act Ephel Duath, as well as Hungarian progressive goth-metallers Without Face, oddball death-grinders T.O.O.H., and Russian genre-blenders Rakoth. Massachusetts label Dark Symphonies was a purely eclectic concern, giving bands such as User Ne and Long Winters' Stare a chance, with their most influential and enduring signing, Maudlin of the Well, releasing three albums between 1999 and 2001 before delving deeper into highbrow realms as the renamed Kayo Dot. But perhaps the most welcoming label home for the late-'90s/early-2000s new wave of avant-garde metal was The End Records.

Cyprus native Andreas Katsambas moved to the U.S. in 1992 and founded The End in 1997, aiming to illuminate strange and unusual metal. Odd U.S. bands Sculptured and Scholomance may have never found a home if not for Katsambas's eclectic tastes. "I couldn't find anything I liked from the mainstream genres," says Katsambas, "so I kept digging deeper into the underground. There were a few really cool underground bands I liked, and I decided to press CDs for them and try to promote and distribute them. Those bands were small but I really liked them and found them fresh and exciting. The goal was to release bands that stood out and were different than what was already out there."

Four years later, Katsambas quit working for Century Media Records, and The End Records became his full-time job. Through the years, The End has championed Norwegian progressives Enslaved, Arcturus, Ulver, Age of Silence, Dødheimsgard, and Frantic Bleep. The label brought Oakland oddities Sleepytime Gorilla Museum to wider acclaim. Voivod—who Katsambas calls "the most progressive metal band ever"—released the curiously straightforward *Katorz* via the label in 2006. Japan's Sigh and Canada's Unexpect also found support through The End Records. The End established itself as the Inside Out Records of avant-metal, performing a service similar to that offered by the legendary prog label on the darker side of the tracks.

With the support of these and other specialty record labels, metal's new avant-garde had arrived. The bands were heavier and more challenging than any metal that came before them, and they would not be ignored. They were simply too bizarre to be ignored.

Until the 1990s, Japan's most well known metal export was Loudness. The Osaka band made it to American major labels and stadium support slots by 1985, and it was expected that their peers in Anthem, EZO, and Bow Wow (aka Vow Wow) might do the same. But the great Japanese metal invasion of America never quite happened. By decade's end, Japan's lustful appreciation for theatrics in music and imagery—not to mention its easy seduction by many aspects of Western culture—found black metal gaining popularity in the Land of the Rising Sun. Tokyo native and young thrasher Mirai Kawashima became entranced by black metal, and with his ever-adventurous listening habits guiding the way, he birthed the oddly named Sigh.

Though Sigh didn't land on The End Records until 2007, their two decades of experimentation naturally led to that appropriate union. Sigh's early demos—*Desolation* and *Tragedies* (both 1990)—and first albums *Scorn Defeat* and *Infidel Art,* wrapped symphonic elements around a mid-paced necro-metal plod. Their synthesizer use was novel, but Sigh never took a great leap into the outer reaches until their third full-length, 1997's *Hail Horror Hail.* Mirroring Voivod's long-term vision, Sigh intended to gradually move into more progressive areas, even in their earliest days. Says Kawashima, "Even back in 1990, we had an idea to mix raw black metal and horror soundtrack–like atmospheric music, but we had no musical ability at that time."

Sigh, sitar and skull, 2005
(*Tenkotsu Kawaho*)

Described by the band as "a horror film without the pictures," *Hail Horror Hail* fulfilled Sigh's cinematic intentions. Throughout the album's nine songs, the influence of experimental composer Karlheinz Stockhausen was felt as strongly as their thrash/black metal loyalties, especially on "12 Souls," which featured a variety of textural complexities and sonic cut-ups. Sigh was embracing technology that allowed them not merely to make music, but to create pieces that were more like aural paintings. "Technology plays a big role in our music," says Kawashima. "With synthesizers and sampling machines, you can now have a big orchestra and a choir. Limitations in composition have been drastically relieved because of technology."

Hail Horror Hail's follow-up, *Scenario IV: Dread Dreams* (1999), was far from conventional, but it wasn't the avant-garde masterpiece many expected. Their next album, 2000's *Imaginary Sonicscape*, blew Sigh's experimental doors wide open. True to its title, *Imaginary Sonicscape* presented an array of outlandish sounds and styles. The album's tone is distinguished by vintage keyboards and an organic sonic texture. The eleven-minute, five-part "Slaughtergarden Suite" referenced everything from Goblin and Tangerine Dream to dark soundtrack music to Mercyful Fate and Mayhem. "A Sunset Song," with its Beach Boys, disco, and *Somewhere in Time*–era Iron Maiden references, placed Sigh on their very own island of individuality. *Imaginary Sonicscape* proved that post–black metal didn't necessarily have to come from Norway. The album could be aligned with what Norway's Arcturus and Solefald were aiming for, but with Sigh's peculiar set of influences, it was run through a completely different filter and arrived at something indelible and singular.

Arriving four years later in 2005. *Gallows Gallery* was unexpected and perplexing. Light-years distant from the elaborate *Imaginary Sonicscape*, *Gallows Gallery* featured a Mercyful Fate–like mid-pace churn with cleanly sung multitracked vocals and unpolished, almost demo-level production. Kawashima's vocals sounded drugged—at once haunting and aloof—while the rhythmic cadence recalled Oktoberfest beer hall dances despite Sigh's ever-present sinister undertow. The album's middle found "The Tranquilizer Song" breaking up the samey feel of the other songs with its seductive, soundtrack–ish sway. *Gallows Gallery* was yet more change from a band that kept fans on their toes, although most of those fans welcomed the more familiar Sigh that returned on 2007's *Hangman's Hymn*.

Sigh described *Hangman's Hymn*, subtitled "Musikalische Exequien," as "a ten-track assault of orchestrated violence, deriving heavy influence from German classical Romantic composers such as Anton Bruckner, Gustav Mahler, and Richard Wagner." *Hangman's Hymn* found Sigh back on the *Hail Horror Hail* track in many respects. This territory was explored further on 2010's *Scenes from Hell*, which included a real string quartet, various brass instruments, and an expansion into even more brutal vocal realms by new member Dr. Mikannibal (who doubles on saxophone, is the band's first female member, and is actually a doctor, holding a PhD in physics).

Kawashima's attitude underscores an intensely important point about what it means to be a progressive musician of any kind: "When bands make efforts only to sound like the leading bands [of their subgenre], it's totally ridiculous. It is nothing creative. The reason so many bands cling to convention is probably that they don't listen to lots of different kinds of music. You need an input for the better output. You have to listen to lots of different music to create something original."

Sigh were not the first avant-garde metal band to arise from Japan. The bizarre and theatrical Doom recorded a series of demos, singles, and albums that were always hard to find outside their own country, but they clearly were one of the first '80s metal bands, from anywhere, to delve into uninhabited weird worlds. They seemed to bear some Voivod influence, and weren't afraid of adding punk and funk into their abrasive, angular metal. The music of Doom—which would never be mistaken for actual doom metal—rarely gelled; just about any given song from the band's catalog has an incomplete and uneasy quirk, as if they tried too hard to be strange at the expense of flow. But their contribution to the forward progression of their genre is duly noted.

Doom and Sigh join a long chain of mold-shattering Japanese bands. In the wider musical spectrum, artists such as Ruins, Koenji Hyakkei, Happy Family, and Pochakaite Malko play music somewhere between dark, unpredictable prog rock and difficult experimentalism. Tokyo's Gonin-ish may as well be considered the metal equivalent of these left fielders.

Gonin-ish ("songs being united by five people") began in 1996 as a tribute to modern Swedish prog rock band Anekdoten. As original songs overtook their cover repertoire, a wild mesh emerged that included death metal, jazz, symphonic prog, and RIO/Zeuhl styles. Like a mammoth creature of incomprehensible shape, their second album, 2005's *Naishikyo-*

At the edge of the cutting edge: Japan's Gonin-Ish (*courtesy of Season Of Mist*)

Sekai, is daunting and frightful. Somehow, they avoid sounding like novelty mishmash. Gonin-ish are serious; their writing is imbued with purpose, and their playing is formidable. The band collectively states that "if ten people were asked to define us by genre, it is likely they would all give ten different responses. We have so many influences and place so many different elements in our music. There are no understandings or misunderstandings; however you feel about our music is right! Therefore, we don't need to be constrained by a genre. In other words: Is this not true progressive music?"

Certainly, liberal genre-blending and the collision of disparate influences is no guarantee of good music. Experimental avant-garde everything-but-the-kitchen-sink metal sometimes sounds no more attractive than a cataclysmic train wreck. Lauded for his band's union of distinctively different genres but rarely considered "avant-garde," Mikael Åkerfeldt of Opeth cautions against forced experimentation: "To deliberately sit down and say, 'Okay, now we're going to create something totally new'—that's not how you should be doing it. If you're going to naturally develop that way, fine, but you need to let it happen on its own, otherwise it's going to be shit."

Musician and fan Chris Roy elaborates: "I think it's hard to break new ground with anything, but envelope-pushing is still happening. The other side of that is that sometimes 'groundbreaking' means it should be buried for not being such a good thing. As much as I'm a Crimson Glory fan, most of the solo material [late vocalist] Midnight put out just sounded insane, which some could call 'groundbreaking.' At least he was trying, but it's definitely not what I would listen to. Between the wackiness of someone like Midnight, experimental bands like Devil Doll, and some of the more technical bands, some kind of basic formula has to be followed or it's like watching a marathon where there's no map and everyone is just running in different circles."

A band like Canada's Unexpect, however, throws every caution to the wind and does everything they're not supposed to. They embrace train wrecks. The challenge of maintaining the delicate balance between "too much" and "not enough" is what makes Unexpect's music as individualistic as it is, though it's not always a smooth ride.

Unexpect's exhausting music is characterized by rapidly shifting tempos, blinding momentum, multifaceted vocals, prominent violin, and nine-string mutated-funk bass guitar. When the middle of "Feasting Fools," from 2005's *In a Flesh Aquarium*, breaks into vocal duets recalling something from *Sweeney Todd*, it's clear they're a metal band of a different stripe. That thread of melodrama actually pervades everything the band does, with influences seemingly coming from Broadway, opera, and underground/independent musical theater as much as, if not more than, standard metal inspirations. Says Unexpect guitarist Syriak: "We are musical sponges, accumulating and dispersing as we see fit. We're free-spirited musical creators with our feet planted on a metal platform. Madness included."

In its own way, Unexpect continues the tradition of cutting-edge metal set forth by fellow Quebecois iconoclasts Voivod, Obliveon, D.B.C., and Gorguts. Unexpect may not be prolific—only two albums and an EP in eleven years—but they have certainly made an impression. Sensory/Laser's Edge president Ken Golden is a fan, as is Dream Theater's Mike Portnoy, who brought the band along on the 2009 European leg of the annual Progressive Nation tour (an installment that also included Opeth and L.A. retro-proggers Bigelf). Along with Swedish opera metal progressives Therion, Unexpect has helped open doors for ever-more bombastic metal-based bands, such as Swedish troupe Diablo Swing Orchestra. Preferring to call their music "riot opera," D.S.O. incorporates cello, synths, female lead vocals, and elaborate costuming—a grandiose metallic mishmash that easily made them what Chris Roy calls the "oddball band" at 2009's ProgPower festival in Atlanta.

A long way west of Unexpect's home, the Pacific Northwest finds Washington's Agalloch and Sculptured forging a dark progressive metal collective. Led by John Haughm, Agalloch has built a tremendous cult following with three albums of elemental, folk-laden metal. Their sound is more akin to the adulterated extreme black/death sounds that emerged from Europe in the '90s than anything happening in their own country. Kin to Opeth and Katatonia, Agalloch embrace their most experimental tendencies via special limited EPs and vinyl-only releases that delve deeper into the post-rock, ambient, and neo-folk sounds that subtly inform their main body of work.

Members of Agalloch are also found in the defiantly different Sculptured. Led by Don Anderson, Sculptured albums, like Agalloch, have released all their albums on The End Records, and while their output is sporadic, the results are compelling. Sculptured's early material—with ornate melodic death metal at its core—featured prominent trumpet, which provided a forlorn undertow to their music, playing a role similar to that of the trombone in Norway's Beyond Dawn. A trombone even appears side by side with trumpet on Sculptured's second album, *Apollo Ends* (2000). Third album *Embodiment* (2008) saw Sculptured dropping the brass and embracing a more teched-out mind-set, for which Anderson found the talents of San Francisco drummer Dave Murray useful. A remarkable artist in his own right, Murray had previously been in gypsy/metal/prog/psych/surf weirdos Estradasphere, and later guided the insanely ambitious Deserts of Träun project as well as tech death monsters Tholus.

Sculptured's Don Anderson
(*Christine Mussen*)

Sculptured's inspirations are multi-fold—the band lists Cynic, Atheist, Mr. Bungle, Naked City, *Awake*-era Dream Theater, Ennio Morricone, and Igor Stravinsky as particularly influential. But for all the intrigue of Sculptured's original compositions, one of the band's greatest achievements came early with a cover of Iron Maiden's eponymous anthem. Appearing on 1998 tribute album *Maiden America*, the version begins with the swing of lounge jazz, turns toward trumpet-laden avant-death weirdness, revisits the bouncy jazz, and concludes with brass-blaring metal. Strange as hell yet surprisingly cohesive—like their original compositions.

Formed around the same time as Sculptured and Unexpect, Boston band Maudlin of the Well are perhaps the most important of the modern avant-garde metal bands outside Norway. Maudlin went from being one of the most obscure bands in the universe in the late '90s to reinventing themselves as Kayo Dot and rubbing shoulders with veteran avant-garde musos just a few years later. The membership fluctuates, but keyboard/woodwind player Terran Olson has been on board with both bands, as has creative center Toby Driver.

Driver—conceptualist, composer, and multi-instrumentalist—never cared to state what Maudlin of the Well were or where the band should have been placed, in terms of genres and categories. While Maudlin were still active, Driver stated, "A lot of metal bands will try to take elements of other genres and use them to enhance their metal, but we are more like a band who plays with metal from the outside looking in. Our compositional style is really different, and it's constantly developing into something that would be as unfair to metal to call us a metal band as it would be to jazz to call us a jazz band."

Maudlin released their 1996 demo, *Through Languid Veins*, in very small quantity, merging the haze of psychedelia, odd timings, and the unpredictability of jazz fusion with the laconic movement of shoegaze music, the abstraction of surrealism, and the bent frame of Norway's post–black metal avant-garde. Threading it all together was a base of diseased death metal, with a particularly revealing influence from eclectic death/doom band My Dying Bride. "They were an extremely significant influence on our writing," admits Driver. "I've never heard My Dying Bride referred to as a progressive band, but they certainly were. At least, until they shamefully cowered at the backlash they received for trying something new with their brilliant 34.788%... *Complete* album, with band members denouncing it as a 'mistake.'"

Another couple demos, more emphasis on brass and woodwinds, and even more spacious arrangements led to Maudlin of the Well's first album, *My Fruit Psycho-bells...A Seed Combustible* in 1999. Two years later, the band simultaneously released companion albums *Bath* and *Leaving Your Body Map*, both quickly achieving recognition as avant-metal masterpieces. With a confidence in their conundrum, Maudlin of the Well out-progged typical Progressive metal bands with the twin offerings, defying any and all metal conventions and, despite their wide stylistic span, writing with more compositional authority and focus than most bands of similar ilk. Praises were heaped upon Maudlin of the Well by various sectors of the metal public, but just as they were on the ascent, a few key members left the fold. Driver decided to rename the band and essentially start anew.

Kayo Dot became the new face of Maudlin of the Well. As Driver puts it, Kayo Dot "was a continuation, but a separation in intent." Kayo Dot's 2003 debut, *Choirs of the Eye*, seemed to be breaking the bonds of the band's metal past to work in an even freer, genre-less area. (Appropriately, the album was released via Tzadik, the label run by legendary avant-garde saxophonist/composer John Zorn.) Successive albums *Dowsing Anemone with Copper Tongue* (2006), *Blue Lambency Downward* (2008), and *Coyote* (2010) took the band further into realms that can only be called "experimental," but they have also been termed "post-progressive," "post-modern," or "post-metal." The band states that their influences include The Cure, Scott Walker, Today Is the Day, Björk, and Gorguts, while people outside the band have likened Kayo Dot to King Crimson, Isis, Jeff Buckley, and Opeth. There is clearly no easy comparison to make between Kayo Dot and others. Driver mused in 2009, "I'm more unclear now than ever on what actually makes something 'metal.' I'm still trying to create intensities, but to do it in ways that are new to me."

Two of a perfect pair: Maudlin Of The Well's simultaneously-released *Bath* and *Leaving Your Body Map*, 2001

While "minimalism" is a tag often thrown at Kayo Dot's music, Driver counters by saying, "People that perceive this music as minimalism surely must not know what minimalist music actually is, and furthermore must not be paying attention to what's actually happening in a Kayo Dot piece. A lot of our songs require patient listening and have slow development, but that isn't even a similar thing to minimalism."

In 2008, Maudlin of the Well fired up its engines for one final recording. Driver and other Maudlin vets had, at various points in their dormant years, revealed that much material was written in the band's lifetime that remained unrecorded. Because Maudlin lacked sufficient capital to record these tracks, fans collected enough money through an online fundraiser for Driver and company to reassemble and crystallize this material. The resulting album, *Part the Second*, was made available as a free download in 2009, via the band's website. The music on *Part the Second* made revealing links between Maudlin of the Well's oppressive metal backbone and the abstracted experimental approach of Kayo Dot, featuring downplayed intensity and greater reliance on dreamlike calm.

While still involved in the first Maudlin phase, Driver revealed his creative philosophies, an approach and attitude he carried into Kayo Dot: "The composition or song, the emotion, those are the important things in music, not the amazing technical ability someone has. I love hearing sloppy punk bands bang the piss out of their instruments to get their point across. Yes, technical prowess is important, because as a musician, you want to be able to express yourself. If you want to write something beyond your ability, it's either important for you to practice it until you can play it, or it's not. It's up to the musician to decide to what extent they want to be able to express themselves. Using this as a basis, it seems that the more virtuosic you are on your instrument or as a composer, the freer you are to express yourself accurately. And again, in the case of a punk guitarist, for example, he might not care to express himself beyond three loud, fast power chords. Unfortunately, some instrumentalists focus so much on the skill that they never learn anything else about music—like emotion or metaphysics—so they believe they're really accomplished when they're really just very isolated."

The continued interest in Maudlin of the Well and Kayo Dot has doubtlessly made it easier for newer left fielders such as Poland's Egoist and Finland's Umbra Nihil to find an audience. But others—such as Italy's Ephel Duath, led by Davide Tiso—have helped widen the field of fiercely avant-garde metal and have been doing it for as long as Toby Driver.

Ephel Duath's 2009 foray, *Through My Dog's Eyes*, found lauded drummer Marco Minnemann bolstering the band's rhythmic pulse. Relating the story of a wandering stray, *Through My Dog's Eyes* is decidedly focused compared to early efforts, although none of Ephel Duath's music is easy to absorb. Angular, dissonant, sometimes confusing, with their early material resembling fractured jazz metal and their newer stuff moving into a more focused, dirgelike area, the band has no albums that provide easy listening. They have been accused of having more style than substance, but they

Esoteric to the core: Toby Driver (right) and Mia Matsumiya of Kayo Dot
(*Yuko Sueta*)

have, at the very least, gotten many people to listen. Legendary label Earache Records is among Ephel Duath's most high-profile supporters, having released five albums by the band since 2002, including *Pain Remixes the Known*, a complete refurbishment of 2005's *Pain Necessary to Know* album.

As a listener, Ephel Duath main man Davide Tiso readily admits a fondness for Norwegian post–black metal bands Ulver and Manes as well as healthy doses of apocalyptic sludge gods Neurosis and smart alt-rock bands Placebo and Radiohead. All this—and surely much more—figures into Ephel Duath's miasma of post-whatever/psychedelic/extreme progressive metal.

Celtic Frost's *Into the Pandemonium* caused tremendous confusion and misunderstanding when it appeared in 1987. The album sat lonely in a heavy metal left field that was waiting to be populated. Ten years later, it finally began finding company. The band, although it took quite some time, were eventually vindicated for the experiment. The paths blazed by Rush, Watchtower, Voivod, Arcturus, and Opeth also made life easier for modern experimental/avant-garde metal bands.

The 2000s have brought wider acceptance of countless unique metal forms than ever before. As genre branches grow, so does the palate of the metal public. Like Dream Theater, Tool became an immensely popular band whose transformative transcendental imagery and musical sophistication brought reward and acclaim instead of the derision and obscurity other iconoclasts before them faced. In August 2001, they hit the road for a short jaunt with King Crimson in tow—and though Tool were rightfully awestruck by the pairing, they were at the same time outselling their heroes. "It was an honor for us," says Tool vocalist Maynard James Keenan. "For our fans, it was something like an education. A lot of our fans weren't really aware where we were coming from, what inspired us. I think to share one stage with King Crimson was important. It showed where our roots are, where we are coming from."

Seemingly simple on the surface, Tool music is deceivingly difficult. "Schism," from 2001's *Lateralus*, illustrates the band's penchant for stealth technique. A flowing, mesmerizing song, its time signature was described by bassist Justin Chancellor as being in the bizarre meter of 6.5/8. "Schism" won a Best Metal Performance Grammy for Tool in 2002, proving highbrow heaviness no longer needed to struggle in the fringes.

Another nearly-impossible-to-fathom Grammy winner, Atlanta's Mastodon—enormous in name and stature—made epic heavy metal acceptable to the mainstream for the first time since the '80s heyday of Iron Maiden and Metallica. Mastodon's metal comes in a different form, but its influences and intentions are clear, and their success deserved. They may not have been the first to play physically demanding metal or drape their imagery in mysticism, legend, and fantasy, but they followed the path blazed by others, held on to their individuality and sense of adventure, and emerged as one of the biggest and smartest metal bands of modern times.

Even instrumental metal is taking a firmer hold with listeners than it did in previous decades. Instrumental metal used to mean guitar shred like David T. Chastain or Tony Macalpine; now a new generation of vocalless bands confound and complicate with involved, technical, highly imaginative metal. When Dysrhythmia, Behold the Arctopus and Canvas Solaris joined together for an East Coast mini-tour in 2008, they proved there was an audience for difficult metal that poses an alternative to the traditional Progressive metal norms. Even younger instrumental tech band Scale the Summit have quickly risen in the ranks, releasing two albums as of 2010 and gaining slots on tours with Dream Theater, Cynic, and Between the Buried and Me.

Metal's current big expansion into uncharted realms, from Hammers of Misfortune and Behold the Arctopus to Deathspell Omega and Between the Buried and Me, among many others, finds barrier-crashing bands still forging their histories, all too "in-progress" for adequate reflection.

Metal certainly wasn't like this in the '80s. Then, it was easy for weird metal bands to stand out from the crowd. Experimentation and innovation were novel, even aberrant. Now, complicated time signatures, unusual instrumentation, and influences outside of metal are common. Tech metal pioneers such as Atheist, Believer, and Cynic find more enthusiastic followings today than they did when they were first active twenty years ago. Their early material wasn't even that adventurous—it was crude thrash/death that only later evolved from its humble origins. Today, evolutionary stages are brief, if nonexistent. Newcomers Obscura and Terminal Function completely bypass the primitive stages of development and dive right in playing refined metal of great complexity. They no longer endure the lengthy journeys of earlier bands that grew up in public and made mistakes out in the open. The modern, honed music of these newer prodigies is impressive on a technical level, but it perhaps lacks the heart and charming naïveté of earlier bands. Add that to the fact that performance standards are higher today than ever before and studio gimmickry far more accessible—suddenly the extraordinary has become ordinary.

Andreas Katsambas has recognized this very phenomenon and shifted The End Records beyond what is expected. In a time when avant-metal bands are now taken for granted, Katsambas has turned yet another corner by putting his energy behind noise rockers Made out of Babies, actor-turned-musician Juliette Lewis, style-spanning violinist Emilie Autumn, electro-punk sensations Mindless Self Indulgence, and monster Finnish rockers Lordi. Not that avant/progressive metal is over for Katsambas, but he noticed a curious thing happening: "When I started the label, I felt metal was the most exciting genre. I always like bands that try different things, and there was a lot of that going on in the late '90s. Now it seems that it has gotten more established. Newer bands follow a lot of stereotypes and try to fit in rather than trying to stand out. Diversity is good and healthy. Our motto is 'Evolve, Explore, Experiment.'"

The viability and malleability of the metal form is no longer in question. And certainly, the genre needs to grow to avoid atrophy—but where can it possibly go from here? Many progressive-minded musicians eventually return to simplicity. For all the delving into the bizarre Dan Swanö did with Pan-Thy-Monium and Karaboudjan, all he really wants is a good song: "Too many progressive bands don't care about adding a pop element to the songs. Even the most complex Gentle Giant songs have a commercial vibe. It means that you can remember it. It's sad when you hear a full record from a band, and the moment it's over you remember absolutely nothing."

While continually amazed at the enormous success of his uncompromising, defiantly progressive band, Opeth's Mikael Åkerfeldt is waiting for the next new thing to emerge in metal. When it does, it just might be more familiar than foreign: "I don't really know if metal's going to be taken further. I'm sure it will, but you'll be able to trace it back to some band from the past. There's something old in everything new."

17. A WAY OUT FROM THE WAY-OUT?

"Music is more about passion than technique. The right single note played, or not played, can have more impact than a thousand notes in its place. Whipping up and down scales is not necessarily good music. Good music happens in the clever places left between notes." —Devon Graves, Deadsoul Tribe/ Psychotic Waltz

ONCE THE MARKS OF METAL'S AVANT-GARDE OUTSIDERS, musical virtuosity, complication, obtuseness, angularity, and total unchecked creative abandon have become features of some of metal's most popular bands. Of course, a fine line still separates originality and white-noise excess. The point when music loses all shape and form is where musicians either revert back to simplicity, or die from a headfirst slam into that wall of complication. As metal moves into its fifth decade, oddities such as Thy Catafalque, Gonin-ish, and Egoist paint the metal machine in new, previously unseen Martian colors. But while attempting to write truly original material, those on metal's fringes risk producing an unapproachable clump of alienating clatter—weird music for the sake of weird music.

Tuomas Holopainen of Nightwish, which is sometimes labeled a progressive act, but more rightly a grandiose power/gothic metal band—an extremely successful one, at that—is skeptical of experimental metal forms. "There's no intrinsic value in doing something differently and breaking the mold," he says. "Originality is one of the most overrated virtues in today's music. If the song rocks, if it manages to stir emotions, then who cares if it reminds you of something that's been done before? Seeking originality for originality's sake is just quasi-artistic bullshit."

As with other arts and life in general, for that matter, black needs white and white needs black—one has no meaning or purpose without the other. So too does simple music need more complicated forms to throw it into relief. Enslaved's Ivar Bjørnson understands the relationship of yin and yang. "Every society needs to have a balance of contraction and expansion," he says. "In metal too you need to have Tool and Motörhead working side by side. There would be no point in expanding and exploring if there was no anchor or center point. And there would be no point in holding back if nobody expanded."

With history in mind, many progressive metal pioneers now understand both sides of these arguments. Some have immersed themselves in technical music so exclusively that the appreciation of what makes complexity extraordinary in the first place becomes blurred. The most interesting progressive metal bands begin as wide-eyed students, learn the craft from their heroes, then dive headlong into frenzied periods of ambition before concluding with a stripped-down approach that emphasizes songwriting over showmanship. Rush, Fates Warning, Psychotic Waltz, and Voivod, to cite just a few examples, persisted long enough to explore both ends of the spectrum and myriad places in between.

Once their playing abilities had reached nearly inhuman levels, the members of Rush became more concerned with composition and less so with bewildering complication. "Once you develop your craft, you're able to wield it more skillfully," says Rush's Neil Peart. "In the early years we were learning to play, and the focus for our first six albums was 'let's get better as musicians.' A lot of stuff was just exercises stuck together, but they had a purpose. It was our postgraduate study, and then we went into songwriting and arranging as specific focuses—and now we try to focus on them all."

Rush's '80s output turned away a segment of their fan base that wanted only grand epics and instrumental wizardry. But the band members remained fans and listeners as well as world-class musicians. As they moved on in their listening, so they did in their playing and composing, and vice versa. Rush never wrote another twenty-minute song after 1978's "Hemispheres" opus, and they never went for easy applause by recording a *2112 II* or a *Still Moving Pictures*. Rush's simplification was part maturity and part technical fatigue.

Rush's "prog" phase was necessary. They were kids raised on the late-'60s proto-metal of Cream and the Yardbirds who became highly energized by the English prog movement in the '70s. Together with the blunt force of early metal, which seeped profusely from their pores at one point, Rush was a big, glorious wrecking ball of hard rock swagger, epic heavy metal glory, and progressive rock grandiosity. While this phase of their career remains the most influential on other progressive rock and metal bands, they're done with it—mostly. "Time and Motion" threw a few tech-y shapes into 1996's *Test for Echo* album, and the band still unveils epic vistas—minus the epic lengths—if songs like "Animate" and "Ghost Rider" are considered.

Despite a handful of fans hoping for a return to the glory days of *Hemi-spheres*, Rush isn't doing badly in its modern guise and has no reason to backpedal. New records still sell by the hundreds of thousands worldwide, their back catalog still moves thousands per year, and they regularly pack arenas and enormous outdoor venues. The 2007–2008 tour for their eighteenth album, *Snakes & Arrows*, netted almost forty million dollars. And if numbers really count, try to do the math on the breadth of eighteen studio albums times the ground covered in forty years of existence times the fact that thirty-five of those years have featured the same lineup. In that equation, a band as "uncool" as Rush stands vindicated for doing the impossible. Now, as when they started, there's never been anything *less* cool than mixing rock's two perennial black-sheep genres. Prog rock and heavy metal have ever been the nerdy outcasts of the rock genre, dismissed by critics and laughed at by hipsters; there's no indication that will change anytime soon, despite the legendary numbers put up by Rush.

Robert Fripp once called King Crimson's '80s material "accessible and exces-sive," but a gnarled heaviness came back into the band's music with their revival in the mid-'90s. In 1994, mirroring Fripp's own awareness of metal music, Bill Bruford spoke of Crimson's forthcoming album boldly: "There is heavier music on *Thrak* than Pantera, Megadeth, and Metallica trebled and sliced and cut up into quarters."

The metal bands that looked to Rush and the English prog godfathers for guidance worked into a less-is-more ethic naturally, not because they were inspired by such streamlined efforts as Rush's *Power Windows* or Genesis's *Abacab*. Many bands come to the light of simplicity after a creatively radical period—which has as much to do with growing as a human being as it does with growing as a songwriter.

Fates Warning in Athens, Greece, 2005, with a returning Frank Aresti (far left)
(*LiveAlive Pictures/Kissadjekian*)

Fates Warning guitarist Jim Matheos began baring his soul in his lyrics in the late '80s, forced to take up the lyric pen after the dismissal of original vocalist John Arch. Songs about growing up, growing old, and facing the cold reality of life's stages paralleled the band's own musical maturation. During the recording of *Disconnected* in early 2000, Mathos stated, "We were thinking about calling the record *Who We Are Now*, because it *is* basically who we are now. A year from now we wouldn't write this record. A year ago we wouldn't have written this record. I don't think we would've had this kind of longevity if we just kept doing the same thing over and over again."

Though Matheos learned a lot from Rush's more-is-more period, he took his band through an ever-changing course to eventually arrive at material that empha-sized songwriting over virtuosity. Fates Warning seemed to go through two less-is-more phases—first with smart, bright-sounding albums *Parallels* and *Inside Out*, and again with the darker, minimal approach of *Disconnected* and 2004's *FWX*.

"To me it's not as drastic a change for us as it was for bands like Rush and Kansas," says Matheos. "They've gone from complex, long songs to really formulaic shorter songs. You can chart their progression—there's a fine point where they went from being really progressive to more commercial, and they stayed that way. For us it's been more of a change from record to record. You can't really split it into two things where we were really progressive and then went to this more 4/4 commercial thing and stayed there."

Released in 1997, *A Pleasant Shade of Gray* proved Fates Warning's unpredictability. The title track, the album's *only* track, was an ambitious twelve-part piece that balanced the refinement of the two previous albums against the wide-scope ambition and instrumental dexterity of their earlier, more sprawling works. As for what awaits on their long-awaited eleventh album, due in 2010, Matheos remains ambiguous. "It's hard to say we wouldn't do something like *Perfect Symmetry* again, something focused more on complexity than songwriting," he says. "I certainly wouldn't copy the *Perfect Symmetry* format, but I am feeling the itch lately to do something long and epic—but I wouldn't know until I got into it."

Disconnected and *FWX* proved Fates Warning no longer had an interest in showboating insane musical chops. As far back as *Parallels*, they discovered the beauty of simplicity—although subtle complexities always wormed their way into the margins. And for every four or five short, simple tracks, the band still offered monsters such as the highly textured, sixteen-minute "Still Remains." Considering both his twenty-two-minute "The Ivory Gate of Dreams" and four-minute "Eye to Eye," Matheos explains, "It's actually easier to write a long song with a lot of difficult parts than it is to try and be really creative in a shorter song and have a lot of different ideas within that space. I hear a lot of people doing a lot of 'progressive' songs now, but they just don't do anything. They just go all over the place and play a lot of fast notes."

One band that never put technique before songwriting is Queensrÿche. Still, 1997's *Hear in the Now Frontier* shocked many fans. The album tipped toward a much simpler approach than anything previously offered, distancing the band considerably from its prime works. Compared to grander, elaborate records of the past, the stripped-down *Hear in the Now Frontier* was a tough pill for some to swallow. The band referenced its progressive past only obliquely within the album, and even less on the curiously unadorned *Q2K* follow-up.

An observant fan review on metalarchives.com notes of 1999's *Q2K*, "Queensrÿche keep evolving, but I don't think they have any clue of what or who they wish to be anymore. *Q2K* shows a band trying to embrace progressive and pop elements and sacrificing the best of both in an attempt to please everyone and spark sales."

Vinnie Apicella of KNAC.com described their supposed return-to-form album, 2003's *Tribe*, as "nap-inducing" and "preposterous." He condemned the band's post-prog material: "Whoever woke up one morning and suggested Queensrÿche become a garage band and play like alterna-metal wankers should seek psychiatric help."

In a risky move, Queensrÿche revisited its most acclaimed era with tenth album *Operation: Mindcrime II*. The 2006 sequel was not exactly the commercial smash of the original, but the band deserved credit for not attempting to mimic the 1988 masterpiece. They pushed forward and stayed true to their modern sound. The main characters were revisited and the story line updated, but the music itself made no attempt to travel back in time.

Dismissing the flak Queensrÿche has taken from the ranks, vocalist Geoff Tate says, "I don't keep up with what other people think about my music. I just came to this conclusion years ago that people hear music differently. You can never get a consensus, because it's a personal journey. Songs move you and some songs don't. Some songs affect you at different times in your life, coinciding with your own experiences, and nobody's on the same path at the same time. It's art. It's not a sport. I follow my own heart and my own muse and what's inspiring to me. I don't recognize if our music is taken badly or good or whatever. I don't pay attention. You know, I've walked through museum after museum on my travels around the world and walked past great works of art and not been interested. There are thousands of paintings you walk by and you glance at them, and 'Ehhh, next...' and then one hits you. And you sit down on the bench and look at it and contemplate it and go 'wow.' You're moved by it. It's that way with music."

Beginning in 2000, Queensrÿche's flood of DVDs, live albums, best-ofs, and covers albums made some wonder if the band would ever record new material. But just when it seemed their creative well was running dry, they answered back with 2009's *American Soldier*. Based on interviews with U.S. troops embroiled in the Iraq and Afghanistan wars, the album is appropriately somber and subdued, still in the

Queensrÿche guitarists Michael Wilton (left) and Mike Stone
on the *Operation: Mindcrime II* tour, 2006
(*Cristel Brouwer*)

"alterna-metal" mold of other latter-day Queensrÿche albums. *American Soldier* took the same kind of beating from the same kinds of fans and reviewers who didn't like their previous several albums, while *Record Collector* magazine called it "superb" and "an essential purchase."

As Tate says, it's art, not a sport. Whether you sit on the bench and listen with appreciation to Queensrÿche's contemporary works, or dismiss them as uninteresting, the band's artistic depth and longevity is something to respect.

In the tech metal world, the longevity of King Crimson or Queensrÿche would be unthinkable. Many bands of this genre imploded prematurely (Watchtower, Spiral Architect), went on lengthy hiatuses (Cynic, Atheist, Believer), or underwent only brief periods of tech obsession (Psychotic Waltz, Pestilence, Loudblast, Oblivéon). Tech-focused bands that showed more staying power with substantial output suffered in obscurity, while only a few found great success.

Mekong Delta still sits at the cult level. As of 2010, the band has produced nine albums, a single, an EP, two compilations, a live album, and a DVD—with more likely to come. Yet despite their ballooning discography, their fan base remains small.

On the other end is Meshuggah, which finds continued success with its uncompromising brain-metal bludgeon. A band as complicated and punishing should have never elbowed its way into aboveground networks, but somehow they have. Endorsements from living legends such as Tool have boosted the Swedes' profile, but perhaps the greatest key to Meshuggah's success is how they've tinkered with their formula only slightly during the past fifteen years. They will probably never make a radical change in sound, and no doubt many of their fans want them to stay just as they are. They are perplexing and difficult enough already.

Then there's Voivod—ever the anomaly. While they haven't been at the cutting edge of tech metal for a couple decades, they do remain unpredictable—progressive in spirit, if not in practice.

Voivod's move from chaotic, technical metal to something much less convoluted evolved over a long period of time and a wide creative arc. After touring extensively for *Nothingface*, the band realized what they were doing was flying over too many heads. Says drummer Michel Langevin, "We did the tour with Soundgarden and Faith No More in 1990, and we realized the world was changing—the groove of the music was changing. Crowds weren't that interested in technical stuff anymore. We spent so much time looking at our instruments—playing our technical songs perfectly and making sure we weren't missing a note—that we didn't even look at the crowd anymore. We decided to switch things a little and write simpler songs that had a vibe. To us, *Angel Rat* seemed like a normal progression, except for some listeners it was quite a departure."

After the original lineup fractured while making 1991's *Angel Rat*, and original vocalist Denis Belanger exited in 1994, Voivod was left a duo in search of a reason to exist. Langevin and guitarist Denis D'Amour did the only thing they could do and carried on. Reshaping Voivod into a trio, they recruited bassist/vocalist Eric Forrest, who had played in little-known bands with regrettable names like Liquid Indian and Thunder Circus. The resulting *Negatron* (1995) revisited the intensity of their early years with an updated, modern production that attempted to strike with the clean, blunt force of Machine Head or Pantera. Follow-up *Phobos* was a wider, deeper, heavier excursion, a cosmic drama that churned with hypnotic, Neurosis-like repetition.

Phobos capped an era of successful reinvention for the band, despite a shrinking audience—then came an era of high hopes, hard times, and outright tragedy. In 1998, Voivod was derailed after Forrest sustained serious injuries in a van accident while touring Europe. After a year of healing, the trio resumed to play high-profile shows with Iron Maiden, Therion, and Neurosis. Shortly afterward, Voivod went on hiatus and eventually the lights went out altogether.

In 2002, original vocalist Belanger came out of hiding and reenergized Langevin and D'Amour. Searching for a new bassist, they joined forces with Jason Newsted, fresh from fifteen loyal years in Metallica, and he infused the band with a ton of fame and money. Newsted had been a fan of Voivod since the '80s, and had befriended them and

Art of simplicity:
Voivod's self-titled 2003 return

even written some music with the members in the '90s. Upon entering the Voivod universe officially in 2002, he said, "I get to live two dreams in one lifetime, and very few people get even a chance for one."

Newsted's presence brought the band much-needed attention, yet the resulting 2003 album, *Voivod*, fell short of high expectations. The thirteen-song album was strong—drummer Langevin claimed it had usurped 1987's *Killing Technology* as his own favorite Voivod album. But the material didn't return to the days of complicated sci-fi metal. And it was too spacey to appeal to Metallica's mainstream contingent. Instead, Voivod simply picked up the thread of *The Outer Limits*, moved into simpler groove-focused territory, and cut guitar soloing to a minimum. Even with songs as different from one another as opening anthem "Gasmask Revival," the churning "Reactor," and psychedelic "Divine Sun," *Voivod* was a rock-obsessed beast that, for better or worse, never looked back to the band's paradigm-shifting glory days.

The following album, *Katorz*, promised to be more expansive, but nobody expected guitarist Denis D'Amour would pass away before its completion. He had battled cancer successfully in 1988. Fifteen years later it crept up on him again. Just before his death, D'Amour—Voivod's songwriting catalyst—had demoed a generous clutch of songs intended for the next album. Knowing his passing was imminent, he told his bandmates where the tracks were located, and asked them to build the songs into an album. Bringing in *Nothingface* producer Glen Robinson, Langevin, Belanger, and Newsted doubled the request—2006 album *Katorz* was the first part of this realization, while 2009's *Infini* closed the book on Voivod's long run with D'Amour's innovative guitar work at the center.

For every stripped-down era visited by a band once so very cutting-edge, in steps a group of young kids eager to explore the furthest reaches; for every *Infini* there comes a band like Between the Buried and Me; for every *American Soldier*, there is an eclectic alternative like Loch Vostok. But the move toward stripped-down material isn't necessarily the death knell for a progressive band. Rush's *Signals*, Fates Warning's *Parallels*, and Voivod's *Angel Rat* are strong albums and favorites of many fans. *Signals* and *Parallels* are, in fact, among those bands' best-selling albums. For Celtic Frost leader Tom Fischer, however, the abrupt turn away from their experimental period was a complete failure—but a necessary step nonetheless.

Celtic Frost's *Cold Lake* debacle of 1988 wasn't so much an artistic less-is-more move as it was a way for Fischer to remain sane. The material allowed the Frost leader to drop all pomposity and pretense and have a little fun. Ironically, and despite the embarrassment it caused, Fischer had to put the band's legacy on the line in order to move forward. "After *Into the Pandemonium* and a year of the worst business difficulties," remembered Fischer in 1995, "we just wanted to go out and party on the next album. Maybe it shouldn't have been released as Celtic Frost, but that was impossible for contractual reasons. As an artist, I hate it, even though at the time it was very liberating to do an album like that."

Hindsight pulls *Cold Lake* into perspective. The tensions created by the band's experimental phase caused an equal but opposite reaction—Isaac Newton's third law of motion.

Celtic Frost's fifth album—1990's *Vanity/Nemesis* on major label RCA Records—made small steps toward regaining the true Frost ethic. But soon the band dissolved, only to reunite twelve years later through a long and arduous rebuilding process. The resulting *Monotheist* was different than any other Frost album before; monolithic and epic, but entirely modern in recording technique and writing approach, with no attempts to look back. *Monotheist* didn't sound much like the old Celtic Frost, though it was still clearly something that could only come from the Frost camp. Well before the band officially reunited, Fischer was adamant about staying current should the beast arise again. "We are looking forward," he said. "If we do new Celtic Frost material and feel that it's not modern, then we'll leave it be. I hate this nostalgia-reunion stuff. I cannot stand that. I cannot do that."

Monotheist was praised by fans and critics, but, crushed under the weight of business demands, fan expectations, and his erratic creative impulse, Fischer exited Celtic Frost in 2008, leaving cofounder Martin Ain to pick up the pieces. Ain quickly decided the band wasn't worth pursuing without Fischer, and Celtic Frost retreated to the shadows once more. When Fischer next surfaced in 2010 with his new band Triptykon, he furthered the modernization of the Celtic Frost ethos. Triptykon's debut, *Eparistera Daimones*, basically carries on where *Monotheist* left off.

In the no-surprises world of the Big Three–influenced Progressive metal scene, deviation from the norm can unsettle listeners used to a steadier musical evolution. One example is Pain of Salvation's controversial *Scarsick,* derided in reviews as "simplistic" and "unsophisticated." Evergrey's *Monday Morning Apocalypse* (2006) was greeted with similar derision, as the band's audience didn't appreciate the album's more direct, carefree, and plain old rocking vibe. Reviewer Murat Batmaz warned on popular prog music site seaoftranquility.org that *Monday Morning Apocalypse* would "alienate some of the band's older fans with its deliberately commercial production, shorter and simpler song structures, and noticeably missing synth work."

The days of expecting progressive bands to excite and surprise with each new step appear to be over for the modern Progressive metal audience. Jim Matheos of Fates Warning finds the stuffiness of some Prog metal fans curious and ironic. "It's like, if the songs aren't all eight minutes long, they aren't good enough," he says. "It's not what you would expect from people who are supposed to be 'progressive.'"

ProgPower festival organizer Glenn Harveston admits that the "traditional" Progressive metal sound is indeed that—a sound that sticks closely to what has come before. "It all goes back to the Big Three," he says, summoning the progressive metal trinity of Queensrÿche, Fates Warning, and Dream Theater. "These newer bands are

Progressive Metal kings Dream Theater in 2009.
No let-up or compromise in sight
(*courtesy of Roadrunner Records*)

basically combining the styles of what we grew up loving in the '80s and '90s. They are simply taking a familiar sound to the next generation of fans."

The kings of the Prog metal heap, Dream Theater, won't be entering a stripped-down less-is-more phase any time soon. They will, by all indications, consistently deliver the kind of sprawling, complex journeys their fans want. Perhaps that's the key to the band's success—they've never made a *Cold Lake* or a *Hear in the Now Frontier*. Dream Theater tinkers only subtly with their formula every album, throwing just enough curveballs that fans stay engaged. Their 2009 album, *Black Clouds & Silver Linings*, is six songs and seventy-five minutes—another epic maze of drama and difficulty, with no outside writers or potential radio hits. Yet it works—massively. *Black Clouds* debuted at number six on the *Billboard* chart in its first week of sales, the highest-ever first-week performance of a Dream Theater album.

The significance was not lost on drummer Mike Portnoy. "To enter the *Billboard* charts in the Top 10 with an album filled with twelve-minute songs, sitting side by side with the Jonas Brothers and Hannah Montana—that was quite a statement," he says. "It was like one small step for Dream Theater and one giant leap for progressive music. And it says a lot for our amazing fan base."

Dream Theater seem conscious always to measure their slick, accessible side against their wilder shred-obsessed personality. "It's a balance," says Portnoy. "Rush, Yes, and Genesis, all those progressive bands through the years, got a little more poppy. We still have that balance. Even for some songs, if the arrangements are a bit more simple, if they sound a little more radio-friendly, we'll balance it with longer instrumentally based songs. We never want to lose that balance. We're not afraid to write short songs. We'll always have a couple songs that are a little more accessible. We're not afraid to admit that we enjoy bands like U2 and Coldplay just as much as Yes and Rush. We're not afraid to do that as long as it's on our own terms—and when it's called for."

Asked if the band would ever simplify in the manner of Rush or Metallica, Dream Theater bassist John Myung states with total confidence, "It would never happen. I couldn't see us having a one-dimensional record. The different areas we might go in that diversify a record will change, but when you do one type of thing, you want to write something different the next time."

Even through his various solo outings, vocalist James LaBrie, arguably the most accessible element of Dream Theater's sound, has never made the stripped-down departure record other prog metal vocalists have. His Mullmuzzler project and the *Elements of Persuasion* album, released under his own name, may not exhibit all-out instrumental insanity, but they remain close neighbors in the Dream Theater kingdom. Many of his vocal peers, however, have gone into drastically different areas. Queensrÿche's Geoff Tate went soft-rock on his 2002 solo outing, which was more like Michael Bolton than most Queensrÿche fans bargained for. Ray Alder's Engine found the Fates Warning vocalist in a modern groove metal mold over two albums between 1999 and 2002. Reception to both the self-titled and *Superholic* albums was lukewarm, but not even close to the cold shoulder given Russell Allen's *Atomic Soul*, an album of hard rock inspired by Bad Company and AC/DC. Some Symphony X fans had trouble accepting that vocalist Allen took a step away from the virtuosity of his main band and did something...different. Go figure.

Even the mighty Dream Theater felt the sting, after all. After Dream Theater made what was, for them, a controversial directional shift with 1997's *Falling into Infinity*, they responded with the conceptually complex *Metropolis Pt. 2: Scenes from a Memory*. Fans responded positively, and Dream Theater were back on course doing what they do best. But as fan-friendly as Dream Theater are, they're careful to keep their creative impulse pure. Mike Portnoy states, "I never want the fans to feel like they're dictating or have control over what the band does."

Portnoy notes that a track from *Octavarium*, "Never Enough," was written in response to the sometimes lacerating opinions of the band's die-hard fan base: "I pay an incredible amount of attention to what the fans say, for better or worse. But 'Never Enough' was kind of a backlash against that, because as much as I love our fans and how dedicated they are, when they can be as critical as they sometimes can be, it really hurts."

Progressive metal needs troublemakers and visionaries; people as ambitious as Daniel Gildenlöw or Toby Driver; as willing to confound as Kristoffer Rygg or Ron Jarzombek. But they and anyone else who bend the very borders of metal walk a precarious path—record one album that the prog audience embraces and you will always be expected to live up to it. Many fans hope for the same kind of album next time—no changes. But if true artists always change, what are these artists to do? As the artist changes as a person, so does the art itself. Should the demands on *progressive* bands by their audience be conditional?

In 2010, Portnoy, Dream Theater, and the progressive music world as a whole are in a comfortable position. Music that provides challenge and demands a long attention span is finding a whole new audience, and a large one at that, if the success of Dream Theater, Opeth, Meshuggah, Mastodon, and Porcupine Tree is anything to go by. Maybe the world at large is finally up for the challenge. Mike Portnoy thinks so. "This is probably as much of a golden age of prog as we've had since the '70s," he says. "I think the term 'progressive' is as big as it's ever been, and probably as accepted or embraced. It's not even necessarily a musical genre, per se; it's more a state of mind—a willingness to be daring. Fifteen years ago, the critics would insult a band like Dream Theater for having long songs, and now the critics are applauding bands for being daring and having long songs. The tide has definitely turned."

Even if the tide has turned and Watchtower returns with its first album in over two decades, will it, the quintessential "cult" band, be as warmly received as Dream Theater, Opeth, or even Cynic? Maybe the better question is—should they even bother rolling with the current tides? Watchtower's members are clearly not in the same life stages as they were in 1989, when their second and still last album was released. Guitarist Ron Jarzombek has continued to play metal in other projects, but Doug Keyser and Rick Colaluca, not exactly typical metalheads even in the band's heyday, are surely even further distanced from the metal headspace than they ever were. Yet, despite many false starts, this is the Watchtower lineup that restarted work on *Mathemat-*

ics yet again in 2009, nearly twenty years after they first started piecing the album together. Of those who care dearly for Watchtower, some hope it will sound exactly like the younger, crazier Watchtower of the '80s; others expect a wiser, more mature band, something different and interesting—another wicked Watchtower curveball.

If *Mathematics* comes out sounding exactly like the Watchtower of twenty years ago, there is some measure of success there. The mere fact of its existence, after years of mythic status, is almost success enough. Should it emerge as a completely new take on the beaten and battered forty-year-old metal frame, something utterly alien to the Watchtower that came before it, incomprehensibly innovative and ahead of its time, it will likely be a big commercial failure. And because no truly *progressive* band does anything by half-measures, then let it be an unforgettable, glorious failure. Let it be, as so many other progressive metal ventures have been, an extraordinary work, even in this extraordinary place.

EPILOGUE:
...AND THE GEEKS SHALL INHERIT THE EARTH

EACH YEAR IN ATLANTA, TWELVE HUNDRED FANS GATHER to worship at the altar of the progressive and power metal elite. The acoustically excellent, tiered theater–style Center Stage venue is an appropriately classy place to host the ProgPower USA festival. Organized by Glenn Harveston, the multiday event consistently sells every one of its limited tickets months in advance—at 120 bucks a pop, that's no mean feat. The entry price is a pretty sweet deal considering headliners such as Fates Warning, Amorphis, Symphony X, Pain of Salvation, Evergrey, and Angra; up-and-coming bands Spheric Universe Experience and Circus Maximus; "oddballs" such as Diablo Swing Orchestra, Therion, and Devin Townsend; a plethora of vendors selling their proggy wares; an incredible networking opportunity with like-minded fans; and a schedule that values quality over quantity.

As Harveston says, "If you want the best, you have to pay for the best."

Glenn Harveston came to progressive metal the way so many others have—dabbling in bits of everything until Dream Theater hit. "I was a child of '80s metal," he remembers. "I was totally into Iron Maiden, Judas Priest, Dio, and early thrash. And I enjoyed all sorts of hard rock and early metal as well. It was during this time that I found Rush and started moving toward music with a bit of complexity. Queensrÿche's *Rage for Order* was the next step in my evolution."

The first ProgPower festival was organized by Rene Janssen, Martijn Balsters, and Annemiek van Dijk and held in the Netherlands in 1999. Through the years it has hosted such names as Cynic, Opeth, Devin Townsend, Vanden Plas, Threshold, and Alchemist, among an enormous number of others. The festival franchise has more recently set up in the U.K. and Denmark, while Harveston has been organizing the American branch since 2001.

He could certainly develop something even bigger out of ProgPower USA. Investors have urged him to take his show on the road—à la Dream Theater's annual Progressive Nation package tour—but Harveston prefers to keep things intimate. ProgPower USA truly has a life of its own.

The success of the festival is testament to the global popularity of both "traditional" Progressive metal—the strain influenced by the Big Three—and of the European power metal sound. Harveston clarifies that "ProgPower" does not mean "the power of progressive music. The name is a combination of two separate genres," he explains. "Progressive metal and power metal. When 2002 became the high point of the festival's history to that point, it was not the progressive metal bands that took me to the next level. It was the power metal bands, as I hosted the U.S. debut for bands such as Blind Guardian, Gamma Ray, and Edguy that year."

While offering a welcome array of big names in modern power and Progressive metal, Harveston strives to feature an "odd band out" each year. "It sounds like an oxymoron," he says, "but I do book an 'oddball' every year at a show with progressive music. Devin Townsend started the tradition. That lead to Mercenary the next year— they were the first band I had with harsh vocals. From there I've gone with hard rock like Pink Cream 69, then we had Orphaned Land and Therion, and we have branched out into a bit of everything since then, with the likes of Freak Kitchen and most recently Diablo Swing Orchestra."

Like 2002's festival, the 2010 installment of ProgPower USA was weighted in favor of power metal bands. Hammerfall, Kamelot, and Nocturnal Rites appeared, while the "oddball" inclusion was Italian hybridists Oceans of Sadness. Even the Norwegian avant-garde sent a 2010 ambassador in Leprous—although only for a pre-show warm-up gig. One hopes the festival will continue to broaden its scope, as its Dutch counterpart has done, perhaps managing a coup like pulling Arcturus out of retirement.

The same year ProgPower launched in the Netherlands, diehard prog rock devotees began flocking to NEARfest—the North East Art Rock festival. Beginning in 1999 in Bethlehem, Pennsylvania, NEARfest has hosted some of the most legendary names in progressive rock history: Van der Graaf Generator, Camel, Porcupine Tree, Keith Emerson, Steve Hackett, Nektar, and Magma, among so many others. The uneasy sounds of old masters Univers Zero cleared much of the auditorium as their set plowed on in 2004, while the remaining devotees sat shocked in a kind of catatonic glee. Newer bands are also welcome: Sleepytime Gorilla Museum and Guapo brought weirdness to the 11 A.M. Sunday slot in 2003 and 2006, respectively, and Wobbler and Beardfish have played their young hearts out too, offering energy and innovation within old-school prog sight lines.

NEARFest's current home, the Zoellner Arts Center, houses the 1,002-seat Baker Hall, a gorgeous theater where the sound is top-notch and every seat is a great one. The audience is reverential, polite and attentive. Vendor rooms offer thousands of CDs by bands new and old, current titles and loads of reissues. Money changes hands throughout the day, to the satisfaction of both vendor and customer. In 2009, there seemed to be no sign that the U.S. economy was in the dumper; one major NEARfest vendor reported record sales. Even in hard times, people need their remastered Matching Mole and Marsupilami CDs.

The NEARfest crowd is largely older, with a median age of around fifty—lots of bald spots and Gentle Giant T-shirts tightly stretched over middle-aged guts. Not all of them love the occasional disturbing performance, like those given by Univers Zero or Present, but no matter. Most of them are open to new things—if they weren't, they wouldn't have gotten into this music in the first place.

If there's another rock outgrowth besides prog well represented by the T-shirt-adorned crowd, it's metal—and not only Dream Theater metal. NEARfest revelers have been sighted wearing the logos of Sigh, Deathspell Omega, Voivod, Cephalic Carnage, Opeth, Master's Hammer, Decapitated, Bathory, even ultra-cult Swedish death metal band Excruciate. Some of the metal-savvy attendees are young, and others were around before Mikael Åkerfeldt even knew what a Camel was.

Each year, Ken Golden of The Laser's Edge lords over the biggest vendor display at the festival. His wares cover five eight-foot tables (forty feet of table space), and he brings enough metal to satisfy those with heavier tastes. CDs by Megadeth, Believer, and Therion have sold to fifty-somethings also purchasing Goblin and Amon Düül II reissues. Clearly some older prog fans have picked up on metal, and surely a band like Opeth is largely responsible for providing that gateway, the same way King Crimson paved the prog path for so many metal fans.

The question is whether metal bands are exerting an influence on progressive rock. There is proof right on the surface that this is happening, depending on which musician you're talking about. Steven Wilson has admitted that, as a listener, writer, and performer, bands like Opeth, Meshuggah, and drone lords Sunn o))) have proven a significant inspiration. Sweden's Beardfish, while certainly in the '70s prog tradition, have evinced a liking for metal on their last several albums, particularly on 2009's *Destined Solitaire*.

Surely the line-blurring and inspired musical richness that has happened in metal, partly thanks to progressive rock's influence, is occurring in reverse with prog rock. The two black-sheep genres have shared commonalities for a long time—it's only natural that they should be strange and very compatible bedfellows at this stage.

Dream Theater's Mike Portnoy is a NEARfest alumnus, having played the festival with Transatlantic in 2000 and Liquid Tension Experiment in 2008. The self-appointed "goodwill ambassador of progressive music," Portnoy offers a view into the tremendous growth of all things prog: "It's interesting how progressive music has branched out. You can hear so many different influences in different bands. How a band like King Crimson would somehow spawn Anekdoten, or a band like Yes or Gentle Giant would spawn Beardfish. And in both of those cases, they would have inspired somebody like Mars Volta or Mastodon. I find it interesting seeing where modern progressive bands' roots come from, and I think maybe there are a lot of younger fans that don't know that history. If you're talking about progressive *metal*, you can't talk about Dream Theater or Queensrÿche or Rush or Fates Warning without knowing what helped form their influences. It's two worlds—progressive, like Yes, Rush, King Crimson, Pink Floyd—and metal, like Judas Priest, Iron Maiden, Metallica, and Black Sabbath. Somewhere in the middle it got thrown into a giant melting pot and that's how progressive metal was born."

As of 2010, I've been to NEARfest six times, and always had a blast. Although the links between progressive rock and heavy metal are clear to those of us who log countless hours in front of the stereo, seeing that intersection firsthand at NEARfest offers proof of the relationship. By now it's inextricable. And it's not just the T-shirts.

Porcupine Tree added a chunkier, riffy element to their music as early as 1996's *Signify*, as underscored by their 2001 NEARfest performance. Their volume levels actually broke a few house lights that year in a sonic experience organizer Rob LaDuca called "punishing." Sleepytime Gorilla Museum's Sunday morning appearance at NEARfest 2003 brought a clattering, banging, dissonant "good morning" to a crowd largely unaware of the band and its beautiful damage. Clad in animalistic costuming and heavy as hell the band had most of the crowd loving every minute. In 2004, Planet X blew the roof of the place with a none-too-subtle set that was equally heavy and virtuosic. Riverside brought extreme vocals and blunt metallic rhythms to more than a few unprepared ears in 2006. And Mörglbl's mixture of jazz fusion, shred, and all-out metal intensity won over hundreds of fans in the surprise breakthrough set of 2008. In metal, prog rock's spectre has never been far behind; now metal seems to be creeping up behind prog rock and scaring it into a whole new level of vitality.

I'll even choose to believe the story about Robert Fripp listening to Voivod and Meshuggah while in the studio recording King Crimson's *The Power to Believe* in 2002. That album had a more deeply embedded metallic vein running through it than anything Crimson had done since 1973's *Red*. Could these younger metal bands whose members grew up listening to King Crimson actually have influenced their heroes in turn?

Sure. Within this musical microcosm, in the relationship between these two weird cousins, much stranger things have happened...

APPENDIX A:
LEST WE FORGET

THE FOLLOWING ARE A VARIETY OF BANDS that didn't fit into the main narrative. Some, like Anathema, are equally important to the forward evolution and expansion of heavy metal as others that received greater focus in the main body of this book. Others—like 3—are barely on the fringes of metal, yet deserve mention. Some are noteworthy only as oddities from the past. Even this is not an exhaustive list.

3

Many prog-minded metal bands have evolved away from the genre (Anathema, Beyond Dawn, Queensrÿche, etc.), but Woodstock, NY's 3, or Three, have inched towards metal from afar. Their early stuff was white teen funk/soul/alt rock with jam band and '70s rock tendencies. Debut album *Paint by Number* (1998) isn't their best, although some tracks hint at greatness. By third album *Wake Pig*, they had morphed into a post-prog/alt rock/melodi-metal hybrid that drew tenuous comparisons to Tool and not-so-tenuous comparisons to Coheed and Cambria. In 2007 they released *The End Is Begun*, which exploited various metal devices on "Battle Cry" and "These Iron Bones." Listeners have picked up a great variety of references, including Dream Theater, Frank Zappa, Fleetwood Mac, Porcupine Tree, Be-Bop Deluxe, Faith No More, Def Leppard, and Spock's Beard. The middle section of the band's "All That Remains" and moments of "Automobile" even recall melodic Euro-metal in the style of Helloween. Basically, 3 sound twenty different ways to twenty different people. The vocals of Joey Eppard run in a similar range to Coheed and Cambria's Claudio Sanchez, and there are familial ties between the two bands. Onetime C&C drummer Josh Eppard was also in 3 with brother Joey in its formative years, as 3 predates C&C. Joey also plays electric guitar in a pickless flamenco style, both rhythm and lead, while other guitarist Billy Riker brings metallic sturdiness to 3's sound and image with his B.C. Rich axes, evil wizard looks, and six-string shredding. The band's versatility has found them matched with headliners as disparate as Porcupine Tree, Scorpions, and Dream Theater. Three has it all: stellar songwriting, excellent live performances, originality, and diversity. Opeth's Mikael Åkerfeldt counts himself a fan: "They're amazing. More so live than on album. Joey's awesome, a great guitar player and singer. I'm definitely interested in them. Whenever they put something new out, I'll buy it." Jim Pitulski, who ran the U.S. Inside Out label office for almost ten years, refers to 3 with a simple gasp: "Oh my God!"

Akercocke

Beginning as an intense and proudly satanic black/death metal hybrid, by third album *Choronzon* (2003) Akercocke turned a sharp corner toward complexity. Fourth album *Words That Go Unspoken, Deeds That Go Undone* (2005) introduced a completely reinvented band with characteristics of '80s new wave and indie rock, vocal melodies reminiscent of bygone prog metallers Anacrusis, exotic touches that recalled Dead Can Dance, and the stated influences of Rush, Sonic Youth, and Killing Joke—all packaged tightly within absurdly brutal death metal. Akercocke appears in photo shoots and live shows dressed to the nines in suits and formal attire, debunking stereotypes about satanic bands and the musicians playing in them, and their music matches their sartorial sophistication and class.

Alchemist

Early Alchemist is truly strange. In 1993, drummer Rodney Holder named their two biggest influences as Pink Floyd and Autopsy, and rightfully the *Jar of Kingdom* debut was wildly idiosyncratic. Underneath the crush of primal death metal—muddy-as-hell guitars with unintelligible, garbled vocals—were curious guitar lines that provided a sole melodic element, ringing above the din with a loopy, silly elasticity. In their own words, the Eastern modalities and peculiar bounce fell somewhere between Richie Blackmore and surf guitarist Dick Dale. *Lunasphere* brought forth Adam Agius's screaming vocals—frightening in their piercing hysteria—and a tribal percussive element in some of the rhythms. Alchemist's cornucopia of sound is best represented on third album *Spiritech* (1997), particularly "Chinese Whispers." With a driving momentum that lurches along like a mid-paced Fear Factory and a chorus with Agius's banshee screeching, the middle section firmly nods to heroes Pink Floyd—and probably hints of Rainbow and Led Zeppelin. After *Spiritech* they released the *Eve of the War* EP, dramatically reworking the lead track from Jeff Wayne's *War of the Worlds*—a 1978 rock opera based on the H.G. Wells novel and featuring members of Moody Blues, Thin Lizzy, and Manfred Mann's Earth Band. Fourth album *Organasm* saw Alchemist integrating their eccentricities deeper into aggressive rhythms. The three-part "Evolution Trilogy" brought the melting pot of their past into tighter focus. Still spacey and hypnotic, if lacking diversity, *Austral Alien* (2003) and *Tripsis* (2007) had a monochrome industrial quality. Based in Australia, Alchemist has had problems touring the rest of the world, but no one else in the world sounds quite like them.

Anathema

Debate rages whether Anathema are truly progressive metal. Their most progressive material is nothing like metal, closer to modern rock/post-prog like Radiohead, Muse, and Porcupine Tree, with Nick Drake added for good measure. Their 1995 release, *The Silent Enigma*, saw influences from Celtic Frost's strangest period seeping in. On follow-up *Eternity*, rife with Floydian melancholy, they left behind their death/doom past entirely. The 1999 album *Judgement* places them in the arena of masterful progressive metal. No matter what they're called or wherever people want to place them, they are probably one of the most undervalued bands on the planet. The year 2010 brought a follow-up to 2003's *A Natural Disaster*, entitled *We're Here Because We're Here*. Signed to Kscope, also home to "post-prog" acts No-Man and the Pineapple Thief, Anathema may have found its perfect partner, a company capable of steering *We're Here Because We're Here* to the audience that will appreciate it most.

Between the Buried and Me

Between the Buried and Me (B.T.B.A.M) rose from the ashes of metalcore band Prayer for Cleansing. Their third album, *Alaska* (the band comes from North Carolina, by the way), was compared to Tool and the Mars Volta by their label, Victory Records. While the hype genuinely reflected their growth into the outer reaches of modern music, the comparisons might have been wishful thinking. Follow-up *Colors* (2007), how-ever, found the band worthy of such respected company. Think Dillinger Escape Plan meets Cave In meets Gorguts meets Mr. Bungle meets Opeth. With lengthy songs, an insanely wide array of sounds and influences, emotive guitar leads, and complete un-predictability, *Colors* doubled the band's following—lots of adventurous metal listen-ers came on board. Being part of Dream Theater's inaugural Progressive Nation 2008 tour (alongside Opeth and 3) didn't hurt. A headlining 2010 tour with Cynic, Devin Townsend, and Scale the Summit cemented a place atop the modern prog metal heap. It's worth mentioning that Canadian progressive metalcore band Protest the Hero gives B.T.B.A.M. a run for the money, equaling the Americans in terms of talent, vi-sion, and ambition—and besting them in the vocal department.

Blue Coconut

Mentioned briefly in chapter 14, these oddly monikered Spaniards sound like some-thing between the most exotic Pain of Salvation music, the Beard bands (Beardfish, Spock's Beard), and the hidden corners of Dream Theater that haven't yet been copied by others. Their eclectic 2008 demo, *End at 953*, is scattered, with rough vocals that border on crappy, but they could very well grow into a seriously good band.

Calhoun Conquer

This Swiss band shared similarities to Sweden's Midas Touch. While not a band any-one could truly love, fans of Voivod, Disharmonic Orchestra, and Mekong Delta can at least appreciate them. Calhoun Conquer were just lackluster. While attempting strange and technical thrash, poor vocals and a garagey feel let their material down. The 1987 *And Now You're Gone* EP and the 1989 *Lost in Oneself* LP/CD are all they left behind. Drummer Peter Haas was a member of Mekong Delta on *Kaleidoscope*, *Visions Fugitives*, and *Pictures at an Exhibition* albums. He also landed in Krokus for a while.

Carnival in Coal

This French duo came to notoriety via their second album, 1999's *French Cancan*, which contained confounding covers of songs by Pantera, Genesis, Gerry Rafferty, Morbid Angel, Michael Sembello, and Ozzy Osbourne, which completely overshadowed the two original tracks. C.I.C. is perhaps the only band to ever cover a Supuration song ("1308.JP.08"), on 2001's *Fear Not* album. Caribbean music, goregrind, disco, and good old heavy metal—they were bound to fail. Carnival in Coal dissolved in 2007 after four admirably absurd albums.

Paul Chain

Italian guitarist Paul Chain found cult adoration via Death SS, whose horror metal dates back to the late '70s. He fled to embark on an ambitious solo career lasting from 1984 to 2003—then officially changed his identity to Paul Cat and burrowed to deep underground obscurity. Intriguing and reclusive, Chain has not seen the vast majority of his many albums released outside Italy. He has almost nothing in common with his country's prolific '70s prog rock wave or the prog metal output of later decades. He never really wrote lyrics; many of his releases state that "the language used by Paul Chain does not exist. It's purely phonetic." Chain's albums were wildly diverse, from old-school doom metal (*In the Darkness*) and free-form experimentation (*Whited Sepulchres*) to spacey jams like the Hawkwind-ish *Sign from Space* and *Cosmic Wind*. Sometimes he was maddeningly dull—for example, 1990's double-length *Opera Decima* and 1993's useless *In Concert*—yet just as often Chain offered majestic, convincing left-field experimental doom as on *Alkahest* (1995) and *Park of Reason* (2002).

Dark Quarterer

These unprolific Italians managed only five obscure albums since 1987, playing epic progressive heavy metal as favored by U.S. bands Manilla Road and Cirith Ungol. After a series of albums with a '70s hard rock/prog aesthetic, they finally flourished with full-on prog metal—emphasis on the "prog"—during 2008's *Symbols*. Only the overbearing accent of vocalist Gianni Nepi keeps them from reaching a wider audience.

Deathspell Omega

The members of this French band never reveal themselves in pictures, nor do they list performance credits. Mysterious from the beginning, they started with an orthodox black metal sound derived from early-'90s Norway. When they released *Si Monumentum Circumspice, Requires* in 2004, anyone already familiar with D.O. was surprised.

Their sound had turned impossibly thick, with great dissonance and more complex, unusual structures. Next came *Kénôse*, a three-song cluster of carefully orchestrated, intellectual black metal with a torrential undertow aligned with total death. With F*as – Ite, Maledicti, in Ignem Aeternum* in 2007, Deathspell Omega ceased making music to be enjoyed. It must be endured—suffered through. Riffs—incredibly dense, protracted phrases—hardly ever repeat. The music is hallucinatory, otherworldly, and unpretentiously highbrow. Each release pushes several kilometers further than the previous benchmark. Although a line runs back to their avant-metal forebears in Norway, Deathspell Omega is something else entirely, and truly progressive.

Egoist

Anyone who listened to Meshuggah in the mid-'90s and imagined how radically the band might evolve over the years is probably disappointed by now. That's where Polish one-man-band Egoist comes in. With ultra-thick guitar tones and odd machinelike rhythmic churning, Egoist builds the Meshuggah foundation into one of the strangest structures ever. The quirky lyrics/vocals of Talking Heads, post-modernism of Ulver, and bleep-bloop messes of *Kid A*–era Radiohead run around the eight confounding tracks of *Ultra-Selfish Revolution* (2009), the second (but first official) Egoist album. Everything is played by Stanisław Wołonciej, except two guitar solos by Pestilence's Patrick Mameli. Wołonciej is also in progressive acts Newbreed and Dream System.

Forgotten Silence

Obtuse. Angular. Abstract. Whether they're enjoyable or not is another story. The Czech Republic's Forgotten Silence began with strange death metal and expanded to other stranger areas. Since their 1994 debut, they have progressed wildly over five full-length albums, each as obscure and difficult to obtain as the next. In 2006 they turned a sharp corner with *Kro Ni Ka*, fully embracing the attitude and aesthetics of '70s prog/jazz rock, wrapped in a modern Porcupine Tree–esque CD package (shortest song: "Mezzocaine," at 17:57). Forgotten Silence's genre has been called "experimental progressive death metal/folk/jazz," but trying to pin them down with absurd genre hybrids is useless. The recent track "Tumulus" suggests a return to heavier, more forbidding areas.

Hammers of Misfortune

A bright hope for truly progressive metal in the 2010s—even if the sea change of 2008's *Fields/Church of Broken Glass* lost the band more fans than it gained. This band relentlessly pushes forward, with a singular vision and a perennially unhip aesthetic. Hammers of Misfortune are pastoral compared to the more cosmic, futuristic vibe of so many other modern prog metal bands. They look back to heroes such as Thin Lizzy and Pink Floyd—plus apparently Kansas, judging by new material—adding traditional metal shapes, organic recording methods, a variety of vocal approaches, and unusual topics. The result is a special and rare breed of modern metal band. Led by guitarist John Cobbett, Hammers of Misfortune began with a harsher sound on 2001 debut *The Bastard*, a three-act, fourteen-song conceptual piece. Next was *The August Engine* (2003), which left extreme vocals behind and showed defiantly progressive epic metal with great songwriting chops. *The Locust Years* (2006) got even more adventurous, and after that a major lineup alteration found the band reinventing again. Double-album release *Fields/Church of Broken Glass* (2008) might stand as Hammers' "transitional" album. Cobbett has a unique creative mind. As he told *Pitchfork*: "'Always Looking Down' has a lot to do with poverty, homelessness, drugs, paranoia, crime, despair, and all that stuff. I like the idea of Ayn Rand as a homeless tweaker, invoking objectivist doctrine as she's breaking into your car."

Heart of Cygnus

Rush-inspired name? Nylon-string acoustic guitars? Epic landscapes on album art? Check to all. It's hard not to like this young Los Angeles band that invokes Blue Öyster Cult, NWOBHM, Mercyful Fate, and Megadeth. They sound like companions to fellow Californians Hammers of Misfortune. Heart of Cygnus could make something uncool very fashionable, for better or worse. Other influences include Pink Floyd, Queen, Kansas, King's X, Dio, Metallica, and Queensrÿche. More power to them.

Hieronymus Bosch

The Russians, sadly defunct as of 2010, nail the 1993-era sound of Obliveon's *Nemesis* and Loudblast's *Sublime Dementia*—yet they claim to have never heard those albums. Perhaps it's a matter of shared influences, as guitarist Vladimir Leiviman holds up

Voivod, Coroner, Destruction, Mekong Delta, Death, and Pestilence as guiding lights. They are more than thrash/death—their progressive metal is thick with modern production, and inspired by Fates Warning, Sieges Even, and Rush. Incredible performances from each member and a sharp, economical songwriting approach, despite the complications of their chosen musical path, made Hieronymus Bosch a band with clear influences that still followed a distinctive path.

Into Eternity

This Canadian band began as a modern, more aggressive answer to the Big Three—or perhaps a more progressive version of the melodi-death blazed by In Flames and Dark Tranquillity. Marked by the guitar-hero leader Tim Roth and bright, infectious vocals, their first several albums carved a niche, but Into Eternity's patented sound (derived from various other subgenres) has already been co-opted by a zillion newer melodi-death bands looking to expand their range and popularity.

Juggernaut

From Texas, the state that spawned Watchtower and Ray Alder, Juggernaut released two quirky albums of semi-technical thrash in the '80s and then disappeared. The second album, *Trouble Within*, features prominent bass by main writer Scott Womack, a completely tweaked guitar tone, and love-'em-or-hate-'em vocals by the late Steve Cooper, a vet of cult Texas band S.A. Slayer. Juggernaut are probably most noteworthy for introducing metal fans to octopus-armed drum prodigy Bobby Jarzombek (brother of Spastic Ink/Blotted Science/Watchtower guitarist Ron), who went on to play with Riot, Spastic Ink, Halford, Iced Earth, Fates Warning, and others.

Kekal

Kekal couldn't be more iconoclastic. From Indonesia, the band began releasing demos in 1995 with a black metal sound but a Christian viewpoint (a subgenre dubbed "un-black" metal). By 2005's *Acidity*, they were incorporating prog rock, electronica, indie rock, psych rock, and trip-hop. They had the good taste to cover Voivod's "The Prow," and could have just as easily originated in Norway, for all their post–black metal/avant-garde aspirations. Unfortunately, they called it quits in 2009.

Orphaned Land

Initially a doom/death hybrid, Israel's Orphaned Land quickly developed an intensely melodic character with female singing, fluid leads, and exotic instrumentation. Folk and Middle Eastern influences saturated 2004's ambitious *Mabool*. Their 2009 album, *The Never Ending Way of ORwarriOR*, was the first metal album Porcupine Tree's Steven Wilson produced after completing three albums with Opeth.

OSI

OSI (or Office of Strategic Intelligence) play chilled, emotional music, spotted by a few heavier outbursts. With an understated vocal approach, simple rhythm-based ideas, samples, and stacks of keyboard/synth layers, metal is only a small part of their modus operandi. Each OSI album unfolds slowly, making for patient, introspective listening. The founders are well-respected: Jim Matheos of Fates Warning, and Kevin Moore, the original Dream Theater keyboardist. Moore has done similar material with his own Chroma Key. And OSI knows how to pick supporting guest musicians. They've called on Mike Portnoy (Dream Theater), Sean Malone (Cynic, Gordian Knot), Joey Vera (Fates Warning), Steven Wilson (Porcupine Tree), Gavin Harrison (Porcupine Tree, King Crimson), Mikael Åkerfeldt (Opeth), and Tim Bowness (No-Man).

Phlebotomized

This Dutch septet was one of the first progressive/avant-garde bands to emerge from the European death metal scene. With prominent keyboard and violins, as well as constantly shifting, unpredictable dynamics and unorthodox (or perhaps inexperienced) songwriting, they stood out in the crowded '90s European underground. Unfortunately, their rickety productions never did the band justice. Second album *Skycontact* (1997) includes the song "I Lost My Cookies at the Disco," which, rather unbelievably, has nothing to do with Cookie Monster's own "Me Lost Me Cookie at the Disco."

Threshold

Early followers of the Big Three, Threshold is very melodic, featuring lots of keyboards, multifaceted arrangements, and background harmony vocals. Tracks range from long epics to short melodic rock songs. The band shares common traits with the

'80s neo-prog movement of their U.K. home, and overall they have more in common with old-school prog rock than most modern Progressive metal bands. Members have played with Arjen Luccasen's Ayreon and Rick Wakeman, among others. Their unassuming name was inspired by Moody Blues album *On the Threshold of a Dream*.

Ufych Sormeer

Appropriately, French band Ufych Sormeer are based on Holy Records, longtime supporters of some of the quirkiest and most experimental metal acts on the planet. With cartoony vocal melodies, whistling, spacey power metal riffs, lighthearted atmosphere, and a complexity that veers into cluttered chaos, they are as likable as they are baffling. Good luck if you attempt to tackle their weirdness.

Urizen

Almost no country with any kind of metal population has gone untouched by the influence of Norway's post–black metal avant-garde, and Urizen are one of America's prime examples. These Texans resemble everything from Arcturus and Solefald to the even weirder electronic-based material by Ulver and Manes. With the *Universe* EP they began incorporating Nintendo and computer-game sounds, moving their material away from Norwegian influence and into something inhabiting a Faith No More or later Thought Industry area. Or, if a more modern comparison is needed, maybe "Horse the Band but weirder" would be apt. And they have played Six Flags over Texas. Curiously—and perhaps unsurprisingly, considering what a risky investment any super-original band can be—they found themselves unsigned as of 2010.

Vanden Plas

These Germans somehow escaped a wider focus in chapter 13, but they epitomize the Big Three–derived Progressive metal sound and attitude. They first surfaced with very slick haircuts for 1986 single "Raining in my Heart," which had a pomp/AOR tone. After eight years, their first album surfaced, and *Colour Temple* presented a much broader scope than the early single. Their approach fit in nicely with the Progressive metal zeitgeist of the mid-'90s, with plenty of melody and bombast packed inside dramatic seven-minute songs. They have worked steadily to expand and improve their style, with later albums *Beyond Daylight* and *Christ o* drawing acclaim from the Progressive metal audience. Somewhere between Symphony X and Dream Theater, they were an early mover in the '90s blitz that defined the Progressive metal style. Vanden Plas ducked out of 2001's ProgPower USA festival, paranoid—as many were—about flying so shortly after the 9/11 attacks. They finally made it to U.S. shores for the 2003 installment of the festival, where they shared the stage with Nightwish, Evergrey, Symphony X, and Redemption, among others.

While Heaven Wept

Though lacking the higher profile of Opeth's Mikael Åkerfeldt, While Heaven Wept leader Tom Phillips has been just as vocal in his love for '70s-era prog rock. WHW's sound rests firmly in epic doom metal, with a decidedly progressive attitude. Heavily inspired by Candlemass, Solitude Aeturnus, and Fates Warning, Phillips also credits prog, classical, and new age bands like Rainbow, Genesis, Marillion, Grobschnitt, Novalis, Devil Doll, Bach, Beethoven, Henryk Górecki, Dead Can Dance, Vangelis, and Kitaro, to name a few. *Of Empires Forlorn* (2003) featured a reworked cover of German band Jane's "Voice in the Wind." On 2009's *Vast Oceans Lachrymose*, Phillips took care to cite an enduring influence: "Although 'To Wander the Void' is as deeply personal as all WHW compositions, it is also something of a tribute to Fates Warning—one of our earliest influences, whose rich musical legacy still continues to inspire us to this day." Despite their deep well of inspirations, While Heaven Wept produce music that is far from derivative, a must-hear for all fans of dark progressive metal.

Windham Hell

Obviously a sinister spin on popular new age record label Windham Hill, this band's moniker incorporates the surname of guitarist Leland Windham. In spirit, this band is a kind of precursor to the even more adventurous bands birthed in Washington in the '90s, such as Agalloch and Sculptured. Windham Hell released three albums of guitar-centric metal with a very heavy classical influence. Although their albums are remarkable to some degree, they are noteworthy for beating Fates Warning, Edge of Sanity, and Green Carnation to the one-song-album idea with 1988's fifty-four-minute single-song demo, *Do Not Fear for Hell Is Here*.

APPENDIX B: PRIME NUMBERS— 50 RECOMMENDED PROGRESSIVE METAL ALBUMS

Angra – *Holy Land* (1996)

Arcturus – *La Masquerade Infernale* (1997)

Atheist – *Unquestionable Presence* (1992)

Ayreon – *Into the Electric Castle* (1998)

Believer – *Dimensions* (1993)

Black Sabbath – *Sabbath Bloody Sabbath* (1973)

Celtic Frost – *Into the Pandemonium* (1987)

Coroner – *Mental Vortex* (1991)

Crimson Glory – *Transcendence* (1988)

Cynic – *Focus* (1993)

Cynic – *Traced In Air* (2008)

Death – *Human* (1991)

Devin Townsend – *Terria* (2001)

Disharmonic Orchestra – *Pleasuredome* (1993)

Dream Theater – *Images and Words* (1992)

Dream Theater – *Awake* (1994)

Dream Theater – *Octavarium* (2005)

Enslaved – *Monumension* (2001)

Evergrey – *Solitude • Dominance • Tragedy* (1999)

Fates Warning – *Awaken the Guardian* (1986)

Fates Warning – *Perfect Symmetry* (1989)

Hammers of Misfortune – *The Locust Years* (2006)

In the Woods – *Omnio* (1997)

Iron Maiden – *Seventh Son of a Seventh Son* (1988)

Maudlin of the Well – *Bath / Leaving Your Body Map* (2001)

Mayhem – *Grand Declaration of War* (2000)

Meshuggah – *Destroy Erase Improve* (1995)

Mind Over Four – *The Goddess* (1990)

Obliveon – *Nemesis* (1993)

Opeth – *Morningrise* (1996)

Opeth – *Still Life* (1999)

Pain of Salvation – *One Hour by the Concrete Lake* (1998)

Pain of Salvation – *Be* (2004)

Pan-Thy-Monium – *Khaooohs* (1993)

Psychotic Waltz – *Into the Everflow* (1993)

Queensrÿche – *Rage for Order* (1986)

Queensrÿche – *Operation: Mindcrime* (1988)

Rush – *2112* (1976)

Rush – *A Farewell to Kings* (1977)

Rush – *Moving Pictures* (1981)

Sigh – *Hail Horror Hail* (1997)

Spiral Architect – *A Sceptic's Universe* (2000)

Thought Industry – *Mods Carve the Pig: Assassins, Toads and God's Flesh* (1993)

Vauxdvihl – *To Dimension Logic* (1994)

Voivod – *Dimension Hatröss* (1988)

Voivod – *Nothingface* (1989)

Voivod – *Angel Rat* (1991)

Watchtower – *Energetic Disassembly* (1985)

Watchtower – *Control and Resistance* (1989)

Zero Hour – *The Towers of Avarice* (2001)

APPENDIX C:
CURIOUS COLLISIONS—
PROG COVERS PROG

"Shadow of Death" – Extol, 2001 (original by Believer, 1989)

"Sorrows of the Moon" – Therion, 1995 (original by Celtic Frost, 1987)

"Circle of the Tyrants" – Opeth, 1996 (original by Celtic Frost, 1986)

"Arc-Lite" – Canvas Solaris, 2007 (original by Coroner, 1988)

"Paralized, Mesmerized" – Sceptic, 2005 (original by Coroner, 1993)

"How Could I" – Aletheian, 2008 (original by Cynic, 1993)

"Soldier of Fortune" – Opeth, 2007 (original by Deep Purple, 1974)

"Prelude to Ruin" – Spiral Architect, 2000 (original by Fates Warning, 1986)

"The Knife" – Dark Empire, 2008 (original by Genesis, 1970)

"Dancing on a Volcano" – Mekong Delta, 1992 (original by Genesis, 1976)

"Mama" – Angra, 2002 (original by Genesis, 1983)

"Mama" – Carnival in Coal, 1999 (original by Genesis, 1983)

"Levitation" – Amorphis, 1996 (original by Hawkwind, 1980)

"Remember Tomorrow" – Opeth, 1998 (original by Iron Maiden, 1980)

"Cross-Eyed Mary" – Iron Maiden, 1983 (original by Jethro Tull, 1970)

"King of Twilight" – Iron Maiden, 1984 (original by Nektar, 1972)

"Epitaph" – In the Woods, 2000 (original by King Crimson, 1969)

"21st Century Schizoid Man" – Voivod, 1997 (original by King Crimson, 1969)

"Cat Food" – Damn the Machine, 1993 (original by King Crimson, 1970)

"One More Red Nightmare" – Realm, 1992 (original by King Crimson, 1972)

"Arctic Crypt" – Sceptic, 2001 (original by Nocturnus, 1992)

"Multiple Beings" – Egoist, 2007 (original by Pestilence, 1993)

"See Emily Play" – 3, 2008 (original by Pink Floyd, 1966)

"Astronomy Domine" – Voivod, 1989 (original by Pink Floyd, 1967)

"Let There Be More Light" – In the Woods, 1998 (original by Pink Floyd, 1968)

"Set the Controls for the Heart of the Sun" – OSI, 2003 (original by Pink Floyd, 1968)

"The Nile Song" – Voivod, 1993 (original by Pink Floyd, 1969)

"When You're In" – Tiamat, 1994 (original by Pink Floyd, 1972)

"Comfortably Numb" – Queensrÿche, 2004 (original by Pink Floyd, 1978)

"Closer to the Heart" – Fates Warning, 1996 (original by Rush, 1977)

"Natural Science" – Devin Townsend, 1996 (original by Rush, 1980)

"YYZ" – Atheist, 2010 (original by Rush, 1981)

"Red Barchetta" – Thought Industry (original by Rush, 1981)

"Fly to the Rainbow" – Therion, 1997 (original by Scorpions, 1974)

"Yellow Raven" – Pain of Salvation, 2009 (original by Scorpions, 1976)

"1308.JP.08" – Carnival in Coal, 2001 (original by Supuration, 1993)

"Rainbow Demon" – Vintersorg, 2000 (original by Uriah Heep, 1972)

"Brain Scan" – Martyr, 2006 (original by Voivod, 1988)

"The Prow" – Kekal, 2005 (original by Voivod, 1991)

(Note: Dream Theater have covered so many other prog bands' songs—even entire albums—their covers are excluded from this list due to space limitations.)

THANKS

SUPER-MASSIVE GRATITUDE AND RESPECT to my cigar-chomping editor in the big city, Ian Christe, who for years encouraged me to write what eventually became this book—thanks for the opportunity, your tolerance of my mini-panics, and your sage advice throughout. Maybe it's a cliché, but "I couldn't have done this without you" is more than appropriate here. I also extend polyrhythmic hails in 13/8 to Hunter Ginn, for his enthusiasm, criticism, suggestions, insight, and, above all, friendship. Equal helpings of gratitude go to Michel Langevin, Steven Wilson, and Polly Watson for providing depth, detail, talent, and that most valuable of currencies, time.

EACH OF THE FOLLOWING PEOPLE OR ENTITIES also played a crucial part in the construction of this book, in some way, shape or form. I'm totally grateful to: Mom, aka Barbara Banyai (for so much); Dirk, Lerxt, and Pratt; Away, Piggy, Blacky, and Snake; Fates Warning (especially *Awaken the Guardian*); Matt Johnsen; Ron Jarzombek (a case of Cheeseburger Helper comin' your way); Paul Masvidal; Jim Matheos; Mikael Åkerfeldt; Mike Portnoy; Jason McMaster; Daniel Gildenlöw; Kurt Bachman; Christofer Johnsson; Dan Swanö; Kristoffer Rygg; Marc Wagner (aka Dad); John Wagner and Nnnnick Wagner for brotherness; Marie Wagner for calling Kiss "cute" and feeding the Kiss addiction when the allowance money ran out; Travis Smith; S. Craig Zahler; Pellet; Heath Hanlin; Jim Pitulski; Ken Golden and Jim Williamson (the Beagle Creek Prog Posse – eat more veggies!); Glenn Harveston; Andreas Katsambas; Monte Conner; Tom Hailey; Tim Hammond (the original "killed by tech"); Garry and Eydie Clifton; Steve Huff; Josh Greer; Derek Sheplawy; Chris Roy; Jasun Tipton; Marianne Moorehead for listening beyond the bluster; Nancy Carlson; Loana dP Valencia; Ula Gehret; Chris Maycock; S. Brook Reed; Tammy Crutchfield; Mike Hope (for a lot, but especially for parking the Nocturnus *Thresholds* CD in the freezer); Nick Terry; Paul Stenning; the Honduras Coffee Company of Stuart, Virginia, for the juice; all the generous photographers who contributed their talents; all who came out of the woodwork when this book was announced and offered their support and help; anyone I overlooked who feels they should have been here; you, for having read this far.

LASTLY AND MOSTLY: Tanja Schoor, for patience, support, love, and natural beauty—I still have much to learn from you; and the amazing Kitty Force: sweetness, adorableness and hilarity incarnate.

ENDNOTES

All quotes in this book are taken from interviews conducted by the author, except for where mentioned within the main text and also the following:

Chapter 1
"King Crimson's first U.S. gig..." King Crimson, *Frame by Frame* box set, 1991
"The fundamental aim..." Ibid.
"'21st Century Schizoid Man'..." *Reflex*, 1991
"We started in 1970..." http://www.blazemonger.com/GG/interviews/derek-rubin.html
"The violin is not..." King Crimson, *The Great Deceiver* box set, 1992
"I think 'Red'..." *Reflex*, 1991

Chapter 2
"Black Sabbath was extraordinary..." *For the Record: Black Sabbath—An Oral History*, Mike Stark, 1998
"'Cities on Flame with Rock and Roll'..." *Blue Öyster Cult: Secrets Revealed!*, Martin Popoff, 2004

Chapter 3
"The question that we tend to ask..." *Exit...Stage Left* concert video, 1981
"They were progressive..." *Contents Under Pressure: 30 Years of Rush at Home & Away*, Martin Popoff, 2004
"There was a lot of pressure..." Ibid.
"The first real blend..." *Rush—Visions: The Official Biography*, Bill Banasiewicz, 1988
"It was uncertain..." Ibid.
"What I did with that..." *Creem Close-Up: Metal Music*, spring 1983
"We wanted to put together..." *Rush—Visions: The Official Biography*, Bill Banasiewicz, 1988
"Certainly the music was over-decorated..." Gehret, *The Aquarian Weekly*, March 9, 1994
"Although we have always..." *Rush—Visions: The Official Biography*, 1988
"Going after fresh rhythmic approaches..." Ibid.
"'Animate' is just as hard to play..." *The Aquarian Weekly*, March 9, 1994

Chapter 4
"I listen to what's out there..." *Power Metal*, April 1990
"Stuff like 'The Musical Box'..." *Run to the Hills: The Official Biography of Iron Maiden*, Mick Wall, 1998
"If I had my way..." Ibid.
"He came in with..." Ibid.
"We just made another..." Ibid.
"Cliff was responsible..." *Justice for All: The Truth About Metallica*, 2004, Joel McIver

Chapter 5
"We're always trying to experiment..." *Metal Forces* #29, July 1988
"We're much more mature..." unratedmagazine.com

"For some bands..." Savatage, *Gutter Ballet* CD reissue liner notes, 2002

Chapter 6
"*Think This* is..." *Metal Forces* #44, November 1989

Chapter 7
"We loved progressive, complex music..." Dream Theater, *The Majesty Demos* CD liner notes, 2003

Chapter 8
"Piggy was the main writer..." *Worlds Away: Voivod and the Art of Michel Langevin*, Martin Popoff, 2009
"We listened to, loved and studied..." Thought Industry MySpace page
"The record company people..." *Voices from the Darkside* #6, 1995
"This band will always take risks..." *Mega Metal Kerrang!* #8, 1987
"straight ahead..." Ibid.
"We approach this album..." *Voices from the Darkside* #6, 1995
"Record companies just aren't risk-oriented..." Ibid.

Chapter 9
"Our music was never..." http://www.designvortex.com/coroner/interviews/exclusiv.htm
"thought it wouldn't sell..." *Metal Forces* #34, December 1988

Chapter 10
"Science and music..." http://www.lordsofmetal.nl/showinterview.php?id=2625
"I thought the way Celtic Frost..." *Snakepit* #9, 2001
"I think it probably would have..." Ibid.
"A record company executive..." Ibid.
"If we have to be pegged in a genre..." *Comedy of Errors* #3, March/April 1991

Chapter 11
"We don't want to be..." *Mega Metal Kerrang!* #9, 1988
"I'm sincerely trying to break down barriers..." *Voices from the Darkside* #6, 1995

Chapter 13
"We are more of a metal band..." punktv.ca
"He's probably the nicest guy..." www.revelationz.net
"Sweeping techniques..." www.sevenstring.org

Chapter 14
"I was just a very young guy..." Megalomaniac Productions, posted on churchoftiamat.com
"The music on..." *Swedish Death Metal*, 2008
"My music will never appeal to the masses..." geocities.com/area51/comet/4847/oxip.html

Chapter 15
"A lot of musicians hide..." *Metal Maniacs*, October 2000
"I listened to *Kveldssanger*..." *Once Upon a Nightwish: The Official Biography 1996–2006*, 2009
"We will never..." *Voices from the Darkside* #7, 1995
"A lot of people..." *Terrorizer* magazine (from clipping, issue unknown)
"*Neonism* was, in a way,..." *Imhotep* #7, 2001

"freeze your heart..." http://shining.no/v1/news.php

"prog, doom, jazz..." Ibid.

"My inspiration and interest..." http://www.rusmetal.ru/vae_solis/drawn.htm

Chapter 16

"I understand why the bands..." metalinjection.net

"When I was twelve..." *Metal Maniacs,* January 1999

"We played Berlin..." Ibid.

"We don't actually change time..." Ibid.

"There were no blast beats..." opeth.com

"I get given a lot of CDs..." rockeyez.com

"Since I did Opeth..." Ibid.

"Even back in 1990..." *Metal Maniacs,* March 2000

"Technology plays a big role..." Ibid.

"When bands make efforts..." Ibid.

"If ten people were asked..." Gonin-ish.com

"We are musical sponges..." seaoftranquility.org

"A lot of metal bands..." http://gnosis2000.net/maudlininterview.htm

"The composition or song..." Ibid.

"It was an honor for us..." NYRock.com, 2003

Chapter 17

"There's no intrinsic value..." *Once Upon a Nightwish: The Official Biography 1996–2006,* 2009

"Once you develop your craft..." *The Aquarian Weekly,* March 9, 1994

"There is heavier music..." electronic press kit for King Crimson's *Thrak,* 1994

"I don't keep up with..." KNAC.com, interview with Geoff Tate by Krishta Abruzzini

"After *Into the Pandemonium...*" *Voices from the Darkside* #6, 1995

INDEX